Cannon County
Tennessee

MINUTE BOOK
VOLUME A
1836–1841

WPA RECORDS

Heritage Books
2024

HERITAGE BOOKS

AN IMPRINT OF HERITAGE BOOKS, INC.

Books, CDs, and more—Worldwide

For our listing of thousands of titles see our website
at
www.HeritageBooks.com

A Facsimile Reprint
Published 2024 by
HERITAGE BOOKS, INC.
Publishing Division
5810 Ruatan Street
Berwyn Heights, MD 20740

Originally published
Feb. 16, 1938

— Publisher's Notice —

Page 12 and page 22 are not in the original manuscript

In reprints such as this, it is often not possible to remove
blemishes from the original. We feel the contents of this
book warrant its reissue despite these blemishes and
hope you will agree and read it with pleasure.

International Standard Book Number
Paperbound: 978-0-7884-8907-5

TENNESSEE

RECORDS OF CANNON COUNTY

MINUTE BOOK VOL. A.
1836 - 1841

HISTORICAL RECORDS PROJECT
Official Project No. 165-44-6999

COPIED UNDER WORK'S PROGRESS ADMINISTRATION

MRS. JOHN TROTWOOD MOORE
STATE LIBRARIAN & ARCHIVIST, SPONSOR

MRS. ELIZABETH D. COPPEDGE
DIRECTOR OF WOMEN'S & PROFESSIONAL PROJECTS

MRS. PENELOPE JOHNSON ALLEN
STATE SUPERVISOR

MISS MATILDA A. PORTER
SUPERVISOR FOURTH DISTRICT

COPIED BY
MISS GLADYS STACEY

TYPED BY
MRS. VIOLET PERRY

Feb. 16, 1938

WPA RECORDS

The WPA Records are, for the most part, carbon copies of the original
that was typed on onion skin paper during the Depression. Since these
records were typed on poor machines by people who did not type well
either and read by persons not always sure of the older handwritten
material, the results are often less that perfect.

We have made every attempt to make as good a copy as can be made from
these older papers. Sometimes there are water stains and burned edges
around the paper.. This is the results of a fire at the home of one of
the workers, Mrs. Penelope Allen, who was over most of the project.

The WPA Records are now very scattered between the State Archives, various
Public and Private Libraries and other collections. Some day, there is
a hope that all of these can be collected and stored in one place. In
spite of their many mistakes and problems, these are still the most complete collection of Tennessee records found anywhere.

CARROLL COUNTY

MINUTE BOOK VOL. A
1836-1841

INDEX

Note: Page numbers in this index refer to those of the original volume from which this copy was made. These numbers are carried throughout the copy within parentheses, as: (p 124)

A

Elledge, Isaac, W. 1, 67, 86, 99,
133, 149, 182, 197, 202, 216,
277, 278, 295, 306, 326, 347,
369, 370, 400, 427, 437, 438,
439, 467, 468, 478, 488, 514
Elledge, T. W. 99, 143
Elledge, Joseph, 271, 273, 277, 287,
295, 514
Elledge, Jas. L. 271, 459
Elledge, Wm. F. 271
Elrod, Adam, 16, 62, 121, 196, 259,
3 59, 495, 504, 542, 543
Eily, 155
Eploy, Geo. 179, 305
Esary, (Esq.) 35, 37, 46
Esary, James, 22, 56, 42
Escue, Charles, 283
Esery, J. L. 23
Essary, James, 550
Essary, Pleasant, 223, 286, 385
Essery, James, L. 63, 67, 98, 133
Estes, Brackot, 110
Estes, John, 198, 540
Estus, John, 200, 209, 210, 298, 365,
484, 487, 520
Estus, Margaret, 32
Etherage, Micheal, 170, 212, 492
Evans, 397
Evans, Andrew, F. 160, 191
Evans, C. C. 35, 37, 79, 80, 85, 223,
245, 248, 252, 268, 269, 276, 279,
284, 285, 286, 288, 321, 327, 328,
329, 341, 342, 346, 379, 381, 382,
383, 386, 396, 397, 410, 411, 412,
422, 423, 424, 428, 431, 433, 436,
437, 439, 440, 443, 444, 451, 452,
460, 461, 462, 464, 465, 470, 476,
478, 481, 483, 498, 502, 503, 505,
508, 512, 515, 518, 526, 536, 540,
552
Evans, Charles, C. 1, 17, 18, 43, 51,
63, 66, 69, 78, 81, 82, 86, 95,
100, 102, 104, 119, 120, 123, 124,
129, 133, 149, 156, 157, 163, 167,
169, 175, 188, 191, 192, 194, 201,
203, 206, 212, 214, 219, 225, 228,
229, 231, 233, 235, 237, 242, 244,
257, 292, 293, 295, 297, 299, 301,
304, 306, 311, 314, 332, 332, 335,
356, 361, 365, 385, 398, 400, 402,
486, 489, 493, 367
Evans, David, 221
Evans, James, 120, 186
Evans, John, H. 160
Evans, Joseph, 20, 42

Evans, Joseph W. 52
Evans, Nathan, 192
Evans, R. 20, 35, 37, 42, 97, 98,
157
Evans, Reuben, 1, 4, 17, 20, 24, 38
67, 86, 94, 97, 99, 100, 110,
119, 120, 123, 129, 149, 156,
163, 167, 170, 175, 176, 178,
185, 187, 201, 203, 205, 214,
216, 231, 233, 235, 237, 242,
244, 247
Evans, Thomas, 20, 94
Evans, William. B. 70, 102, 269, 410
Evans, William. B. Sr. 52
Ewell, Dabney, 456, 457, 460

F

Fagan, R. L. 44
Fagan, Robert, 56
Falkenberry, Catharine, 230
Falkenberry, David, 230, 530
Falkenberry, Hugh, P. 230
Falkenberry, Jacob, 19, 23, 29, 34
44, 105
Falkenberry, William, 44, 56, 69
Farles, Burrel, 186, 187
Farles, John, 127, 128, 478
Farles, Patton, 540
Farles, Thomas, 136, 339
Farley, Thomas, 364
Farmer, John, 31
Farrington, 53
Farrington, J. M. 150, 158
Farrington, Joshua, M. 9, 21
Ferrell, Charles, 188, 191, 195, 223
Ferrell, Edmund, 391
Ferrell, Elizabeth, 391
Ferrell, Enoch, 385
Ferrell, James, 6, 7, 24, 55, 60,
134, 151, 181, 391, 532
Ferrell, John, 195
Ferrell, Leighton, 2, 5, 7, 9
Ferrell, Robert, S. 391
Findley, 35, 37, 79, 96
Findley, Daniel, 51
Findley, Isaac, 63, 66, 67, 78, 81,
82, 106, 191
Findley, John, 79
Finley, 97, 98, 130, 131, 156, 157
Finley, Alexander, 54, 182
Finley, Britton, 225
Finley, Edmund, 121
Finley, Daniel, 128, 422, 433

Y

Young, A. 106
Young, Alexander, 102,113,132
Young, Henry, 105,106,113,196
Young, Isaac, 22,54,68,101,
    128,531
Young, John, 70,101,160,223,244
Young, Sam'l, 160
Young, Thomas, 58
Young, Thos. R. 318,362,431
Young, William, 16,24,25,68,102,
    143,196,209,440,497
Youngblood, 546
Youngblood, A. 507
Youngblood, Arthur, 395,420,459
Youngblood, Josiah, 9,61,102,125,
    138,221
Youngblood, Ransom, 141,164,200
Youree, Thos. N. 462,463,516,517

CANNON COUNTY

MINUTE BOOK VOL. A
1836 - 1841

(p 1)   State of Tennessee)
          Cannon County   )   May Term 1836
pursuant to the 2nd section of the act of the General Assembly of the State
of Tennessee rased   at Nashville on the 31st day of January in the year
of one thousand eight hundred and thirty six Entitled an act to Establish
the County of Cannon. In which it is(proved) that for the due Administration
of Justice that the different Court to be holden in said County of Cannon
shall be held at the House of Henry D. McBroom untill the seat of Justice
for said County shall be located and a suitable House is Erected for that
purpose (SC) . And induced the Commission from his Excellency Newton Governor
in and over the State of Tennessee to the following Worshipfull Justices
of the peace elect for said County viz:

Thomas Powell & Isaac Finley for District No. 2
Allen Haley & Joseph Simpson for District No. 3
Blake Sedgley & James L Dssary for District No. 4
John Pendleton & Isaac W. Elledge for District No. 5
Elijah Stephens, J.H. Brown & T.L. Turner for District No. 6
John Melton & Charlie C. Evans for District No. 7
Samuel Nance & William Dates for District No. 8
William B. Foster & John Martin for District No. 9
John Frazier & Martin Phillips for District No. 11
Reuben Evans & Lemuel Moore for District No. 13
James Goodner for District No. 14
Peter Reynolds and James Beatie for District No. 15
Joel Cheatham & Jonothan Fuson for District No. 16
who being duly sworn into Office by (p 2)   Ely Daily Esq. one of the
Justices of the Peace for the County of Warren took there   seats and pro-
ceeded to hold the first County Court for Said County of Cannon as the Law
directs. On Motion the Court proceeded to Elect a Chairman to preside over
there deliberations untill the first Monday in January next A.D. 1837.
And untill his successor shall be elected and on the first Ballading the
Worshipfull Thomas Powell Esq. was duly elected and proceeded to Discharge
the duties of said Office in the further buisnes of the Court.————

On Motion San'l J. Garrison produced a certificate from Leighton
Perrell Shiriff of Warren County which shewed to the satiffaction of the
Court that he had been duly and constitutionally elected Clerk of Cannon
County Court. And on motion the Oath of Office were administered to the
said Garrison by Ely Daily Esq. one of the Justices of the peace for Warren
County according as the law directs(&C) After which he entered into bond
together with his Securities approved by the Court viz: T.W. Duncan,
Tillman, Bethell, L.S. Gilliam, Benjamin Blade, Benj. Avant and Reuben
Evans in the sum of five thousand Dollars payable to his Excellency
Newton Cannon Governor and his successors in office conditiond as the
Law directs. And he also entered into bond together with his securities viz.

T.W. Duncan, Tilman Bethell, L.T. Gilliam, Benjamin Blade, Benjamin Avant,
& Reuben Evans in the sum of One Thousand Dollars payable to the Worshipfull
Thomas Powell Esq. Chairman of the Said Court and his successors on office
conditioned as the law directs (&C) viz; ————————————————————

Know all men by these presents that we Samuel J. Garrison, T.W. Duncan,
L.S. Gilliam, Tilman Bethell, Benjamin Avant, Benjamin Blade and Reuben
Davis, all of the County of Cannon and State of Tennessee are held and firmly bound unto Newton Cannon, Governor and his successors in office in the
Sum of Five Thousand Dollars to which payment well and truly to be made
we bind ourselves Our Executors, Administrators and assigns jointly
severally, and firmly by the presents sealed with our seals and dated this
2nd day May 1836.

The condition of the above obligation is such that whereas Sam'l J.
Garrison has been duly and constitutionally elected Clerk of Cannon County
Court for the term of four years from this date. Now if the said Samuel J.
Garrison shall and truly and faithfully Keep all the records of Said
Court properly belonging to his office according law during his continuance
therein . Then shall this obligation be void. Otherwise to remain in full
force and virture.

                    Sam'l J. Garrison (seal)
                    Benjamin Avant   (seal)
                    L.S. Gilliam   (seal))
                    Reuben Evans   (seal)
                    Benj. Balde   (seal)
                    Tillman Bethell (seal)
                    T.W. Duncan   (seal)

(p 4) Know all men by these presents that we. Samuel J. Garrison, T.W. Duncan
L.S. Gilliam, Tilman Bethell, Benj. Avant, Benj. Blade and Reuben Evans all
of Cannon County Tennessee are held and firmly bound unto Thomas Powell
Chairman of Cannon County Court and his successors in office in the sum of
One Thousand Dollars to which payment well and truly to be made and don we
bind ourselves Our heirs Executors Administrators and assigns jointly and
severally firmly by these presents sealed with our seals and dated this 2nd
day May 1836.

The condition of the above obligation is such that whereas Samuel J.
Garrison has been duly and constitutionally elected Clerk of Cannon County
Court for the ensuing four years. Now if the said Sam'l J. Garrison shall
well and truly pay all monies that shall come into his hands for the use
of the County to the County Trustee or any other person or persons Legally
authorized to receive the same or any monies that may come into his hands
for the use of others by virture of his office aforesaid. To them there
agents or attornies Lawfully authorized to receive the same. Then this
obligation to be void else to remain in full force and virture.

                    Sam'l J. Garrison (seal)
                    Reuben Evans   (seal)
                    Benj. Avant   (seal)
                    Benj. Blade   (seal)
                    L.S. Gilliam   (seal)
                    Tilman Bethell   (seal)
                    T.W. Duncan   (seal)

(p 5) On Motion of George Gruzzle came into Court and produced a certificate
from Leighton Ferrell sheriff of Warren County which shewed to the satisfaction of the Court that he had been duly and constitutionally elected sheriff
of Cannon County for the term of two years from this date. And Motion
the oaths of office well administered to him by Ely Daily Esq. one of the
Justices of the peace for Warren County. After which he entered into bond
payable to N. Cannon Governor and successor in office together with his
securities approved of by the Court Viz; William Gunter, J.G.W. Rose and
William Campbell in the sum of Twelve Thousand five hundred Dollars conditioned as the law directs To wit;
(Know all men by these presents that we George Gruzzle, William Gunter, J.G.
W. Rose, and William Campbell All of the County of Cannon and State of Tennessee are held and firmly bound unto Newton Cannon Governor and his successors in office in the Penal Sum of Twelve Thousand five hundred dollars/which
payment well and truly to be made and done we bind ourselves our heirs &c
jointly and severaly firmly by these presents sealed with our seals dated
this 2nd day of May 1836.

    The condition of the above obligation is such that whereas the abound-
ed George Gruzzle has been elected sheriff of Cannon County for the term of
two years from this date now if the said George Gruzzle shall well and truly
Execute and due returns make upon all process and precepts to him directed
and pay and satisfy all fees and sums of money by him received or laid by
vittue of any (p 6) process unto the proper office by which the same shall
be due his, her or there agents or attornies and shall in all things will
truly and faithfully Execute the office of sheriff according to law during
his continuance therein. Then this obligation to be vied else to remain in
full force and virtures.

                    George Gruzzle   (seal)
                    William Gunter   (seal)
                    J.G.W. Rose   (seal)
                    William   (seal)

    On Motion Alexander F. McFerrin came into Court and produced the
certificate of Leighton Ferrell sheriff of Warren County which shewed to
the satisfaction of the Court that he had been duly and constatutionally
elected Register of Cannon County. And on Motion of the oaths of office
were Administered to him by Eli Daily one of the Justices of the peace
for Warren County. After which he entered into bond together with his
securities approved of by the Court in the Penal Sum of Twelve Thousand
five hundred dollars payable to Newton Cannon Governor and his successors in
offices Conditioned as the Law Directs. &C Viz;

Know all men by these presents that we Alexander F. McFerrin
                                       B.L. McFerrin
                                       Joseph Simpson
                                       D.M. Stewart
                                       John Barkley
                                       James Ferrell
All of the County of Cannon and State of Tennessee are held and firmly
bound unto Newton Cannon Governor and his successors in (p 7) office for
which payment well and truly to be made we bind ourselves our Executers, Administrators and assigns jointly severally and firmly by these presents sealed
with our seals and dated this day May 1836

    The conditions of the above obligation is such that whereas the said

Alexander F. McFerrin has been elected Register of Cannon County in the ensuing four years from this date. Now if the said Alexander F. McFerrin shall well and truly and faithfully Execute all of the duties of his office as also to keep safe all of the records of belonging to his office during his continuance therein. Then this obligation to be void or otherwise to remain in full force and virture.

Alexander F. McFerrin	(seal)
B.L. McFerrin	(seal)
Joseph Simpson	(seal0
D.M. Stewart	(seal)
John Barkley	(seal)
James Ferrell	((seal)

On Motion Job Stephens came into Court and produced the certificate of Leighton Ferrill sheriff of Warren County which showed to the satisfaction of the Court that he had been Duly and constitutionally elected Trustee for Cannon County And on motion the oaths of office were Administerd to him by Eli Baily Esq. one of the Justices of the peace for Warren County after which he entered into bond together (with his securities) which were approved of by the Court in the sum of Five Thousand Dollars (p 8) payable to Thomas Powell Chairman of Cannon County and his successors in office conditioned as the law directs &C Viz:

Know all men by these presents thar we -- Job Stephens
                                          Archibald Stone
                                          J.G.W. Rose
                                          Asa Smith
                                          Joseph Clark

All of this County of Cannon and state of Tennessee are held and firmly bond unto Thomas Powell Chairman of Cannon County Court and his successors in office in the sum of Five Thousand Dollars to which payment well and truly to be made we bind ourselves our heirs Executors, Administrators and assigns jointly severally and firmly by these presents sealed with our seals dated this 2nd day May 1836

The condition of the above obligations is such that whereas Job Staphens has been duly and constitutionally elected Trustee for Cannon County for the Term of two years from this date. Now of the said Job Staphens shall well truly and faithfully account for and disburse all County monies that shall or may come into his hands by virture of his office of County Trustee During his continuance therein and shall in all things appartaining to his said appointment discharge the duties of said office of County Trustee, according to Law. Then This obligation to be void, otherwise to remain in full force and virture.

Job Stephens	(seal)
Archibald Stone	(seal)
J.G.W. Rose	(seal)
Joseph Clark	(seal)
Asa Smith	(seal)

(p 9) On Motion of the following Gentlemen, Constables elect came into Court and produced their certificates severally from Leighton Ferrell sheriff of Warren County which showed to the satisfaction of the Court that they had been severally Duly and constitutionally elected constables for the County of Cannon and in the following District Viz:

In District No. 2 — Roswell Soap
In District No. 3 — Jonothan Bateman
In District No. 4 — Richard Holt
In District No. 5 — Isham Pelham
In District No. 6 — Josiah Youngblood & William F. Covington
In District No. 7 — James Helton
In District No. 8 — G.B. Sapp
In District No. 9 — B.L. Johnson
In District No. 10 — Jasper Rugle
In District No. 11 — John Johnson
In District No. 12 — Charles D. Markham
In District No. 13 James Pendleton
In District No. 14 — Thomas V. Ashworth
In District No. 15 — Abram W. Ford
In District No. 16 — Joshua M. Farrington

Who being duly sworn into office by Eli Daily Esq. one of the Justices of the peace for Warren County Entered Bond severally together with there securities approved by the court in the sum of one Thousand Dollars each payable to Newton Cannon Governor and his successors in Officecondi- tioned as the Law directs.

Malaciah Cummongs)
    To   )
Robert G. Spicer)   Deed for 160 acres of Land from Malaciah Cummings to Robert G. Spicer lying in Howard County State of Missouri and baring date 2nd day May Anno Domoni 1836 was produced in open Court for probate and was duly acknowled in open Court by Malaciah Cummings the Bargainor and ordered to be certified for registration.
(p 10) On Motion the worshipfull court was adjorhed untill 9 00 O'clbck tomorrow .

        Thomas Powell Chairman
        James M. Brown
        Elijah Stevens
        John Milton

Tusday morning May 3rd 1836 The Worshipfull Court meet Pursuant to adjourn- ment a quoram present.

On Motion the Court proceeded to the Election of a Coronor for said County of Cannon to serve for the term of Two years from this date And Alexander McEnight was duly and constitutionally elected to that office And on motion the oaths of office were administered to him after which he entered into bond together withrhis securities in the sum of three thousand dollars payable to the Governor and his successors in office conditioned as the law directs .

On Motion the court proceeded according as the law directs to elect five Commissioners to superentend theLaying off and selling of the lots of the county site and for other purposes and on the first Ballading
                Joseph Clark
                Archabald Stone
                T.W. Duncan
                Jno D. Stone and
                John Brown

wore duly Elected commisioners (p 11) as aforesaid And T.W. Duncan de-
clining to serve as one of said comicsi nors to fill said vacancy and on
the first Ballading it appeared that William Bates was duly elected said
commissioner . After which the said Joseph Clark

A. Stone

J.B. Stone

John Brown and

William Bates

Entered into bond together with there securities severally in the sum of
five thousand dollars payable to Thomas Powell Chairman of Cannon County
Court and his successors in office which securities being approved of by
said Court they severally took the oath of office as commissioners according as the Law directs.

On Motion the court proceeded to elect a ranger for the County of Cannon
to serve for the Term of two years from this date and on the first Ballading
Henry H. Clifton was duly and constitutionally elected to that office who
being first duly sworn as the Law directs Entered into Bond together with
his Securities approved of by the Court in the sum of five Hundred dollars
payable to Thomas Powell Chairman of Cannon County Court and his successors
in office conditioned as the Law directs.

On Motion the Court proceeded to elect an Entry taker for the County of Cannon
and the first Ballading William Stone was duly and constitutionally elected
to that office. And on Motion the oaths of office were Administered to him
after which he entered into bond together with his securities approved of
by the Court in the Penal Sum of Ten Thousand dollars conditioned as the
Law dir cts payable to the Governor and his succesors in office (&C)

(p 12) On Motion the court proceeded to the election of a surveyor for the
County of Cannon to serve for the Term of four years from this date And
Hugh Robenson was duly and constitutionally elected to that office . And
after being duly sworn into office as the Law directs he entered into bond
together with his securities approved of by the Court in the sum of Ten
thousand dollars payable to the Governor and his successors   in office
conditioned as the Law directs.

John Wright &)
Pumphry Byrun)
    To   )
Charles Espy)   Deed for 72 acres of land from John Wright & pumphry
Byrum to Charles Espry lying in Cannon State of Tennessee baring date the
8th day of may 1835 was produced in open Court for probate and was duly
proven by the oaths of Hugh Robinson the suscribing witness thereto and was
ordered to be certified for registration.

  Benjamin Pendleton   )
      To   )
  Benjamin C. Stephens)   Deed for 79½ acres of land from Benj. Pendleton
to Benjamin C. Stephens Lying in Cannon County Tennessee Baring date the
1st day June 1835 was produced in open Court for probate and was duly
acknowleded by said Pendleton on oath and was ordered to be certified
for registration.

Transfer of

Lemuel Duncan   )
    To   )
Hiram Smithson)   lot of certificate of 40½ acres of Land from Lem Duncan
to Hiram Smithson lying in Cannon County Tennessee was produced in open
court for Probate and was duly proven by the oaths of Lewis A. Leray and
Charles Leray the suscribing witnesses thereto and bares   date the 15th
March 1836.

(p 13)
Washington Keneday)
        To   )
Benj. C. Stephens)   Deed for about ᵗᵗ acres of land from Washington
Keneday to Benj. C. Stephens lying in Cannon County Tennessee and baring
date the 4th of/October 1835 was produced in open court for probate and was
duly acknowleged on oath by the Bargainer to be his act and Deed for the
Purpose therein contained and ordered to be certified for Registration.

James Taylor   )
    To   )
John S. Russworm &)
JOnothan Webster   )
Commissioners &C   )   Deed for 20 acres & 21 poles land from James Taylor
to John S. russworm & Jonothan Webster Commissioners appointed to purchase
a tract of land upon which to lay off the seat of Justice for Cannon County
Lying in and near the Town of Danville in said county of Cannon and state of
Tennessee and baring   date the 15th of April 1836 - was produced in open
Court for probate and was duly Proven by the oaths of W.Y. Henderson & John
Drown the suscribing witnesses thereto and was ordered to be certified for
Registration.

On Motion William B. Wit Attorney at law came into Court and qualified
as the Law directs and was Permitted to Practise at the Bar of Said Court.

On Motion Henry Trott Jr. came into Court and presented a report from
Jonothan Webster and John S. Russworn Commissioners appointed by act of the
General Assembly of the state of Tennessee passed at Nashville January
31st. 1836 to Establish the county of Cannon . In which the said Russworn
& Webster were appointed to Locate the County seat of said County of Cannon
Viz:

(p 14) State of Tennessee)
    Cannon County   )   To the Worshipfull County Court of Cannon County
The undersigned being a majority of the commissioners appointed to lay off
designate, locate and name a SCITE for the establishment of a seat of
justice within and for your County have proceeded to Locate the same upon
the scite and adjoining the scite of the town of Danville and have procured
a tittle in fee simple for said scite according to the Boundries of a
Deed for the same Herewith submitted to your worshipful court the said Deed
containing sixty two acres of uncncumbered Land, consisting of Land and Lots
Purchased and donated to the undersigned as appears by said deeds and as will
more fully by deed and report which the undersigned are redy to make to such
commissioners for said Town as your worship shall appoint according to Law.
The undersigned also report to your worship that the said scite for the said
town was by them Located and the Title to the Land procured as above by them

on the 15th day of April 1836.

Being within the time prescribed by law. And furthermore the undersigned report to your worship that as by law fully impowered they have given the name of Woodbury in honor of the Hon. Levi Woodbury of New Hampshire to the seat of Justice by which it will be hereafter designated and known unless changed by law. The undersigned are ready to make the conveyance and Deeds required (p 15) by law and a full report of there proceedings herewith to the comissioners required by you to be appointed or elected for the said Town as soon as they shall be appointed all of which is respectfully submitted.

April 15th 1836

We have issued certificates to the following Persons for land and Lots Purchased and Expences incured for the following sums Viz:

To James Taylor ————————————————— $ 2.00
To H.D. & A.McBroom ————————————————— 7.00
To Martha Gannon ————————————————— 40.20
To Wm. Cunningham for surveying ————————— 2.00
To S.H. Laughlin for professional services
in Examining tittle making conveyences &C 75.00

} John S. Russworm
} Jonothan Webster

All of which was accepted and approved of by the court except so much of the certificate Isued by said Commissioners as relates to the fee allowed S.H. Laughlin for his services which was left open to be considered of by the next or any subsequent Term of this Court.

(p 16) On Motion the last Will and Testament of Joel Mears dec'd was produced in open court and duly proven by the oath of Benjamin C. Stephens one of the suscribing witnesses thereto. The other witness Ishum Pelham not appearing to qualify to the same. And on Motion Benjamin C. Stephens was appointed Administrator of said Estate with the will anexed who being duly sworn as such entered into bond together with his securities John Eastes in the sum of three Hundred dollars payable to Newton Cannon Governor and his sucessors as the law directs. And letters of Administration Granted him upon said Estate.

W.Y. Henderson)
Nathan Neely)
Adam Elrod)
Joseph Peckerton)
Henry Trott Jr.)
Abel McBroom)
H.D. McBroom)
Robert Vinson)
William Young)
Patsy Gannon)
Mary Gannon)
To)

Deed for about 42 acres land from the Individuals Herin named. To the commissioners herin named Lying in Cannon County Tennessee baring date 15th April 1836 was produced in open court for probate and was duly proven by the oaths of Daniel Shacklefood & E. Stephens the suscribing witnesses thereto and ordered to be certified for Registration.

John S. Russworm &)
Jonothan Webster   )
commissioners &C   )

(p 17) On Motion ordered by the court that M.S. West be appointed overseer
from the two mile post from alexander (on the stage road) to the four mile
post toward Liberty and to have the same hand hereto allowed.

On Motion ordered by the court that
Alexander Higgins
James melton
Lemuel Turney
Jasper Bugle
Isiah Neely and
Francis Spurlock
be appointed a jury of men to view and mark out a road from the mouth of the
rock House Fork of Stone River to entersect   the road leading from Liberty
to McMinnville near the mouth of the Canal Fork. And make return to the next
term of this court.

On Motion ordered by the court that Jesse Lawrence be appointed overseer to work the road leading from the top of the ridge above George St.
Johns to William West and have the same hands that have been working on
said road.

On Motion ordered by the court that Francis Boyd be appointed overseer
of the stage road from the two mile post near Isaac Greys to Boyd Spring .
And Reuben Evans & Jonothan Tuson furnish him with a list of hands &c.

On Motion ordered by the court that Vincen Paily be appointed overseer
of the road from John B. Stones to Ezekiel Hammond and Aply to Thomas L.
Turner Esq. for a list of hands.
(p 17)
On Motion ordered by the court that Nathan Neely be appointed Overseer
to work the road leading from Woodbury to the Wilson County Line and that
he apply to Elijah Stephens Esq. for a list of his hands.

On Motion ordered by the Court that James Pendleton be appointed overseer, to work the road from William West to the Warren County Line and that
he have/hands that heretofore work said road.

On Motion ordered by that John Boyd be appointed Overseer of the road
from William Cummings to the fork of the Hollow above the Warrens and apply
to Esq. Evans for a list of hands.

On motion ordered by the court that Joseph Clarks be overseer of the road
from the fork of the Hollow above the Warrens (to the county line) of the road
leading by John Martins Esq.

On Motion ordered by the Court that Peachman Gannon be appointed overseer on the road leading from Woodbury to the top of the ridge above George
St. Johns.

On Motion ordered by the Court that Thomas Lawrence be appointed overseer of the road from the ford of Smiths Fork (the mouth of Dismal Creek) to the Smith County line near Peter Reynolds and have the same hands that Randall Wilson had.

(p 19)   On motion ordered by the court that Benjamin Avant be appointed overseer of the road from the top of the Dismal hill to the mouth of Dismal creek and hands and bound as heretofore.

On motion ordered by the court that Clinton B. Reynolds be appointed overseer of the road from the Smith County line near William Malone and that James Peatie and Peter Reynolds Esq. allot the hands.

On motion ordered by the Court that Henry Hays be appointed overseer on that part of the stage road leading from the ford of the River below Stewarts Mils to Wm. Suttons and have the same list of hands as formily

On Motion ordered by the Court that Matthew Whitfield be appointed overseer on the dug Hollowroad from William Grays to the Coffee County line and be allowed the same hands that formily belonged to said road.

On motion ordered by the Court that William Ring be appointed overseer of the road leading from Silas L. Roberts to William Grays &C.

On Motion ordered by the Court that James Taylor be appointed overseer commencing on the stage road at J.M Woods to Jacob Falkenberry and have the same hands as heretofore.

On motion ordered by the Court that Alex Sutton be appointed overseer of the stage road from Mrs. Suttons to Woodbury and have same hands as former overseer.

(p 20) On motion ordered by the Court that Thomas Cavatt be appointed overseer of the road leading from Joseph Eledges to Manchester as fare as the road leading from Woodbury to R. Blues and G.B. Sapp be appointed overseer from that point to the stage road and apply to Sam'L Lance and William Bates for a list of hands.

On motion ordered by the Court that Thomas Evans be appointed of the stage road from Liberty to the two mile post near Isaac Grays and that he apply to Reuben Evans & Jonothan Fuson Esq. for a list of hands.

On motion by the court that Joseph Evans be appointed overseer of the stage road from Liberty to the two mile post in the direction of Alexandria and that R. Evans & L. Moore Esq. furnish him a list of hands.

On motion by the Court that Elijah Scott be appointed overseer of the road from the Smith County line to the first mile post toward Liberty at Benj. Garrisons.

On motion ordered by the Court that John S. Keneday be appointed overseer of the stage road from the one mile post at Benj. Garrison to the two mile post at Philip Haas.

On motion ordered by the Court that John Vantrees Jr. be appointed overseer of the stage road beginning at the two mile post at philip Haas to the three mile post towards Liberty.

(p 21) On motion ordered by the Court that William Bennett be appointed overseer of the road from the top of the dismal hill to its junction with the stage road near Phillip Haas.

On motion ordered by the Court that L.Y. Davis be appointed Overseer of the stage road from Alexandria to the Wilson County line toward Nashville.

On motion ordered by the court that James Goodner and P.A. Thomason be appointed to allot and devid and allot hands to the following overseers to wit:

  Elijah Scott
  Lewis Y. Davis
  J.S. Keneday
  John Vantrees Jr.
  William Bennett &
  Joel Coffee
  Overseers &C

On motion ordered by the Court that Joel Coffee be appointed Overseer of the road from Alexandria to the Smith County line near Lucy Prestons.

On motion ordered by the Court that
     Robin Forestor
     Henry Heart
     Joshua M. Farrington
     Matthews Sellers &
     Pleasant C. Watson
be a jury of men to vew and mark out a road the nearest and best way commencing at the stage road near William Williams runing up the dry fork of Smiths fork to the top of the ridge near Grayhams old place and they make a report to the next Termof this Court.

On motion and petition ordered by the Court that Joseph Knox
     Absolam Bowen
     Learner Watson
     James Hollis &
     William Bowen
be appointed a jury of men to (p22) vew and mark out a mill road begining at Harrod Lasseters to Mitchells mill and report to the next term of this Court.

On motion and petition ordered by the Court that Robert George
     Ezekiel Hays
     James L. Deary
     Hugh Robinson &
     Charles Alexander.
be appointed a jury of men to vew and mark out aroad begining   at the Town of Woodbury Creek near Jonothan Jones . And make report at the next term of this Court.

In District No. 5 — F.W. Eledge
In District No. 6 — J.M. Brown
In District No. 7 — John Melton
In District No. 8 — Sam(l Lance
In District No. 9 — John Martin
In District No. 10 — Lemuel Turney
In District No. 11 — John Frazeur
In District No. 12 — Watson Cantrell
In District No. 13 — Lem'l Moore
In District No. 14 — James Goodner
In District No. 15 — James Beatie
In District No. 16 — Jonothan Fuson

On Motion the Court appointed the followinf person as jurymen to attend the next Circuit Court viz:
In District No. 1 — David McKnight & Robert Cummins
In District No. 2 — Charles Alexander & D.M. Stewart
In District No. 3 — Joseph Knox Sr. & S. Roberts
In District No. 4 — Alexander Petty & B.B. Pickens
In District No. 5 — Washington Keneday & Martin Cox
In District No. 6 — J.E. Sullivan & William Young
In District No. 7 — Vinson Ba'ly & Thomas Cavatt
In District No. 8 — Reuben Balem & Wm. Cummins
In District No. 9 — Archibald Hicks & J.G.W. Rose
In District No. 10 — James Dood & Nathan Sellers
In District No. 11 — Thomas Wood & Allen Johnson
In District No. 12 — John Charles & Washington Cameron
In District No. 13 — Reuben Evans & John Reed
In District No. 14 — P.A. Thomason & John Waters
In District No. 15 — William Bennett & Wiley Jones
In District No. 16 — Thomas Lawrence & Hugh Alton

By request of James Ferrell the court permitted the clerk Aninister the oath of office to him as deputee

(p 25) The Worshipfull Court adjoined tall tomorrow 12 O'clock

                                        Thomas Powell cherman
                                        James M. Brown
                                        Elijah Stephens
                                        John Melton
                                        William Bates
                                        Thomas L. Turner
                                        John Martin

State of Tennessee)
Cannon County   )   Wednesday May 4th 1836
The worshipfull Court met pursuant adjoinment present the worshipfull
                                        Thomas Powell chrn   &C
                                        James M. Brown
                                        Elijah Stephens
                                        John Melton
                                        William Bates
                                        John Martin
                                        Thomas L. Turner Esq.

On motion the Court appointed W.B. Foster Esq. to allot hands to
Joseph Clark overseer.

On motion and petition ordered by the Court that William S. Clark
                                                William Preston
                                                Wm. Young
                                                Alexander Petty &
                                                Solomon Long
be appointed a jury of men to vew and mark out a road the nearest and best
way from Woodbury to Manchester the seat of Justice for Coffee County and
make return to the term of this Court provided that said Jury of men are
not required to extend there vew further than the County line. &C

On motion and petition ordered by the Court that Nathan Neely
                                                James Smith
                                                Alexander McKnight &
                                                Richard Tenpenny
be appointed a jury men to vew and mark out aroad from the Town of Woodbury
by way of Nathan Neelys to the widdow Travis on Andrews Creek thence to
the Lebanon Road in the McKnight settlement Thence to the settlement about
Milton and make report to the next term of this Court.

There being no further buisniss before the Worshipful Court On motion
it was adjoined till Court In course in May 4th 1836
                                                Thomas Powell Jr.
                                                John Martin
                                                Thomas L. Turner
                                                James M. Brown
                                                William Bates
                                                Elijah Stephens
                                                John Melton

                    Woodbury June 6th 1836
(p 27)
State of Tennessee)
Cannon County   ) June Term County C. 1836
The Worshipfull County Court pursuant to adjorcument mett on this day
6th of June 1836 At the House of M.D. McBroom as the Law directs present
the worshipfull Thomas Powell chairman &C together with a sufficient
number of the justice to form a Quorum to do county buisniss &C

On motion ordered by the Court that William Gilley be appointed overseer
of the road from Archibald Hixs to the Warren County line near Reuben
Blues and William Foster Esq. furnish him with a list of hands.

The Clerk presented before the Court Commissioners from the Governor
for the following Justices for said County And on Motion the clerk was
ordered to qualify them which being done they took there seats and proceeded with the balance of the court to the further deliberations of said
Court Viz: J.C. Martin
                                                Lem'l Turney
                                                F.A. Thomason
                                                Jonothan C. Doss

Thomas Simpson
Watson Cantrell and
David   Fisher

On Motion ordered by the Court James S. Cism be appointed overseer of
the road leading up the middle fork of Stones River begining at the mouth
of the horse spring fork up to the said Cisms and have the former hands.

On motion ordered by the Court that Jonothan Wherry be appointed
overseer commencing at the ford of the river at D.M. Stewarts runing to the
County line near John H. Woods and apply to J.C. Martin Esq. to furnish a
list of hands.

(p 28) On motion ordered by the Court that Evan Pateman be appointed overseer of the road begining at the ford of the river below David Pattons
saw mill runin g In a direction towards murfreesboro to the county line
and have the following hands. Viz:

Silas Robertson
George Hamilton
A.P. Gowen & hand
Mark Stacey & sons
James Monahan & sons
and John K. Casley.

On motion ordered by the Court that Thos. Lawrence be appointed overseer of the road from the ford Smiths fork near the mouth of dismal creek
down to the ford near JohnReynolds Blacksmith Shop and have the same hands
be firmley had.

On motion ordered by the court that Wm Self be appointed overseer of the
road from the ford of the creek at John Reynolds Shop down to the Smith
County line and have the same hands that Randall Wilson formily had.

On motion ordered by the Court that John Allen be appointed overseer
of the road from purtets creek from where it crosses the Wilson County line
to where it intersects the stage road near Joseph Johnsons and have the
same hands and bounds that Joel M. West had.

On motion ordered by the Court that Thomas Uavatt be appointed overseer
of the road from Joseph Eledges to the road leading from Woodbury to
Reuben Blues in a direction toward Manchester and apply to John Martin
Esq. for a list of hands &c

(p 29)   On Motion ordered by the court that G.B. Sapp be appointed overseer of the road from Blues Road to John Pendletons and apply to Sam'l
Lance Esq. for a list of hands. &c.

On motion ordered by the Court that Jacob Falkenberry be appointed
overseer of the road from Tuckers Blacksmiths shop to Strouds on topp
of the hill and have the same hands and bounds that Jonothan Jones had.

On motion ordered by the Court that Martin S. Pack
R. McGinnis
B. Atnip
Thomas Clark and

Isaac Gallon

be appointed a jury of men to vew and mark out a road begining at the
mouth of Holms Creek where it runs into the Caney Fork runingup same creek
to the point of the ridge runing down from Woods old place Thence to run
up said ridge or around the same as may be most property so as to intersect
with the said road runing by word old place runing to the Camp Ground And
make report to the next term of this Court.

On motion ordered by the Court That Thomas Lawrence be appointed Guardian
of Elijah Duncan (who it has been represented to this court) is so far so
impaired with old age that he is not capable of taking care of his Estate
And the said Lawrence entered into bond together with his securities John
Davis and Solomon Davis in the sum of five hundred dollars conditioned
as the Law directs for his Faithfull purformance as such and was sworn
in open Court as the Law directs in such case.

(p 30)   The jury of men heretofore appointed at the last term of this
Court to vow and mark out a road begining at Jonothan Jones runing so as
to intersect the stage road at or near Laswells mills reported to the present
term of this court upon which objections were urged and the said report
was set aside by the court and the Following persons were appointed a jury
men Viz:

            Dan'l M. Stewart
            Alexander Petty
            Thomas Williams Sr.
            B.B. Dickens &
            James M. Brown Esq.
to vew and mark out a road the nearest and best way from Woodbury to intersect the Hickory Creek Road at or near Jonothan Jones and make report
to the next term of this court.

The jury men (or a majority thereof)
                Joseph Knox Sr.
                Absolom Bowen
                James Hollis &
                William Bowen
who were appointed at the last term of this court to vew and mark out a
m ll road from Harros Lasseters to Mitchells mill make report as follows
viz: that they vewed and marked the same begining at the ford of the
river at James Mitchells Thence West with Parson Curlus fence leaving
it on the right hand thence west to said Curlees upper plantation leaving
it on the left runing west to Isham Adams line thence west with said Adams
fence up the branch to the mouth of Luke Lasseters Lane and with Lane to
Harrod LasseterAnd on motion ordered by the Court that the same be adopted
and that Thomas Hodges be appointed overseer of said road.

On motion Thomas J? Hix The constable elected in the first District
presented acertificate from Joshua Nichols certifying that he had been duly
and constitutionally elected constible in said district. Who being duly
qualified in open court intered (p 31) into bond together with his securities approved by the Court conditioned as the law directs.

On motion George Aspy represented to this court that an orphan Boy By
the name of John Farmer about 10 years of age, is in a helpless situation

and deserves protection and is destitute of any/and proposes to this court
that he is willing to have said John Farmer bound to him by order of this
court untill he arrives to the age of twenty one years and proposes to give
him twelve months schooling when he shall have arrived to the age of fourteen years, and six months more when he shall have arrived to the age of
eighteen years And that hecwill Give him in addition thereto at the Expira-
tionof his servitude two Good suits of home spun clothing and will keep him
comfortably clothed during his servitude and treat him well in all things&C.
All of which being agreed to by the court the said Aspy Entered into bond
payable to the chairman of said Court and his successors in office together
with his securities approved of by the court in the sum of five hundred
dollars conditioned as per agrement with said court as the Law directs .

On motion ordered by the Court that

> Abram Overall
> Abram Adams
> Frances Turner
> Robert Vinoen and
> William Stone

be appointed a jury of men to vew and mark out aroad from the Town of
Woodbury the nearest and best way so as to intersect the road leading from
the Gapp of the short mountain to Liberty Somewhere between Tittle School
House and Abram Overalls and make report to the next term of this court.

(p 32) On motion Archalous Prater about sevebty years of age personally
appeared in open court and made oath that he was acquainted with Joel Mears
in his lfetime and that Margaret his wife (Formerly Margaret Estes) and
deponent further states that on or about the 30th Sept. 1827 he being an
authorized minister of the Gospel married the said Margaret to the said
Joel, deponant states that sometime in the latter part of the year of 1835
the said Joel mares deceased in Warren County Tennessee.

On motion Isham Pelham one of the suscribing witness to the last will
and testament of Joel Mears (deed) which was produced at the last term of
this court and proven by the other witness came into open court and made
oath that he saw the said Joel sign seal and execute the same and heard
acknowledge it in like manner to be his act and deed for the pur poses therein
contained.

A. McKnight)
     To   )
Drury Matthews) A deed from Alexander McKnight to Drury Matthews for 28
acres and 70 poles of land in Cannon County baring date the 4th day of
April 1836 was this dayproduced in open court for probate and was duly
acknowledged by Alexander McKnight (the Bargainer) to be his act and deed
for the purposes therein contained and the same was ordered to be certified for Registration.

(p 33) On motion a mortgage from J.B. Robinson to Josiah Harrod for personal property that is to say One Black Horse for the consideration therein
named was this day produced in open court for probate and was duly
proven by the oaths of James Dillard and Hugh Robinson.

The Chairman of the Court presented the resignation of Roswell Soap Constible in the 2nd District and on motion the same was ordered to be made of Record and that the Sheriff advertise and held an election to fill said vancy as the Law directs.

James Dillard To)
Thos Hopkins) Bond for Deed from James Dillard to Thomas Hopkins for two hundred and twenty four acres of land Lying in Cannon County baring date the 22nd day of August 1835 was this day produced in open court for probate and was duly Acknowledged by James Dillard (the Bargainer) to be his act and deed for the purposes therein contained and ordered to be certified for Registration.

Hugh Reed)
    To)
John Cooper) Deed for fifty eight acres of land lying in Cannon County baring date the 3rd day of November 1835 was this day produced in open court for probate and was duly acknowledged by Hugh Reed (the Bargainers) al and ordered to be certified for Registration.

Michael Beachel)
    To)
B.L. McFerrin) Deed from Michael Beachel to B.L. McFerrin for 90 acres of land lying in Cannon County baring the date the fifteenth day May 1832 was this (p 34) day produced in open court for probate and was duly proven by the oaths Micajah Petty and Jacob Falkenberry who being first sworn depose and say that they heard him acknowledge the same to be his act and deed for the purpose therein contained and the same was ordered for Registration.

On motion ordered by the court that R.L. Shaw be appointed overseer of the road from the ford of the cave spring Branch to the School House near Sam'l Tittles and that he apply Lem'l Turner Esq. for a list of his hands. &C

On motion ordered by the Court that Henry Powell be appointed Overseer (p 35) of the road from the school House near S. Tittles to the topp of the Big Hill and that he apply to Sam'l Turney Esq. for a list of hands.

On motion ordered by the court that John Planton be appointed overseer of the road from the topp of the Big Hill to Archibled Hixe And apply to Wm. B. Foster Esq. for a list of hands.

On motion the court proceeded to levy a tax for County purposes and there being a majority of all of the Justices of said court present viz:
Esqrs. Phillips/Frazeur
        Sadgely
        Lance
        Bates
        T. Simpson
        Turney
        Cheatham
        I. Simpson
        Fisher Cantrell
        R. Evans
        Findley

C.L. Evans
Thomason
Fuson
Doss
Batie
Reynolds
Esary
Goodner and
Powell 22

It was proposed and adopted unanimously that a tax Equal to the state tax
be levied on all property & poles liable to taxation in the state and that
the tax upon the priveledges and occupation be levied Equal to the one
half of the state tax ordered by the Court that the clerk be and he is hereby Authorized and required to demand and receive the county taxes assesed
by the court upon all of the priveledges and occupations that are not at
present Licensed when he may be applyed to for a Licence for priveledges
and occupations that have been Licenced in the county and the amts. that
they are respectivelly subject to ay for county purposes and hand the same
to the shiriff who shall be and is hereby authorized to collect the same
when collecting other taxes.

The jury of men that were appointed at the last term of this court to
vew and mark out a road the nearest practicable rout for a road from the
Town of Woodbury to the point of the ridge where the dug Hollow road crosses the said ridge. have reported with only two names of said jury signed to
the same which was set aside by the court.

(p 36) On motion ordered by the court Harman James be appointed Administrator
of the Estate of Daniel James deceased who came into Court and qualified And
together with his securities athan Neely and James Mears entered into bond
in the sum of fifteen hundred dollars conditioned as the aw directs And
letters of Administration are granted him upon Estate &C

On Motion the last will and Testament of Margaret Petty was produced in
open court for probate and was duly proven by the oaths of Hugh Reed and
James L. Esary, the suscribing witness thereto who being first sworn
depose and say they heard her acknowledge the same to be her act and deed
for the purposes the ein contained which was ordered to be spread upon
reccord .

Joel Cherry)
    To   )
William Craft) Deed for 100 acres of land from William Craft to Joel
Cherry Lying in Cannon County baring date the 2nd day May 1836 was produced
in open court for probate and was duly proven by the oaths of Lewis M.Pleasant M.
Lemay the two suscribing witness thereto who being first sworn depose
and say that they saw him sign seal and Execute the same which was ordered
to be certified for Registration.

On motion ordered by the court that Liscence to keep an ordinary with
priviledges to retail spirituous Liquors be granted to B.F. Browning for
the term of one year from this date he having entered into bond with security approved by the Court in the sum o f five hundred dollars conditioned

as the Lawddirects and taken the oath required in such cases.

Ordered by the Court that Licence to James Powell to keep ordinary in Cannon County for the term of one year from this date he having entered into Bond together (p 37) with his security approved of by the Court in the sum of five Hundred Dollars conditioned as the Law directs.

On motion ordered by the court that a licence be granted to Henry D. McBroom to keep an ordinary in Cannon County for the term of one year from this date He having Entered into bond together with his securities approved of by the court in the sum of five hundred dollars conditioned as the Law directs.

On motion the Court next took up that part of the report J.S. Russworm and Jonothan Webster Com &C which was made at the last term of this court And there being twenty two of the justices of said court present to wit
Esqrs.   Phillips
           Frazuer
           Sedgely
           Lance
           Bates
           T. Simpson
           Turney
           Cheatham
           I. Simpson
           Fisher
           Cantrell
           R. Evans
           Findley
           C.C. Evans
           Thomason
           Duson
           Doss
           Patie
           Reynolds
           Peary
           Goodner and
           Powell
It was unanimously concured in that so much of said reports as relate to the fee allowed S.H. Laughlin, was illegal and ought not to be allowed. And it is on motion further ordered by the court that the clerk notify the Town commissioners that were appointed at the last term of this court not to pay said fee out of any money that is or may come into there hands all of which was adopted by the court.

(p 38)
Jessee Sapp)
   &o   )
G.B. Sapp   )   Articles of agreement between Jesse Sapp and G.B. Sapp was this day produced in open court for probate and was duly proven by the oaths of James H. Lance the suscribing witness thereto who being first sworn depose and say that they saw the parties sign seal and Execute the same on the day and date it purports to be written and the same was ordered

to be certified for Registration .

On motion the worshipfull court was adjorned <u>till</u> tomorrow morning
nine oclock.

> Thomas Powell Chmr.
> Reunen Evans J.P.
> Watson Cantrell J.P
> Joel Cheatham J.P.
> Joseph Simpson J.P.
> James Goodner J.P.

Woodbury June 7th 1856

(p 39) The Worshipfull County court meet pursuant to adjornment present
the worshipful Thomas Powell chairman &C together with <u>twenty six</u> other
justices which being a sufficient number to transact any <u>Business</u> before
siad court.

On motion ordered by the court that they reconsider the order made
yesterday the 6th day of June It being the first day of the present term
of this court levying a tax for county purposes upon <u>priveledges</u> and
<u>occupations</u> and whereas by said order It was made the <u>duty of the clerk</u>
to demand and receive the one half of the amt. of the tax upon all <u>pri-</u>
<u>vidgeles</u> and occupations (by him to be hereafter <u>Licences</u>) for county
<u>purposes</u> And by an <u>order</u> made this day twenty three <u>justices</u> voting in
the affirmative.

It was ordered by the court that the <u>Licence</u> hereafter be <u>Isued</u>
by said clerk that he shallonly be <u>required to</u> demand and receive the one
forth of the amount of the state tax upon <u>priveledges</u> and occupations
for County purposes and that said clerk is hereby required to refund to
those who have taken such Licence seize the adoption of the order on the
first day of this term (<u>requiring</u> one half of the amount of the state tax
to be collected for County purposes) the one half of the amt. so received
for County purposes and that (p 40) the <u>receits</u> of such persons for the
same shall be a good voucher to said clerk <u>with</u> the county Trustee for all
such sums that the said clerk may be liable for from the Granting of said
<u>Licence</u> under the said first order made at the present term of this Court.
And <u>it</u> is further ordered by the court that the clerk shall only be required
to furnish the <u>shiriff</u> with aduplicate list for the one <u>forth</u> of the
amount of the <u>statetax</u> upon those who have taken out <u>Licence</u> for <u>priveled-</u>
<u>ges</u> and <u>occupations</u> prior to the first day of the present <u>term</u> of this court
or prior to the adoption of the rate of taxes for county purposes on the
said first day of the present term and that the said <u>shiriff</u> shall only be
required to collect the same <u>off</u> for <u>priveledges</u> and Occupations &C

On motion ordered by the court that they reconsider the order rating
the taxes upon property real and personal for County purposes nineteen
Justices voting in the affirmative which being a majority of the justices
in the County it was carried And a proposition being made to reduce the
rate of the County tax layed on the first day of the present term of this
court from the amount of the rate of the state tax twenty justices voting
in the affirmative . It was carried and the clerk ordered to report the

in Wilson County which Lies in Cannon County and have Dennet Ruckers hands.

On motion ordered by the Court that

Joseph Knox
Alfred P. Gowen
Matthew Edwards
Silas A. Robinson and
Allen WAhitfield

(p 45) be appointed a jury of men to vew and mark out aroad from the ford of the river at Calvin Curlees to

On motion ordered by the court that Charles C. Evans, Thomas L. Turner and Sam'l Lance Esqrs. be appointed to allot and divide the hands between James Wood

>Vincen Daily
>
>John Boyd and
>
>G.B. Sapp

And that they mets at Moses Cummins on the 18th June Inst. for to make said devide.

On motion ordered by the Court that John Barkley be appointed overseer of the road leading from Lebanon to manchester begining at the forks of the road near Ephriam Andrews from thence to the stage road near John C. Martins field and have the following hands. viz:

>Alexander McKnight & hands
>
>Sam'l H. McKnight
>
>John A. Travis
>
>Sam'l Travis
>
>William Travis
>
>Jefferson Hix
>
>Joshua Nichols
>
>John Andrews
>
>Sam'l H. Andrews
>
>Pereson Andrews
>
>Lazerous Holeman
>
>Alexander Porterfield
>
>Sam'l Porterfield
>
>James A. Steel
>
>Swenfield Smith
>
>James Henderson
>
>Miles F. Travis
>
>E.A. Orr
>
>James D. Orr
>
>James Suttin
>
>John W. Price and
>
>Joseph C. McGee

On motion ordered by the court that Robert Shepherd be appointed overseer of the Lebanon and manchester Road commencing where it crosses the stage road/thence up Brawleys fork to C.S. Roberts and apply to Esqs. Haly and Simpson for a list of hands.

(p 44)   On motion ordered by the court that Peter Fleming

>Jacob Falkenberry
>
>Cornelius Brandon
>
>B.L. McPerrin and
>
>Joseph Knox Sr.

be appointed a jury of men to vew and mark out a road commencing on the Shelbyville road at or near the end of Joseph Knoxs lane thence to the nearest and best way so as to intersect the McMinnville road at or near the end of Jonothan Jones Lane and also the road that is proposed to be opened from said Jones to the Town of Woodbury and report to the next Court

On motion ordered by the court that

>Wm. Falkenberry Esq.

R.L. Fagan
Azariah Gather
James R. Taylor &
Hampton Sullivan

be appointed a jury of men to vew and mark out a road a road from the upper end of David Hollis Lot or field to intersect again at the most suitable place toward Woodbury and make report at the next term of this court.

On motion ordered by the Court that William McCormac be appointed overseer of the road from the County line of Warren near John Martin Esq. to the Camp Ground and apply to John Martin Esq. for a list of hands.

On motion ordered by the Court that James Pendleton Sr. be appointed overseer of the road from West to the County line of Warren and apply to William Rates & John Pendleton Esq. for a list of hands &C.

(p 45) On motion ordered by the Court that Sirus S. Roberts Be appointed overseer of the road commencing at his own house on the Lebanon Road and thence to William Grays and apply to Esqs. Haly and Simpson to furnish a list of hands. William Ring having appointed the overseer at the last term of this court and being overage would not serve.

On motion ordered by the Court that Joel Maxey be appointed overseer of the road from the creek near David McKnights to the foard of the river near Readyville by said Maxys own House and have the following hands viz.

Phillip Maxey
Andrew Brown
James Mitchell
Thomas Bernett
James Bernett and
David F. Boyd

On motion ordered by the Court that William Adams be appointed overseer of the road begining on the road leading fro Liberty to McMinnville near the widdow Turneys, runing to Richmonds mills and have the same hands that James Grooms (former overseer) had.

On motion ordered by the court that WM Boyd be appointed overseer of the road from the Rutherford County line near John Wetherspoon to the Rutherford line near Robert Boyd (leading to Murfreesboro and have the following hands, viz.

William Boyd
Caleb Horton
Robert Boyd Jr.
Robert Boyd Sr. & hands
David McKnight & hands and
John M. McKnight

On motion Robert George, Ezekiel Hays and Hugh Robinson, three of the jury of men appointed at the last term of this court to vew and (p 46) mark out aroad begining at the Town of Woodbury runing so as to intersect the road leading from Lebanon by Readyville to Hickory Creek near Jonathan Jones , make report that they have vewed and marked out the same according

to the order and report the same to which objections were raised and was
set aside and on motion a jury of men was appointed.

On motion the jury of men that were appointed at the last term of
this court to vew and mark out a road from John Boyds runing   by Henry
Lance through the gap of the short Mountain in a direction of Reuben Blues
to the Warren County line make report that they have vewed and marked out
the same viz leaving the short mountain road at or near John Boyds runing
by the House of Henry Lance intersecting the road leading from Hammonds
(old place) to the Gap of the m ountain at Hammonds and from there to intersect the road leading from William Cummins to Reuben Blues at or near where
the Hicker Jack trace crosses said road , which was adopted.

On motion the jury of men that were appointed at the last term of
this court to vew and mark out a road the best way up the mountain to
commence at the South West corner of B.B. Dickens plantation to intersect
at the top of the ridge make report that they have vewed and marked a
road in conformity with said order which was adopted and ordered by the
court that overseer Richard Holt be appointed overseer of the same and
apply to Esqrs. Sedgley and Emary for a list of hands.

(p 47)

Arthur Warren)
     To   )
Joseph Fowler)   Deed from Arthur Warren to Joseph Fowler for thirty three
acres of land Lying in Cannon County (original Warren County) baring date
the 13th day March 1828, was this day produced in open court for probate
and the Execution thereof was acknowledged by Arthur Warren the (Bargainer)
to be his act and deed for the purposes thereincontained and was ordered
to be certified for Registration.

Abel And H.D. McBroom   )
     To Joseph Clark & others, Town com.) Deed for one Town lot in the
Town of Woodbury (formily Danville) From Abel McBroom and Henry D. McBroom
to Joseph Clark
Archibald Stone
John R. Sane
John Brown and
William Bates (commissioners appointed at the may term of this court to Lay
off and sell the lotts in the Town of Woodbury and for other purposes)
Baring date the 13th day May 1836, was this day produced in open Court for
probate and was duly proven by the oaths of Henry Trott Jr. and John R.
Sullivan the suscribing witners thereto, who being first sworn depose and
say that they heard the Bargainor acknowledge the execution thereof to be
there act and deed for the purposes therein contained and the same was
ordered to be certified for Registration.

Elizabeth & D.D. Brown)
     To   )
Hale Barton   )   Bill of sale from Elizabeth Brown and David D.
Brown To Hds Barton for a negro woman named Tody baring   date the 3rd
day March 1834 was this day produced in open court for probate and the
Execution thereof was duly proven, in part by the oath of Alexander Sullivan.

one of the suscribing witness   thereto the other witness not appearing to qualify.

(p 48) Abel & H.D. McBroom)
            To   )
      Joseph Clark   )   Deed for a half acre town lot in Town of
Woodbury(original Danville) from Abel and Henry D. McBroom to Joseph Clark

Archibald Stone none
John B. Stone
John Brown and
William Bates

(commissioners appointed at the last term of this court to lay off and sell the lots in the Town of Woodbury and for other purposes baring date the 13th day of May 1836 was this day produced in open court for probate and the Execution thereof was duly proven by the oaths of Henry Trott Jr. and John R. Sullivan the suscribing witnesses thereto, who being first sworn depose and say they heard the Bargainers acknowledge the same to be there act and deed for the purpose therein contained which was ordered to be certified for Registration.

On motion the clerk was permitt the oath of office to Thos. Elkins Deputie Shiriff . The Worshipfull Court then adjourned till   tomorrow twelve oclook innorder to Give the clerk time to write up the minutes of this days Buisniss .
                Signed
                (Thomas Powell hrm.
                (J.N. Brown
                (Thomas L. Turner
                (J. Pendleton

            Woodbury 8th June 1836

(p 49)   The Worshipfull County Court meet pursuant To adjornment presensent the worshipful Thomas Powell, chairman
                Thomas/Brown
            Thomas L. Turner and
            John Pendleton Esqrs.
which being a fouram   to transact the Buisness of appointing Overseer &C On motion it was ordered by the court that James/Brown
                Thomas L. Turner and
                Elijah Stephens Esqr.
be appointed to allot & divide the hands Between Jessie Lawrence and Beacham Cannon Overseers &C

The jury of men that were appointed at the last term of the Court to vew and mark out a road from the Town of Woodbury by way of Nathan Neelys to the widdow Travis on Andrews Creek Thence to the Lebanon road in the McKnight settlement, Thence to the settlement about Milton, Have reported favorable to the following, viz. from Woodbury, by Nathan Neelys House there Thence across the mountain to the widdow Smiths Thence to James McKnight thence to S.F. McKnights, Thence to the Lebanon Roadat Col, Jarrets all of which is adopted by the Court.

On motion ordered by the court that
> R.W. Lemay
> Thomas Cooper
> John E. Sullivan
> John Wood Sr.
> James James
> B.H.F. Phillips &
> B.C. Stephens

be appointed a jury of men to vew and mark out aroad the nearest and best way commencing at or near the east end of H.D. McProoms tract of land on the stage road leading through Woodbury to McMinnville thence to the topp of the ridge above R.W. Lemays so as (p50) to intersect the old road leading from Dansville to the stone fort and Jacksborough thence to the Warren County line in a direction to Jacksborough and make report to the next term of this court.

There being no further Buisness before the Court it was adjurned til court in Cources.
Signed
  | Thomas Powell ohr.
  (James M. Brown
  (T.L. Turner
  (J. Pendleton

                    July Term
(p 51)
State of Tennessee)
Cannon County   ) at the County Court held for Cannon County at the Court House in the Town of Woodbury on the first Monday in July it being the 4th day A.D. 1836 and the sixtieth year of American independance — Present the Worshipful

> John C. Martin
> Isaac Finley
> James L. Escart
> Allen Hailey
> Elijah Stephens
> Thomas L. Turner
> James M. Brown
> John Melton
> Charles C. Evans
> John Pendleton
> John Martin
> Wm. B. Foster
> Watson Cantrrell
> Thomas Simpson
> Lemuel Moore
> William Bates
> John Frazour
> James Goodner and
> Jonathan C. Doss Esqrs.

Whereupon the following orders were made (to wit.
Whereas the Worshipfull Thomas Powell chairman of said court being absent on motion ordered that James M. Brown Esquire be appointed to act as chairman protem during the Term of the present Court.

On motion ordered that Daniel Findley be appointed overseer of the road that leads up Carsons fork from the foot of the ridge to the Hollow Springs and the aforesaid Findley & James Sisson divide the hands on said creek

On motion ordered that the road be Turned for the benefit of James Goodner on the right hand side of a small field.

On motion ordered that Samuel Daily be appointed overseer of the Statesville road beginning at Moses Fites running to the Wilson County line and have the same hands that John Turner Former overseer had.

(p 52) On motion ordered that Anson Thompson be continued as overseer of the road beginning at the mouth of Cavender fork running up the same to the Wilson County line and have his former hands and bounds.

On Motion ordered that Robert Pallett be appointed overseer in the manchester road beginning at Lyon L. Roberts running up to D.C. Dickens in place working to Capt. Grays.

On motion ordered that Joseph W. Evans be appointed overseer of the road leading from Liberty to Lancaster and that he work the said road that L.B. Vick former overseer worked and have the same hands and bounds.

On motion ordered that
> William A. Nusmith
> Peter Hayes
> L.B. Vick
> Samuel H. Burton
> David Fite
> James Pendleton and
> Lemuel Moore

be appointed a jury of men to vew and mark out a road commencing at Neils shop on Dismal Creek the nearest and best way to Liberty and report to the next term of the court.

On motion ordered that —
> William B. Evans Sr.
> William Stone
> John Halpain
> Richard B. Ford and
> William Elkins

be appointed a jury of men to vew and make a road the nearest and best way beginning at the mouth of the rook house fork running up the same and across the ridge to the Wilson County line below Wily Ratleys and make report to the next term of this court.

(p 53) On motion ordered that
> John C. Kanaday
> Enoch Jones
> Henry Kersey
> Samuel Purger and
> Archibald Zane

be appointed a jury of men to vew and mark a road the nearest and most convinient way commencing at or near Lincolns Ferry on the Caney Fork running thence to the headwaters of Stones River and make report to the next term of this court.

On motion and partition ordered that

William Braswell
Henry Hart
Nathan Sellers
John Dutton &
Flemming Jirmal

be appointed a jury of men to vew and mark a road from the mouth of the Lyclmore fork the nearest and best way running by the muster- ground thence the nearest and best way so as to intersect the McMinnville road at or near Mrs. Farringtons and make report to the next term of this court.

On motion and partition ordered that

Davis Patton
William Haney
Zachariah Dush
Wiley Willis and
Jessie Gilley

be appointed a jury of men to view and make a road from David Pattons Cabinet Shop(on the stone fort Road) passing near Wells meeting house and Jessie Gilleys and continue the same course towards manchester so far as the Coffee County line And make report to the next term of this court.

(p 54) On mo tion and partition ordered by the Court that Moses Shelby

Alexander Finley
David D. Hipp
Isaac Young and
John Craft

be appointed a jury of men to vew and mak a road from the Town of Woodbury towards manchester in Coffee County crossing the road leading from McMinnville to Shelbyville at or near Mr. Darnells and make report to the next term of this court.

On motion and partition ordered by the court that Peter W. Clark

James J. Bogle
Osborn Mullinox
John Turner
Elijah Trewit
Henry Fite and
Daniel Force

be appointed a jury of men to vew and work a road commencing on the stage road at or near James Allens, Thence the nearest a d best rout passing John Turners and Nathaniel Hays so as to intersect the road leading from Richmonds Hill to the Short mountain at or near I. Bogles and make report to the next term of this court.

On motion and partition ordered that

Robert Baily
John Boyd
Francis Spurlock
Henry Lance
John Herriman

Jessie Sullins and William Cummings be appointed a jury of men to vew
and mark a road leaving the Short - mountain road at or near William
Cummings running by Robert Bailys thence the nearest and best way so as to
intersect the clear fork and Short mountain road at or near Frances
Spurlocks and make report to the next term of this court.

(p 55) On motion and partition   ordered that
                                    Barton B. Dickens
                                    William Ring
                                    Peterson Gilley
                                    Robert Pallett and
                                    James Lee
be appointed a jury of men to vew and mark a road Beginning at David
Pattons Saw mill running thence so as to intersect the Dug hollow road at or
near the House of William Grays and make report to the next Term of this
court.

        On motion and partition   ordered that
                                    John Henderson
                                    James Ferrell
                                    F.G. Hamilton
                                    John H. Smith
                                    John Bragg and
                                    John C. Cannon
be appointed a jury of men to vew and mark out a road leading from Woodbury
with the stage road to Samuel Taswells newground fence thence by the way
of Sam'l Underhills crossing Lar - Creek between Fos Travis and Levi
Porkers thence by way of widow Smiths down Andrews creek to the county line
and make report to the next term of this Court.

        On motion and portition   ordered that
                                    Thos. Vance
                                    William Givens
                                    John Salls
                                    Moses McKnight
                                    Edwin J. Rosebury and
                                    Drewry Mathis
be appointed a jury of men to vew and mark a road Beginning at the most
suitable place between Thomas Vances and the top of the ridge on the road
leading from Woodbury to Lebanon running thence on said ridge to some point
between Lazerous Holemans and John Salls and thence the most suitable way
to the Rutherford County line near Col. Jarratts and make report to the next
Term of this court.

        On motion ordered that
                                    Robert Vinson
                                    Joseph Pinkerton
                                    Hamon Barrett
                                    Richard Tenpenny and
                                    John A. Dunn
be appointed a jury of men to vew and mark a road leading from woodbury
up the mossy cane hollow to the Wilson County line and make report to the
next Term of this Court.

On motion ordered that –

      William Falkenberry Esq.

      Robert L. Fagan

      Azariah Gather

      James R. Taylor and

      Hampton Sullivan

be continued a jury of men to vew and mark a road from the upper end of
David Hollis lot or field and to intersect it again in a direction towards
Manchester insted of Woodbury as ordered by the last term of this Court.

      Richard U. Lemay

      Thomas Cooper

      John F. Sullivan

      James James &

      Benjamin C. Stephens

a part of the jury of men appointed at the last Term of this court to vew
and mark a road the nearest and best way commencing at the east end of H.D.
McBrooms tract of land on the stage road leading through Woodbury to McMinnville) Thence to the top of the ridge above R.U. Lemays so as to intersect
the old road leading from Danville to the stone fort and Jacksborough to the
Warren County line towards Jacksboro make report as follows to wit (p 57)
Beginning near the east end of H.D. McBrooms tract of land running thence
with the stage road to Beacham Cannons stable leaving it on the right hand
leaving the stage road running thence with a line of marked trees up Hills
Creek to Ragsdale shop thence with the oald road leading from Danville To the
stone fort and Jacksboro to the Warren County line to the top of the ridge
above Richard A. Lemays all of which was approved of and adopted by the
Court, as a road and on motion ordered that Benjamin C. Stephens be appointed overseer of said road an apply to James M. Brown and Thomas L. Turner
for a list of hands.

      Baxter B. Dickens

      Alexander Petty and

      Thomas Williams

a part of the jury view appointed at the last term of this court to vew
and mark a road the nearest and best way from Woodbury to intersect the
Hickory Creek road at or near Jonathan Jones make report as follows (to wit)
That they have vewed and marked said road commencing at Jonothan Jones,
Thence by the wodow McGills and up the hill by Joseph Brandons leaving siad
Brandons on the left into the Low Cap on the ridge southwest of Benj. Hayes
field Thence through one corner of said Hayes field and down the hill cross-
the upper corner of Alexanders field crossing the Creek at the best place
Thence up said creek to the mouth of Dashams Hollow Thence with said Hollow
through Robert Georges field (by his Gin) Thence crossing James (p 53)
Taylors field running as to intersect the stage road at or near the ford of
the river SC.

To whichreport objections were raised upon the ground of damage &c. And the
same was suspended for the time being and the following persons were appointed as a jury revew – to wit. Milton Fowler

      Joseph Warren

      Daniel M. Stewart

      Henry Hayes and

      Ezekiel Hayes

to proceed and Revew said road as designated in said report and to see if
the same could not be so changed and placed upon other Ground so as to prevent a damage and if not to say what damage shall be awarded the injured
parties if any And make report to the next Term of this Court.

Alford P. Gowen
Joseph Knox
Silas Robinson and
William Whitfield

a part of the jury of men appointed at the last term of this court to vew and mark out a road from the ford of the river at Calvin Curlees to Blake Sagelys Esqrs. and make report as follows (to wit) Beginning at the ford of the river at Calvin Curlees running so as to strike the mouth of Joseph Knoxs lane Thence to the mouth of Thomas Goings lane (now supposed to belong to the heirs of Thomas Hopkins) Thence with the old road to Blake Sagelys Esqrs. Thence to the Coffee County line all of which was approved of by the court and adopted as a road And on motion ordered Jonathan Bateman (p 59) be appointed overseer of said road and have the following hands tooclear out and work the same (to wit)

Joseph Knox
William Knox
T. Perry
T. Watson
James N. Watson
J. Bateman
J.W. Bateman
E. Bateman
Isaac Bateman
M. Edwards
H. Edwards
R. Pallet
James Alexander
Alexander Lothing
William N. Moore & brothers
T.P. Stacey
Josiah W. Stacey
John R. Woosley
Isham Adams and hands
Partenous Pack
Richard McGinnis and
Isaac Gallon

a part of the jury of men appointed at the last term of this court to vew and mark a road beginning at the mouth of Holmes Creek where it runs into the Caney Fork running up said creek to the point of the ridge (that runs down from Wards old place) Thence to run up said ridge (or round the same as may be most proper) so as to intersect with the road running from Wards old place to the Camp Ground make report as follow (to wit) That they have vewed and marked the same according to the calls of said order all of which are adopted and approved of by the court as a road And on motion ordered that Richard McGinnis be appointed overseer of said road and apply to Joel Cheatham and John Frazeur for a list of hands to clear out and work the same.

(p 60) James Ferrell Deputy Shff. present to the court a sertificate from George Cannon, B. Moore and Sam'l Burke, judges appointed to judge an alection held at the house of Cahrles Alexanders on the 23rd day of June A.D. 1856 to elect a constable in the forth civil District to fill the vacancy occasioned by the resignation of Roswell Soap who certify that Thomas Hayes was duly elected to said office And on motion the said Hayes came into court and after being duly qualified entered into bond together with his securities (to wit) Henry Hays and John Hayes) in the sum of One thousand dollars conditioned as the Law directs.

On motion ordered that Jonathan Bateman and William L. Covington Cons. be appointed to wait upon the court and jury at the next circuit Court.

John Melton)
   Deed)
Stephen Cantrell) A deed of conveyance from John Melton to Stephen Cantrell for Fifteen acres of land lying in Cannon County(originally WarrenCounty) bearing date 15th of August A.D. 1834 (p 60) was this day produced in open court for probate and was duly acknowledged by John Melton the Bargainor and ordered to be certyfyed for registration.

(p 61) Ancil Melton)
      Deed)
Stephen Cantrell) A deed of conveyance from Ancil Melton to Stephen Cantrell for thirty acres of land lying in Cannon County(originally Warren County) bearing date the 15th day of August A.D. 1834 was this day produced in open court for probate and was duly acknowledged by Ancil Melton the bargainer and ordered to be certifed for registration.

James Melton)
   Deed)
Stephen Cantrell) a deed of conveyance from James Melton to Stephen Cantrell for Ten acres of land lying in Cannon County(originally Warren County) bearing date the 12th day of August A.D. 1834 was this day produced in open court for probate and was duly acknowledged by James Melton the bargainor and ordered to be certifyed for Registration.

James Wood)
  Deed)
Josiah Youngblood) a deed of conveyance from James Wood to Josiah Youngblood forninety and one half acres of land lying in Cannon County (originally Warren County) bearing date 19th December A.D. 1834 was this day produced in open court for probate and was duly acknowledged by JamesWood the Bargainor and ordered to be certifyed fr Registration.

(p 62) Joseph Clark & others)
       Deed)
James Taylor   ) a deed of conveyance from Joseph Clarke
                                        John/Stone
                                        John Brown
                                        William Bates and
                                        Archibald Stone
Commissioners &c for one town lot lying and being in the Town of Woodbury and known in plann of said Town Lot No. 54. bearing date 13th day June A.D. 1836 was this day produced in open court for probate and was duly proven by the oaths of James Rasey and Adam Elrod two of the suscribing witness thereto and ordered to be certifyed for Registration.

On motion ordered that William Moore Be appointed Guardian for Jacob Moore minor heir of Jessie G. Moore dec'd who together with his securities Joseph Ramsey and Arthur Warren Came into Court and entered into Bond payable to Thomas Powell Chairman and his successors in office in the sum of Two thousand five Hundred dollars conditioned as the Law directs.

Elizabeth & D.D. Brown)
)
  Bill Sale   )
)
Hale Barton   ) was this day produced in open court by an for probate and duly provenod by the oath of Henry Clifton one of the suscribing
witness thereto who failed to appear at the last court to qualify to the
same and was ordered to be certifyed for registration.

(p 63) On motion ordered that William Moose be appointed Guardian for
Elizabeth Jane Moore minor heir of Rowland Moore dec'd who together with
his securities Henry Clifton and Arthur Warren came into Court and entered
into Bond payable to Thomas Powell Chairman of the Court and his successors
in office in the sum of three hundred dollars condition as the Law directs.

On motion the court proceeded to the consideration of adopting plans
for building the Court house and jail in the Town of Woodbury present the Worshipful
    John C. Martin
    Isaac Findley
    James L. Essary
    Allen Haily
    Thomas L. Turner
    James M. Brown
    John Melton
    Charlis C . Evans
    John Pendleton
    John Martin
    Wm. B. Foster
    Watson Cantrell
    Thomas Simpson and
    William Bates Esqrs.
who being a majority of all the justices of the county and the questions
being put whether or not the court would proceed to the consideration
of the above subject at this Term of Court and on taken the ays and noes
there being eight of said justices voting in the affirmative the qustion
was carried and on motion ordered that --
    John Melton
    John Martin
    Thomas L. Turner
    William Bates and
    John C. Martin Esqrs.
be appointed a committee for the purpose of examining into plans for the
constructing and probible cost of said buildings and report as soon as
practicable at the present Term of this court who with drew for the above
purposes &C.

(p 64) The committa appointed at the present term of this court for
the purpose of examining into proper plans for constructing a court house
and jail for the County (to wit)
    John Martin
    John Melton
    Thos. L. Turner
    William Bates and
    John C. Martin Esqrs.

have presented to the Court a written report of their deliberations so
far which was read and approved of by the court and in motion ordered to
be spread upon the minuets which is as follows (to wit) We the undersigned committa appointed at the July Term of the Cannon County Court
for the purpose of examinging into the plan and dementions for the
constructing of a court house and jail have had before them a partial plan
of the Court house in Bedford County which they approve of and have appointed three of their said committa to proceed to Shalbyville and there
examine and ascertain the proper dimentions of the said Court house
and also the cost of the same and to obtain any other such information
as may be necessary concerning said buildings, and make report to the next
Term of this court and have appointed as said sub committa

> John C. Martin
> John Melton and
> John Martin

Given under our hands this the 4th day of July A.D. 1836 signed
(p 65)
> John Martin
> John Melton
> John C. Martin
> Thomas L. Turner &
> William Bates

There being no further business on motion the worshipfull Court adjorned
until tommorrow 2 oclock signed

> James M. Brown Chairman
> Thomas Simpson protem
> John Melton
> William Bates

Woodbury July 5th day A.D. 1836 The worshipfull court met persuant to adjournment present the worshipful —

> James M. Brown chr. pro.
> Elijah Stephens
> Thomas Simpson
> John Melton &
> William Bates Esqrs.

Whereupon the following orders &C were made (to wit)

On motion ordered that John Vance be appointed overseer of the road
beginning on the Lebanon at Nathan Neelys thence along the same as marked
to Joseph Mo Cains field and apply to James Smith and George Gannon for
a list of hands.

(p 66) On motion ordered that Francis G. Hamilton be appointed overseer
of the road (new) beginning at Josiah McCains field to Andrews creek
and apply to David McKnight and and Edward Fragg to furnish a list of
hands.

On motion ordered that Sam'l F. McKnight be appointed overseer of the
new road beginning at Andrews creek running to Col Jarretts as marked and
apply to Col. Jarrett & David M. McKnight for a list of hands.

> James M. Brownchr pro
> Thomas Simpson
> John Melton
> William Bates

State of Tennessee)
Cannon County   )   At a County Court began and held on the first Monday
of August it being the first day of said month A.D. 1836 present the
Worshipfull

> Thomas Powell chr. &C
> John Frazeur
> Blake Sagely
> Samuel Lance
> Joel Cheatham
> Allen Hailey
> Martin Phillips
> Watson Cantrell
> William Bates
> David Fisher
> Elijah Stephens
> John Pendleton
> Isaac Findley
> Charles C. Evans
> John C. Martin
> James L. Essary
> James M. Brown
> John Martin
> Lemuel Moore
> Jonathan C. Doss
> JamesGoodner
> James Beatie
> Jonathan Fuston
> Lemuel Turney and
> William B. Foster Esqrs

(p67)
Samuel J. Garrison Clerk of our said court presented a commission from his
Excellency Newton Cannon Governor &C to Alexander McKnight as a justice
of the peace for Cannon County Whereupon the said McKnight came into open
Cpurt and was duly quallifyed   into office as such.

    Then Court then proseded   to appoint a Venice faceas for the next
circuit court whereupon the following persons were appointed (to wit)
John C. Martin & Alexander McKnight in Dist. No 1
Thomas Powell & Isaac Findley in Dist No. 2
Allen Hailey & David Patton in Dist No. 3
James L. Essery & Blake Sagely in Dist. No. 4
John Pendleton & Isaac W. Elledge   "   "   5
Elijah Stephens & Benj. Pendleton   "   "   6
John Melton & Charles C. Evans   "   "   7
Ezekiel Hammonds & gabriel Lance   "   "   8
Harvey Johnson & John Martin Sr.   "   "   9
Lemuel Turney & Thomas Martin   "   " 10
Friley Martin & John Parsley   "   " 11
Isaac Adcock & James Coger   "   " 12
John Jenkins
Lemuel Moore
Reuben Evans
German Gosset
Joseph Adamson

George L. Given & James Bryant in Dist NO 13
John Vantrees & Hesekiel Powers   "   "   14
Benjamin Avant & Peter Hayes   "   "   15
David Taylor SR. & Ezekiel Taylor   "   "   16

(p 68)
    On motion ordered by the Court that

                              Charles C. Evans
                              William West
                              Moses Cummings
                              Arthur Warren
                              William Dates
                              Henry Ford
                              Joseph Ramsey
                              William Young
                              William Preston
                              Robert George
                              Samuel Laswell &
                              Richard Tenpenny

be appointed a jury of men to vew a road lately vewed and marked by a
jury of men appointed at the June term of the Court Beginning at or near
John Woods on the stage road running up Hills Creek through the plantations
of the said John Wood & Arch'd Stone then thereexamine said road and see
whether or not if the same could not be placed upon other ground equally as
much to the public without an injury to the said Wood & Stone and if not
to say what damage if any shall be awarded them upon their complaint and
make report to the next term of this court.

                              Moses Shelby
                              David D. Hipp &
                              Isaac Young

a part of a jury of men appointed at the last term of this court to vew
and marke a road from Woodbury towards Manchester crossing the road from
McMinnville to Shelbyville at or near Mr. Darnels. And make report as
follows: (to wit) running with the stage road to John Woods thence up the
branch to Lemays thence up the ridge with the old road to the forks of the
road in the barrons thence near Mrs. Pelmsthence near William Crafts
thence on the ridge on the (p 69) east side of the White oak slash crossing
the creek near the ford where the Nashville road crosses the same Thence
on the ridge to Darnells and on motion ordered that the same be established as a county road. On motion ordered by the court that the decission
of the jury of men appointed this term to assess damages &C upon the road
leading from John Woods up Hills Creek to the top of the riadge
Richard U. Lemays shall rule and govern this :
that part of this road running through the fa
Wood & Arch'd Stone.

                              William Falkenberry
                              Hampton Sullivan and
                              Azariah Cather

a part of the jury of men appointed at the last term of this court to
vew and mark a road from the upper end of David Hollis lot or field and
to intersect it again towards Manchester and make report as follows,
(to wit) that they have agreed to lay said road so as to intersect the old
road below Thomas Stokes dwelling & shop and on motion the same was established as a county road.

William Cummings
Frances Spurlock
John Harriman
Jessie Sullens
Robert Baily &
Hury Lance
the jury of men appointed at the last Term of this court to vew and mark
a road leaving the short mountain road at or near William Cummings, running
by Robert Ballys, the nearest and best way so as to intersect the Clear Fork
& short mountain road at or near (p 70) Frances Spurlocks and make report
as follows (to wit) Leaving the road near William Cummings thence up the hollow
by Robert Baileys thence to John Youngs Thence to Cyrell Durhams Thence down
the clear fork intersecting the short mountain road at Francis Turners and on
motion that the same be established as a county road.

William Stone
William Elkins
William B. Evans
John Halpain
the jury of men appointed at the last Term of this court to vew and mark a
road the nearest and best way beginning at the mouth of the rock House fork
running up the same and across the ridge to the Wilson County Line below
Wily Ratleys and make report as follows (to wit) beginning at the mouth of
the rock House fork running up said fork through the corner of Benjamin Allens
field, Thence to James Stone, Thence to the Wilson County line and on motioned
ordered that the same be established as a county road.
Jessie Gilley
William Haney
William Winnis and
Zachriaj Dush
a part of the jury of men appointed at the last Term of this court to vew and
mark a road from David Pattons passing near Wells meeting House towards Manchester to the Coffee County line and make report as follows (to wit) that
they have vewed marked the same agreeable to the Order of the court and report
favorable. And on (p 71) motion ordered that the same be established as a county
road and that William Haney be appointed overseer of the same from the beginning of said road at Pattons Cabinet shop to the line between Willes & Bushes
And that James Marchbanks be appointed overseer from said line to the old
road near Mrs. Herrods on top of the mountain. And on montion ordered that
Baxter B. Dickens and David Patton furnish the said overseers with a list of
hands to clear out and work said road.
Robert Vinson
Hayman Barrett
Joseph Pinkerton &
John A. Dunn
a part of the jury of men appointed at the last Term of this court to vew and
mark a road leading from Woodbury up the mossy cave Hollow to the Wilson
County line and make report as follows (to wit) Beginning at the ford of the
river at James Sullivans running Thence with the old fence rowe between
James M. Browns and Mrs. Sullivans Thence up the Branch to Mrs. Brownsfields
Thence to Joseph Pinkertons, Thence up the mossy cave Hollow to Alexander
Vinsons, Thence up the mane Hollow to the Wilson County line.
And on motion ordered that the same be established as a county road and

that Robert Vinson be appointed Overseer of the same and apply to James
M. Brown & Elijah Stephens for a list of hands to clear out said road and
keep the same in repare.

        Drewry Mathis
        Thomas Vanse
        Moses McKnight
        John Salls

a part of the jury of men appointed at the last term of this court (p 72)
TO VIEW and mark out a road beginning on the top of the ridge at the most
suitable place between Thomas Vances and the road leadingfrom Woodbury
to Lebanon running thence to some point between Lazareth Holemans and
John Salls And thence the most suitable way to the Rutherford County line
near Col Jarratts And make report as follows (to wit) Leaving the big
road above William Givens running on the said ridge until opposite
Lazareth Holemans there leaving the ridge and running to the Rutherford
County line near Col. Jarratts And on motion ordered that the same be
appointed overseer of said road beginning at the Lebanon road and from
thence to the top of the ride to a marked popular. And that Alexander
McKnight Sr. be appointed overseer from the marked poplar to the top of the
ridge at Lazareth Holemans And that E.J. Rosebury be appointed overseer from
the topof the ridge at Lazareth Holemans to the Wilson County linenear Col.
Jarratts And it is further ordered by the Court that

        Thomas Vance
        Lazareth Holeman &
        Samuel McKnight

furnish said overseer with a list of handsto clear out said road and keep
the same in repair.

        Milton Fowler
        Daniel M. Stewart
        Henry Hayes and
        Joseph Warren

a part of the juty of men appointed at the last term of this court to
revew and examine a road as layed out by a jury of men appointed at the
June Term of this (p 73) Court beginning and running as follows (to wit)
commencing at Jonathan Jones Thence by the widow McGills and up the hill
by Joseph Brandons (leaving said Brandons on the left) into the low gap
on the ridge southwest of Benjamin Hays field and down the hill crossing
the upper corner of Alexanders field crossing the creek at the best place
Thence up said creek to the mouth of Bashams hollow Thence with said hollow
through Robert Georges field (passing his fince) so as to intersect the
stage road at or near the ford of the river then there to examine said road
as marked out and see whether or not the same could be changed and put
upon other ground to answer as well for the public conveinance and if not
see what damages shall be awarded the complaining parties as follows (to
wit) after examining said road as marked out by the former jury of men
have agreed to change said road as follows (to wit) running from the widow
McGills Through Jessie Todds Lot, Thence up the hill to the low Gap south
west of Benjamin Hayes field Thence down the hollow by James P. Todds to
the lower end of Milton Fowlers lane Thence up the creek toAkelus Alexanders intersecting the aforesaid road as first marked out And on motion
ordered that the same be established as a county road And that Gideon
Duke be appointed overseer of said road from the lower end of Jonathan
Jones lane to the top of the ridge between Joseph A. Brandons and James
Todd And that Britton Moore be appointed overseer from thence to Bashams
Gap and William P. George be appointed overseer from thence to the ford of
the river.

(p 74) On motion ordered by the Court that Peter W. Clarke & others be continued as a jury of view persuant   to an order made at the last Term of this court and that they report to the next term &C

On motion ordered that John S. Canady and others be continued a jury of men persuant   to an order made at the last term of this court and they report to the next term &C.

On motion ordered that William Braswell and others be continued a jury of view persuant   to an order made at the last term of this Court and they report to the next term &C

On motion ordered by the Court that John P. West
Joel H. West
James Garrison
Benjamin Garrison and
Andrew Pickett
be appointed a jury of men to vew and mark a road in a direction from Alexandria to Woodbury begining on the stage road near Benjamin Garrisons Thence the most practicable way so as to intersect the Wilson County line near John P. West and make report to the next term of this court.

On motion ordered by the court that Levi Parker be appointed overseer of the stage road from the ford of the river at Daniel M. Stewarts to the to the crossroads near John C. Martins field and that Hale Barton and John C. Martin be appointed to furnish him with a list of hands to keep said road in repairs.

On motion ordered by the court that Benjamin Clark be appointed (p 75) overseer from the Gap of the ridge near Indian Creek to the old Warren County line and that Joel Cheatham furnish with a list of hands to work said road and keep it in repare

On motion ordered by the Court that Joel Cheatham be permitted to rebuild his mills on Holmes creek upon his own land and at his own Expence &C

On motion ordered by the court that James Manahan be appointed overseer of the road from Milton to Shelbyville begining at the Cross roads at Marke Staceys thence to William Grays, and be allowed the following list of hands (to wit)
I. Alexander
Alexander Lothing
William H. Moore
Ephriam Moore
G. Manahan
B. Stacy
P.R. Stacey
J.W. Stacey
Robert Pallet
Osee Manahan
James Manahan &
Hiram Self

On motion ordered by the court that David McKnight

James D. Orr &
Phillip Maxey

be appointed to allot and divide the lands between —

Joel Maxey
John Barkley and
William N. Boyd overseer

any order made by the court heretofore not withstanding.

Benjamin C. Stephens Administrator of the Estate of Joel Mears deceased made report of the account of sales of said Estate and on motion the same was ordered to be spread upon records in the Proper Book.

Harman James Administrator of the Estate of Dan'l James deceased made report of the account of sales of the property of said Estate as also a list of notes &c which on motion was ordered by the court to spread upon record in the proper book.

(p 76) Thomas Lawrence, Guardian of Elijah Duncan came into Court and report that said Duncan has recovered his proper mind and wishes to take charge of his Estate and affect again Whereupon the Court appointed John Reynolds as Commissioners to settle with the said Lawrence and make report of the same to the next or succeeding term of this court.

John Brown)
  Deed)
Thomas Barrett) A deed of conveyance from John Brown to Thomas Barrett for ten acres of land Lying in Cannon County baring date the 30th day of October 1835 was this day produced in open Court for acknowledgement by the said John Brown (the bargainer) to be his act and Deed for the purposes therein mentioned and on motion ordered that the same be certified for Regis.

William Parton)
  Deed)
John Pendleton) A deed of conveyance from William Parton to John Pendleton for fifty two acres of land Lying in Cannon County (originally in Warren County) Baring date the 15th day of March 1856, was this day produced in open court for acknowledgement and was duly acknowledged by Wm. Parton (the Bargainer) to be his act and deed for the purposes therein mentioned and upon the day it bares date And on motion Ordered by the Court that the same be certified for Registration.

Arthur Warren)
  Deed)
Henry Warren) A deed of conveyance from Arthur Warren to Henry Warren for 89½ acres of land Lying in Cannon County 'originally Rutherford County)(p 77) baring date the 20th day December 1825 was this day produced in open court for probate and was duly acknowledged by Arthur Warren (the bargainer) to be his act and Deed for the purposes therein mentioned And on motion ordered that the same certified for Registration.

Edmund Jones)
  Deed)
Hamon Barrett) A deed of conveyance from Edmond Jones to Hamon Barrett for fifty acres of Land Lying in Cannon County Baring date the 29th day of July 1856 was this day produced produced in open court for probate

and was duly proven by the oaths of William Barton and William V. Henderson subcribing witnesses thereto and ordered the same to be certified for Registration.

John Martin & John C. Martin Esq. a part of the subb Committee appointed at the last term of this court to proceed to Shelbyville to Examine the Bedford Cort House , Jail &C make report as follows (to wit) The undersigned a subb Committee appointed at the County Court for Cannon County fro the purpose of proceeding to Shelbyville to asertain   the cost, the plan and the dimintions of the court House of Shelbyville do hereby certify that from certain information derived from certain Gentlemen of the bare we were induced to beleave it would be a useless trip &C

Signed
John C. Martin and
John Martin

did not think it conveninet to go to Shelbyville &C and on motion ordered by the Court that the said Committee be discharged from further duties &C

John C. Martin Esq. presented for the consideration of the court a partial plan of the Court H. in (p73) Rutherford County, whereupon On Motion the court proceeded to consideration of said plan present the worshipfull

Watson Cantrell
JohnnFrazour
Elijah Stephens
Joel Cheatham
Wm. B. Foster
Thomas Simpson
Alexander McKnight
Lemuel Turney
Jonothan Fuson
Charles C. Evans
John Melton
John C. Martin
James Beatie
David Fisher
James M. Brown
Isaac Findley
John Penileton
Thos. L. Turner
Sam'L Lance
James Goodner
Allen Hailey
Jonathan C. Doss
Isaac W. Eledge
Johh Martin and
Thomas Powell Esqrs.

Whereupon On motion the question was taken by ays and noes whether or not the Court would suspend the further consiration of the subject at this time and on taking the question by ays and noes the same was decided in the affirmative.

On motion ordered by the court that Henry Warren

Charles Alexander
Joseph Warren
Sam'l Lacefield &
William Moore

be appointed a jury of men to vew and change the road leading from Jones
to Woodbury from the point at the end of Milton Fowlers lane so as to
intersect the stage road near Joseph Ramseys. And report to the term of this
Court.

On motion ordered by the Court that James Todd Sr. be appointed overseer
of the road leading from Woodbury near Jonathan Jones - begining at the stone
fort above said Jones - runing to the top of the mountain near John
Findleys field to a marked tree and apply to John Brown and Isaac Findley
Esq. to furnish a list of hands.

On motion Thomas G. Wood is appointed and quallified as deputy clerk
of this court.

(p 79) On motion ordered by the Court that Ezekiel Hays be appointed
overseer of the road leading from Woodbury near Jonothan Jones begining
on the top of the mountain near John Findley field runing to a tree
marked for that purpose by Esq. Findley and apply to John Brown & Esqrs.
Findley for a list of hands to clear out and and keep the same in repare.

On motion ordered by the court that William George be appointed overseer if the road leading from Woodbury by Jonathan Jones beginning on
a marked tree for that purpose runing to intersect the stage road near
Bridge in Stones River And apply to John Brown and Esq. Findley for a list
of hands to clear out and keep the same in repare.

Nathan Parker one of the deputic shiriffs Came into open court and
on motion of George Grizzle High sheriff the said Parker was qualified
into office and on motion ordered that the same be spread upon the minuets
of the court.

The Worshipful Cout then adjorned till tomorrow morning eight oclock.

                    Thomas Powell Chrn.
                    John Melton
                    Samuel Lance
                    Thomas L. Turner
                    C.C. Evans
                    Lemuel Moore
                    J. Pendleton

(p 80) Tuesday Morning Augt.the 2nd 1836.
    The Worshipful cort meet pursuant adjornment -- the worshipful

                    Thomas Powell Chmr.
                    Charles C. Evans
                    John Melton
                    Sam'l Lance
                    William Bates
                    John C. Martin
                    Alexander McKnight
                    Isaac Finley
                    John Pendleton
                    Isaac W. Eledge

James H. Brown
Thomas L. Turner &
Lemuel Moore Esqrs.

On motion ordered by the Court that R.E. Ford be appointed overseer of the New road from the mouth of the rock House fork to the Wilson County line below wily Ratleys as marked &C and that Charles Evans Esqr. be appointed to furnish him with a list of hands to clear out said road and keep the same in repare &C

On motion ordered by the Court that Milton Fowler and Esqr. Findley be appointed to furnish Gideon Duke and Britton Moore overseers &C with a list of hands.

On motion made by James H. Brown Esq. the question was taken by ays and noes whether or not the court would reconsider the vote taken on the first day of this term upon refering the adopting of plans for the building of a court house and jail, and upon counting the votes taken by ays and noes it was unanimously decided in the affirmative - Lemuel Moore Esqr. refusing to vote and Esqr. Bledge being absent.

William Bates Esq. one of the Town commissioners handed into Court for the consideration of the same (81) a petition signd by himself Archibald Stone, John B. Stone and John Brown others of said commissioners shewing to the Court that they had proceeded according to Law to sell out the lots in the Town of Woodbury and that they had securied in their hands from twelve to fourteen thousand dollars in notes. And that they were now ready to receive plans under the order of the court for the publich buildings and that they were desirous that the Court should give then such orders and instructions as they deem necesary so that they may proceed as soon as practical with said Building as they beleave the Good of the publich very much required the same to be done And that they would suggest to the court the propriety of instructing them in the orders that may be made by the Court to set the same under contract on Wednesday the 31st day of the present month.

Thereupon John C. Martin Esqr. again presented a partial plan of the Court House in the Town of Murfresborough And on motion of James H. Brown the court proceeded to vote by ays and noes whether or not the court would approve of said law for the plan of a Court House to be built for Cannon County in the Town of Woodbury Thereupon on calling the names of the members of the Court who were present it was unanimously adopted all the members present voting in the affirmative (to wit)

Sam'l Lance
James H. Brown
Isaac W? Bledge
Isaac Findley
John Melton
John Pendleton
William Bates
Charles C. Evans
John C. Martin
Elijah Stephens

Thos. L. Turner
Alexander McKnight and
Thomas Powell Esq.

On motion of Sam'l Lance Esqr. the following order was unanimously
adopted by the Court there present the worshipfull (p 82)

John C. Martin Esq.
Isaac Findley
Sam'l Lance
John Melton
Charles C. Evans
Thomas L. Turner
John Pendleton
Alexander McKnight
James M. Brown
Isaac W. Eledge
William Dates
Elijah Stephens and
Thomas Powell Esqrs. (to wit)

Ordered by the Court that the court house for Cannon County be erected
in the center of the publich square in the Town of Woodbury and that the
five commissioners appointed by the County Court of said County of Cannon
to Lay off and sell the Lots in said Town and there successors in office
Be and they are hereby directed to let the same out to be built according
the plans of the court house in the Town of Murfresborough Rutherford
County Tennessee, presented to the Court by John C. Martin Esqr. which
said plan has this day been unanimously adopted by said court for the
erection of the same. The building in every manner of the said Murfresborough Coutt House with the exception contained in said plan presented
by John C? Martin as aforesaid, and with the following exception (to wit)

The walls of said Court House are to be built up, both inside and out
and penciled off like the Murfresborough Court house is outside and
also the said court house Is to have a nice cupola erected in the top of
the same. And the said five commissioners are hereby ordered and directed
to contract for the building of such a one as they may deem necessary
or most suitable and it is further ordered by the court that the said
five commissiners let the same out on the 31st day of Augt. 1836 in the Town
of Woodbury to the Lowest bidder or bidders provided that he she or
they will Give satisfactory bond to said commissioners in the sum of (p 83)
Ten Thousand dollars according to the act of the general assembly in
such case made and provided. Also the he she or they will undertake
to have said building or court house completed on or before the 1st
day of October 1837. But if he she or they should fail to give the bond
as above required on the said 31st day of Augt. as aforesaid , then
and in that event the said five commissioners are hereby ordered and
directed to accept of the next best bid (if they shall be the judges)
which may have been offered for the same or which may be offered on
that day And provided also that the next best Bider whose bid may be
accepted shall undertake to build the said court house in the time
above mentioned or specified.

On motion ordered by the court that the chair appoint a comittee consisting of there of their own body to draft some plan or dimentions for the building of a jail in the County of Cannon And whereupon the following persons were app inted as said committee (to wit.)

James/Brown
John C. Martin &
Alexander McKnight Esqrs.

Whereupon said Committee withdrew for the above purpose &C

On motion ordered by the Court that John Ealem be appointed over-seer of the road from the Warren County line to Washington Kenadys And that James Pendleton Sr. be appointed overseer from said Kenadys to William Wests And that they apply to William Dates and John Pendleton Esqrs. for a list of hands to work said road &C

(p 84)

James H. Brown
John C. Martin and
Alexander McKnight Esqr.

who were appointed on this day day to draft plans for a jail for said County have made a written report to the Court which was red and app-roved by the court and ordered to be spread upon the mineuts of the court and is in the following words (to wit) We the undersigned being a commi-ttee appointed by the County Court of Cannon County after due deliber-ation have agreed to instruct the five commissioners appointed by the County Court of Cannon County to Let out and contract for the building of the jail on Lot 110. Known in the plan of the Town of Woodbury. On the following plan (to wit) That the above commissioners are hereby Authorized to let out and contract for the above building of the above jail upon the same plan that other jails are built upon & that they may consider the best and most suitable plan for the construction of said jail and the above jail be Let out at the same time that the court house is Let out and contracted for and to be completed at the same time that the Court House is to be completed to wit on or before the 1st day of October 1837.

On motion it is ordered by the Court, the five Town Commissioners forthwith advertise the Letting out of the Court House and jail on the 31st. day of Augt. 1836 in the Town of Woodbury And that the advertise-ments be made in the Nashville Republican the Central Gazette at McMinn ville, the Murfresborough Moniter And in one of the papers printed in Shelbyville.

(p 85) The worshipful Court then adjorned until Court in Course.

Thos. Powell Chrn.
C.C. Evans
John C. Martin
Sam'l Lance
Thomas L. Turner
John Felton
Jas. H. Brown

(p 86) September The 5th A.D. 1836   September Term

State of Tennessee)
Cannon County   ) September Term of the County Court A.D. 1836 —

The Worshipful County Court met pursuant to adjournment, present The
Worshipfull:

> John C. Martin
> Alexander McKnight
> Isaac Finley
> Joseph Simpson
> John Pendleton
> Isaac W. Elledge
> John Milton
> Charles C. Evans
> James M. Brown
> Elijah Stephens
> Sam'l Lance
> William Bates
> John Martin
> William B. Foster
> Thomas Simpson
> Lemuel Turney
> Martin Phillips
> Watson Cantrell
> Dav'd Fisher
> Reuben Evans
> Pleasant A. Thomason
> Joel Cheatham and
> Thomas Powell Esqrs. &C

The last will and Testament of Robert Stephens deced. was produced in
open court for probate and was duly proven in open court, by the oaths
of J.G.W. Rose and E.C. Seal, suscribing witnesses thereto, and on
motion the same was ordered to be recorded. Whereupon Robert K. Stephens
one of the executors named therein, came into Open Court and qualified
as such, now, together with the securitys Joseph Clark and J.G.W. Rose
entered into bond in the sum of one thousand dollars, payable to his
Excellency, the Governor and his successors in office conditioned as
the Law directs. Whereupon letters of Testamentary were granted &C The
other executor named in the will not appearing to (p 87) Samuel J.
Garrison clerk of our said Court presented before the court a duplicate
Tax list containing a statement of the taxes due and payable to the state
and County for the present year and from an abstract statement also
exhibited it appeared therefrom the amount of Taxes due to the state was
Five hundred and forty three dollars and twenty eight cents whereupon
George Grizzle high shff, and collector of the taxes for Cannon County
Came into Court and entered into Bond together with his securitys
approved of by the Court (to wit) Samuel E. Burger and of Abram Burger
In the sum of One Thousand and eighty four dollars conditioned as the
law directs. And is in the following words and figures (to wit)
Know all men by these presents that we George Grizzle

> Samuel Burger &
> Abraham Burger

all of the County of Cannon & state of Tennessee are held and firmly
bound unto Newton Cannon, Governor in and over the state of Tennessee and
his successors in office in the sum of One Thousand and eighty four
dollars which sum well and truly to be made we bind ourselves, our heirs,

executors , administrators and assigns jointly and severally and firmly by these presents sealed with our seals and dated this the fifth day of September 1836.

The condition of the above obligations is such that whereas the above bound George Grizzle high sheriff of the aforesaid County of Cannon has this day been appointed by the County Court of said County to collect the taxes due and payable in said County for the year 1836.(p 88) Now if the said George Grizzle shall well and truly pay to the Treasurer of the state all Taxes that he may collect (or ought to have collected) in said County on or before the first day of January 1837 then the above obligation to be void else to remain in full force and virture witness our hands and seals this the first day and year first above written

George Grizzle (seal)
Samuel Burger (seal)
Abraham Berger (seal)

Whereas it appearing to the satisfaction of the court from the abstract statement as exhibited by the chr. of our said court that the County taxes due and payable to the county amounts to the sum of three hundred and fifteen d ollars and t wenty cents for the present year Thereupo George Grizzle high Sheriff and collector of the taxes for Cannon County came into Court and suscribed the oath as required by law And entered into bond together with his securities approved of by the Court (to wit) Samuel D. Burger and Abraham Burger in the sum of Six hundred and thirty dollars and forty one cents payable to Thomas Powell Chairman of the County Court of said County and his successors in office conditioned as the law directs and is in the following words and figuers (to wit)

Know all men by these presents that We George Grizzle
Samuel Berger &
Abraham Burger

all of the County of Cannon and State of Tennessee are held and firmly bound unto Thomas Powell Chairman of the County Court of the aforesaid (p 89) County of Cannon and his successors in office in the sum of six hundred and thirty dollars and forty one cents which payment well and trult to be made We bind ourselves our heirs, executors, administrators and assigns jointly and severally and firmly by these presents sealed sealed with our seals dated this the 5th day of September 1836. The condition of the above obligations is such that whereas the above bound, George Grizzle high shiriff of the aforesaid County of Cannon has this day been appointed by the County Court of said County to collect the taxes due and payable in said County for the year 1836. Now if the said George Grizzle shall well and truly collect and pay to the County Trustee of the aforesaid County of Cannon all money (for Taxes) that he may collect (or should have collected) for said County on or before the first day of January 1837 then the above obligation to be void else to remain in full force and virture witness our hands and seal this the day and year first above written.

George Grizzle (seal)
Samuel Burger (seal)
Abraham Burger (seal)

William McCormac)
    Deed of Trust)
Richard Butcher)   The execution of a deed of Trust from William

McCormac to Richard Butcher for personal property as named therein bearing date the 3rd day of August 1836 was this day produced in open court for probate and was dulu acknowledged by the bargainer to be his act and deed fot the purposes therein named and was ordered to be certifyed for registration.

(p 90)
John E. Sullivan)
    deed   )
Richard U. Lemay) The execution of a deed of conveyance from John E. Sullivan to Richard U. Lemay for one hundred and fifty Acres of land lying in Cannon (originally Warren County) bearing date the 29th day of december 1834 was this day produced in open court for probate and was duly acknowledged by the bargainer to be his act and deed for the purposes therein contained and ordered to be certifyed for Registration.

Henry Bullard)
deed of gift)
Elisha Bullard) The execution of a deed of gift from Henry Bullard for Elisha Bullard for personal property as therein contained bearing date the 1st day of June 1836 was this day produced in open court for probate and was duly acknowledged by the said Henry Bullard to be his act and deed for the purposes therein contained and ordered to be certifyed for registration.

Elijah Stephens)
    Deed   )
Benj C. Stephens) The execution of a deed of conveyance for Elijah Stephens to Benjamin C? Stephens for Town lot No. 22 in the Town of Woodbury Cannon County bearing date the 27th day of August 1836 was this day acknowledged in open Court by the bargainor to be his act and deed for the purposes therein contained and ordered to be certifyed for registration.

On motion ordered by the Court that Robert George
                          Nathan Neely
                          James Soap
                          John Basham and
                          Daniel Tenpenny
be appointed a jury of men to vew and mark out a road (p 91) leading from Edmond Taylors mill to Jonathan Jones that part of said road that leads through the plantation of James Taylor (to wit) from a Branch in the north side of the said plantation unto a branch running down from the south where Pleasant Henderson formily lived and report to the next term of this court . And that the overseer suspend operation till the jury report.
Daniel Ford
Peter W. Clarke
John Turner
Elijah Trewit and
Osburn Mullinox a jury of men appointed at the July Term of this court 1836 and continued as such at the August term of this court to vew and mark a road commencing at or near James Allens on the stage road running to intersect the road leading from Richmonds mill to the Short Mountain at or near J.J. Bogles and make report as follows (to wit) we the jury of

men have found and marked a road agreeable to this order &C to which onjections was raised by Nathaniel Hayes on account of the aforesaid road passing through his plantation whereby he considered himself damaged And on motion ordered that the sheriff summons a jury of from seven to twelve Good and lawful men to revew said road as marked or layed out and see whether the same could be placed upon the ground upon other ground to answer the public convenance And if not say what damages shall be awarded him on his complaint and make report to the next term of this court.

On motion ordered by the court that John K. Salls be appointed overseer in place of Alexander McKnight Sr. on that part of the (p 92) road lately cut out by the said McKnights.

      Henry Warren
      Charles Alexander
      Joseph Warren
      Samuel Laswell and
      William Moore

a jury of men appointed at the last term of this court to vew and change the road leading from Jones to Woodbury from the point at the end of Milton Fowlers lane so as to intersect the stage road at Joseph Ramseys make report that they have changed the road from the end of Milton Fowlers lane to run by Joseph Warrens and from there to Henry Warrens so as to intersect the stage road at or near Joseph Ramseys which was approved of by the court and on motion ordered that Joseph Warren be appointed overseer of the same.

      John F. West
      Joel N. West
      James Garrison
      Benjamin Garrison and

Andria Pickett a jury of men appointed at the last term of this court to vew and mak a road in a direction from Alexandria to Woodbury leaving the stage road near Benjamin Garrisons Thence the most practical way so as to intersect the Wilson County line near John F. Wests Report that a road may be made according as marked which was approved of by the Court and is established as a county road And on motion ordered that John F. West be appointed overseer of the south end and James Garrison of the North end and that they meet at the corner of Thomas West fence (near some peach trees) and that James Goodner & Jonathan C. Doss Esqrs. furnish them with a list of hands.
(p 93)

On motion and petition ordered by the court that the part of the road as layed out by the jury of men appointed at may term 1836 from Smiths to Garretts be annulled.

On motion and petition ordered by the court that Henry Ford
      James Barkley
      Henry D. McBroom
      Elijah Mears and
      James Woods

be appointed a jury of men to vew and make a road leaving the old road above Ansons Thompson running up the hollow pass John Prestons spring and up the ridge near said Spring so as to intersect the old road leading down the Herricane fork near the Wilson County line and also to intersect

the road leading up the Sycamore fork in the County of Wilson at the Cannon
County line and make report to the next term of yhis court.

On motion ordered that Alford P. Gowen and James Mannahan be appointed
to allot dire hands between Evans Bateman and the said Mannahan Overseers.

Peter Reynolds and John Reynolds commissioners appointed at the last term
of this court to settle with Thomas Lawrence Guardian of Elijah Duncan
have made report which was receved by the court and ordered to be spread
upon record in the Guardian Book. And the original filed in the office And
on motion the said Thomas Lawrence he was released of his guardianship
for the said Elijah Duncan holdinh himself accountable for all arrearages
in his hands, of the said Duncans effects.

(p 94)   On motion and upon the application of John Davis Ordered by t'e
Courtthat the sheriff summons Twelve Good & lawful men (to wit)

> James Tubb
> William Williams
> Reuben Evans
> James Beatie
> Pater Reynolds
> Faris Lawrence
> Jonathan Fuson
> John Fite
> Thomas Evans
> John Reynolds
> Abner Self and
> James Pistoll

to proseed to Elijah Duncans then and there to examine the said Duncan
with regard to the state of his mind and see whether or not in their
opinion he is capable of taking care of his own Estate as also his person
and report to the next term of this court.

On motion ordered by the Court that

> John Davis Jr.
> Jonson Parris
> David Morrow
> David Adcock and
> James Delong

(made void through error)

be appointed a jury of men to vew and mark a road from Shipping port on the
Cany for the nearest and most practical rout leading on to the Gap of
the Short Mountain intersecting or crossing the clear fork road , and
intersecting the road leading from Woodbury to the Gap of the mountain.

On motion ordered by the court that

> Enoch Jones
> Henry Kessey
> John C. Kennedy
> Samuel Burger
> Joseph Banks
> Pater Cantrell
> Abraham Taylor
> John Charles

Joseph Cantrell
John Lynder
James Adcock and
Washington Cannon

be appointed a jury of men to vew and mark a road Commencing at shipping port on the Caney fork the nearest and most practicable rout leading on through the Gap of the (p 95) Short mountain intersecting the road leading from Woodbury to the Gap of the short mountain and maker report to the next term of this court.

On motion ordered by the court that Martin Fouch be appointed overseer of the road commencing u on the Smith County line near old Centerville Thence to heltons creek near William Fouchs and to apply to Esqrs. Goodner & Thomason for a list of hands to work the same.

Samuel J. Garrison Clerk of our said Court presented to the court an account against Cannon County for Books furnished for the use of the County And official services rendered &C for Books to the amout of Fifty four dollars which was unanimiously allowed by the Court There being twenty two justices upon the bench voting in the affirmative.

John C. Martin
Alexander McKnight
Isaac Finley
Joseph Simpson
John Pendleton
James M. Brown
Elijah Stephens
William Bates
Samuel Lance
Charles C. Evans
John Melton
John Martin
William B. Foster
Lemuel Turney
Thompson Simpson
Martin Phillips
Watson Cantrell
David Fisher
Reuben Evans
Pleasant Thomason
Joel Cheatham and Thomas Powell
Esquires.

And on motion ordered by the Court that the Trustee pay the same out of any money in his hands(or that may come into his hands) not otherwise appropriated or the same be settled with the said Garrison out of any moneys he may be liable to pay to the Trustee as collected by him officially (p 96) Whereupon the further allowance was made to the said Garrison (to wit) the sum of twenty dollars for furnishing the sheriff or collector with a duplicate tax list for the Taxes due and payable for the present year and also for the sum of one dollar for furnishing the Sheriff with a list of the taxes due and payable from persons excersizing the priveledges and occupations who was licensed by the payment of the stateTax prior to the levying of the County Tax

(In numbering typed pages, Page 54 left out, Old book pages numbered correctly)

for the present year and also the sum of Ten dollars for recording the Revenue commissioners report in a book kept for that purpose and the further sum of one dollar and fifty cents for three chairs furnished for the use of the office making in allthe sum of Thirty Two dollars and fifty cents Whereupon the ayes and noes were taken upon the same and when the names of the members of the court (present) were called those who voted in the negative were —

Esquires Findley
Joseph Simpson
Bates
Charles R. Evans
Lance
Foster
Turney
Thoms
Simpson
Cantrell and
Fisher

and those voted in the affirmative were Esquires John C. Martin

McKnight
Pendleton
Brown
Stephens
Melton
John Martin
Phillips
Reuben Evans
Thomason
Cheatham &
Powell

12 who being a majority of all the justices present and the lawful number to make appropriations under fifty dollars And whereupon it was ordered by the court that the same be allowed and paid by the Trustee for the County out (p 97) of any moneys (not otherwise appropriated) that are in his hands or may come into his hands in virture of his office.

Alexander F. McFerrin Register presented an account against the County for an allowance of the sum of thirteen dollars & fifty cents for a Record Book Pat for the use of the County which was considered by the Court to be reasonable and was unanimously allowed There being present.

Esquires John C. Martin

McKnight
Finley
Joseph
Simpson
Pendleton
Melton
Charles C. Evans
Brown
Stephens
Lance
Bates

John Martin

                                              Foster
                                              T. Simpson
                                              Turney
                                              Phillips
                                              Cantrell
                                              Fisher
                                              R. Evans
                                              Cheatham
                                              Elledge and
                                              Powell

     And on Motion ordered by the Court that the Trustee pay the same out of
any moneys that are in or may come into his hands by virtue of his office not
otherwise appropriated.

Thomas C. Wood Clerk of the Cannon Circuit Court, presented and account
against Cannon County for an allowance of the sum of thirty one dollars and
eighty seven and one half cents for Books furnished by himself for the use of
his office includeing a writeing table for the use of the same which was
unaninously adopted by the court, There being present
                                    Esquires John C. Martin
                                              McKnight
                                              Finley
                                              Joseph Simpson
                                              Pendleton
                                              Brown
                                              Stephens
                                              Pates
                                              Lance
                                              Melton
                                              John Martin
                                              Foster
                                              Turney
                                              Thoms
                                              Simpson
                                              Phillips
                                              Cantrell
                                              Fisher
                                              Reuben Evans
                                              Cheatham and
                                              Powell

(p 98) who being a majority of all the justices of the county and a proper
number to make appropriations under the sum of fifty dollars. And on
motion ordered by the Court that the same be allowed and paid out of any
moneys that is or may come into the Trustees hands by virture of his office n
not otherwiseappropriated.

The Court then proceeded to making allowances to the Revenue commissioners
for takeing in a list of the taxable property for the present year and the
question being taken it was decided in the afermative that they receive an
equal amout for their serveses as such. And on motion ordered that they be
entitled to receive the sum of three dollars each for such servisesand are taking the questions by ayes and noes. Those who voted in the negative were
Esquires Melton
         Lance
         Elledge
         Cheatham

         John C. Martin
         Turney

R. Evans and
Powell

And those who voted in the affirmative were Esquires Joseph Simpson
Cantrell
Phillips
John Martin
Foster
Thomas
Simpson
Fisher
Bates
Charles C. Evans
McKnight
Stephens
Finley and
Brown 14

who being a proper number and authorized by law to make appropriations under
the sum of fifty dollars. The same was allowed and on motion ordered by the
Court that the clerk Issue seperate certificates to each of said Revinue
commissioners for the said sum of three dollars each (to wit)

John C. Martin
Isaac Finley
Larkin Hensley
James L Essary
Isaac W. Elledge
James M. Brown
John Melton
Samuel Lance
John Martin
Lemuel Turney
John Frazeur
Watson Cantrell
Lemuel Moore
James Goodner
James Beatie and
Jonothan Duson

(p 99)

the said Revinue commissioners And on motion it further ordered by the court
that the Trustee pay the same out of any moneys in his hands or may come into
his hands not otherwise appropriated.

On motion ordered ordered by the Court that John C. Martin & Watson
Cantrell be appointed Commissioners of the County Revenue for the present year
to settle with the clerks and other officers concerned in collection of County
moneys and to perform such other dutys as by law they are bound to do.

The Worshipfull Court then adjorned till tomorrow morning 10 o'clock.
Thos. Powell Chrn.
John Melton
Charles C. Evans
William Bates
James M. Brown
Reuben Evans
David Fisher
C. Stephens
T.W. Elledge
Lemuel Turney

(p 100) Tuesday morning Sept. the 6th 1836 The Worshipfull Court met pursuant to adjornment   present the Worshipfull

> Thomas Powell
> William Bates
> John Martin
> John Melton
> David Fisher
> Elijah Stephens
> James M. Brown
> Charles C. Evans
> Isaac W. Elledge
> Isaac Finley
> Reuben Evans and
> Lemuel Turney

John R. Sullivan presented to the Court an account against the county for a writting table furnished the Clerk of the County Court for the use of the County for the sum of four dollars which in the opinion of the court was a higher price than the same is worth. And a proposition being made to curtail the act to the sum of two dollars and fifty cents which was carried. The question was then taken by ayes and noes upon the allowance of the said sum of two dollars & fifty Whereupon it was decided unanmiously decided in the affirmative there being present

> Esqrs. Powell
> John Martin
> Melton
> Fisher
> Stephens
> Brown
> Charles C. Evans
> Eledge
> Finley
> Reuben Evans and
> Turney 12

who being a lawful number to make appropriations not Exceeding fifty dollars th the same was allowed. And on motion ordered by the court that the same be paid by the Trustee of the County Out of any monies in his hands (or that may come into his hands) not otherwise appropriated.

On motion ordered by the Court that Sirol Durham be appointed overseer of the new road commencing at Francis Turners runing up the clear fork by the said Durhams to the foot of the ridge between said Durhams and Youngs and apply to Esqrs. Lance for a list of hands.

(p 101) On motion ordered by the court that John Young be appointed overseer of the new road begining at the foot of the ridge between said Youngs & Sirol Durhams and from thence by Robt. Bailys to the mountain road at William Cummings and apply to Esqr. Lance for a list of hands.

On motion ordered by the Court that David D. Hipp be appointed overseer of the New road from Woodbury to the the Coffee County line in a direction to Manchester Commencing commencing at Farnells runing to the ford of the creek above Isaac Youngs And apply to Esqrs. Eledge & Pendleton for a list of hands, to clear out and work the same.

On motion ordered by the court that Jonothan Wimberly be appointed Overseer of the new road from Woodbury to the Coffee County line in a direction toward Manchester Commencing at the ford of the creek above Isaac Youngs to the top of

the ridge above Lemays and apply to Esqrs Eledge & Pendleton for a list of hands
to clear out and keep the same in repare.

On motion ordered by the Court that Joseph Clark Overseer of the road from
the mouth of the hollow above the narrow to the County line, near Esqr. Martins
have the following hands in addition to his former hands viz. the Mr. Mullins,
Daily and Merrimans and that he commence at the forks of the Hollow at the foot
of the hill and work to the road landing from A. Hicks to R. Blues.

(p 102)   On motion ordered by the Court that

> John Idding Sr.
> William Preston Sr.
> Jesse Hollis
> H.D. Holbroom ans Alexander Young

be appointed a jury men to vew and mark a road from Woodbury to Hardy Spicers
and make to the next term of this court.

On motion ordered by the Court Thomas Reaves be appointed overseer of the
road from Collins old cabin to the County line near Esqr. Martins and that he
apply to Esqr. Martin for ——— and he is directed to Give a list of hands east
of the road leading from Hicks to Blews.

On motion ordered by the Court that

> Robert Vinson
> John Felton
> Elijah Stephens
> William B. Evans
> Jesse Lawrence
> Joseph Pinkerton
> John A. Dunn
> James Scott &
> Josiah Youngblood

be appointed a Jury of men to revew so much of the road that leads from
Woodbury to the Coffee County line and to Jacksborough as runs through the en-
closures of John Woods And Archibald Stone and see if the same can be put on as
good ground as it now runs for the convebience of the County and if not to say
what damages the said Wood and Stone will Sustain by said road runing where it
now does And report to the next term of this court.

William Young
Joseph Ramsey
William West
Robert George
Charles C. Evans
William Pates
Samuel Laswell
Arthut Warren and
Richard Tenpenny
a part of a Jury of men appointed at (p 103) the last Term of this Court to
revewed road road vewed and marked out a jury of men appointed at the June Term
of this Court beginning at or near John Wood Sr. on the stage road runing up
hills creek through the plantations of the said John Woods & Archibald Stones
make report as follows viz. – Sept. 1st 1836. We the undersigned met in conformity to the written order on the date above written and an Examination
agreed to change the road so as to begin at an Elm on the stage road and Thence
to run with the dividing line between John Wood and Arch'd Stone to an Elm
(marked tree) near the line Between Arch'd Stone and John Browns thence with the
dividing line between said Stone and said Brown to the Creek and agree that John

Wood is damaged to the Amt. of twelve dollars which report was set aside by
the Court &C.

James Pendleton
Peter Hayes
William A. Beesmith
Sam'l M. Durton
L.R. Vick
L. Moore

a part of a jury of men appointed at the July Term of this Court and continued
at the Augt Term to vew and marke a road begining at Neils Shop on dismal creek
the nearest and best way to Liberty have made report which is objected to on
account of conditiond therein to obstruct the same with Gates &C which the
Court think illegal. &C.

On motio: ordered by the Court that William George overseer shall not be
required to work that part of his road as runs through Robert Georgees plantation untill the crop is Gather and that a copy of this be sent him by the clerk
or sheriff.

(p 104) On motionnordered by the Court that the bounds heretofore Given to
Prittain Moore overseer be changed agreeable to the change made in said road,
to intersect the stage road near Joseph Ramseys and that Joseph Warren be released from the appointment of overseer.

Baxter B. Dickens
William Ring
Peter Gilley
Robert Pallet and
James Lee

the jury of men appointed at the July Term of this Court to vew and mark a
road Beginning at David Pattons saw mill running thence so as to intersect
the dug Hollow road at or near the house of William Grays have made report
&C which was made void and set aside by the Court- On account of its not being
returned in due time according to the requestions of the orders, And Also on
account of Other objections raised by the petitions of sundry Individuals &C.

The Worshipfull Court then adjorned till Court in Course.

Thos. Powell Chrm.
John Melton
Charles C. Evans
James M. Brown

(p 105)   Woodbury October 1836
                    October Term
State of Tennessee)
Cannon County   )   October Term 1836

The Worshipfull County Court met pursuant to Adjournment. It being the first
Monday And 3rd day of October 1836, present the Worshipful
                    Thomas Powell
                    Isaac Finley
                    John C. Martin
                    Alex'r McKnight
                    Blake Sedgley
                    James M. Brown

John Melton
Jonothan C. Doss
Lemuel Moore
Thomas Simpson
John Martin
William B. Foster
John Pendleton &
Watson Cantrell   Esqrs.

On motion ordered by the Court that Elijah Stephens Esq. be appointed to allot hands to Henry Young Overseer

On motion ordered by the Court that

Thomas Williams
John A. Brown
Robert Carson
be appointed to devide hands between Jacob Falkenberry
James Todd and
James Scism overseers.

On motion ordered by the court that Anson Thompson released from serving any longer as overseer and that Mack Crabtree be appointed in his place and have the same hands that Thompson the former overseer had and that he work the same road to the foot of the hill above the said Thompsons thence the new road As marked to the Wilson County line.

On motion ordered by the court that Edwin J. Rosebury, overseer be released from working (p 106) that part of his road that leads through the lands of John Weatherspoons until the mind of the neighbors can be assertained.

On motion and petition ordered by the Court that the Sheriff summons a Jury of twelve good and lawful men as a jury of men to vew so much of a road lately vewed and marked out (leaving the stage road at or near Joseph Ramseys) as passes through the enclosed lands of Mary Sutton and see whether or not the same could be put upon other groud to answer as wellthe public convenience if not say what damage shall be awarded hwr on her complaint and make report to the next Term of this court.

John Eddings
Henry D. McBroom
Jesse Hollis
A. Young and
William Preston
a jury of men appointed at the last Term of this court to vew and marke a road from Woodbury to Hardy Spicers & make report as follows. (to wit) from Woodbury to William Prestons, Thence to Thomas Wallaces Thence up the Laurel point Thence to Hardy Spicers and the same is established as a county road And on motion ordered by the Court that Henry Young be appointed overseer from Woodbury to the foot of the Laurel point and that JohnnEddings be appointed overseer from the foot of the Laurel point to Hardy Spicers And thatHenry D. McBroom and Isaac Findley Esqr. furnish the said overseers a list of hands to open said road and keep the same in repair.
(p 107) On motion ordered by the Court that Solomon Long be appointed overseer of the Lebanon Road running from the Hollow Springs to the Coffee County line and have the following hands(to wit)   James McLean
John Williams
Oliver C. Duncan
Dennis R. Hawkins and

Aaron R. Thomas

On motion ordered by the court that
Tilman Bethell
Daniel Ford
James Dodd
William Goggin and
George L. Given
be appointed a jury of men to vew the old mountain road beginning on the stage road between Daniel Fords and James A lens running in the said mountain road to Francis Turners and make such alterations in the same as they may think necessary and make report to the next Term of this court.

On motion ordered by the court that
Jonathan C. Doss
James Threeatt
Daniel Smith and
James Powell
be appointed a jury of men to vew and mark an alteration in the road from Alexandria to Statesville leaving the stage road near James Powells running up the branch to the Wilson County line and make report to the next Term of this court.

On motion ordered by the court that Samuel Burton and Peter Hayes overseers be allowed the use of the crowbar and leave same in the hands of Benjamin Avant overseer.

(p 108) On motion and petition ordered by the court that
William Ring
Baxter B. Dickens
Cyrus L. Roberts
Ira L. Blair and
Silas A. Robinson
(p 108) be appointed a jury of men to vew and mark a road commencing near David Pattons Saw mill running south so as to intersect the Dug Hollow road at or near William Grays on said old road and make report to the next Term of this court.

John Charles
Abraham Taylor
Joseph Cantrell
John Lynder
Peter Cantrell and
James Adcock
be part of the jury of men appointed at the last Term of this court to vew and mark a road commencing at shipping port on the Caney Fork Thence the nearest and most practical rout leading through the Gap of the short mountain intersecting or crossing the road and intersect the road leading from Woodbury to the gap of the mountain on the top of the Stones River hills, report that they have found and marked a road agreeable to the order of said court and the same is established on a country road as marked. And on motion ordered by the court that James Delong be appointed overseer on said road from shipping port to the upper end of John Lynders field, and that Peter Cantrell be appointed overseer of from John Lynders field vth district and that Enoch Jonson be appointed overseer from the line of the twelvth district (p 109) to the dry fork road and that John Patterson be appointed overseer from the dry fork road to his own house and that James Hawkins be appointed overseer from John Pattersons to the top of the Stones river hills and on motion it is further ordered by the court that Watson Cantrell, David Fisher and

William Foster

Esquires furnish siad overseers with a list of hands to clear out said road
and keep the same in repair.

> Nathan Neely
> James Soap
> John Basham and
> Daniel Tenpenny

a part of the Jury of men appointed at the last Term of this Court to revew
and mark out a road leading from Edmond Taylors mills to Jonathan Jones, that pa
part of said road that leads through James Taylors plantation and &C make report
as follows (to wit) that they think the road round James Taylors fence will
answer the purposes &C And on motion ordered by the court that William George
overseer work the road agreeable as established by this report insted of working as heretofore marked out through the said Taylors plantation.

James Barkley
Henry D. McBroom
Hebry Ford
James Wood and
Elijah Mears

a jury of men appointed at the last term of this court to vew and mark out a
road leaving the old road above Anson Thompsons running up the hollow passing
John Prestons Spring and up the ridge so as to intersect the old road leading
down the harrican fork near the Wilson County line and also to intersect the road
leading up the sycamore fork in Wilson County at the Cannon County line make
report as follows (to wit) That they vewed (p 110) and marked the same agrec-
able to said order.

On motion and petition ordered by the Court that a report made at the last
term of this court by William A Neesmith and others (jury of men) upon a road
from heels shop through Lemuels Moores plantation to Liberty be revewed and
the same is established agreeable to said report as a county road.
And on motion it is further ordered by the Court that Peter Gays be appointed
overseer on thatpart of the road commencing at Heels shop running to the top
of the ridge above Lemuel Moores and that Samuel H. Burton be appointed overseer of said road beginning on top of the ridge above Lemuel Moores running
thence to Liberty and that Reuben Evans and Lemuel Moore Esquires furnish said
overseers with a list of hands to clear out said Road and keep the same in
repair.

Hiram M. Fite
Charles Jenkins
Wells Adamson
Bracket Notes
James J. Bogle and
Samuel C. Porterfield

a jury summoned by the Shff. to review that part of a road lately vewed and
marked out passing through the plantation of Nathaniel Hays make report that
they have reviewed the same and have established the same as heretofore marked out and are of opinion that the said Hayes should have an allowance of
ten dollars made him for damages &C to which part of said report the court
objected but established the road as heretofore marked out And (p 111) on
motion ordered by the Courtthat Samuel Bryson be appointed overseer of said
road and apply to Lemuel Moore & Lemuel Turney Esquires for a list of hands
to clear out said road and keep the same in repair.

On motion and petion of the contending parties heretofore upon the road leading from Woodbury up hills creek Ordered by the court that the same be permanantly established by the consent of the contending parties and with the assent of the court so as to run agreeableto a report of the Jury of men made at the last Term of this court that is to say leaving the stage road at an Ellem tree on the stage road near Beacham Cannons at the foot of the hill Thence with the line between John Wood & Arch'd Stone up hills creek to the boundary line between JohnBrown and Archibald Stone Thence with said Browns & Stones line so as to intersect the road as vewed and cleared out heretofore at or near where the road now crosses the said creek And thence with said road as heretofore vowed and marked to the top of the ridge above Richard U. Lemoyn , And on motion it is further ordered by the Court that Benjamin C. Stephens br released from further serving as an overseer upon said road and that John H. Ragsdale be appointed in his rheum and sted and that he be entitled to the same hands that was heretofore allowed said Stephens former overseer for to clear out and keep the same in repair.

(p 112) On motion ordered by the court

Stephen Cantrell
Moses Cummings
Usibious Stone and
William Stone

be appointed to visit and inqure into the situation and condition of Sarah Melton and see whether she has meant ot is able to maintain herself And make report to the next term of this court.

personally appeared in open court Andrew McCabe and deposed in due form & law that he knew Joel Mears in his life time that said Joel departed this life in Warren County (now Cannon) on the 21st December A.D. 1835 which is ordered by the Court to be certyfied

On motion ordered by the court that Solomon Beasley be permitted to have his account for surveying certain lines of Cannon County spread upon the records of this court which is in the following words (to wit) April 16th 1836 Solomon Beasley Commissioner for running and marking the East & West boundary line of Cannon County Employed 8 days Expence $4 which is sworn to in open court.

Thomas G. Wood makes known to the satisfaction of the court that he has been appointed as a Deputy of A.F. McFerrin Register of Cannon County And on motion ordered by the court that he be qualiffed as such and the same be made of Record Thereupon the said Thomas G. Wood Esq. came into open Court and took the oath to support the constitution of the United States and of the State of Tennessee also an oath to discharge the duties of the office of Deputy Register.

(p 113) On motion ordered by the Court that Henry R. Perry be appointed Amr. of the Estate of Jessee L. Perry deceased Thereupon the said Henry R. Perry came into open court and qualifyed as the Law directs who together with his securities James M. Brown

William J. Henderson and
John B. Stone

entered into bond in the sum of one thousand dollars payable to Newton Cannon Governor and his successors in office conditioned as the Law directs and letters of Administrations granted &C whereupon on motion it is further ordered by the court that

John Melton
James M. Brown and
Usioious Stone

be appointed to lat off to the widow Ann M. Perry one years provisions out of said Estate.

On motion ordered by the Court that Al exander Young be appointed Administrator of the estate of Archibald Edwards deceased, whereupon the said Alexander Young came into open court and qualifyed as the law directs who together with his securities Hanry Young and John Eddings entered into bond in the sum of one hundred and twenty five dollars payable to Newton Cannon Governor and his successors in office conditioned as the law directs and letters of administratora granted &C Whereupon on motion it is further ordered by the court that

>   Isaac Finley
>   Robert George and
>   James Taylor

be appointed to lay off to the widow of the said Arch'd Edwards deceased one years provisions out of said Estate.

(p 114) John Davis represents to the court that one Elijah Duncan of this County is very much on the decline of life and inpared in mind and is in his opinion incapable of taking care of his person or estate, upon which information It is ordered by the court that the sherriff summons (Instanter) a jury of twelve Good and Lawful men to assertain from the best means in their power the true state and condition of the said Duncan And report to the present Term of this court which being don the jury of inquest report as follows (to wit) We the undersigned after hearing all the testimony in our Power to collect do believe that the said Duncan is incapable of either taking care of his person

or property. We also understand from the witnesses that the said Duncan has

the following property that is to say about four acres of corn, one horse, 6

head of cattle and between 20 and 30 head of sheep, some 15 or 20 head of hogs

two beds and some other household furnature and one hundred and twenty five

acres of land signed

>   Joseph Clark
>   David D. Hipp
>   Jacob Berger
>   Moses Cummings
>   John Edding
>   William F. George
>   Arthur Warren
>   Thos. Cavatt
>   Daniel M. Stewart
>   James Smith and
>   Robert Baily

Jury of Inquest.

Whereupon motion ordered by the court that John Davis be appointed Guardian of the said Elijah Duncan with power to sell(by giving the Legal notice) the whole or so much of the perishable property of said Duncan as he may think necessary. Whereupon on motion the said John Davis together with his securities Solomon Davis & Joseph Davis came into open Court (p 115) entered into bond payable to Thos. Powell Chairman of Cannon County Court and his successors in office in the sum of one thousand dollars conditioned as the Law directs &C.

On motion ordered by the court that James W. Williams have bound to him as an apprentice to the House Carpenter Puisness George Holland a minor and illegi-

timate son of Omey Holland who it has been represented to the satisfaction of
this court is about the age of six years and is without protection Except the
mercy of the publick And the said Williams agrees to Give the said George Two
years schooling between the age of twelve to sixteen years, and when he shall
have arrived to the age of twenty one years to Give him a horse, saddle, and
Briddle worth sevebty five dollars in cash at that time Also a suit of clothes
worth say twenty five dollars And to take all other care and protection of the
siad Ceroge that he of right should do. Whereupon on motion the said James W.
Williams together with his securities B.L. Johnson & Thomas Cavatt came into
open Court and entered into Bond payable to the Chairman of the countyCourt for
the time being & his successors in office in the sum of five Hundred dollars
conditioned as the Law directs.

John H. Smith)
    Deed   )
Samuel Burger) A deed of conveyancefrom John H. Smith to Samuel E. Burger
for one thousand acres of land lying in Cannon County bearing date the 3rd day
of August (p 116) 1836 was this day presented in open court for probate and
was duly proven (in part) by the oath of Jacob Burger one of the suscribing
witnesses thereto.

Tabner Martin)
  To Deed) 20)
Edward W. Edge)) a deed of conveyance from Tabner Martin to Edward W. Edge
for twenty acres of land lying in Cannon County bearing date the 26th day of
September 1836 was this day duly acknowledged in open court by the said Tabner
Martin (the bargainor) to be his act and deed for the purposes therein contained
and ordered to be certified for Registration.

Tabner Martin   )
  Too Deed) 180)
Edward W. Edge) a deed of conveyance from Tabner Martin to Edward W. Edge
for one hundred and eighty acres of land lying in Cannon County bearing date
26th day of September 1836 was this day acknowledged in open court by the said
Tabner Martin (the bargainor) to be his act and deed for the purposes therein
contained. And ordered to be certified for registration.

James King   )
Transfer) 156)
William Daely) a Transfer of a plot and certificate from James King to William
Daely for one hundred and fifty six acres of land lying in Cannon County(originally Warren County) bearing date fourth of December 1834 was this day produced
in open Court for probate and was fully proven by the oath of Alexander Patty
and David Patton the suscribing witnesses thereto.

(p 117)
Solomon Redman)
Deed (269)   )
John Davis   ) A deed of conveyance from Solomon Redman to John Davis for
two hundred and sixty nine acres of land lying in Cannon County bearing date
the 29th day of August 1836 was this day produced in open Court for probate
and was duly proven by the oaths of Watson Cantroll and Tillmon Patter suscribing witnesses thereto and ordered to be certified for registration.

Josias Hendrickson   )
    Deed (50)   )
Cynthia Kemp and John Gardner) a deed of conveyance from Josias Hendrickson to

Cynthia Kemp for fifty acres of land lying in Cannon County (originally Smith County) bearing date the 17th day of June 1834 was this day fully proven in open court by the oath of William Vanover one of the suscribing witnesses thereto the other witness names therein(to wit) James Goodner having deposed to the same out of term time to wit, the 1st day of August1836. And on motion the same is ordered by the court to be certifyed for registration.

Court then adjourned until tomorrow morning at 10 o'clock.

> Thos. Powell Chrm.
> Elijah Stephens
> John Melton
> James M. Brown

(p 118) Tuesday morning, October the 4th day 1836.
The Worshipfull court met pursuant to adjornment present the Worshipfull
> Thomas Powell
> James M. Brown
> John Melton /
> Elijah Stephens Esqr.

Robert K. Stephens Executor of the Estate of Robert Stephens decd. made report of an Inventory of said Estate And on motion Ordered by the Court that the same be spread upon reccord in the Inventory book.

The Worshipfull court then Adjorned till court in course.

> (Thos. Powell Chrm.
> (John Melton
> (Jas. M. Brown
> November Term of the County Court.

(p 119)
State of Tennessee)
Cannon County   )   November Term
of the County Court 1836

At a county court began and held at the court house began and held at the court house in the town of Woodbury on the first mondy it being the 7th day of November 1836. Present the worshipfull John C. Martin
> Joseph Simpson
> Allen Haley
> Blake Sagely
> John Pendleton
> James M. Brown
> Elijah Stephens
> Charles C. Evans
> John Martin
> William Bates
> Thomas Simpson
> Martin Phillips and
> Reuben Evans Esquires

Robert Forrester presented before the court the last will and Testament of William Forester dec'd which was duly proven in open court by the oath of Frances Forester one of the suscribing witnesses thereto and ordered by the court that the same be spread upon reccord in the proper book And on motion it is furthered ordered by the court that Robert Forester be appointed Aministrator of said Estate with the will annexed who together with his securities John Martin and Reuben Evans Came into open court and entered into bond in the sum of three thousand dollars payable to the Governor and his successors in office conditioned as the law directs Thereupon letters of administration were granted &c

Samuel Garrison Clerk of this court presented the resignation of Grsen Berry S Sapp as constable of the eight civil district which accepted by the court and ordered to be made of reccord And that the sheriff proseed to hold an election to fill said vacancy as the Law directs.

(p 120) On motion and upon the petition of Hany Sullivan widow of the late William Sullivan dec'd (whereas it appearing to the sattisfaction of the court from the official indorsement thereon that a copy of said petition had been legally served upon all the legities of said Estate that was of lawful age) it is ordered that a prosess issue to the sheriff of Cannon County to summon five good and lawful men to proceed upon the premises of the said William Sullivan dec'd and then there examine the said premises and set apart the one third of the lands belonging to the said estate To the said widow as a dower and make report to the next term of this court.

Whereas as it has been represented to this court that James Evans late of this county has deceased leaving no will or Testament And on motion ordered by the Court that Reuben Evans be appointed administrator of the estate of the said Reuben Evans together his security John Turner came into open court and entered into bond in the sum of one hundred dollars payable to the Governor and his successors in office conditioned as the law directs. And letters of administration were granted &C.

Blake Sagely Esquire presented the resignation of Richard Holt as Constable in the 4th cival district which was accepted of by the court And ordered to be made of reccord And that the Sheriff proceed to hold and election in said district to fill said vacancy as the law directs.

(p 131)
On motion ordered by the court that Charles C. Evans
John C. Martin
Joseph Simpson
William George and
William Hollis
be appointed a jury of men to revew a road lately vewed and established by the court from Woodbury to Harvey Spicers and see whether the same can be placed upon other ground to answer as well for the public conveniance and if not say what damages shall be awarded to Adam Elrod & Woodson Northcutt upon their complaint for the same passing through their lands and make report to the next term of this court.

Thomas Elkins one of the deputy sheriffs of this county returned and order executed) made at the last term of this court (with no other indorsement thereon) appoining Stephen Cantrell
Moses Cummings
Usibius Stone and
William Stone
to inquire into the situation & condition of Sarah Melton &C

Milton Fowler

Robert G. Spicer
John Hollis
Anderson Bennett
Thomas Hayes
Henry Warren
Henry Hayes
Joseph Warren
A. Alexander
Jonathan Pasham
Isaac Finley and
Edmund Finley

a jury of men summoned by the sheriff pursuant to an order made at the last term of this court to revew so much of the road that leads from the state road near Joseph Ramseys to Jonathan Jones as passes through the enclosed lands of Mrs. Mary Suttons have made a sumaryreport in which they have said a damage should be allowed the same Mary Sutton of the sum of thirty dollars upon her complaint &C Whereupon the said Mary Sutton presented a Counter petition praying the court that the (p 122) said road be disanulled And for satisfactory reasons disclosed to the court the same was accordingly done &C.

On motion and upon petition of aundary citizens living near the road that leaves from the stage road near James Allens intersecting the road that leads from Richmonds mill to the short mountain near J.J. Bogles the same is disannulled .

Silas A. Robinson
Scyrus L. Roberts
and Ira L. Blair

a part of a Jury of men appointed at the last term of this court to vew and make a road commencing near David Pattons saw mill running south so as to intersect the old dug Hollow road at or near William Grays on said old road, make report that they have vewed and marked the same according to the calls of the order and the same is established by the court as a county road And on motion ordered That Thomas Ting be appointed overseer of said road and apply to Allen Haly & Blake Sagely for a list of hands to clear out and keep the same in repair.

Alexander McKnight Coroner of Cannon County presented to the court a verdict of a jury of inquest held under his direction by James D. Orr and others over the dead body of Jane Nichols deceased And upon the examination of the said jury upon their oaths do say that they believe the said Jane Nichols came to her death by having a fit and (p 123) Falling into the Spring of Joshua Nichols did then and there strangle, drown &C
And on motion ordered by the court that the Clerk certify the same as being correctly reported as contemplated by law in such case made and provided.
And it is further ordered by the Court that the Trustee of Cannon County pay the Coroner his lawful fee (to wit) the sum of five dollars) out of any moneys in his hands not otherwise appropriated for the servises rendered thereinkc

The Court then adjourned till tomorrow morning Nine Oclock.

Reuben Evans
John C. Martin
Charles C. Evans
James M. Brown

Tuesday morning Nov. the 8th 1836.
The Worshipfull court meet pursuant to Adjornment presents the Worshipfull
John C. Martin
Charles C. Evans
Reuben Evans
James M. Brown and
James L. Essary

On motion the Court was adjourned till court in Course.

Reuben Evans
John C. Martin
Charles C. Evans

December Term

(p 124)
State of Tennessee)
Cannon County   )

Be it remembered that a county court was began and held
at the House of Henry D. McBroom in the Town of Danville (woodbury) the place
appointed by Law for Holding the county court for said county untill the
court house for said county shall be erected on the first Monday, it being
the 5th day of December 1836, present the Worshipfull Charles C. Evans
John Helton
John Pendleton
Isaac Finley
Pleasant A. Thompson
Thomas Simpson
Sam'l Lance
Lemuel Moore
Jonathan Fuson
James M. Brown
Lemuel Turney
William Pates and
Thomas Powell Esqrs.

Whereupon the following orders were made (to wit)

On motion ordered by the Court that Allen Whitfield be appointed administrator of the estate of Willis Whitfield deceased whereupon the said Allen
Whitfield came into open court and quallified as such; Ansel Whitfield and
Thomas Y. Whitfield entered into bond in the sum of nine hundollars payable
and conditioned as the law directs whereupon Letters of Administration were granted &C.

On motion and upon the petition of Rhody Whitfield widdow of the late
Willis Whitfield deceased ordered by the court that William King
Hugh Robinson and
Jessie Gilley
be appointed commissioners to Lay off to the said Rhody Whitfield one years
support out of her said husbands Estate and make report of the same to the
next Term of this court.

(p 125) Thomas Elkins one of the deputy sheriffs of this county returned
into Court a certificate from under the hands of the judges of an election
held by Him in the 8th civil district of Cannon County certifying to this
court that James H. Lance had been duly and constitutionally elected a constable in said district for the Term of two years from the 6th day of March

last in place of Green B. Sapp, resigned And on motion the same James H. Lance
came into open court and was duly qualified as such whereupon he the said
Lance together with his securities

John Pendleton

Gabriel Lance and

Benjamin Pendleton

who being approved of by the court entered into bond in the sum of one thousand
payable and conditioned as the Law directs.

Thomas Elkins one of the deputy sheriffs of Cannon County returned a certificate from under the hands of the judges of an election Lately held by him
in the 5th civil district of said County, certifying that William W. Milligan
had been duly and constitutionally elected a constable in said district for
the term of two years from the 6th day of March last in place of Josiah Youngblood resigned And on motion the said William W. Milligan came into open
Court and was duly qualified as such whereupon he the said Milligan together
with his securities Thomas St John

James M. Brown and

JohnnB. Stone

who being approved of by the Court entered into Bon in the sum of one thousand
dollars conditioned and payable as the Law directs.

(p 126) Henry R. Perry Administrator of the estate Jesse L. Perry deceased
returned in open court an account current of the amount of sales together with
an Inventory of the effects of said said estate that has come into his hands
by vitture of his Administration And qualified to the same whereupon On
motion ordered by the court that the same be spread upon record in the proper
book &C.

On motion ordered by the court that Joseph Turney be appointed Guardian
of Sally Turney

Francis Turney and

George Turney

minor heirs of the estate of Isaac Turney deceased in place of John A. Spurlock
Former Guardian whereupon the said Joseph Turney together with his securities
Lem'l Turney and Polly Turner come into open court and entered into bond in
the sum of one thousand dollars payable to Thomas Powell Chairman of the county
Court of Cannon County and his successors in office conditioned as the Law
directs &C.

On motion ordered by the Court that John D. McBroom be appointed administrator of the Estate of Elizabeth Jane Moore deceased whereupon the the said
John D. McBroom came into open court and was duly qualified as such who together with his securities Henry Trott Jr. and John A. Dunn being approved of
by the court entered into bond in the sum of three thousand two hundred dollars
payable and conditioned as the Law directs. Thereupon letters of Administration were granted &C

(p 127) On motion and petition ordered by the court that Jacob Fite

Moses Fite

Henry Fite and

Andrew Fickett

be appointed commissioners to make a division of the negroes belonging to the
heirs of Frank S. Kenner deceased Between the said heirs equally that is to
say Between Jefferson H. Johnson an heir at Law by virtue of his marriage to
the widdow of the said F.S. Kenner dec'd and Daniel and Thomas Kenner minor
heirs of said Estate And make report to the next term of this court.

Moses Cummins

Joseph Moore
John Farles
Robert Vinson and
Henry Ford

commissioners summoned by the sheriff of this county by virture of a writ directed to heirs in pursuance of an order made at the last term of this court to set apart the one third(as a dower Wright of the land belonging to the Estate of William Sullivan Jr. deceased make report as follows (to wit) We the undersigned commissioners and Sheriff after Examining the Land and Tenements belonging to the estate of William Sullivan dec'd have alloted to Hamy Sullivan the widdow of the said William Sullivan deceased forty five acres of Land bounded North by the Land of Richard Vinson East by the Land of James McBroom south by the land belonging to the heirs of William Sullivan dec'd which boundary line is to be adm east and west line so as to include the above no. of acres in the dower of the said Hamy Sullivan also bounded West by the Land of Edmund Taylor which is a part of the Tract of Land that the said Hamy Sullivan now lives in which we think to be one third part in value of all the Lands and Tenements belonging to the Estate of the said William Sullivan dec'd we have we have also put the widdow in possession of the Dwelling house that she now lives in with other out houses upon the above Land.

Given under our hand this the 19th day of November 1836 signed

Moses Cummins
Joseph Moore
John Farles
Robert Vinson and
Henry Ford

And motion ordered that the same be certified for Registration On motion the court proceeded to appointed a Verure Facies For the next Circuit Court to be held for this county whereupon the following persons were appointed (to wit)

For District No. 1 Hale Barton, James D. Orr
For District No. 2 Thomas Hays and Milton Fowler
For District No. 3 Joseph Simpson and Alfred P. Gowen
For District No. 4 Hugh Reed and Daniel Finley
For District No. 5 John Pendleton and Isaac Young
For District No. 6 James Mears and Richard W. Lenny
For District No. 7 Robert Baily and William Elkins
For District No. 8 Sam'l Lanes and John Farles
For District No. 9 William B. Foster and William Wood
For District No. 10 Thomas Simpson and John Harriman
For District No. 11 Curtis McDowell and John E. Drake
For District No. 12 John Durham and Thomas Allen
For District No. 13 Peter M. Clark and H.M. Fite
For District No. 14 William Floyd and Jonathan C. Doss
For District No. 15 James Tubb and James Beatie
For District No. 16 Samuel Williams and Joel Cheatham 32

On motion the court proceeded to appoint a revenue commissioner for each cival district for the county to take in a list of property and poles in said county for the year 1836, whereupon the following persons were appointed to wit.

For District No. 1 Alexander McKnight
For District No. 2 Thomas Powell
For District No. 3 Joseph Simpson
For District No. 4 Blake Sagely

(p 129)

For District No. 5 Isaac W. Dledge
For District No. 6 James M. Brown
For District No. 7 Charles C. Evans
For District No. 8 Sam'l Lance
For District No. 9 John Martin
For District No. 10 Thomas Simpson
For District No. 11 Martin Phillips
For District No. 12 David Fisher
For District No. 13 Reuben Evans
For District No. 14 Pleasant A. Thomason
For District No. 15 Peter Reynolds
For District No. 16 Jonathan Fuson Esqrs.

James Taylor and Isaac Finley two of the commissioners appointed at the last term of this court to set apart to widdow of Archabald Edwards deceased one years provisions out of said Estate make report as follows.

We who have been appointed to lay off one years provisions for the widdow of Archabald Edwards do say that we beleave she ought to have twenty five barrels of corn one thousand pounds of pork, one barrel of salt, ten pounds of coffee & 25 pounds suger Dated December the 5th 1836 signed James Taylor &
Isaac Finley

Thomas Hays a constable of this county in the 2nd cival district this day returned in open court his sigmation as such And on motion ordered by the coutt that the same be made of reccord and that the shiriff proceed as the Law dirāots to hold an election in said District to fill said vancy &C .

Samuel Turney Esqr. reports to the Court that Jasper Ryle a constable for this county in the 10th cival district has removed of the state whereupon his office has became vancant And on motion ordered by the court that the same be made of reccord. And that the sheriff proceed forthwith as the Law directs to hold an election to fill the vancy occasioned by said removal.

(p 130) Lemuel Moore Esqr. presented to the Court for allowance on account from German Gossett, for making a coffin for Daniel Grant a trancient man who drawned himself in the limits of this county and on exmmation had no money or other effects wherewith to satisfy the same, And charges for the same four dollars, whereupon the names of the members of the court who were upon the bench being caled and the vote taken by ayes and noes, the vote stood as follows, to wit, Those who voted in the affirmative were

Esqrs. Charles C. Evans
Finley
Turney
Thos. Simpson
Pendleton
Melton
J.C. Martin
Powell and
Lance.

And those who voted in the negative were
Esqrs. Bates
Moore
Fuson
Brown

Whereupon the same was allowed And on motion ordered by the court that the clerk certify the same to the Trustee for payment out of any monies in his hand not otherwise appropriated.

Beacham Cannon Overseer of the stage road from Woodbury to the top of the ridge above George St. Johns having moved out of the bounds of his said road returns his commission as such and on motion ordered by the court that John D. McBroom be overseer in his room and sted upon said road with the same hands and Bounds.

Robert L. Shaw overseer of the road from Liberty to the short mountain (to wit) from the Cave Spring Branch to Tittle school house Returns his commission And is released from further serving as such Whereupon on motion ordered by the court that Isaac Turney be appointed Overseer in his room and sted with the same hand and bounds that the said Shaw overseer had .

(p 151) On motion ordered by the court that the road leading from Woodbury to Hardy Spicers be turned so as to run with the line of Francis Northcutt old place to the corner of the said Northcutts Land that the widdow Finley now lives on till it intersects with said road as vewed and out out heretofore.

Whereas it has been made known to the court that Nathan Neely Former overseer of the road from Woodbury to his own house in a direction of Statesville or Lebanon has removed out of the county and thereby his part of said road become vacant as to a overseer, whereupon on motion ordered by the court that Sam'l Vance be appointed overseer, with the same hands and bounds and that an order Issue to that effect.

Polly Turney)
  power atty)
Lem'l Turney) The execution of a power of Attorney from Polly Turney to Lem'l Turney to collect monies therein names bearing date the 5th day of December 1836 was this day duly acknowledged in open court by the said Polly Turney to be her act and deed for the purposes therein contained And on motion ordered that the same be certified for Resignation.&C.

Whereas Thomas Powell Chairman of this court being absent at the opening of the court On motion ordered by the Court that Charles C. Evans Esq. take the chair and preside over the deliberations of this court during its present term.

(p 152) Court then adjorned till tomorrow morning nine OBlock.
                              Charles C. Evans
                              John Pendleton
                              Isaac Finley
                              John C. Martin

Tuseday Morning December the 6th 1836 Nine O'clock to worshipfull cort meet pursuant to adjournment present the Worshipfull
                              Charles C. Evans
                              Isaac Finley
                              John Pendleton
                              John C. Martin
                              William Bates
Whereupon the following proceedings were had and don (to wit)

Alexander Young Administrator of the Estate of Archibald Edwards deceased returned in open court an account current and an amount of sales of the property and effects of said Estate that had come into his hands by virtue of his Administrators of said Estate and was duly qualified to the same. Whereupon motion ordered by the court that the same be spread upon <u>record</u> in the proper book.

   Ther being no further <u>Buisness</u> Court adjorned till Court in Course.
          Charles C. Evans
          Isaac Finley
          John Pendleton

       January Term

(p 133)
State of Tennessee)
Cannon County   ) January term of the County Court.

At a county court began and held at the house of Henry D. McBroom in the Town of Woodbury it being the place appointed by law for holding the County Court in said County until the court house shall be erected &C it being the second day of January A.D. 1837 and the Sixty first year of the American <u>Independance</u> Present the Worshipfull
      Thomas Powell
      Isaac Finley
      Alexander McKnight
      John C. Martin
      Joseph Simpson
      James L. Essery
      Isaac N. Elledge
      John Pendleton
      James McBroom
      Elijah Stephens
      John Melton
      Charles C. Evans
      Sam'l Lance
      John Martin Sr. and
      Watson Cantrell Esqrs.
Whereupon the following orders were made (to wit)
  On motion ordered by the Court that Henry Heart be appointed Guardian of Elizabeth Jane Kelly
 William Jasper Kelly and
 John R. Kelly
minor heirs of John Kelly deceased. Whereupon the said Heart came into open court and <u>qualifyed</u> as such who together with his securities Sam'l Tittle Senr. (being approved of by the court) entered into bond in the sum of <u>sevin</u> hundred dollars payable to Thomas Powell Chairman of the County Court and successors in office <u>condition</u> as the law directs.

Henry Heart Guardian of
    Elizabeth Jane Kelly
    William Jasper Kelly and
    John R. Kelly
minor heirs of John Kelly deceased returned into open court an account (p 134) current of the effects belonging to the said orphans and <u>quallified</u> to the same Whereupon on motion ordered by the court that the same be spread upon <u>record</u> in the guardian Book.

James Ferrell one of the deputy sheriffs of Cannon returned into open court a certificate from the judges appointed to hold an election in the fourth <u>cival</u>

district in Cannon County for to elect a constable for said district from which certificate appeared to the sattisfaction of the court that Alexander F. Todd was duly elected to said office. Whereupon the said Alexander F. Todd came into open court and qualifyed as such who together with securtys Hiram Wilson and Jonathan Bateman entered into bond in the sum of one thousand dollars condition and payable as the law directs.

George Grizzle sheriff of this county returned into open court as certificate of an election held in the tenth cival district for constable from which certificate it appeared to the sattisfaction of the court that Lemuel Tittle was duly elected to said office whereupon the said Tittle came into open court and qualifyed as such who together with his security Samuel Tittle senr. (being approved of by the court) entered into bond in the sum of one thousand dollars conditioned and payable as the law directs.

On motion ordered by the court that Thomas Given be appointed guardian of William Bratton and Henry Bratton minor heirs of Henry Bratton deceased in place of George (p 135) L. Given former guardian of said minors who was heretofore appointed by the Smith County County Court as such whereupon the said Thomas Given came into open court and qualifyed as such who together with his securities Joseph Clark and George L. Givens (approved of by the court) entered into bond in the sum of three hundred and thirty dollars payable to Thomas Powell Chairman of the county court and successors in office condition as the law directs.

Whereas it appearing to the satisfaction of the court that William Moore entered as guardian for Elizabeth Jane Moore at the July Term of this court 1836 with Henry Clifton And Arthur Warren his securities and whereas it appearing to the satisfaction of this court that the said Henry Clifton had given the said William Moore the Lawfull notice that he should appear before this court to move against him the said Moore to compell him to Give other counter security Whereupon the said William Moore came into court and acknowledged the service of the said notice and offered Russell Lewis as said counter security who being approved of by the court, he the said Lewis came into open court, and assigned as said counter security the bond given by the said Moore, Warren and Clifton at the July Term of this court. Whereupon on motion ordered by the court that said Clifton be released from any further liability as the security of the said Moore an said Guardain previous to this date.

(p 136) On motion ordered by the court that
Andrew Pickett
Jacob Fite
Moses Fite &
Henry Fite
commissioners appointed at the last Term of this court to devidethe negroes belonging to the estate of F.S. Kenner deceased between the legaties of said Estate be contined as commissioners to make said devision And make report to the next term of this court.

On motion and upon the petition of Jefferson H. Johnson Guardain of the minor heirs of F.S. Kenner deceased Ordered by the Court that
William Floyd
Peter W. Clark
Henry Fite
Moses Fite and
Matthias S. West

be appointed commissioners to divide the lands belonging to the estate of F.S.
Kenner deceased (to wit)

                    Thomas Kenner
                    Daniel Kenner

and the said Jefferson H. Johnson, and make report to the next Term of this
court according as the law directs.

On motion ordered by the court that the clerk of this court Issue and
order commanding the shiriff of this county to summons a jury of twelve Good and
Lawful men to proceed to the house of Robert Gibson in the first district and
then and there to examine into the state of the mind of Patsy Gibson and report
the same at the next term of this court.

Edwin J. Roseberry came into and proposed to have Thomas Farles bound to
him untill he arrivided to the age of twenty one years And proposed to instruct
the said Thomas in the act and mistery of the Blacksmithing Buisness or cause
the same to be done and also to constantly find the said Thomas meet drink and
Lodging And also good apparel And have the said Thomas taught in arithmetic to
the rule of three and (p 137) to treat him the said Thomas in all the respects
with Humanity &C which proposuals were accepred of by the court. Whereupon the
said E.J. Roseberry together with his security Alexander McKnight came into
open court and entered into bond faithfully to perform the Injunctions agreed
upon when the said Thomas Farles shall arrive at the age of twenty one years.

Benjamin F. Odom came into open court proposed to have bond to heir
William Patrick an orphan of Levi Patrick deceased and proposed to instruct
the said William in the act and mistery of farming and to read write and cipher
to the rule of three also to constantly find the said William sufficient Lodging washing and apparel both in sickness in Helath and also to take care of
his morels and treat him with Humanity and at the end of the time to Give him a
Horse, bridle and saddle worth seventy five dollars and one Good suit of jeans
clothing and a good fur hat. Which proposition being accepted of by the court
The said B.F. Odom together with his security W.C.Odom came into open court and
entered into bond for the faithfull performance of the same payable and condition-
as the law directs.

Thomas Cavatt)
Deed 98½ acres)
William Woods)   The execution of a deed of conveynnce from Thomas Cavatt
to William Wood for ninety eight and one half acres of land lying in Cannon
County bearing date the 11th day of July 1836 was this day duly aclnowledged
in open court (by the bargainor) to be his act and deed for the purposes
therein contained and on motion ordered that the came be certified for registration.

(p 138)
Thomas Cavatt)
Transfer to   )
William Wood)   The execution of a transfer or an assignment upon a plot and
a certificate for three hundred acres of land lying in Cannon County bearing
date the 12th day of December 1836 was this day acknowledged in open court by
the assignor to be his act and deed for the purposes therein contained And on
motion ordered that the clerk of this court certify the same.

David Byford)
Transfer to)
Amuel Rains)   The execution of a transfer or assignment of a plot and certifi-

cate from David Dyford to Anuel Rains for seventy four acres of land lying in Cannon County bearing date the 4th of August 1836 was this day proven in open court by Hardy Dyford and William Leigh subscribing witnesses thereto And on motion ordered by the court that the Clerk of this court certify the same.

Robert Stephens)
Deed 5 acres   )
Jessee Johnson) The execution of a deed of conveyance from Robert Stephens to Jessee Johnson for five acres of land lying in Cannon County (originally Warren County) Bearing date the 30th day of June 1835 was this day duly proven in open court by Joseph Clark and Reuben Blue subscribing witnesses thereto and on motion ordered that the same be certifyed for registration.

George T. Ford   )
Deed 140 acres   )
Josiah Youngblood) The execution of a deed of conveyance from George T. Ford to Josiah Youngblood for one hundred and forty acres of land lying in Cannon County bearing this date 2nd January 1837 (p 139) was this day duly acknowledged in open court by the bargainor to be his act and deed for the purposes therein contained And on motion ordered that the same be certifyed for registration.

William Parton &)
William Bates   )
Deed 500 acres) The execution of a deed of conveyance from William Parton to Washington Canady for five hundred acres of land lying in Cannon County (originally Warren County) bearing date the 8th April 1835 was this day duly acknowledged in open court by the bargainor to be their act and deed for the purposes therein contained and on motion ordered that the clerk certify the same for registration.

Stanford Smith)
Deed in trust)
Henry Hayes   ) The execution of a deed in trust from Stanford Smith to Henry Hayes for personal property therein contained bearing date the 24th day of December 1836, was this day duly proven in open court by Thomas Hayes and John Bevirts subscribing witnesses thereto and on motion ordered that the same be certified for registration.

On motion ordered by the court that William Higgins
Nelson Owen
Hiram Tittle
James Milligan and
James McAdoo
be appointed a jury of men to vew and Marke a road Begining at the Cannon and Wilson County line runing up the Harlcain Creek so as to intersect with th road leading from Woodbury to Liberty up the Cavanaugh Creek on top of the ridge and make report to the next term of this court.

(p 140) On motion ordered by the court that Epy Francis be appointed Overseer of the road begining at the widdow Coopers running to the Wilson County line and that he have the same hands heretofore alloted on said road by the Wilson County Court.

On motion ordered by the court that Francis Cooper be appointed Overseer of the road from the widdow Coopers to Richard L. McKnights and have the same hands heretofore appointed by the Wilson County Court &C.

On motion Ordered by the Court that James Reed be appointed Overseer of the road from the Forks of the creek at John W. Summars to the top of the ridge towards Woodbury And have the same hands heretofore appointed by the Wilson County Court &C.

On motion ordered by the court that William L. Covington & James H. Lance Constables be appointed to attend the next Circuit Court and on motion it is further ordered by the Court that the Clerk of this Court Issue to the shff. an order to that effect.

On motion ordered by the court that Christopher Owen be appointed Overseer of the road from Thomas Leaches to the top of the ridge between Wilson and Rutherford Counties and have the same hands that were heretofore appointed by the Wilson County Court.

On motion ordered by the Court that Sam'l Corn be appointed Overseer of the road from Leaches (p 141) to the Cannon County line and have the same hands heretofire appointed by the Wilson County Court &C.

On motion ordered by the court that Sam'l Tittle Sr.
Henry Dennis
John Hollensworth
George Ashford
Josiah Fuston
Jeremiah L. Reaves
Robert Dogle &
Alexander Armstrong
be appointed a jury of men to vew and marke a road Begining at the School House on the clear fork near Sam'l Tittles runing up the Canal Creek the nearest and best way so as to intersect the Rock House fork road in the Hollow below Wily Ratleys and make report to the next term of this court.

On motion ordered by the court that Christopher C. Alexander be appointed Overseer of the road from Leaches Blacksmith shop to Richard L. McKnights and have the same hands and bounds Heretofore allowed by the Wilson County Court to J.B. Summars and A. Cooper Former Overseer had.

On motion Ordered by the Court that Sterling Almon be appointed Overseer of the Streets in the Town of Woodbury and have the following hands to clear out and keep said streets in order (to wit)
John R. Sullivan
John Denton
Gabriel Williams
William Y. Henderson
Henry Trott
Ransone Youngblood
William L. Almon
T.G. Almon
John A. Dunn
A.B. Capps
Wm. L. McLin and
James O. George Sr.

Whereas it appearing to the satisfaction of this court that an act was passed at the last regular session of the General Assembly of the state of Tennessee annexing a portion of the county of Wilson to the (p 142) County of Cannon provided there should be a surpluss in said Wilson County after leaving six hundred and twenty five square miles to be assertained on a survey to be made by the surveyors of Sumner County And whereas it appearing to the satisfaction of this court that said survey had been regularly made and that said surveyor has made a return to the Governor of said survey as the Law directs she shewing from his plot and Certificate of said survey that there was a surplus in said Wilson County of ————square miles after leaving the Constitual Limits in Wilson County And it further appearing to the satisfaction of this Court that his Excelency the Governor has Issued his proclimations declaraing that the said surplus therein Contained And all the citizens residing in said district or Teritory shall have and are now and was on the Issuing said proclimation Intitled to all the rights and priveledges of other citizens of said Cannon County And on motion it is further ordered by the court that the shiriff of this County proceed on Friday the 20th to open and Hold an election in said district (to be caled district No. 17) to elect two justices of the peace and one Constable for said district and make report of the same as the Law directs.

On motion ordered by the court that William C. Odom be appointed a revinue commissioner for the 17th cival District in Cannon County to take in a list of the poles and taxable property in said district for the year 1837 and make return as the law directs.

On motion Micajah Petty presented before the court a petition sworn to in open court praying this (p 143) court to instruct there Clerk To make out a transcript of all the records of this court had and done before the same upon a paper writing purporting to be the Last Will and Testament of Margaret Petty deceased at the June Term of this Court 1836. And whereas it appearing to the satisfaction of this court that the prayer of the petitioners is reasonable and ought to be granted. Whereupon on motion ordered by the Court that the Clerk of this court make out a full and complete transcript of all of the proceedings had and done at the said June Term of this court as also at this term upon the said paper writing purporting as aforesaid to be the Last Will and Testament of the said Margaret Petty deceased by the said Micajah Patty (who shews in his said petition to the satisfaction of this court that he is a Lawful heir of the said Margaret Petty deceased) Giving bond with approved security faithfully to prosecute said suit Whereupon the said Micajah Petty together with his security William Young (being a proved of by the court came into open court and entered into bond in the penal sum of Five hundred dollars payable to Alexander Petty faithfully to prosecute said suit he being the only distribute names in the said paper writing purporting as aforesaid to be the Last will and Testament of the said Margaret Petty deceased (there beingno execution appointed in said Will to whom to execute said bond, as directed by law, And that Notice Issue of this proceeding to the said Alex'r Petty as the Law directs. Court then adjorned till tomorrow morning 10 o'clock.

Thos. Powell Chrn.
E. Stephens
I.W. Elledge

(p 144) Tuseday morning January the 3rd 1837
The Worshipfull court met pursuant to adjornment present the Worshipfull

Thomas Powell
Isaac W. Elledge
John Melton
Elijah Stephens and
James M. Brown Esq.

Whereupon the following orders were made (to wit)

Daniel Nichols came into open court and proposed to the court to have bound to him Jesse Smith (an orphan born on the 29th day of September 1825) until he attains the age of twenty one years and proposed to learn him the said Jesse in the art and mistery of the farming Buisness and have him taught to read and write and the arithmetic to the single rule of three and to give him at the end of his servitude a horse saddle and bridle worth seventy five dollars and a good jeans suit of clothing and a fur hat and such other good comfortable clothing during his servitude &C . Which proposition being approved by the court the said Daniel Nichols entered into bond together with his secuity William Nichols and Silas Gather approved of by the court faithfully to perform said agreement.

Josiah McElwin came into court to have bound to him William Smith (orphan boy born on the 17th day of January 1824) Untill he arrived to the age of twenty one years and proposed to learn him or have the same done in the art and mistry of the farming Puisness and to have him taught to read write and the arithmetic to the single rule of three and at the end of his servitude to (p 145) give him a horse, saddle, and bridle worth seventy five dollars and also a good suit of jeans clothing and a fur hat and such other clothing as is necesary and comfortable during his servitude and to furnish him in good wholesome diet &C which prosuals being approved of by the court, the said Josiah McElwen entered into bond together with his security Thos.Vance (being approved by the court) faithfully to perform the above agreement &c.

Joseph C. McGee came into court and proposed to have bond to him Barnit G. Smith (an orphan Child) born the 22nd of October 1827 untill he shall have attained to the age of twenty one years and proposes to teach him in the art and mistery of the farming Puisness and in addition thereto proposes to give him at the expiration of his servitude a horse, saddle and bridle worth seventy five dollars and a good suit of jeans and a fur hat and such other comfortable clothing as is necessary during his servitude and to furnish him the said Barnet G. Good Holesome diet, lodging &C. Which proposuals being approved of by the court the said McGee together with his security Joseph Ramsey (being approved of by the court entered into bond faithfully to execute the above covenent.

Whereas it appearing to the satisfaction of the court that Margaret Petty late of our county is deceased and having left a paper writing purporting to be her last will and Testament which being presented to this court at the June Term 1836 for probate and was duly (p 146) proven and at the present Term of this court upon the petition of Micajah Petty is ordered to be sent to the Circuit Court there to try the validity of the same Whereupon On motion ordered by the court that Micajah Petty be appointed Administrator of the estate of the said Margaret Petty deceased . Whereupon the said Micajah Petty came into open court and quallified as such who together with his securitys Henry Trott and Joseph Ramsey (being approved of by the court) entered into Bond in the sum of Four Thousand dollars payable to his Exceleney Newton Cannon Governor and his successors in office conditioned as the Law directs. Whereupon on motion ordered that Letters of Administration be granted.

February Term

(p 149)
State of Tennessee)
Cannon County   )

At a County Court began and held for the County aforesaid at the House of Henry D. McBroom in the Town of Woodbury (it being the place appointed by law for holding the Court for said county until publick Building are erected &C) On the first Monday It being the sixth day of February A.D. 1837 and the sixty first year of American Independence present the Worshipfull Thomas Powell Chrm.
John C. Martin

Isaac Finley
Joseph Simpson
James L. Essary
Blake Sagely
Isaac W. Elledge
John Pendleton
Thomas L. Turner
Elijah Stephens
James H. Brown
Charles C. Evans
John Helton
William Bates
Sam'l Lance
John Martin
Lem'l Turney
Thomas Simpson
Martin John Fraseur
Watson Cantrell
Reuben Evans
Lemuel Moore
Pleasant Thomason
James Beatie and
Jonathan Fuson &
James Goodner Esqrs.

Whereupon the following orders and rules were made (to wit)

On motion the court proceeded to the election of a chairman for the Term of twelve months from the Jany. Term of this court 1837.
Whereof James Goodner and John C. Martin Esqrs. were put in nomination and upon the first Balloting John C. Martin Esqrs. was found to be duly elected have received 17 votes and James Goodner Esq. having only 10 votes. Whereupon the present incumbent resigned the chair to the Chairman Elect who accepted of the sum and proceeded to discharge the duties of that office.

(p 150)
Francis Cooper & William Bryson the justice Elect in the 17th district in Cannon County (it being in that part of said county detached from the County of Wilson) presented there Commissioners from his Excelency the Governor And on motion the said justices came into open court and were duly qualifyes as such.

George Grizzle Esqr. shiriff of Cannon County presented a certificate of the judges appointed to hold the election for district Officers in the 17th district and it appeared from said certificate to the satisfaction of the court that Alexander Milligan was duly elected as constable in said district On motion the said Alexander Milligan came into open court and was duly qualified as such who together with his securities William R. James and James Higgins came into open court and entered into bond in the sum of One thousand dollars Conditioned and payable as the Law directs.

Matthew Parker Esqr. one of the deputy shorriffs of Cannon County presented before the court a certificate from the judges appointed to judge an elected in the 16th district to elect a constable for said district to fill the vancancy accationed by the removal of J.M. Farrington Former constable of said district from which certificate appeared to the satisfaction of the court that Benjamin Curtis was duly elected. Whereupon he the said Benjamin Curtis came into Court and was duly qualified as such Who together with his securities Jonathan Fuson and William Boyd entered into bond in the sum of one thousand dollars conditioned and payable as the Law directs.

James Ferrell Esqr. one of the deputy sherriffs in Cannon County presented before the court a certificate from the judges appointed to judge an election held in the secondn district in Cannon County to elect a constable in said district in place of Thomas Hays resigned from which certificate it appeared to the satisfaction of the court that Jesse Hollis was duly elected, Whereupon the said Jesse Hollis came into open court and was duly qualified as such who together with his securities Isaac Finley and William Hollis came into open court and entered into bond in the sum of one thousand dollars conditioned and payable as the Law directs.

Hugh Robinson produced in open court the last will and testamentof John Bullard deceased late of our county, which was duly proven in open court by the oaths of Hezekiah Clements and Isaac Winberly suscribing witnesses thereto and on motion Ordered that the same be recorded in the proper Book. Whereupon Hugh Robinson (having been appointedto excute said will by the Dictator) came into open court and was duly qualified as such who together with his securities David Patton & Joseph Knox entered into bond in the sum of one thousand dollars conditioned and payable as the Law diricts Whereupon on motion Ordered that Letters Testamentory be granted.

Joseph Turney Guardian of Sally L. Turney , Frances Turney and George Turney minor heirs of the Estate of Isaac Turney deceased returned in open court an account Current of his said Guardianship and was qualified to the same in open court andon Motion Ordered that the same be spread upon record in the proper Book.

(p 152)

John Davis Guardian of Elijah Duncan Returned in open court on account Current of his said Guardianship and qualified to the same And on motion Ordered that the same be spread upon reccordin the proper Book.

Allen Whitfield Administrator of the estate of W.llis Whitfield deceased returned into court an account of sales of the said Willis Whitfields Estate by virture of his administration and qulified to the same on motion Ordered that the same be spread upon reccord in the proper Book.

Hugh Robinson
William Ring and
Jessie Gilley
commissioners appointed at the December Term of this court 1836 to lay off one years provisions to the widdow of Willis Whitfield deceased, make report that they have laid off the said widdow the following atticles (to wit) thirty Barr els of corn, five hogs of her choice out of the stock, twenty five pounds of coffee fifty pounds of sugar two hundred and fifty pounds of flower and one hundred pounds of salt dated December the 15th day 1836.

Henry Sauls)
Deed 100 acres)
Andrew Boyle) The execution of a deed of conveyance from Henry Sauls to Andrew Boyle for one hundred acres of land lying in Cannon County bearing date the 28th day of October 1836 was this day duly proven in open court by the oaths of William Bryson & John W. Summer subscribing witnesses to the same and on motion ordered that same be cettified for Registration. William W. Milligan one of the constables in the sixth district in Cannon County this day returned into Court his resignation as constable in said district and on motion ordered that the shiriff held an election to fill said vancy

(p 153)

Lemuel Turney)
Deed 41 acres)
Abram Adams) The execution of a deed of conveyance from Lemuel Turney to
Abram Adams for forty one acres of land lying in Cannon County bearing date the
8th day of January 1837 was this day duly acknowledged in open court by the said
Lemuel Turney (the bargainor) to be his act and deed for the purposes therein
contained And on motion ordered that the same be certified for Registration.

Benjamin Pendleton)
Deed 60 3/4 acres)
William West) The execution of a deed of conveyance from Benjamin
Pendleton to William West for sixty and three forth acres of land lying in
Cannon (originally) Warren County bearing date the third day of September 1830
was this day duly acknowledged in open court by the said Benjamin Pendleton
(the bargainor) to be his act and deed for the purposes therein contained and
on motion ordered that the same be certified for Registration.

Sam'l Boyle & his wife)
Isabel Boyle)
Deed 33 1/3 acres)
James Odom) The execution of a deed of conveyance from Sam'l
Boyle and his wife Isabel Boyle to James Odom for thirty three and one third
acres of land lying in Cannon County bearing date the sixth day of February 1837
was this day duly acknowledged in open court by the bargainor to be there act
and deed for the purposes therein contained and on motion ordered to be certified
for Registration.

James L. Essary one justice of the peace Cannon County in district No. 4 this
day returned in open court his resignation as such And on motion ordered that
the shiriff hold an election to fill said vanvancy.

(p 154)
Jacob Fite
Moses Fite and
Henry Fite
a part of the commissioners appointed at the December Term of this court 1836
and continued at the January Term 1837 to devide the negroes belonging to the
estate of Frank G. Kenner dec'd Between the heirs of said Estate equally to wit
Jefferson H. Johnson one of the heirs at law by vitture of his marriage with
the widdow of the said F.G. Kenner and Thomas Kenner minor heirs of the said
Estate make report as follows. (to wit)

State of Tennessee)
Cannon County) January the 25th 1837
We the undersigned commissioners appointed by the Worshipfull County Court of
Cannon County make a devision of the negroes of the estate of F.G. Kenner &
Thomas Kenner minors and J.H. Johnson and wife, lawfull heirs of said Estate
report as follows, first we gave to J.H. Johnson and wife Elizabeth ——
Tom at four hundred dollars ————————————————————————$ 400.00
Dafney, his wife at one hundred and fifty dollars ————— 150.00
Nancy and child Hansford at —————————————————— 850.00
Handy (a boy at —————————————————————————— 900.00
Caroline (a girl at ————————————————————————— 700.00
                                                         3000.00
The above Class is indebted to Daniel Kenner sixteen dollars and Thomas Minor
heirs sixty eight dollars. ——
Second Daniel Kenner minor heir he gave as follows;

Harriet at	$ 500.00
Lucy at	725.00
Rach at	425.00
Mary at	200.00
Watsey at	700.00
Jane at	350.00
	$ 2900.00

The third calse Thomas Kenner minor heir of Estate we give as follows

Hannah (a girl at	700.00
Easter (a girl at	500.00
(p 155) Amount over	1200.00
Bethiah at	300.00
Elizabeth at	300.00
Emily at	250.00
Lucinda at	200.00
Mercer (a boy) at	600.00
	2850.00

All of which is hereby submitted and Given under our hands the day and date above written and signed by

Henry Fite
Moses Fite
Jacob Fite Commissioners

Which report being sworn before Jonathan C. Doss one of the justices of the peace for Cannon County the same was received and ordered to be spread upon the minuits of this court.

Alexander McKnight Coroner of Cannon County returned into open court, a report of a jury of inquest held under his direction at the House of Thomas L. Todd on the 31st day of Jan. 1837 over the dead body of Joshua Vasser. And from the evidence before them they beleave that he was braught to his death by violence inflicted upon him by one of Roswell Soap as Is more fully set forth in said report. And it appearing to the satisfaction of the court that the duties performed by the said Corner in the above inquest have been done and perforned in accordance with the acts assembly in such cases made and provided. It is therefore ordered by court that the clerk certify the same to the county Trustee and that he pay the coroner the fees allowed by Law for such servises   out of any monies in his hands not otherwise appropriated.

(p 156) William Higgins came into court and made known to the court that he had under his care an orphan boy about nine years old by the name of Jesse Patrickson of Levi Patrick deceased who he believed ought to be taken consideration by the court and proposed to him bouhd to him untill he arrived to the age of twenty one years and proposed to give fifteen months schooling between the ages of fifteen and twenty years and give him a horse, caddle and Bridle to be worth seventy five dollars one good suit of jeans clothing, one fur hat, and to furnish him constantly Good strong and comfortable clothing and good Holesome diet &C during his servitude with him which proposition being agreed to by the court the said William Higgins entered into bond with Joseph C. McGee his security faithfully to comply with the said proposition)

On motion the court proceeded to Levy the taxes for the present year and after various propositions the following rate was fixed upon the priveledges and Occupations (to wit) the one half of the amount od the state taxes, And upon taking the question by ayes and noes upon the above rate(It being laid for county purposes indiscimenately Those who voted in the affirmative were Esqrs.

John Martin
Thomason
Cantrell
Frazeur
Phillips
Moore
Patie
Fuson
Thomas
Simpson
Sedgely
Lance
Joseph Simpson
Melton
Bates
Finley
Stephens
Turner
Cooper
Bryson
Reuben Evans
Pendleton
Powell
JohnnC. Martin
twenty three.
Those who voted in the negative were Esqrs.
Charles C. Evans
Lemuel Turney
Isaac W. Elledge and
James M. Brown
Four.
Whereupon after various propositions the following Rates (p 157) were fixed
upon as the tax forcounty purposes indiscriminately upon the property real and
personal and white polls (to wit) Equal to the state tax upon the same And
upon taking taking the vote by ayes and noes upon the above propositions,
Those who voted in the affirmative were Esqrs.
Thomason
C. . Evans
Lance
Joseph Simpson
Melton
Bates
Finley
Stephens
Turner
Cooper
Bryson
R. Evans
Pendleton
Brown
Powell
Elledge and
J.C. Martin — seventeen — And those who voted in the negative were;
John Martin
Cantrell
Fraqeur
Phillips
Moore

Patie
Fuson
T. Simpson
Sedgely
T. Turney, Ten

On motion ordered by the court that Samuel J. Garrison Clerk of this court be authorized and Required to receive the amount of the County Taxes severally from all of those Hereafter to be Licenced to exercise any of the priveledges and Occupations in this state. When granting said Licence and that he pay over and account to the County Trustee in manner and form as the Law directs for the same . And it is alos further Ordered by the Court that the said clerk furnish the shiriff or Collector for the present year a list of all who have been Licenced sence the first day of september 1836 together with the amount of County taxes due from each Individuals or firm of Copartners who have been Licenced by him agreable to the rates fixed upon at the present Term of this Court. And it is moreover Hereby further ordered by the Court that the said sherriff is Hereby authorized and required to collect the same when collecting other co nty taxes for the present year of 1837 and that the said shiriff or collector pay over and account to the County Trustee for the same as the law dirkcts.

(p 151) On motion ordered by the court that Hereafter It shall be a standing rule of this cort for the government of the same that any order or rule made on any day of Term of this court shall stand and not be reconsidered By a less number of the justices of said court then were present at the adoption of such rule or order any former practices of this court to the contrary notwithstanding.

On motion ordered by the court that Joseph Boyle be appointed Overseer of the road from Leaches shop to R.L. McKnight in place of C.C. Alexanderrremoved out of his bounds and that he have the same hands Heretofore allowed by the Wilson County court and bounds.

On motion ordered by the court that Sam'l L. Tyree be appointed Overseer of the road from the Caney fork river at Allens Ferry to the two mile post towards Liberty and have the same hands and bounds that Jesse Allen Overseer had.

On motion ordered by the court that Finley Martin be appointed Overseer from the two mile post on the Allens Ferry road to Tavner Martins old place and have the same hands that Tavner Martin the former Overseer had.

On motion Ord red by the court that Curtis McDowell be appointed Overseer on the Allens Ferry road from Tavner Martins old place to the forks of the road near the old Canadt place and have the same hands and bounds that Bartemicus Pack Former Overseer had.

(p 159) On motion ordered by the court that
William Foster
Enoch Jones
John Foster
John C. Canady and
Thomas Ward
be appointed a jury of men to vew and change the road about a forth of a mile

where the same runs through the lands of San'l E. Burger if practicable and report the same to the next term of this court.

On motion ordered by the court That Ezekiel Hays one of the Overseers on the road from Woodbury to Jonathan Jones have the following list of hands to work the same (to wit)
Henry Dasheur
Peter Maxey
John Hollis
Wm. Hollis Jr.
Wm. Hollis Sr.
Charles Bowen
Dossen McGlockin
Jonathan Dashaw
John Dashaw
Benjamin T. Hays
Meshac Warren
Richmond Cogwell
Achilus Alexander
Benjamin Hays
James Todd
Charles P. Alexander and
James Soap.

On motion ordered by the court that Archabald Stone have leave to change the stage road so as to run the same strait commencing at the crook in said road near said stones own house and to intersect again near where Elisha Miles lives and that when the said Stone shall have put the same in good repare the Overseer on that part of the road will work the same.

On motion ordered by the court that John Boyd one of the Overseers of the road from Woodbury up stones river to the Cap of the short mountain have the following list of hands, (to wit)
Elijah Gilley
James Sullens
Melberry Brashers
Lewis Starr
Alman Rigeby
Abram Walker
Henry Sullins
Dickson Cummings
Mansfield Thompson
Ezekiel Merriman and
Robert Baily one black hand.
(p 160)
On motion ordered by the court that John Young Overseer have the following list of hands (to wit)
William Halpain
Joseph Molton
James Melton
Jesse Sullins
Richard Sullins
Thomas Sullins
Edward Gilley
San'l Young
Canady Almon

David Carder &
Henry Sewell
And that he commence at the shelving rock at the <u>moth</u> of the Hollow leading
from James Phillips field.

On motion ordered by the court that Joseph Moore be appointed Overseer of
the ——— from Liberty to Woodbury commencing at the mouth of the rock house
fork leading up this fork and over the ridge to Rackleys and that he have the
following list of hands and bounds to keep the same in <u>repare</u>.(to wit)
William Sullins
Alexander Higgins
James Higgins
Jesse Melton
James Cantrell
William L. Melton
Powell
Perry
Thomas Pitman
William Elkins
Andrew F. Evans
John N. Evans
Joseph Halpain
Elisha Melton
James Melton
Henry R. Perry and
Elisha Cantrell

Sam'l Tittle Sr.
Henry Dennis
John Hollensworth
Josiah Fuston
George Ashford and
Robert Bogle
the jury of men appointed at the last term of this court to vew and marke a road
Beginning at the school House near Sam'l Tittles running up the <u>Carmal</u> fork the
nearest and best way so as to intersect the rock House fork road in the Hollow
below Wiley Rachleys make report that they have <u>vewed</u> and marked the same
according to said order And on motion it is further Ordered By the court that
the same be established as a County road and that John Hollinsworth be Overseer
of the same to Wily Rachleys and that he have the following list of hands to
clear out said road (to wit)
(p 161)
Adam Tittle
Sam'l Tittle Sr.
Elijah Higgins
Elisha Harris
William Dennis
John Cann
Britton Cann
George Ashford
Josiah Fuston
Josiah Hollinsworth
Naoman Hollensworth
Hector Smith
Jerry T. Reaves

Alex'r Armstrong
John Boyle
Daniel Boyle
Hugh Ledbetter
William Blair
James Blair
John Anderson
Hiram Morris
Miles Spurlock
Jefferson Ledbetter
John Herriman
Josiah Herriman
Wily Hendrickson
Peter P. Hyres
Francis Turner
Francis Spurlock
Fountain Owens
Benjamin Hail Jr.
John McGee
Wm. McGee
John Craddock
Abner Craddock
Green Craddock
Robert Tittle
Archabald McDougle
Edmond Collins
John Blair

On motion ordered by the court that William Pratt be appointed Overseer of the road from Neils shop on dismal creek to Liberty commencing at said shop and running to the top of the ridge above Lemuels Moores and have the same hands and bounds that Peter Hays former Overseer had.

On motion ordered by the court that James Wilson be appointed Overseer of the road in place of Joel Coffee removed and that he have the same hands and bounds.

On motion ordered by the court that Epaproditas Francis Overseer of the ——— from the Wilson County line to the widdow Cooper have the following list of hands to keep the same in repare (to wit)
Robert Landsden
Robert Marshall (black hand)
Armsted Francis 2
James Odom 2
Reding M. Odom
Shadrack Odom
E. Francis
One of the widdow Cooper 1
Benjamin B. Cooper
M. Francis
L.B. Moon
William Johnston and
Aaron Duggan

On motion ordered by the court that Sam'l E. Burgar be appointed Overseer of the road from the county line near John Martins Esqr. to Burgars store and apply to John Martin Esqr. for a list of hands to keep the same in repare.

On motion ordered by the court that

Joseph Adamson
Abram Overall
Wills Adamson
Moss Allen
James Barrett and
William Melton

be appointed a jury of men to vew and mark a road from the Overalls up the clear fork by way of Joseph Adamson so as to intersect the McMinnville road at or near Wm. Meltons and make report to next Term of this court.

On motion ordered by the court that the shiriff of this county summons from five to twelve Good and lawfull men free holders as a jury of men to vew and marke such alteration as may be practicable in the road from Liberty to Woodbury commencing on the stage road at the most suitable place between Thomas Dales and Joseph Clarks runing in the direction of Woodbury as fare as the sholl house on the Clear fork near Sam'l Tittles and that they make report to the next term of this court.

Holsen Owens
William Higgins
Hiram Tittle
James Milligan and
James McAdow

a jury of men appointed at the last term of this court to vew and marke a road Begining at the Cannon County line runing up the Herican Creek so as to intersect with the road leading from Woodbury to Liberty up the Cavannughs Creek on top of the ridge at the old Wilson County line above John Prestons make report that they have vewed and marked the same according to said order And on motion the same is established as a County road. And on motion (p 163) It is further ordered by the court that John Higgins Jr. be appointed Overseer of said road ad and that he have the following list of hands to clear out said road and keep the same in repare (to wit)

William Cock
Hiram Tittle
James Higgins
Sam'l Bryson
John Higgins
William Higgins
Elbert Owens
William James
David Milligan
Thomas Standley
Robert Milligan
William Standley
Harrison Standley
Moss C. Standley
William Willard
Joel Willard
Sam'l C. Odom
William C. Odom
Benjamin F. Odom
Nelson Owens
James Milligan
Charles Hancock
James McAdow
Allen Wilson and

John Riggins

Court then adjourned till tomorrow morning 12 oclock.
J.C. Martin Chairn.
John Melton
William Bates
James Beatie
Isaac Finley
James M. Brown

Tuseday Morning   Feby. 7th A.D. 1837
The Worshipfull Court met pursuant to adjournment present the worshipfull
John C. Martin Chairman
Isaac Finley
James M. Brown
Thomas L. Turner
Elijah Stephens
Charles C. Evans
John Melton
Sam'l Lance
William Bates
Reuben Evans
James Goodner
James Beaty
William Bryan and
Francis Cooper Esqrs.
Whereupon the following orders and rules were made (to wit)

On motion ordered by the court that Abner D. Alexander be appointed Overseer of the road from the widdow   (p 164) Coopers to Richard L. McKnights in
place of Francis Cooper Former overseer Resigned and that he have the same hands
that were appointed upon said road by the Wilson County Court.

On motion ordered by the court that John C. Martin & James M. Brown be
appointed commissioners of the County Revenue for the present year of 1837 for
the purpose of settling with the officers of the county concerned in the collection of the Publick Revenue.

On motion ordered by the court that Jane Gannon be appointed overseer of
the road leading from Woodbury to Lebanon commencing at Woodbury runing to
James Smiths and have the following list of hands.
Edmund Taylor 3
Sam'l Gannon
James Smith
Beacham Gannon
John Marke
G. Elkins
Ranson Young
John Wood
Gabriel Hume

On motion Ordered by the court that
Arnet Jones
Vinson Gather
Hampton Sullivan
Thomas B. Jones

Peter Fleming

be appointed a jury of men to vew and change that part of the road that leads through the lands of John H. Woods which road leaves the stage road near Capt. Brandons running up Brawleys fork and that they report to the next term of this court.

On motion ordered by the court that Sam'l Vance be appointed overseer of the road leading from Woodbury toward Lebanon that is to say from James Smiths to the old Wilson County line and have the following list of hands (to wit)
(p 165)
George M. Connelly
Jesse Givens
Munford Tenpenny
Joseph Tenpenny
William Givens Jr. and
John Vance

On motion Ordered by the court that Jonathan Wherry one of the Overseers of the stage road from the ford of the river at Col. Stewarts to the county line below John H. Woods, procure a crow bar and Hammer for the use of said —— and that said tools when purchased shall be for the use of three overseers (to wit)
the said Wherry
Levi Parker and
John Barkley
And it is further ordered by the court that the said tools shall not be used in any other way than for said publick roads .

On motion Ordered by the court that Lewis Y. Davis overseer of the stage road from Alexandria to the Wilson County line procure a crowbar and Hammer for the use of the Publick roads in the vicinity of Alexandria and that he Exhibit his account to the court for payment.

On motion ordered by the court that John Paris be appointed Overseer from thetop of the big hill to Archibald Hicks in place of John Blanton Former Overseer removed.

John D. McBroom Administrator of the Estate of Elizabeth Jane Moore deceased returned in open court an account current of said Estate and qualified to the same in open court. And on motion Ordered that the same be spread upon record in the proper Book.

(p 166) John McClain represents to this court that John Askue an orphan boy about the age of fourteen years wishes to be bound to him till he arrives to the age of twenty one years. And the said McClain proposes to the court that he is willing to take the said boy and have him learned to read write and cipher well to the rule of three and to furnish him Good strong and comfortable clothing and diet during his servitude and when he shall arrive to the age of twenty one years to Give him a Horse, saddle and briddle worth seventy five dollars and a Good fur hat and suit of janes clothes which which proposition being agreed to by the court the said John M. McLain together with his security Isaac Finley entered into bond faithfully to perform said contract or agreement.

On motion the court the court proceeded to the Election of a Ranger for said County to fill the vacancy occasioned by the resignation of Henry Clifton Former Ranger. And upon the first Balloting James Barkley was duly elected to said office whereupon the said James Barkley came into open court and was duly qualified as such who together with his security Hugh Robinson and Wm. Y. Henderson entered into bond in the sum of five hundred dollars conditioned and payable as the Law directs faithfully to perform the duties of His said office.

Isaac W. Eledge one of the justices of the peace for Cannon County presented before the court his resignation as such whereupon it is ordered that the shiriff proceede to hold and election to fill said vancancy.

(p 167)
Benjamin Pendleton jailor of Cannon County presented a Claim against the County for the sum of twenty five dollars & 36¾ cents for allowance which was adjudged by the Honorable Circuit Court to be paid by the County of Cannon when the county coutt shall allow the same which accrewed in the case the state against Allen Nedham and Kinehen Jarnagin. And it appearing to the satisfaction of this court that the Attorney General had examined and certified the same to be correct the same was allowed by the unanimous vote of this court there being present the Worshipfull
James Goodner
William Bates
James Beatie
Thomas L. Turner
Reuben Evans
Isaac Finley
William Bryson
Charles C. Evans
Francis Cooper
John Melton
James M. Brown
Elijah Stephens and
John C. Martin Esqrs.
Whereupon on motion Ordered by the court that the clerk of this court Certify the same to the County Trustee for payment out of any monies in his hands not otherwise appropriated.

Benjamin Pendleton jailor of Cannon County presented before the court for Allowance an account which was adjudged by the Honorable Circuit to be paid by the county of Cannon when the county court shall allow the same of the amount of Forty Four dollars fifty six and one half cents which is the whole cost that accrued in the circuit court in the case the state against Marks A. Pope upon an Indictment for an assault and Batery And it appearing to the satisfaction of this court that the same had been examined and certified by the Attorney General to be correct, the same is allowed (p 168) by the unanimous vote of the court there being present the worshipfull
James Goodner
William Bates
James Beatie
Thomas L. Turner
Reuben Evans
Isaac Finley
William Bryson
C.C. Evans
Francis Cooper
John Melton
James M. Brown
Elijah Stephens and
John C. Martin Esqrs.
Whereupon on motion it is ordered by the court that the Clerk of this court Certify the same to the County Trustee for payment out of any monies in his hands

not otherwise appropriated.

    On motion the court then adjourned <u>Till</u> court in Course.
J.C. Martin Chair'n.
Isaac Finley
Thos. Powell

(p 169)
State of Tennessee)
Cannon County   ) At a county court Began and held for said county at the
Home of Henry D. McBroom in the Town of Woodbury (it being the place appointed
by Law for holding the court of said county until the courthouse shall be r
erected &C) on the first Monday (it being the 6th day of March 1837) and the
61st year of the American Independence present the Worshipfull
John C? Martin
Alexander McKnight
Joseph Simpson
Allen Haily
Blake Sagely
John Pendleton
Elijah Stephens
Thomas L. Turner
Charles C. E vans
Thomas Simpson
David Fisher
Reuben Evans
Jonathan C. Doss
Pleasant A. Thomason
James Beatie
Peter Reynolds
Jonathan Fuson and
Francis Cooper Esqrs.
Whereupon the following orders were made (to wit)

Thomas Pendleton)
appointed   )
Constable   ) Thomas Elkins one of the deputy <u>shiriffs</u> of Cannon County
presented in open court a certificate of the judges of an election held in the
6th <u>cival</u> district in said county for a constable in said district to fill the
<u>vanancy occationed</u> By the resignation of William W. Milligan from which cer-
tificate it appeared to the satisfaction of the court that Thomas Pendleton had
been duly elected to said office Whereupon the said Thomas Pendleton came into
open court and was duly qualified as such who together with his securities
Benjamin William West, Sam'l Lance and Thomas Elkins (who were approved of by
the court) entered into bond in the sum of one thousand dollars conditioned and
payable as the Law <u>directs.</u>

(p 170) Henry Heart Apt.   )
    Administration   )
    Michael Etherage dec.) The Last Will and Testament of Michael
Etherage dec. was this day produced in open court for probate and was duly proven
by the oaths of <u>Nelson</u> Taylor and Shadrick Tramel subscribing witnesses thereto
and was <u>Admitted to reccord.</u> And it appearing to the satisfaction of the court
that the said Testator had left no executor in said will to execute the same on
motion ordered by the court that Henry Hart be appointed Administrator of said
Estate with the said will annexed, Whereupon the said Hart together with his
Securities Sam'l Draswell and Reuben Evans came into open court ans entered into
bond in the sum of one thousand dollars conditioned & payable as the Law directs.

Whereupon the said Hart was duly qualified as such And letters of Administration were granted &C.

Woodson Northcutt appt.)
    Administration   )
Francis Northcutt dec.) Whereas it has this day been made Known to the satisfaction of the court that Francis Northcutt late of this county is deceased and having left no will or testament On motion it is ordered by the court that Woodson Northcutt came into open court and was duly qualified as such who together with his security William West entered into Bond in the sum of one hundred dollars conditioned and payable (p 171) as the Law directs, Whereupon letters of Administration were granted.

Sam'l Braswell appt   )
Administration   )
Nathan Sellers deceased) Whereas it has this day been made known to the satisfaction of the court that Nathan Sellers late of this county is deceased and having left no will or Testament, On motion it is ordered by the court that Sam'l Braswell be appointed Administrator of said Estate. Whereupon the said Sam'l Braswell came into open court and was duly qualified as such who together with his securities Henry Hart and Samson Braswell entered into bond in the sum of Four Thousand dollars payable to his excelency the Governor and his successors in office conditioned for the faithful performance of said Administration And letters of Administration are granted &C

Henry D. McBroom)
Benjamin Sapp appt.)
Executors   )
James Barkley   ) Henry D. McBroom produced in open court a paper writing purporting to be the last will and Testament of James Barkley deceased, which was duly proven in open court by the oaths of Henry Trott Jr. And John A. Dunn Subscribing witnesses thereto and was admitted to record. And it appearing to the satisfaction of the court that Henry D. McBroom and Benjamin Sapp were appointed in said will to execute the same they came into open court and were duly qualified as such who together with their securities Henry Trott Jr. and Job Stephens entered into bond in the sum of one Thousand dollars payable to his excelency the governor and his successors in office conditioned for their faithful performance as such Whereupon Letters Testamentory were granted &C.

Baldy H. Summars)
Apprentice to   )
Thomas D. Summars) Thomas D. Summars this day makes known to the satisfaction of the court that Baldy H. Summars an orphan about the age of thirteen years deserves the protection of this court. And proposed to have the said Baldy H. Bound to him as an Apprentice to the occupation of Farming till he arrives to the age of twenty one years and also to Learn him to write, read well and cipher to the rule of three and Give him at the expiration of said term a Horse, saddle and Bridle worth one hundred dollars and to treat him with all the Humanity in other respects as is due to an apprentice which proposals being accepted of, The said Thomas D. Summars his security in open court entered into Bond payable to John C. Martin chairman of the county court and his successors in office faithfully to perform the same.

Hugh Thomas)
Apprentice   )
Elihu B. Jewell) Elihu B. Jewell has this day made known to the satisfaction of the court that Hugh Thomson an orphan boy about the age of Eleven years Kneeded the protection of the court. And proposed to have the said Hugh Bound

to him as an apprentice to the Blacksmith Buisness until he attains the age of twenty one (p 173) Years and also to Lear him to read, write well and cipher to the rule of three or have the same done if he have capacity sufficient and also to give at the expiration of the term aforesaid a Horse, saddle and Bridle worth one hundred dollars and a suit of Broadcloth and a fur hat, And all other things necessary and suited for the comfort of an apprentice and also to treat him with Becoming Humanity which proposition being accepted of by the court, the said Elihu B. Jewell together with his securities Iverson J. Thomas and E.A. Fisher Entered into Bond in open court payable to John C. Martin chairman of the court and his successors in office faithfully to perform the same.

Matthew Summars)
Apprentice)
James B. Summars) James B. Summars this day made known to the satisfaction of the court that Matthew Summars an orphan about the age of eight years kneeded the protection of the court and proposed to have the said Matthew bound to him untill he attains the age of twenty one years as apprentice to the occupation of Farming and have him taught to read and write well and cipher to the rule of three and Give him at the expiration of the term aforesaid a Horse Saddle and bridle worth one Hundred dollars and a suit of Broad cloth and to do and perform all other things suited to the comfort of an apprentice which proposual being accepted of by the court, the said James B. Summars together with his security Thomas D. Summars together with his security Thomas D. Summars entered into Bond in open court payable to John C. Martin chairman of the county court and his successors in office faithfully to perform the same.

(p 174)
John W. Hatfield)
Apprentice)
Dennison Hogwood) Dennison Haywood has this day made known to the satisfaction of the court that John W. Hatfield an orphan about the age of nine years kneeded the protection of the court and proposed to have the said John W. Bound to him as an apprentice to the taning buisness until he attains the age of twenty one years And agrees to have him taught to read and write well and cipher to the rule of three and at the Expiration of the term aforesaid Give him fifty dollars in money and a good suit of broad cloth and a good fur hat and all other necissariessuited to an apprice which proposual being approved of by the court the said Dennison Haywood entered into Bond together with his securities Joseph C. McGee and Joseph Simpson payable to John C. Martin chairman of the county court and his successors in office faithfully to perform the same.

Patsey Gibson)
To)
An Allowance) Whereas it appearing to the satisfaction of the court from the report of a jury made at the last term of this court who had been summoned for that purpose that patsy Gibson of this county is in a helpless situation without means to support upon and also void of judgement or reason sufficient to take care of herself and that they were of the opinion that the court would do well to make an allowance out of the county revenue to be appropriated to her support to be placed in the hands of a (p 175) suitable person to be appointed as Guardian for her for that purpose Whereas it was proposed that the sum of thirty six dollars be set apart and allowed for that purpose And on taking the voice of the court by ayes and noes It was allowed by the unanimous vote of the court present the Worshipfull
Blake Sagely
Joseph Simpson
Jonathan C. Doss

Alexander McKnight
Sam'l Lance
Thomas Simpson
Reuben Evans
John Pendleton
William Bates
Elijah Stephens
Francis Cooper
Charles C. Evans and
John C. Martin Esqrs.
13 Justices. And on motion ordered by the court that the Clerk certify the
same to the county Trustee for payment out of any monies in his hands not
otherwise appropriated and deliver the same to such person as may be appointed
Guardain for the said Patsey Gibson.

Elizabeth Spence)
    To   )
An Allowance   ) Moses Shelby this day represents by his petition to the
satisfaction of the court that Elizabeth Spence of this county is an old woman
in her Dotage Blind, very infirm and without means to support upon and that the
court would well to make an appropriation out of the county Revenue to applyed
to her support . Whereupon it was proposed that the sum of thirty six dollars
be set apart for that purpose. And on taking the voice of the court upon said
Appropriation by ayes and noes it was unanimously allowed present the worship-
full
Thomas L. Turner
Francis Cooper
William Bates
Jonathan C. Doss
Alexander McKnight
Sam'l Lance
Thomas Simpson
Reubin Evans
John Pendleton
Elijah Stephens
Charles C. Evans
Joseph Simpson and
John C. Martin Esqrs.

(p.176) 13 Justices. And on motion ordered by the court that the Clerk certify
the same to the countybTrustee for payment out of anf monies in his hands not
otherwise appropriated and deliver the same to such person as shall be appointed Guardain of the said Elizabeth Spence.

Polly Spicer)
    To   )
An Allowance) Samuel Lance Esq. this day represents to the satisfaction of
the court that Polly Spicer of this county is in a helpless and afflicted situation not able to support ot take care of herself upon any means subject to
her control and that the court would do well to make an appropriation for her
Benifit out of the county revenue Whereupon it was proposed that the sum of
thirty six dollars for the present year be allowed and set apart for that purpose And on taking the voice of the court upon said appropriation by ayes and
noes it was unanimously allowed present the worshipfull
Reuben Evans
William Bates
Sam'l Lance
Alexander McKnight

Thomas Simpson
Joseph Simpson
Allen Haily
Thomas L. Turner
John Pendleton
Francis Cooper
Elijah Stephens
John C. Martin Esqrs.

12 And on motion Ordered by the court certify the same to the County Trustee for payment out of any monies in his hands not otherwise appropriated And deliver the same to such person as may be appointed Guardain of the said Polly Spicer.

Ephriam Andrews)
Guardain of)
Patsey Gibson) On motion ordered by the court that Ephriam Andrews be appointed Guardain of Patsey Gibson a (p 177) pauper in this county for the purposes of receiving and applying to the use of the said Patsey Gibson in the way and manner that he may think the most advisable all such monies as may come into his hands either from the county or in any other way for the use and Benifit of the said pauper. Whereupon the said Ephriam Andrews came into open court and was duly qualified as such . Who together with his security Alexander McKnight entered into Bond in the sum of one hundred dollars payable to John C. Martin chairman of the county court faithfully to perform the same.

Moses Shelby)
Guardain of)
Elizabeth Spence) On motion ordered by the court that Moses Shelby be appointed Guardain of Elizabeth Spence (a pauper in this county) for the purpose of receiving and applying to the use and benefit of the said Elizabeth Spence in such manner as he shall think most advisable all mones that may come into his hands either from the county or otherwise for the use and benefit of the said pauper. Whereupon the said Moses Shelby came into open court and was duly qualified as such who together with his security William Bates Entered into bond in the sum of one hundred dollars payable to John C. Martin Chairman of the county court and his Successors in office faithfully to perform his said Guardainship &C.

Peter Crips)
To)
Hanry Hart) The execution of a quit claim deed from Peter Crips to Henry Hart for occupant write to a certain parcel of land and improvement (p 178) lying in Cannon County bearing date the 16th day of August 1836 was this day proven in part in open court by the oath of Reuben Evans one of the subscribing witnesses there to the other witness J.W. Farrington not appearing to qualify.

Daniel Parkhrust)
Deed 20 acres)
Jessee Johnson) The execution of a deed of conveyance from Daniel Parkhrust to Jessee Johnson for twenty acres of land lying in Cannon (originally) Warren County bearing date the 30th day of June 1835 was this day duly proven in open court by the oaths of Joseph Clark and A. Stone Subscribing witnesses thereto and was ordered to be certified for Registration.

Rachel Palmer)
Hannah Davis &)
John D. Jones)
Deed of Trust)
P.A. Thomason) The execution of a deed of Trust from Rachel Palmer, Hannah

Davis and John D. Jones to P.A. Thomason for Real and Personall property
therein mentioned lying and being in Cannon County bearing date the 4th day
of February 1837 was this day duly proven in open court by the oaths of A.W.
Walker and Edmund Palmer Subscribing witnesses thereto and on motion the same
was ordered to be certified for Registration.

Thomas West)
P. of Attorney)
Isaac C. West)   The execution of a power of attorney from Thomas West to Isaac
C. West for certain purposes therein expressed bearing date the 28th day of
February 1837, was this day duly proven in opene court by the oaths of P.A.
Thomason and Jonathan C. Doss subscribing (p 179) Witnesses thereto And was
the eupon ordered to be certified &C.

Joshua Williams)
   Transfer   )
John Williams)   The execution of a transfer or assignment of a plot and
certificate from Joshua Williams to John Williams for six hundred and forty
acres of land lying in Cannon County (originally Warren County) Bearing date
the 3rd day of April 1833 was this day duly proven in open court by the oaths of
William Cummings and George Epley subscribing witnesses thereto and the same is
ordered to be certified.

Shadrick Capps)
   Transfer   )
Lewis Starr   )   The execution of a Transfer plot and certificate from
Shadrick Capps to Lewis Starr for 60 acres of land lying in Cannon (originally Warren County) bearing date the 13th day of February 1837 was this day
duly acknowledged in open court by the said Capps (the assignor) to be his ——
and deed for the purposes therein contained And the same was ordered to be certified.

Joseph Bryson   )
Guardain   )
Heirs of Wm. Bryson)
deceased   )   Joseph Bryson Guardain of the minor heirs of William
Bryson deceased makes report of his said Guardianship and and was duly
qualified to the same in open court and on motion the same is admitted to
recoord.

Thomas Simpson & others   )
     Commissi ners   )
To lay off one years provision)
to N. Sellers widdow   )   On motion ordered by the court that Thomas
Simpson, Fleming Jenny and Robert Forester be appointed as (p 180) Commissioners to lay off and set apart one years provisions to the widdow of Nathan Sellers
deceased out of said estate and make report to the next term of this court.

William Foster)
  & others   )
Jury of men   )   William Foster
                   Enoch Jones
                   John C. Canady and
                   Foster
a part of the jury of men appointed at the last term of this court to vew and
change the road about a fourth of a mile where the same runs through the lands
of Samuel Burger make report that they think it most practicable that the road
should run through said Burgois lane which isn approved of and Established
by the court.

Sam'l Vance   )
  Appointed   )
Overseer of road)   On motion ordered by the court that Sam'l Vance be appoint-
ed overseer of the roadfrom Woodbury to the top of the ridge at the old Wilson
County line toward Statesville And have the following hands to work the same
(to wit)
Edmund Taylor 3
Beachan Gannon
James Gannon
Sam'l Gannon
James Smith
L.C. Polin
Mumford Tenpenny
Tobias Tenpenny
Joseph Tenpenny
Christopher Coble
Jesse Givan
Jesse Denton
William Givens and
George W. Connally
all former orders to the contrary notwithstanding

Cabb Early   )
  Appointed   )
Overseer of road)   On motion ordered by the court that Cabb Early be appoint-
ed overseer of the road from Woodbury to the top of the ridge above Richard
Lemayz.

(p 101) William Thweatt)
            appointed   )
            Overseer of road)   On motion ordered by the court that William Thweatt
be appointed overseer to cut out and work a road as fare as the Wilson County
line vewed and marked out by a jury of men appointed by this court - leading
from Alexandria to Statesville leaving the stage road at James Powells and
apply to James Goodner & Jonathan C. Doss, Esquires for a list of hands.

James Fletcher   )
  appointed   )
Overseer of road) On motion ordered by the court that James Fletcher be
appointed overseer of the road from the forks of the Hollow above the Sulpher
Spring to the McMinnville road in the place of Joseph Clark former overseer
and to have the same hands & bounds that was granted to the aforesaid Clarks.

Arnett Jones & others)
Appointed   )
Jury of men   )   Arnett Jones
                             Thomas B. Jones
                             Hampton Sullivan and
                             Vinson Gather,
a majority of the jury of men appointed at the las   term of this court to
change the part of the Drawleys fork road that runs through the lands of John
H. Wood, make report as follows that they have vewed marked out and changed
the same leaving the stage road at the corner of George Brandons field running
thence up the Branch South on the line between the said Brandon & John H. Wood
to the corner of the said Wood & James Ferrell thence running East so as to
intersect the old road at the mouth of the lane between the said Wood and
Ferrell, and the same is approved by the court.

(p 182)
John Jarul   )
appointed   )
Overseer of road)   On motion ordered by the court that John Jarrel be appointed overseer of the road from Blues Todd to John Pendletons in place of Green-
bury Sapp former overseer, and have th e same hands that the said Sapp had
allowed to him.

John Hollensworth)
)
Overseer of road)   On motion Ordered by the court that John Hollensworth
overseer of the canal fork road have the following hands in addition to the
hands already given him, to wit,
Wily Ratley
Jonas Hapes
William Capeham
Melton Dodd
Joseph Dodd
John Haley
Martin Owens
William Bryant
Thomas Hoakes and
Daniel Taylor

John Simpson & others)
    appointed   )
Jury of men   )   On motion and petition ordered by the court that
John Simpson
Ezekiel Taylor
Shadrick Trammel
Lewis Parker
Archibald McIntire and
Barnabus Page
be appointed a jury of view to vew and marke a road beginning near Zekiel
Taylors on Indian creek the nearest and best way so as to intersect the stage
road at or near William Hayes on Dry Creek and make report to the next Term
of this court .

John Craft et al)
appointed   )
Jury of men   )   On motion ordered by the court that
John Craft
James Cherry
Joseph Harper
Alexander Finley
Isaac W. Elledge
Levi Craft
Jacob Spangler and
John Pendleton
be appointed a jury of men to vew and marke a road beginning at or near
Hardy Spicers running the nearest and best way so as to intersect the Man-
chester road (p 183) at or near John Brandons and make report to the next
Term of this court.

Henry Fite et al
  appointed
Jury of vew

On motion ord red by the court that
Henry Fite
William Goggin
Daniel Ford
Moses Allen
Abram Overall and
Leonard Lamberson
be appointed a jury of vew to vew and mark such alterations as they may deem
expedient in the road leading from Liberty to Woodbury beginning on the stage
road at the most suitable place between Joseph Clarkes and Thomas J.G. Sales
up the clear fork to Tittles school house - and that they pay due regard to
private property as well as to the public convenience all former reviews and
reports to the contrary notwithstanding.

On motion ordered by the court that Jesse Givens and Christopher Coble,
be taken from a list of hands belonging to Meritt Givens overseer and attached
to Samuel Janes overseer and that Price Richardson & George Debinport be taken
from James Reed overseer and be attached to Meritt Givens and that Warren
Debinport be attached to John H. Salls overseer.

William Willard)
List of hands)
Overseer of road) On motion ordered by the court that William Willard overseer
of the Harrican fork road have the following list of hands, to wit,
James McAdoo   3
Allen Wilson
William Wilson
William C. Odom 2
James Milligan
Almon Pullinax
Alexander Milligan
Charles Hancock
Sam'l C. Odom
Joel Willard
Nelson Owen
Aaron Duggin and
Henry Hagans ---
(p 184) And that the said Willard work said road beginning at the Wilson
County line below James McIdors running up the said Harrican creek to the
upper corner of John Hagans Jr. field.

Peter Reynolds)
Exempted)
From double tax) Peter Reynolds this day filed his petition in open court
praying the court to release him from double taxes for the (present) year
of 1837. And for satisfactory reasons disclosed to the court in said petition-
eris released from doble taxes And the said petitioner also discloses to
the satisfaction of the court Good reasons why his father or the heirs of John
Reynolds deceased should also be exorated from double taxes for the present
year. And on motion ordered that the Clerk of this court when making out the
tax list Observe this order.

Thomas L. Turner)
  Elected)
County Ranger) Whereas it appearing to the satisfaction of the court

that James Barkley Ranger of Cannon County has dec'd On motion the court
proceeded to Elect a Ranger for said County to fill the vacancy Occationed
by said deceased , And upon the forth Balloting Thomas L. Turner having
received a majority of the votes that were Given in said Election was ordered to be duly elected Whereupon the said Thomas Turner came into open court
and was duly qualified as such who together with his securities William Bates
and Francis Cooper entered into (p 185) Bond in the sum of Five Hundred
dollars payable to John C. Martin Chairman of the county court and his
successors in office conditioned for the faithfull performance of the said
Ranger —

Joseph Clark & Others)
      Report   )
Town Commissioners   )   Joseph Clark
                             John Brown
                             John B. Stone
                             Archibald Stone and William Bates
commissioners of the Town of Woodbury This day returned in open court a statement of there proceeding (in part) up to this day by virtue of there appointment which was was ordered by the court to be filed in the office of the
clerk of this court.

Court then adjorned til tomorrow Eleven oclock ————
J.C. Martin Chmr.
Reuben Evans
Elijah Stephens
T.L. Turner

Tuseday morning March 7th A.D. 1837
The Worshipfull court met pursuant to adjornment present the worshipfull
John C. Martin Chrm.
Reuben Evans
Thomas L. Turner
William Bates
Elijah Stephens and
John Melton Eeqrs.
Whereupon the following orders were made to wit.

Washington Canady)
    appointed   )
Overseer of road)   On motion ordered by the court that Washington Canady be
appointedoverseer of the stage road (p 186) of which John Halen was former
overseer and have the same hands and bounds that the said Halen former overseer
had allowed to him.

Reuben Evans   )
Admrs. of   )
James Evans dec.) Reuben Evans Administrator of the estate of James Evans
deceased Returned in open court an Inventory of all of the effects of said
estate that had come to his possession and was duly qualified to the same And
on motion the same was admitted to reccord.

John B. Stone)
   Appointed)
Jury of vew   )   On motion ordered by the court that John B. Stone
                                            Thomas Elkins
                                            Edward White
                                            William Pears

Benjamin Pendleton and
William West
be appointed a jury of vew to vew and mark out a road from the mouth of the
dry Branch near John E. Stones to the top of the ridge By way of Thomas L.
Turners so as to intersect the stage road at Benjamin Pendletons and make
return to the next term of this court.

On motion Ordered by the court that the road leading up the Branch between James M. Brown and Isaac McBroom and so on up said Branch as has formily
been used be and the same is hereby declared nul and void.

Durrel Farles)
   Apprentice)
Thomas Elkins)   Thomas Elkins this day represents to the satisfaction (p 187)
of the of the court that Durrel Farles an orphan boy about the age of nine years
kneeds the protection of the court and proposes to have the said Durrell Bound
to him until he attains the age of twenty one years and agrees on his part to
learn him the occupation of Farming and to take good care of him the said
Durrell in every respect as is due to an apprentice and at end of the Term
aforesaid Will give him a horse saddle and Bridle worth seventy five dollars and
a good suit of jeans clothing and a fur hat and such other things as is suited
to an apprentice which proposual being approved of by the court ; the said
Thomas Elkins together with his security William Bates and Philip Hoodenpyle
in open court entered into Bond payable to John C. Martin Chairman of the County
Court and his successors in office faithfully to perform the same.

Joseph Adamson)
  & others   )
Jury of Vew   )   On motion ordered by the court that
Joseph Adamson
Abraham Overall
Will Adamson
Moses Allen
James Jarrett and
William Melton
a jury of vew appointed at the last term of this court to vew and mark a
road to be continued and report to the next term of this court.

Court then adjorned til court in course.
J.C. Martin Chm.
Wm. Bates
Reuben Evans

(p 188)
State of Tennessee)
Cannon County   ) At a county court begain and held at the House of Henry
D. McBroom in the Town of Woodbury (it being the place appointed by law
for holding the county court of said county untill the court House shall
be erected &c) on the first Monday (it being the 3rd day of April A.D. 1837
And of the American Independence the 61st year.
Present the worshipfull
John C. Martin
Elijah Stephens
Francis Cooper
William Bryson
John Melton

Charles C. Evans
Sam'l Lance
Isaac Finley
WilliammBates
Joseph Simpson and
James H. Brown Esqrs.
Whereupon the following orders were made (to wit)

George Grizzle Esq. shiriff of Cannon County produced in open court Commissioners from his Excellency the Governor for Hugh Reed and Moses Shelby as justices of the peace for Cannon County. Whereupon they come into open court and were duly qualified as such and took their seats upon the bench.

The Clerk of this court produced a duplicate of the taxes due and payable in Cannon County for the year 1837 prepared for the shiriff or Collector of the same Whereupon in pursuanceof the statues in such cases made and provided George Grizzle Esq. shiriff of Cannon County was duly qualified as such who together with his securities
Charles Ferrell
Jonathan Bateman
Samuel Braswell and
John Melton (p 189)
(being approved of by the court) entered into bond payable to his Excellency the Governor and his successors in office in the sum of one thousand two hundred and twenty six dollars and fifty three cents conditioned for the collection and payment of the state Tax in the time and manner prescribed by Law. Also one other bond in sum of one thousand six hundred and sixteen dollars and fifty three cents payable to John C. Martin Chairman of the county court of Cannon County and his successors in office conditioned for the faithfull Collection and payment of the county Taxes on the time and manner directed by Law. Which several Bonds are in the following words and Figures (to wit)

Know all men by these presents that we
George Grizzle
Charles Ferrell
Jonathan Bateman
Sam'l Braswell and
John Martin
all of the county of Cannon and state of Tennessee are Held and Firmly bound unto Newton Cannon Governor in and over the state of Tennessee and his successors in office in the Penal sum of one thousand two hundred and twenty six dollars and fifty three cents to which payment well and truly to be made we bind ourselves, our heirs, executirs, administrators and assigns jointly and severly firmly by these presence sealed with our seals and dated this the 3rd day of April 1837- The condition of the above obligation as such that whereas In purance of the statues in such case made and provided the above bound Ceroge Grizzle shiriff of Cannon County has this day been appointed by the County Court of said county Collector of the publick taxes due and payable in said county for the year of 1837.

(p 190) Now if the said George Grizzle shirriff and collector for said county shall and well and truly collect and pay over to the Treasur of the state (or to other such other person or persons as may be by Law autherized to receive the same) all such sum or sums of money as by Law he is bound to collect, or should have collected for the use of the state on or beforethe first Monday in October next then the above obligation to be void else to be and remain in full force and virtue. In testimondy whereof we have hereunto set our hands and seals this the day and year first above written.

Geo. Grizzle (seal)
Charles Ferrell (seal)
Jonathan Bateman (seal)
Sam'l Braswell (seal)
John Melton (seal)

Know all men by these presents that we
George Grizzle
Charles Ferrell
Jonathan Bateman
Samuel Braswell and
John Melton
all of the county of Cannon and state of Tennessee are held and firmly bound
unto John C. Martin chairman of the county court and his successors in office
in the Penal sum of one thousand six hundred and sixteen dollars and fifty
three cents to which payment well and truly to be made we bind ourselves our
heirs Executors administrators and assigns jointly severly Firmly by these
presence sealed with our seals and voted this the 3rd day of April 1837. The
condition of the above obligation is such that whereas in pursuance of the
statues in such case made and provided (p 191) the above bound George Grizzle
has this day been appointed by the county court of Cannon County as Collector
of the publick taxes due and payable in said county for the year of 1837.
Now if the said George Grizzle shiriff and collector for said county
shall well and truly collect and pay over to the county Trustee of the aforesaid County of Cannon all such moneys as by Lawhe is bound to collect or
should have collected for the use of the county on or before the first Monday
in October next then the above obligations to be void else to be and remain
in full force and virtue.
In Testimony whereof we have hereunto set our hands and seals this
day and year first above written.
(George Grizzle (seal)
(Charles Ferrell (seal)
(Jonathan Bateman (seal)
(Samuel Braswell (seal)
(John Melton (seal)

On mtoion ordered by the court that the following persons be appointed
as jurors for the next Term of the Circuit Court (to wit)

District No.
1. Joshua Nichols and Hinden R. Jarratt
2. James Taylor Jr. and Isaac Findley
3. John K. Woosely and James Hollis
4. William Holt and John Brown
5. Moses Shelby and Moderate Duke
6. James Smith and Henry Ford
7. Charles C. Evans and Androw P. Evans
8. Reuben Balem and William Bates
9. Abraham Burger and Henry Kersey
10. Henry Heart and Lemuel Turney
11. Moses Pedigo and Alexander Martin
12. Watson Cantrell and Sam'l H. Allen (p 192)
13. Leonard Lamberson and David Fite
14. James Goodner and Andrew Pickett
15. Nathan Evans and Peter Reynold
16. Jonathan Puston and Pharis Lawrence

17. William Bryson and Francis Cooper
And Alexander Milligan and Charles Marcum Constables to wait upon the court
and jury.

Whereas it has this day been made Known to the satisfaction of the court, that
Barkley Couch an orphan boy, son of Elizabeth Couch is in a helpless situation
and that he deserves the protection of the court, Whereupon on motion ordered
by the court that the sum of thirty six dollars be and the same is hereby
appropriated for the Benifit out of the county Treasury to be placed in the hands
of a Guardains that may be appointed for that purpose. And it is further order-
ed by the court that the clerk certify the same to the County Trustee for payment
out of any monies in his hands or that may come into his hands not otherwise
appropriated which order on taking the voice of the court by ayes and noes
was unanimously adopted, present the worshipfull
John C. Martin
Isaac Finley, Joseph Simpson
Hugh Reed
Moses Shelby
James M. Brown
Elijah Stephens
Charles C. Evans
John Melton
William Bates
Samuel Lance
William Bryson and
Francis Cooper Esqrs.

On motion ordered by the court that William Bates be appointed Guardain
of Polly Spicer a (a pauper thrown upon the Charities of the county at the
last term of this court) Whereupon the said Bates was duly qualified as such
(p 193) who together with his securities Moses Shelby and Samuel Lance entered
into bond in open court in sum of one hundred dollars payable to John C.
Martin chairman of the county county court and his successors in office conditioned for the faithfull performance of his said Guardainship as the Law
directs &C.

On motion ordered by the court that William Bates be appointed Guardain
of Barkely Couch an orphan and pauper thrown upon the charties of the county
at the present term of this court. Whereupon the said Bates was duly qualified as such; who together with his securities John Melton and Moses Shelby
Entered into bond in open court in the sum of one hundred dollars payable
to John C. Martin chairman of the county court, and his successors in office,
conditioned for the faithfull ----of his said Guardianship.

On motion the court proceeded to the consideration of an allowance to
Solomon Beasley one of the commissioners appointed by the Legislature to run
and mark the west and east boundrylines of Cannon County. And it appearing to
the satisfaction of the Court that the said Beesley was eight days imployed
in runing said lines and also that he had necessaryly spent the sum of four
dollars in said survises. It was proposed that he be allowed the sum of two
dollars per day for said service and the said sum of four dollars by him expended. And on taking the voice of the court by ayes and noes it was unanimously agreed to present the worshipfull
John C. Martin
Isaac Finley
Joseph Simpson
Hugh Reed

Moses Shelby (p 194)
James M. Brown
Elijah Stephens
Charles C. Evans
John Melton
Sam'l Lance
William Bates
William Bryson and
Francis Cooper Esqrs.

And on motion is further ordered by the court that the clerk certify the same
to the county Trustee for payment out of any monies in his hands not otherwise appropriated .

Hugh Robinson one of the commissioners appointed to run the west and east
boundry lines in Cannon County presented in open court and wasqualified to the
same an account for twelve days serves in runing said lines also four dollars
Expenseswhile thus engaged whereupon it was proposed that he be allowed the
sum of two dollars pr. day for said servises And on taking of the voise of the
court by ayes and noes upon the same it was unanimously agreed to present the
worshipfull
John C. Martin
Isaac Finley
Joseph Simpson
Hugh Reed
Moses Shelby
James M. Brown
Charles C. Evans
John Melton
Sam'l Lance
William Bates
Francis Cooper and
William Bryson Esqrs.
And it is further ordered that the clerk of the court certify the same to the
Trustee for payment out of any monies in his hands not otherwise appropriated.

    On motion and petition ordered by the court that Sam'l Reynolds be per-
mitted to Build a grist and saw mill on smithsfork about six miles below
Liberty and about two hundred yards below where the old mill formilystood provided the same be in the bounds of Cannon County.

(p 195) Micajah Petty administrator of the Estate of Margaret Petty deceased
this day returned in open court an Inventory of the amount of sales of the ef -
fects of said Estate that has come into his possession as also the amount of
the hire of two negroes (to wit) Michal and Nancy his wife; and was duly qualified to the same. And on motion the same is admitted to reccord

Robt. Forrester
Thomas Simpson and
Fleming Janey
commissioners appointed to Lay off one years provisions out of the Estate of
Nathan Sellers Decd. to his widdow make report that in pursuance of said
appointment they have Layed off and set apart to the said widdow all the corn
all of the bacon (But two hogs) all the Lard, all the salt on hand &wheat twenty
five pounds of coffee & twenty five pounds of sugar all the spun yarn and
cotton on the place and that the administrator M. Braswell Furnish two good
sides of leather one of upper and one of under. Signed &C.

On motion and upon the petition of Charles Ferrell ordered by the court
that, Green D. Murphey
    Newton Murphey
    John Parsly Jr.
    Robert Parsley
    John Blanton
    John Ferrell and
    Moses Pedigo
be appointed a jury of vew to vew and mark a road Leading from the moth of
the Herican creek to intersect the Allen Perry road at or near Tavner Martins
old place and make report of the practicability of the same at the next or any
subsequent term of this court.

(p 196) On motion ordered by the court that Henry Young Overseer of the road
from the Town of Woodbury to Hardy Spicers have the following list of hands to
work the same (to wit)
William Young
Adam Elrod
Thomas St. John
Henry Medford
Washington Mears
John Ealem
Nathan Finley
William Preston
Wm. Elkins
John Cannon
John Melton
Gabriel Hume

On motion ordered by the court that
Sam'l E. Purgar
Enoch Jones
Dennis Neel
Josiah Wade &
Thomas Ward
be appointed a jury of vew and change the road near the house of Henry Persey
upon such ground as he may clear out himself provided that if in their judge-
ment the same shall be as good a rout as where the road now runs and make
report to the next term of this court.

On motion ordered by the court that Caleb Early Overseer work the road from
John Woods to the top of the ridge above R.W. Lemays insted of from Woodbury
and that he have the following list of hands to work said road (to wit)
J.T.D. Wale
John Harris
William Kirk
John H. Ragsdale
Thomas Lemay
Samuel Lemay
Thomas Cooper
John Brown
John M. James and
R.G. James

On motion ordered by the court that Henry Wilson be appointed overseer of
the road in place of Joel Coffce insted of James Wilson with the same hands.

On motion ordered by the court that Haman Barrett

James Mears
William James
Elijah Mears and
Stephen Herrman
be appointed a jury of vew to vew and change the ————————Woodbury up Jones
Valley (that part near Mrs. Brownfields Spring, upon such Ground as Thomas
Barrett may clear out for the same provided that the same may appear to them
Expedient and make report to the next term of this court.

On motion ordered by the court that William F. George overseer of the road
from the stage road near Esqr. Taylors to the top of the Hill near Bashan have
the following hands to work the same (to wit)
Robert George
John G. Taylor
David Tenpenny
Alfred Tenpenny
Sam'l Burke and
James Cooper

John Craft
Joseph Harper
James Cherry
Isaac W. Elledge
Levi Craft and
Jacob Spangler
a majority of the jury of vew appointed at the last term of this court to vew
and mark out a road from Hardy Spicers the nearest and best way so as to intersect the Manchester road at or near John Brandons make report that they have
vewed mared said road from Spicers to Coxes field from Thence to John Crafts
Thence to San'l Spanglers Thence to the county line near John Brandons all of
which is approved of by the court and adopted as a county road And upon motion
ordered by the court that Joseph Harper be appointed overseer of said new
road as marked from Hardy Spicers (p 108) to John Crafts and that John Craft
be appointed overseer of said new road from his own house to the Sweat Gum
swamp and that James Cherry be appointed overseer from the sweet gum swamp
to the county line near John Brandons.

Personally appeared in open court
Margaret Mears
Andrew McCabe and
John Estes
all of Cannon County and and upon their oaths have satisfactorily proved to
the court here that she the said Margaret Mears was the lawful wife of the
late Joel Mears of said County deceased and that her said husband died on
the 21st day of December one thousand eight hundred and thirty five and at
the time of his death he had been placed on the roll of Revolutionary pinsion-
ers of the United States under the act of Congress of the 7th of June 1832
and further that he was the identical Joel Mears named in the original certificate that had not reached him at his death and which is here shown to the
court &c And she the said Margaret Mears further testifies that her late husband
the said Joel Mears deceased was entitled to a pension at the rate of twenty
dollars per annum from the 4th day of March 1831 up to the date of said certificate when he died and that at the time of his death he resided in Warren
County (but now Cannon County) and had resided there for the space of twenty
five years past and previous thereto he resided in Duncomb County State of
North Carolina.
Sworn to and subscribed in open court here signed Margaret M. Mears, Andrew

McCabe and John Moses Estes
And on motion ordered that the Clerk of this court certify that the above affi-
davits were duly (p 109) made here in open ———&C

Margaret Mears)
 To Pow ty   )
John Nelson   )   The execution of a power of attorney from Margaret Mears to
John Nelson for certain purposes therein expressed was this day duly acknowledged in open court by her the said Margaret Mears to be her act and deed for the
purposes therein contained . And on motion ordered that the clerk of this court
certify the same together with all other proceedings relative to said pension
claim in manner and form as directed by the several acts of Congress in such
case made and provided.

        Court then adjorned till tomorrow 12 O'clock.
J.C. Martin Chrm.
Wm. Bates
William Bryson

Tuseday12oclock April the 4th 1837
Court met pursuant to adjornmentpresent the worshipfull
John C. Martin
Elijah Stephens
William Bates and
William Bryson Esqrs.
Whereupon the following orders were made (to wit)

        On motion ordered by the court that Alexander Sutton overseer of the road
from Woodbury to the old Rutherford County line have the following hands to
work the same (to wit)
Sterling Almon
William T. Almon
Thadious Almon
Phillips Hoodenpyle
Gabriel Williams
James Taylors hands
Elijah Harwood
Sherwood Moss
Nathaniel N. Taylor &
William Sutton
And that he commence working at the publick square in the Town of Woodbury.

(p 200)   On motion ordered by the court that Archd Stone be appointed overseer
of the stage road commencing at the publick square in the Town of Woodbury
runing to the foot of the ridge at George St. Johns and have the following list
of hands.
Parker F. Stones hands
Elisha Miles
F.G. St. John
John St. John
Alexander McBroon
Ranson Youngblood
William Elkins Jr.
John Estes
Murphy G. Elkins
John R. Sullivan
John A. Dunn

Thomas C. Word
Cole Word
Abel McBroom & 1 Black hand
Wm. L. Covington
James O. George
Henry Trott 2
William Y. Henderson
E.A. Fisher
C.R. DAvis
John Fisher
One Black hand
E D. Stephens &
Wm. Wharton

On motion ordered by the court that Epy Francis Overseer of the road from the Wilson County line to the widdow Coopers have the following hands in addition to his former list (to wit)
Wm. C. Leach & hands &
Samuel Bell

On motion the court then adjorned til court in course.
J.C. Martin Chrm.
E. Stephens
William Dryson

(p 201)
State of Tennessee)
Cannon County   )   At a county court began and held at the court house in the Town of Woodbury on the first Monday (it the first day of May A.D. 1837 And the 61st year of the American Independence present the worshipfull
John C. Martin
Isaac Finley
Allen Haily
Joseph Simpson
Hugh Reed
Moses Shelby
John Pendleton
James M. Brown
Elijah Stephens
Charles C. Evans
John Melton
Sam'l Lance
John Martin
William B. Foster
Martin Phillips
Reuben Evans
James Goodner
Jonathan Fuson
William Dryson and
Francis Cooper Esqrs.

Whereupon the following orders were made (to wit)

Whereas it has this day been made known to the Satisfaction of the court here the William Allison Late our County deceased And having left no will or Testament On motion ordered by the court that Thomas Allison be (at his request) appointed Administrator of the Estate of the said William Allison deceased. Whereupon the said Thomas Allison came into court and was duly qualified as such who together with his securities Manson M. Brien and James Goodner Entered into bond in the sum of two hundred dollars payable to his Excelency Newton Cannon Governor & his successors in office conditioned as the Law directs for the faithfull Administraton &C whereupon Letters of administration were Granted &C.

(p 202)

Baxter B. Dickins)
   Deed 100 acres)
Joseph Nivins   )   The execution of a deed of Conveyance to Joseph Nivens for one hundred acres of land Lying in Cannon (originally Rutherford County bearing date the 6th day of April 1836, was this day duly acknowledged here in open court by the said Baxter B. Dickins (the bargainor) to be his act and deed for the purposes therein contained. And on motion ordered that the same be certified for Registration.

Oran Stroud   )
Deed 200 acres)
Jessee Milligan)   The execution of a deed of conveyance from Oran Stroud to Jessee Milligan for Two Hundred acres of Land lying in Cannon County bearing ————— the 21st day of December 1836, was this day proven in open court by the oaths of Isaac Elledge and William Nivens subscribing witnesses thereto and on motion ordered by the court that the same be certified for Registration.

Woodson Northcutt   )
   Adm of   )
Francis Northcutt decd.)   Woodson Northcutt Adm. of the estate of Francis Northcutt deceased this day returned in open court an account current of the Sales of property of the said Francis Northcut deceased and was duly qualified to the same And on motioned ordered that the same be admitted to reccord .

(p 203)

Thomas Given   )
Guardain of   )
William Pratton et al)   Thomas Given Guardain of the minor heirs of Henry Pratton decd. to wit Willaim Pratton and Henry Bratton This day returned in open court an Inventory of the effects in his hands belonging to the above mentioned words and was duly qualified to the same And on motion the same is admitted to record.

Sam'l J. Garrison)
     To   )
An Allownce   )   Sam'l J. Garrison this day presented an account of Cannon for the sum of Twenty five dollars and sixty two and one half cents for the following Books furnished by him for the use of his office to wit

```
1  Minuets Book  cost ——————————— $9.00
1  Road Book  cost ——————————— 7.50
1  Tax Record Book cost(balllance)—m 4.00
1  Revenue Dockett Book  cost ————— 1.06¼
1  Commissioners Book  cost ————— 1.06¼
1  Free Negro Record Book cost ———— 1.00
1  Revenue commissioners oath Book— 1.00
1  Mark and Brand record Book cost  1.00
                                   $25.62½
```

And taking the voice of the court the same was unanimously allowed present the

worshipfull
Martin Phillips
Joseph Simpson
John Martin
John Melton
Isaac Finley
Reuben Evans
Charles C. Evans
John Pendleton
Moses Shelby
Sam'l Lance
William Bryson
Francis Cooper
Jonathan Fuson
William B. Foster
Elijah Stephens and
John C. Martin Esqrs.
And on motion ordered that the clerk of this court certify the same to the
county Trustee payment out of any monies in his hands not otherwise appropriated.

(p 204) Also a claim or charges against the same for Recording the revenue
commissioners returns for 1837 in the Tax Record Book. Whereupon the sum of
fifteen dollars was proposed as a compensation for said serviceswhich on
taking the vote of the court by ayes and noes was approved. Those who voted
in the affirmative were Esqrs.
Martin Phillips
Allen Haldy
Joseph Simpson
Charles C. Evans
William Bryson
Reuben Evans
Sam'l Lance
Moss Shelby
Jonathan Fuston
Francis Cooper
John Martin
James Goodner
William B. Foster
James M. Brown and
John C. Martin
And those who voted in the negative were Esqrs. Isaac Finley
                                                John Melton
                                                John Pendleton and
                                                Elijah Stephens
And on motion ordered that the clerk of this court certify the same to the
county Trustee for payment out of any monies in his hands not otherwise
Appropriated. Also a claim or charge against the same for furnishing the
shiriff with a list of the Taxable property and poles for the year of 1837.
Thereupon the sum of seventeen dollars was proposed as an adequate compensation
for the same. Which on taking the vote of the court by ayes and noes was
approved of. Those who voted in the affirmative were Esqrs.
Martin Phillips
Joseph Simpson
Charles C. Evans
Isaac Finley
John Melton
William Bryson

Reuben Evans
Moses Shelby
James M. Brown
Jonathan Fuson
Francis Cooper
John Martin
James Goodner
William B. Foster and
John C. Martin
And those who voted in the negative were Esqrs.
Sam'l Lance
John Pendleton and
Elijah Stephens
And on motion ordered that the clerk of this court certify the (p 205) same
to the County Trustee for payment out of any monies in his hands not otherwise
appropriated . Also a claim or charge against the same for ex officio
servises in writing the minutes of the court Issuing the orders therefrom
&c. Whereupon the sum of forty dollars was proposed as an adequate compensa-
tion for said servises And on taking the vote of the court by ayes and noes
the same was approved of by the unanimously vote of the court present the
worshipfull
Martin Phillips
Allen Haily
Joseph Simpson
Charles C. Evans
Isaac Finley
John Melton
Reuben Evans
Sam'l Lance
John Pendleton
Moss Shelby
Elijah Stephens
James M. Brown
Jonathan Fuson
John Martin
James Goodner
William B. Foster and
John C. Martin Esqrs.

And on motion ordered that the clerk of this court certify the same to the
county Trustee for payment out of any monies in his hands not otherwise appropriated.

Hugh Robinson executor)
        of   )
John Bullard decd.   ) Hugh Robinson executor of the last will and
Testament of John Bullard dec'd this day rendered in open court and was duly
qualified to the same an inventory of the effect belonging to said Estate that
had come into his hands by virtue of his appointment And on motion ordered
that he be admitted to reccord &c.

On motion ordered by the court that Sarah Reynolds and Flewford Q. Reynolds
be permitted to build a saw and Grist mill on Smiths fork on their own land
about six miles below Liberty and about (p 206) and about two hundred yards
below where the old mill formerly stood.

George Grizzle
    To An Allowance

George Grizzle shiriff of Cannon County This day presented for the consideration of the court a claim of charge against the county of Cannon for Exofficio serivses rendered the county aforesaid for the last twelve months. Thereupon it was proposed that the sum of fifty dollars be allowed him for said servises and taking the vote of the court upon the same by ayes and noes the same was approved. Those who voted in the affirmative were the worshipfull
Martin Phillips
Joseph Simpson
Isaac Finley
Charles C. Evans
John Melton
Moses Shelby
Elijah Stephens
James Goodner
Jonathan Fusen
John Martin
James M. Brown
William B. Foster Esqrs.
And the negative votes stood Thus:
John C. Martin Esqr.

And on motion ordered by the court that the clerk certify the same to the County Trustee for payment out of any monies in his hands not otherwise appropriated. Also a claim or charge against the same for the sum of two dollars for firewood furnished during the November Term of the circuit court, present the worshipfull
M. Phillips
Jo. Simpson
J. Finley
J. Melton
M. Shelby
E. Stephens
Jas. Goodner
J. Fuson
J. Martin
Jas. M. Brown
Wm. B. Foster and
John C. Martin Esqrs.

And on motion ordered that the clerk of this court certify the same to the county Trustee for payment out of any money in his hand not otherwise appropriated .

(p 207) Robert J. Summars This day makes known to the satisfaction of the court that Telithia Summar an orphan girl about the age of nine years is in a helpless situation and lneded the protection of the court. And at the same time proposed to have the said Telithia Bound to him until she attained the age of eighteen years, and proposed to Learn (or have the same done) her to read and write well and cipher to the rule of three, and at the expiration of the Term aforesaid to give her a good featherbed & clothing and good waring clothes &C which proposual being approved by the court The said Robert J. Summar together with his securities Francis Cooper and Willdiam Bryson entered into bond faithfully to perform the same.

On motion ordered by the court that the commissioners appointed at the May Term of this court 1856 to Lay off and sell out the Lots in the Town of Woodbury and other purposes be and they are hereby authorisedpursuant to the

acts of Assembly in such case made and provided to retain of the funds in
their hands originating from the proceeds of the sale of the Lots in said Town
for said services the sum of two dollars per day to
John Brown
John B. Stone
Archibald Stone and
William Bates and to Joseph Clarks the sum of two dollars and fifty cents
per day that is to say for so much of these time as they may be necessarily
engaged. And it is further ordered by the court that the clerk of this court
certify a copy of this order to the said commissioners.

(p 208)
James Barkley widdow   )
    To   )
Pension certificate rev.)   Personally appeared in open court here Sarah
Barkley Henry D. McBroom and Benjamin Sapp all of Cannon County and upon their
oaths have satisfactorilly proved to the court here that she the said Sarah
Barkley was the lawfull wife of the Late James Parkley of said county deceased
and that her said husband died on the 26th day of February 1837. And at the
time of his death he had been placed on the roll of Revolutionary pensioners
of the United States under the act of Congress of the seventh of June 1832
and further that he was the identical James Barkley deceased was intitled to
a pension at the rate of twenty three dollars and thirty three cents per
annum from the 4th of March 1831 to the 4th of September 1836 to which time he
was last paid to the 26th day of February 1837, when he died an account of
servises rendered the United States during the Revolutionary War and at the
time of his death he resided there for the space of twenty four years and previous there to resided in the State of North Carolinsa Rowan County and
moved to Tennessee in 1808 and · resided in Rutherford County Tennessee from
the year 1808 1813 - signed, sworn to and subscribed in open court here the
day and year first above mentioned.
                         Sarah Barkley
                         H.D. McBroom
                         Benjamin Sapp

(p 209) And on motion ordered by the court that the clerks of this court certify the same together with all other papers relative to the said pension claim-
ed.
    Sarah Barkley   )
      To Power of)
  Attorney   )
  William Young   )   The execution of a power of Attorney from Sarah Barkley
to William Young for certain purposes therein Expressed bearing this date
was this day duly acknowledged here in open court by the said Sarah Barkley
to be her act and deed for the purposes therein expressed which is also ordered by the court to be certified by the clerk of this court in manner and form
as the Law directs.

       Personally appeared in open court here Margaret Mears
                                 Andrew McCabe and
                                 John Estes
all of Cannon County and upon their oaths have satisfactorily proved to the
court here that she the said Margaret Mears was the Lawful wife of the Late
Joel Mears of said county deceased, and that her said Husband died on the 21st
day of December 1835 and that at the time of his death he had been placed on
the roll of Revolutionary pensioners of the United States under the act of
Congress of the 7th June 1832 and further that he was the Identical Joel Mears

named in an original certificate that had not reached him at his death and
which came to hand after his death and is here shown to the court &C. And she
the said Margaret Mears further testifies that her late Husband the said Joel
Mears deceased was intitled to a pension at the rate of Twenty dollars per
annum from the 4th day of March 1831, the date of his pension certificate to the
(p 210) 21st day of December 1835 the date he died and that at the time of his
death he resided in Warren County (But now Cannon County) and had resided there
for the space of twenty five years last past. And previous thereto he resided in Buncoln County state of North Carolina Sworn to and suscribed in open
court here the day and year first above mentioned Signed Thus:
Margaret Mears (seal)
Andrew McCabe (seal)
John Bates (seal)
And on motion ordered that the clerk of this court certify the same together
with all other papers and proceedings relative to said pension claim.

Margaret Mears)
Power of Atty.)
John Nelson   )   The execution of a power of Attorney from Margaret Mears
to John Nelson for certain purposes therein Expressed bearing this date was
this day acknowledged in open court hereby the said Margaret Mears to be her
act and deed for the purposes therein mentioned which is also ordered that the
clerk of this court certify the same in manner and form as the Law directs in
such case made and provided.

        John Pendleton one of the justices of the peace for the county of Cannon
this day presented in open court his resignation as such which was accepted by
the court . And on motion ordered that the shiriff of Cannon County proceed
to open and hold an election in the said Pendletons cival district as the
Law directs to fill said vacancy. (p 211) Court then adjourned till tomorrow
morning Eleven O'clock.

J.C. Martin chairm.
Elijah Stephens
James M. Brown

Tuesday morning May the 2nd A.D. 1837.
The worshipfull court met pursuant to adjornment   present the worshipfull
John C. Martin
James M. Brown and
Elijah Stephens Esqrs.

        There being no further Buisness the court was adjourned til court
in course.
J.C. Martin chairm.
James M. Brown
Elijah Stephens.

                        June Term
(p 212)
State of Tennessee
At a county court began and held for the County of Cannon at the House of
Henry D. McBroom (it being the place appointed by Law for Holding the county
court for said county &C) on the first Monday it being the 5th day of June one
thousand eight hundred and thirty seven. And the American Independence the
sixty first year present the worshipfull

John C. Martin
Alexander McKnight
Joseph Simpson
Blake Sadgely
Moses Shelby
Sam'l Lance
Charles C. Evans
John Melton
Thomas Simpson
William Bryson and
Frances Cooper Esqrs.

Whereupon the following orders were made to wit On motion the court adjorned to John D. McBrooms New House. The shiriff of Cannon County presented a
commission from his excelency the Governor to Thomas Hays as a justice of the
peace for Cannon County, Whereupon the said Hays came into open court and was
duly qualified as such and took his seat.

Henry Heart Administrator with the will annexed of the estate of Micheal
Etherage decd. returned into court an account of the Sales &C of said estate
and was duly qualified to the same and on motion ordered by the court that the
same be admitted to reccord.

Sam'l Braswell Administrator of the Estate of Nathan Sellers deceased (p 213)
returned into court an account of the s les &C of said estate and was duly
qualified to the same And on motion ordered by the court that the same be
admitted to reccord.

Benjamin Sapp & Henry D. McBroom exctrs. of the Last Will and Testament of James
Barkley decd. returned into open court an account of sails of the said estate
and were duly qualified to the same And on motion ordered by the court that the
same be admitted to reccord.

On motion and petition ordered by the court that
Ebenezor Wright
Pater Clark
John Turner
Francis Turner and
Joseph Adamson
be and they are Hereby appointed commissioners to devidethe negroes belonging
to the Estate of Henry Braughton decd. amongst the Heirs of the said Henry
Braughton decd. And that they report to the next Term of this court.

On motion ordered by the court that
John Melton
Charles C. Evans and
Archibald Stone
be and they are Hereby appointed commissioners to settle with Benjamin C.
Stephens Administrator with the will annexed of Joel Mears decd. And make
report to the next Term of this court.

John M. McKnight   )
Deed 2 acres &94 poles)
Drewry Matthews   )   The execution of a deed of conveyance from John M.
McKnights to Drewry Matthews For two acres & 94 poles of Land lying in Cannon
County bearing date the 23rd day (p 214) of January 1837 was this day duly
acknowledged in open court by the said John M. McKnights to be his act and deed

for the purposes therein contained. And on motion ordered that the same be certified for Registration &C.

There being no further Buisness Court adjorned till court in course.
J.C. Martin chrm.
C.C. Evans
Blake Sadgely

Tennessee State)
Cannon County) At a county court began and held for the county aforesaid at the House of Henry D. McBroom (it being the place appointed by law for holding the county courts of said ---- until the courthouse shall be erected &C.
On the first Monday (it being the 3rd day of July A.D. 1837. And of the American Independence the 61st year present the Worshipfull
John C. Martin
Reuben Evans and
Isaac Finley esq.

Whereupon the following order was made to wit.
     On motion ordered by the court that they adjoun to a house in the Town of Woodbury belonging to Campbell and Wallace It being considered by the court to be for the Better convenience for (p 215) holding the same-

     Washington Kenedy came into open court and presented a commissioner from his Excelency Newton Cannon Governor of our state as a justice of the peace for Cannon County. And on motion he the said Kenedy was duly qualified by the clerk of this court as such, after which he took his seat and proceeded to the further Buisness of the court.

E. Wright et al)
Commissioners)   E. Wright
                     John Turner
                     Francis Turner
                     Peter W. Clarke and
                     Joseph Adamson
Commission appointed at the last term of this Court to Divide the negroes belonging to the Estate of Henry Bratton decd. Report as follows to wit.

     In pursuance of an order of court Issued by the clerk of Cannon County Court at the June Termof said ---- for 1837. We have proceeded to devide the negroes apecified in said order among the heirs of Henry Bratton decd. and have agreed that the two children of said Bratton shall have the negro woman and child valued at six hundred and forty dollars and that Ausburn Mullinax shall have the oldest boy named Stephen valued at two hundred & sixty five dollars & that the said Mullinax shall be paid out of the money rec'd for the hire of said negroes the sum of thirty seven dollars & 66 2/3 cents to make his share equal all of which is respectfully submitted &C.

(p 216) Given under our hands this 27th day of June 1837 (signed)
E. Wright
Peter W. Clarke
John Turner
Francis Turner &
Joseph Adamson
upon which was the following certificate to wit.

     This is to certify that I have qualified the within names men and

they proceeded to, and made the within report this 27th June 1837
(signed) Reuben Evans (J P)

James Cherry)
Constable   )   George Grizzle Esqr. sheriff of Cannon County by his deputy
Thomas Elkins this day returned into court the certificate of an election open-
ed and held at the House of John Craft on the 29th day of June 1837 to elect
a constable in the fifth cival district in Cannon County to fill the vacancy
Af Isham Pelham Resignedm which certificate it appeared to the satisfaction of
the court that James Cherry came into open court and was duly qualified as
such, who together with his securitys   Isaac W. Elledge ard Thomas Elkins
Entered into bond in the sum of one thousand dollars payable to his Excelency
Newton Cannon Governor and his successors in office faithfully to execute his
said office &C

Green B. Sapp)
Deed 125 acres)
Henry Warren)   The execution of a deed of conveyance from Green B. Sapp
to Henry Warren for one hundred and twenty five acres of land lying in Cannon
County (p 217) bearing this date (3rd July 1837) was day duly acknowledged
in open court by the said Greensbury Sapp (the bargainor) to be his act and
deed for the purposes therein contained And on motion ordered by the court that
the same be certified for registration.

James Williams This day came into open court and makes known to the satisfaction
of the court that he is desirious of being exonotated from any further liability
upon bond by him given on having one George Holland bound to him at the October
Term of this court 1836, And for regens made known to the court to the satisfaction the same is granted. Provided that this order shall not be so Construded
as to release the said William nor his securities from any fualt alredy hapinning
upon said bond.

John Halpain)
Constable   )   George Grizzle shiriff of Cannon County by his deputy Thomas
Elkins this day returned in open court the certificate of an election by him
opened and held at the house of John Melton on the 1st. day of July 1837 to
elect a constable in the seventh cival distriact in Cannon County to fill the
vacancy occasioned by the Resignation of James Melton from which certificate It
appeared to the satisfactin of the court that John Halpain was duly elected to
said office Whereupon the said John Halpain came into open court and was duly
qualified as (p 218) such who together with his securities William Halpain.
P.D. Cummings and
James H. Alexander
entered into bond in the sum of one thousand dollars payable to his excelency
Newton Cannon Goveror and his successors in office conditioned as the Law
dareots &C.

On motion ordered by the court that the commissioners for the Town of
Woodbury appointed at the may Term of this court 1836 In pursuance of an act
of the General Assembly of the State of Tennesseepassed at Nashville January the
31st 1836 Entitled an act to Establish a new County of the name of Cannon be
and they are hereby authorised to make any alteration in the plans Heretofore
Laid down by the court with the contractor for building the court house for
Cannon County that they may deem necessary and proper proved they shall not
authorised to make any ateratlons that may amount to a radical change to the
plans heretofore Laid down for the Building of said court House that say be
inderogation of the plan of the court house in the town of Murfreesboro Rutherford County which plan the court have heretofore always contemplated to Build

after for the County of Cannon (p.219) There being no further Buisness
court adjourned til court in course.
J.C. Martin Chairm.
Isaac Finley
Washington Kenneday
Moses Shelby

State of Tennessee
        At a county court began and held for the ---- of Cannon at the House
of Henry McBroom (it being the place appointed by Law for the court for said
county - the publick Buildings are erected &c , on the first Monday(it being
the 7th day of agust 1837, and of the American Independence the 62nd year present the worshipfull
Martin Phillips
Joseph Simpson and
Thomas Hays Esqr.
Whereupon the following order to wit.

        On motion ordered by the court that it adjourn to the House of John
Fisher in the Town of Woodbury for the better convenienced of Holding the
same And after having met pursuant to said adjournment there was present the
worshipfull
John C. Martin
Elijah Stephens
Charles C. Evans
Alexander McKnight
Watson Cantrell
James M. Brown
Lemuel Turney
William Bryson
Thomas L. Turner
Hugh Reed
Moses Shelby
Blake Sagely
Washinton Kennedy
John Melton and
Sam'l Lance
Isaac Finley
William Bryson and
Francis Cooper Esqrs.

(p 220) Henry Frazeur Represents to the satisfaction of the court Here that
Sam'l Hunt late of our county is deceased and having left no will or Testament
On motion ordered by the court that Henry Frazeur be appointed be appointed
Administrator of said Estate whereupon the said Henry Frazeur together with
his security Matthew Hunt entered into bond in the sum of three Hundred
dollars, conditioned and payable as the Law diricts. After which the said
Frazeur was duly qualified as such in open court.

Henry Trott Jr. Having this day made known to the satisfaction of the court
Here that John Y. Commings late of our county is deceased and he having left
no will or Testament, On motion ordered by the court that Henry Trott Jr.
be appointed Administrator of said Estate. Whereupon the said Henry Trott Jr.
was duly quallified innopen court as such who together with his securities
John Brown entered into bond in the sum of two Hundred dollars conditioned and
payable as the Law diricts , faithfully to perform said Administration.

        George Grizzle shiriff of Cannon County By his deputy Thomas Elkins this

day returned into open court a certificate from the clerks and judges of an .. election opened and held by him in the 6th cival district in said county on the 29th day of July 1837 to elect a constable in said district to fill the ...... vacancy occasioned by the resignation of Thomas (p 221) Pendleton resigned and and from said certificate it appeared to the satisfaction of the court that John Brown was duly elected to said office Whereupon the said John Brown came into open court and was duly qualified
as such who together with his securities Josiah Youngblood and James M. Brown entered into bond in the sum of one thousand dollars conditioned and payable as the law directs faithfully to perform the duties of said office.

John Woods Sr.)
   Deed   )
James Parkley)   The execution of a deed of conveyance from John Wood Sr.
to James Parkley
   David Evans
   Benjamin Allen
   John Wood and
   William Middleton
Trustiese &C for a small portion of Land lying in Cannon County (originally Warren) county baring date the 13th day of January 1824 was this day duly acknowledged in open court by the said John Wood Sr. (the bargainor* to be his act and deed for the purposes therein contained and on motion ordered by the court that the same be certified for Registration.

Thomas Woodall)
 Deed 50 acres)
Joseph Turney)   The execution of a deed of conveyance from Thomas Woodall
to Joseph Turney for fifty acres of land lying in Cannon County bearing date the 27th day of July 1837 was this day duly proven(in part) in open court by Lemuel Turney , one of the subscribing witnesses thereto (the other witness not appearing to q alify.

(p 222)
Beverly Pearce)
 Deed 1 lot   )
James Taylor)   The execution of a deed of conveyance from Beverly Pearce
to James Taylor for one town lot in the town of Danville bearing date the 9th day of November 1829 was this day duly acknowledged in open court, by the said Pearce (the bargainor) to be his act and deed for the purposes therein contained andon motion ordered that the same be certified for Registration.

Francis Cooper)
   Deed 60 acres)
Enes S. Wetherspon) The execution of a deed of conveyance from Francis Cooper
to Enes S. Wetherspon for fifty eight ac res of land lying in Cannon county bearing date the 5th day of Aug. 1837 was this day duly acknowledged in open court by the said Francis Cooper to be his act and deed for the purposes there-in contained and on motion ordered that the same be certified for Registration

     On motion ordered by the court thatatthat William Moore be permitted to build a grist mill on Stones River upon his own land and also to join his dam to the oposit bank upon the land of John D. McBroom provided that the said McBroom may not have any objections to the same.

     On motion ordered by the court that Joseph Simpson and Hugh Reed Esqrs. be appointed a committee to examin into and report to the next Term of this court (p 223) the condition and what assistance Jane Peyton an idiot child of Polly Peyotn of Cannon County may knead as a pauper.

On motion ordered by the court that Charly C. Evans and Sam'l Lance be appointed a committee to examine into the condition and means of Sarah Metton a pauper in Cannon County and see what assistance she may kneed and report to the next term of this court &C.

On motion ordered by the court that the following persons be appointed as jurors for the next Term of the Circuit court for Cannon County commincing the 3rd Monday in November next and that the shiriff summons the same to wit.

Joel Maxey
Ephriam Andrews
Henry Hays
Jesse Hollis
Joseph Knox
Sirus L. Roberts
William Leigh
Baxter B. Dickens
Washington Kennedy
William West
Elijah Mears
Benjamin Pendleton
John Young
Robert Baily
Sam'l Lance
Pleasant Essary
Sam'l E. Burgan
Enoch Jones
Fountain Owens
Robert Tittle
Thomas Bradford
Charles Ferrell
Hardin Cantrell
James Delong
Joseph Clarke
Tilman Bethell
Andrew Pickett
Thomas Price
Benjamin Avant
Samuel Vannatta
Ezekiel Taylor
William Williams
Abner Alexander
Richard Hancock

And it is also ordered By the court that the following persons be appointed as constables to wait upon the next Circuit Court to wit Sam'l Tottle and Jefferson Hicks.

(p 224)
Joseph Soap   )
Deed 100 acres   )
Charles P. Alexander)   The execution of a deed from Joseph Soap to Charles P. Alexander for one Hundred acres of land lying in Cannon County bearing date the 7th day of October 1836, was this day duly proven in open court by the oaths of Calvin Curlee & James Soap Susoribing witnesses thereto and on motion ordered that the same be certified for Registration.

Joseph Soap   )
Deed 100 acres)
Joseph Warren)

The execution of a deed of conveyance from Joseph Soap to Jos. Warren for one hundred acres of Land lying in Cannon County bearing date the 7th day of October 1836, was this day duly proven in open court by the oaths of Calvin Curlee and James Soap Subscribing witnesses thereto and on motion ordered that the same be certified for Registration.

On motion ordered by the court that David Taylor and Jonathan Fustons be appointed commissioners to lay off and set apart one years provisions to the widow of the late Sam'l Hunt deceased and make report to the next Term of this court.

Court then adjorned till acourt in corse
J.C. Martin chairm.
Elijah Stephens
Thomas Hayes
John Melton

State of Tennessee
At a county court began and held for the County of Cannon at the House of John Fisher (It being in pursuance of the adjornment of the last Court) on the first Monday And fourth day of September 1837, present the worship-full
Elijah Stephens
Lemuel Moore
Charles C. Evans
Thomas Simpson
Joseph Simpson
P.A. Thomason
Moses Shelby
William Bates
Hugh Reed and
Francis Cooper, Esqrs.

Thereupon the following orders were made to wit
On motion ordered by the Court that Elijah Stephens Esqr. be called to the chair to act as chairman during the present term of this court to fill the vancy occasioned by the absence of John Martin Esqr.

James Malone represents to the satisfaction of the court here that Winey Scribner late of our coubty is deceased and having left no will or Testament On motion ordered by the court that James Malone be appointed Ad-ministrator of said Estate whereupon the said Malone came into court and was duly qualified as such who together with his security Britton Finley and P.A. Thomason Entered into Bond in the sum of two Hundred dollars condition-ed and payable as the Law directs.

(p 226)
William Dale)
Deed 26 acres)
John Vantrees) The execution of a deed of conveyance from William Dale to John Vantrees for 25 acres of land lying in Cannon County bearing date the 31st day of August 1837, was this day duly proven in open court by the oaths of Thomas Glover and James Fulton subscribing witnesses thereto and on motion ordered that the same be certified for Registration.

Thomas Glover)
Deed 89 acres)
John Vantrees) The execution of a deed of conveyance from Thomas Glover

to John Vantrees for Eighty nine acres of land lying in Cannon County bearing
date the 20th day of Augt. 1836 was this day duly acknowledged in open court
by the said Thomas Glover (the bargainor) to be his act and deed for the purposes therein contained. And on motion ordered that the same be certified
for Registration.

Henry Haas this day filed in open court a declaration containing Facts with
Reguardtto his servises as a Revolutionary Soldier and was duly qualified to
the same Also personally appeared in open court Henry Fite a clergeman and
Lemuel Moore and Pleasant A. Thomas Esqr. and made oath with reguard to the
character of the Henry Haas And on motion ordered by the court that the same
be certified in manner and form as required by the several acts of Congress
in such case made and provided.

(p 227)
David Taylor
Ezekiel W. Taylor and
Jonathan Fuston
Commissioners appointed at the last term of this court to Lay off one yeart
provisions out of the estate of the late Sam'l Hunt decd. to his widdow, make
report that they have given to the said widdow the following articles as a
support for one year to wit Ten Barrels of corn All the Hogs on the place to
make her meet one Bushel of salt, five dollars worth of sugar and coffee, five
dollars worth of flour , one dollar to buy peper and spice &C and the chick-
ens and vegetables on the place which apart being adjudged by the court to be
correct, the same is ordered to be made record on the minuits of the court
as above.

Hugh Reed Esq. one of the members of this court makes known to the same that
there are idiots, to wit Jane Peyton and Jane Oliver, in the district which
he represents that are objects of charity and Beleaves also that they are
such persons and in such conditions as require the notice of the court. And
whereupon on motion ordered by the court that the shiriff of Cannon County
summons a jury or juries of twelve Good and Lawful men and proceed to examine
into the condition meens of support &C of the said tow Idiots and make report
of the same to the next court in order that the court maybe prepared to take
legal steps with the same.

(p 228) There appearing no further Buisness the court then adjorned till
tomorrow morning twelve o'clook.
E. Stephens
C hermon Proten
Charlws C. Evans
Thomas Hayes

Tuseday morning Sept. the 5th 1839.
Court meet pursuant to adjornment present the worshipfull
Elijah Stephens
Thomas Hayes and
Charles C. Evans Esqrrs.
Court then adjorned till court in course.
E. Stephens
Thomas Hayes
Charles C. Evans

October Session 1837

(p 229)
State of Tennessee

At a county court began and held at the House of John Fisher (It being according to the adjournment of the last tem) on the first Monday (it being the 2nd. day of October 1837 - And of the Indipence of the United States the 62nd/ year. Present the worshipfull
John C. Martin
Charles C. Evans
Elijah Stephens
Joseph Simpson
Saml. Lance
William Dates

Whereupon the following orders were made to wit.

Lewis Parker represents to the satisfaction of the court that Ephriam Parker late of our county is deceased and having left no will or testament On motion ordered by the court that Lewis Parker be appointed administrator of said Estate Whereupon the said Lewis Parker together with his security Matthew Parker entered into bond in the sum of two Hundred dollars payable to the Governor for the time being and his successors in office faithfully to discharge his duty as administrator. Whereupon letters of Administration were granted him.

John Barkley)
Mortgage)
John L. Moore) The execution of a mortgage for for one hundred and two acres of land lying in Cannon County from (p 230) Barkley, to John L. Moore bearing date the 12th day of September 1837, was this day proven in part in open court, by the oath of Elihu Saunders one of the subscribing witnesses thereto (the other witness) not appearing to qualify.

Thomas Williams one of the deputy shirriffs of Cannon County this day returned into court the report of a jury of Inquest by him summoned in pursuance of an order that was Issued at the last Term of this court, to inquire into the condition of Jane Oliver and Jane Peyton Daughter of Polly Peyton, And there not being a court sufficient to act upon an allowance On motion ordered that the clerk of this court file the same in his office until the same shall be called for a subsequent term.

On motion ordered by the court that Joseph Simpson be appointed Guardain of
Hugh P. Falkenberry
Catherine Falkenberry and
David Falkenberry deceased Whereupon the said Joseph Simpson was duly qualified as such who together with his security entered into bond in the sum of five hundred dollars payable to John C. Martin chairman of this court and his successors conditioned as the Law directs.

(p 231) Court then adjorned til court in course.
J.C. Martin chairman
Charles C. Evans
E. Stephens

State of Tennessee
At a county court began and held for the county of Cannon at the House

of John Fisher in the Town of Woodbury on the first Monday and sixth day of
November in the year 1837 And of the American Independence the 62nd. year
Present the worshipfull
John C. Martin chairm'C
James Beatie
Peter Reynolds
Reuben Evans
Thomas Simpson
Charles C. Evans
Joseph Simpson
Elijah Stephens
William Bryson
Francis Cooper
Isaac Finley
Alexander McKnight
John Melton
Watson Cantrell
Thomas Hayes
Washington Kenedy
James M. Brown
William Bates Esqrs.
Whereupon the following orders were made to wit --

Henry Frazeur Administrator of the estate of Sam'l Hunt decd. this day returned in open court an account current of the sales (p 232) of the property belonging to said Estate and was duly qualified to the same and on motion ordered by the court that the same be admitted to record &C.

On motion ordered by the court that James Odom be appointed Guardain of
Sarah Odom wife of ------ Odom formily Sarah Owens, Whereupon the said James
Odom came into open court and together with his security Benjamin F. Odom en-
tered into Bond in the sum of three hundred dollars payable to John C. Martin
Chrm. of the county court of Cannon County and his successors in office con-
ditioned as the law directs &C.

On motion ordered by the court that the commissioners appointed by
this court for the purposes of laying off the Town of Woodbury and for other
purposes be and they are hereby instructed to Give the contractor for the
Building of a court house for Cannon County the further time of four months
from the maturity of the bond to complete the same.

Lewis Y. Davis this day produced in open court an account against the County
of Cannon for the sum of eight dollars and Eighty four cents for monies by him
Expended in purchasing a Pro bare sledge hammer and one set of boreing tools
pursuant to a former order of this court And in taking the voice of the court
upon the allowance (p 235) of the same by ayes and noes, Those who voted in
the affirmative were Esqrs.
James Beatie
James M. Brown
Charles C. Evans
Peter Reynolds
Thomas Simpson
Isaac Finley
Thomas Hays
Reuben Evans
Washington Kenedy
Francis Cooper
Alexander McKnight

Elijah Stephens and
John C. Martin
Which being the number required by law for making appropriations under the sum
of fifty dollars the was allowed And on motion ordered by the court that the
Trustee of Cannon County pay the same out of any monies in his hands not
otherwise appropriated

Henry Trott JR. This day produced in open court a joint account from
Jonathan Webster and John S. Russworm against the County of Cannon for five
days serviceseach as commissioners appointed by law to purchase the county
site for Cannon County at the rate of three dollars per day, each making in
all thirty dollars, And on taking the voice of the court upon the same those
who voted in the affirmative were Esqrs.
James Beatie
James M. Brown
Pater Reynolds
Thomas Simpson
Charles C. Evans
Joseph Simpson
Isaac Finley
Thomas Hays
Washington Kennedy
Elijah Stephens
Alexander McKnight and
John C. Martin
which being the number required by law for making appropriations under the
sum of fifty dollars the same was Allowed whereupon on motion ordered by the
court that the Trustee of Cannon County pay (p 234) the same out of any
monies in his hands not otherwise appropriated.

Thomas G. Wood Clerk of the Circuit courts for Cannon County this day
produced in open court five diferent accounts against the County of Cannon
to wit. The State of Tennessee against John Melton upon an Indictment for
an affray, the whole amount of cost in said cause $9.18¾ . The State of
Tennessee against Littleton Hullet and Sarah Hullet upon an Indictment for
an assault and Battery, the whole amount of the cost in this cause 15.12½
The State of Tennessee against Eli Paily upon a presentment for an affray
the whole amount of the cost in this cause $8. 37¼. The State of Tennessee
against Charles Ross upon an Indictment for an assault and Patery the whole
cost in this cause $7.00.
The State of Tennessee against Richard and James Eddings upon a recognizance for a riot the whole cost In this cause $3.25 making in all upon the
above described five charges the sum of forty three dollars and forty three
and three fourth cents. And it appearing to the satisfaction of the court
from the diferent records accompanying the several accounts as above; that
Honorable judge of the circuit court hand adjudged the same to be paid by
the County of Cannon when the county court should allow the same And also
it appearing further to the satisfaction of the court that the Attorney
General had examined (p 235) and certified the said accounts to be correct.
On motion the court proceeded to vote upon the allowance of the same, And
taking the voice of the court by ayes and noes those who voted in the
affirmative were Esqrs.
JamesBeatie
James M. Brown
Pater Reynolds
Thomas Simpson
Charles C. Evans

Joseph Simpson
Isaac Finley
Thomas Hays
Reubin Evans
Francis Cooper
Washington Kenedy
Elijah Stephens
Alexander McKnight and
John C. Martin
which being the number requests it to make an appropriation under fifty
dollars the same was allowed. Whereupon on motion ordered by the court that
the Trustee pay the sameout of any monies in his handsnot otherwise appropri-
ated .

On motion ordered by the court that Thomas Elkins Depty Shiriff be
fird the sum of five dollars for negligence and absence from the place of
holding court during the setting of the same and that Execution Issue
against him for said fine together with the cost of Entries Execution &C.

Court then adjorned till tomorrow morning 12 O'clock
Reubin Evans
William Bates
E. Stephens

Tuseday morning November the 9th A.D. 1837

Court meet pursuant to adjornment present the worshipfull
Reuben Evans
Elijah Stephens and
Willaim Bates Esqrs.

Whereupon the following order was made to wit.

Whereas from the absence of John C. Martin Esqr. Chairman of this court, On
motion ordered by the court that Reuben Evans take the chair for the time
being.

Whereupon it appearing to the satisfaction of the court that there was no
further Buisness that the present court could attend to - On motion the
court adjorned till court in course.
Reuben Evans
William Bates
E. Stephens

(p 237)
State of Tennessee
At a county court began and held for the county of Cannon at the House
of John Fishers in the Town of Woodbury on the first Monday and 4th day of
December in the year of our Lord one thousand eight hundred and thirty seven
And of the American Independence the sixty second year, present the worship-
full
Sam'l Lance
Alexander McKnight
Thomas Hayes
Joseph Simpson
Hugh Reed
Washington Kenedy

Charles C. EVans
James M. Brown
Elijah Stephens
William Bates
Thomas Simpson
Reuben Evans
James Goodner
Jonathan Fuson
Francis Cooper and
William Bryson Esqrs.

Whereupon the following orders were made to wit.
Whereas it appearing to the satisfaction of the court that John C. Martin
chairman of the court was absent from the county and in all probability
would not appear to take his seat during the present Term of this court.
Thereforeon motion of James M: Brown Esq. Sam'l Lance Esq. was called to the
chair to preside over the Deliberations of the court during the present Term
thereof.

A paper writing purporting to be the last will and Testament of Robert
George decd. late of our county was this day produced in open court for probate and was duly proven by the Oaths of
John Finley
James D. George and
James Taylor
subscribing witnesses thereto and on motion the same was (p238) admitted
to record and to be certified &C. And it appearing to the satisfaction of the
court that James O. George and John George were appointed in said last Will to
executethe same, the came into open court and were duly qualified as such
who together with their securuties John Finley and William F. George Entered
into Bond on Open court in the ---- sum of Ten thousand ---- conditioned and
payable as the law directs. And letters Testamentory are granted &C.

On motion Ordered by the court that James Taylor
                                John Finley and
                                Daniel Tenpenny
be --------- and they are hereby appointed as commissioners to lay off and set
apart one years provisions out of the Estate of Robert George decd. to the
widdow of the said Robert George decd. and make report to the next Term of
this court.

James Malone Administrators of the Estate of Winney Scribner decd. this day
returnedin open court an account of the sales of the property belonging to said
Estate and was duly qualified to the same And on motion the same is admitted
to reocord.

On motion and upon the application of Charles P. Alexander he is here-
by constituted and appointed Guardain of
Calvin Sullivan
Caswell Sullivan
Andrew Sullivan
Colwell Sullivan
Lucinda Sullivan and
Milisy Sullivan
minor heirs of the Estate of William Sullivan decd. who together with his
securitys Joseph (p 239) Warren and Akelus Alexander came into court and
entered into Bond in the sum of sixteen hundred dollars conditioned and payable
as the Law directs.

On motion and upon the application of Rebecca F. Bennitt and Richard S. Bennitt minor heirs of John M. Bennitt decd. Thomas S. Bennitt is hereby constituted Guardain of the said Rebecca F. Bennitt and Richard S. Bennitt who together with his securities came into court and entered into bond as such conditioned and payable as the Law dericts in the sum of six hundred dollars.

On motion and upon the application of William Bennitt Jr. he is hereby constituted and appointed Guardain of
Sophia Bennitt
Elizabeth Patterson
John M. Patterson
William M. Patterson and
Judith C. Patterson
heirs at law of the Estate of John M. Bennitt decd. and choldren of Joab Patterson of the state of Illenois who together with his securities Thomas S. Bennitt and William Bennett Sr. came into Court and Entered into bond in the sum of three hundred dollars conditioned and payable as the Law directs.

William Patterson)
  and others)
Petition to divide lands) This day came Matthias S. West & William Patterson Administrator of the Estate of John M. Bennitt decd. heirs at Law of the estate of James Brown decd. by virtue of purchase from the heirs of the said Jas. Brown as is shown in said petition as also by a certified copy of the last will and Testament of the said Brown praying this court to appoint five commissioners Good and Lawful men to divide (p 240) the lands belonging to the Estate of the James Brown decd. agreable to said last will and Testament And it appearing to the satisfaction of the court that the prayer of the said petitioners is reasonable and ought to be granted. Therefore on motion Ordered by the court
Jonathan Griffith
Ephriam Garrison
James Goodner
Moses Fite and
Moses Allen
be and they are hereby appointed commissioners with full authority to divide the before mentioned lands belonging to the legal representatives of the aforesaid James Brown decd. between the heirs at law of said Estate according to the calls of the last will and Testament of the said James Brown decd. and make a full report of their proceedings upon the same under oeth to the next Term of this court.

William Patterson et)
  Admr.)
Petition to divide lands) William Patterson this day filed a petition in open court praying the court here to appoint five Good and Lawful men to lay off and set apart the one third part of the lands belonging to the Estate of John M. Bennitt decd. (Including the Mansion House) to Judith Bennitt widdow of the John M. Bennitt decd. And It appearing to the satisfaction of the court hear that the same never has been done and that in consiquence of which the prayer of the petition is reasonable and ought to be granted. Therefore It is ordered by the court that Jonathan Griffith
                Ephriam Garrison
                James Goodner
                Moses Fite and
                Moses Allen
be and they are hereby constituted and appointed for the purposes aforesaid

with full authority to proceed to and upon the premises aforesaid and then and there to Lay off and set apart to the said Judith Bennitt the one (p 241) third part of the lands belonging to the Estate of the aforesaid John M. Bennitt decd. Including the Mansion House and make a full report of the same under oath to the next Term of this court.

William Patterson et al)
     Petition   )
To devide Lands   ) This day came William Patterson one of the heirs at Law of the estate of John Bennitt decd. and William Bennitt an heir at law of said estate on his own behalf and as Guardain of
Sophia Bennitt
Elizabeth Patterson
John M. Patterson
William Patterson and
Judith C. Patterson
(heirs at law of said Estate Also Thomas S. Bennett an other of the heirs of law of said Estate for himself and as Guardain of Rebeca F. Bennitt and Rich'd S. Bennitt minor heirs of the aforesaid John M. Bennitt decd. And filed their petition in open court praying the court to appoint five Good and Lawful men to lay off and divide the lands of the said John M. Bennitt decd. Between the legal heirs of said Estate (after seting the widdows dower out of the same) And it appearing to the satisfaction of the court that all of the heirs of said Estate by themselves and their legally appointed Guardains had assigned the aforesaid petition and that the prayer of said petitioner is reasonable and ought to be granted therefore It is ordered by the court that Jonathan Griffith
                Ephriam Garrison
                James Goodner
                Moses Fite and
                Moses Allen
be and they are hereby appointed as commissioners for the purposes aforesaid with full autherity to proceed to and upon the premises aforesaid and then and there to divide all the lands belonging to the aforesaid Estate of John M. Bennitt decd (p 242) (over and above the widdows dower) and make a full report of the same under Oath to the next term of this court.

        On motion (the following justices present to wit
Joseph Simpson
Jonathan Fuson
Thomas Simpson
Thomas Hays
Charles C. Evans
Alexander McKnight
Reuben Evans
James M. Brown
James Goodner
 Sam'l Lamce
Francis Cooper and
Hugh Reed Esqrs.
All voting in the affirmative (the following allowances was made to Authur Warren to wit the sum of two dollars and forty seven and a half cents as a return of monies by him paid to the shiriff as taxes which accrued by an overcharge in the valuation of his property by the revenue commissioners of his District when listing property for taxes for the year 1837.
And it is further ordered by the court that the county Trustee pay the same out of any monies in his hands not otherwise appropriated.

December Term

On motion the following justices present to wit

Charles C. Evans
Washington Kenedy
Thomas Hays
Alexander McKnight
Reuben Evans
Jonathan Fuson
Thomas Simpson
Elijah Stephens
James Goodner
James M. Brown
Sam'l Lance and
William Bryson Esqrs.

which being the number requisit for making appropriations under the sum of fifty dollars, all voting in the affirmative an allowance of thirty six dollars was made for the Benefit of Jane Peyton (Daughter of Polly Peyton who has been at a previous Term of this court represented by a jury summoned by the shff for that purpose as being in a Helpless (p 243) condition and without means to support upon or evenly able to take care of her person to be placed in the hands person appointed Guardain Special for that purpose. And it is further ordered by the court that the Trustee of the county pay the same to such person as may be appointed as aforesaid out of any monies in his hands not otherwise appropriated.

On motion and upon the application Micajah Petty he is hereby constituted and appointed Guardain to Jane Peyton for the special purpose of receiving and administering to her wants such allowances as have been or may hereafter be set apart and allowed by the county court out of the county Treasurer for here special benefit whereupon the said Petty together with his security Akelus Alexander came into court and entered into bond as such in the sum of Eighty dollars conditioned and payable as the law directs.

Parker F. Stone This day came into court and made application to the same for an order to be made Instructing the commissioners appointed to lay off the lots in the Town of Woodbury and for other purposes to settle with and pay him for additional work by him done to the publick jail for Cannon County. Whereupon a question arose among the court whether such authority now belong to the court after having alredy instructidsaid commissioners to build such jail as was common to be built for other counties whereupon on motion the ayes and noes were taken upon the (p 244) same when all the justices present to wit.

Charles C. Evans
Washington Kenedy
Thomas Hays
Jonathan ———
Thomas Simpson
Joseph Simpson
James Goodner
Hugh Reed
William Bates
Francis Cooper
William Bryson
Elijah Stephens
James M. Brown
Alexander McKnight and
Sam'l Lance Esqrs.

voting in the negative was at once thereby declaring that the authority of making all such settlement belonged Specially to those with whom the contracts were made.

On motion the court proceed to appoint the following persons to serve as jurors at the next Term of the circuit court for Cannon County commencing on the third Monday in March next at the court House for said county in the Town of Woodbury to wit

Lewis Patton
Joshua Nichols
John Hollis
Sam'l Durke   (p 244)
David Patton
Azariah Cather
Jonathan Wimberly
John Young
Elijah Stephens
Elijah Keely
Charles C. Evans
George T. Ford
Reuben Ealem
Sam'l Lance
Sam'l Denby
James Hawkins
Thomas Simpson
Henry Heart
James Simpson
William Parsley
John Cas key
John Bevirte
Reuben Evans
Lem'l Moore
Thomas Tyree
A.W. Brien
James Tubb
Benjamin Avant
William Fite
John Simpson
Francis Cooper and
Washington Mathis.
And it is further ordered by the court that the shff of Cannon County summons the same when an order shall Issue &C

(p 245) On motion the court proceeded to appoint the following to take in a list of the taxable property and poles for their Respective districts in Cannon County for the year 1838, to wit
District No 1 —Alexander McKnight
         2nd — Thomas Hays
         3rd — Joseph Simpson
         4th — Hugh Reed
         5th — Washington Kenedy
         6th — William Y. Henderson
         7th — John Melton
         8th — Sam'l Lance
         9th — John Martin
         10th — Thomas Simpson

11th - Martin Phillips
12th - Watson Cantrell
13th - Reuben Evans
14th - James Goodner
15th - Peter Reynolds
16th - Jonathan Fuson
17th - William Bryson
It is therefore ordered by the court that the clerk of this furnish each of
the above named revenue commissioners with a copy of his appointment as also
a copy or form containing a list of the Items of property and poles that are
taxable agreable to the acts of assembly in such case made and provided &C.

        On motion the following justices present to wit
Jonathan Fuson
Reuben Evans
William Bryson
Joseph Simpson
Hugh Reed
James Goodner
James M. Brown
Samuel Lance
Washington Kenedy and
C.C. Evans Esqrs.
voting in the affirmative And
Thomas Simpson
Thomas Hays and
Alexander McKnight
voting in negative - And there being a majority of the same voting in the
affirmative an Allowance of four dollars each is made to the commissioners
appointed to take in a list of the Taxable property and poles for (the present)
year of 1837, to wit
Alexander McKnight
Thomas Powell
Joseph Simpson
Blake Sadgely
Isaac W. Elledge
Jas, M. Brown
Charles C. Evans
Sam'l Lance
John Martin
Thomas Simpson   (p 246)
Martin Phillips
David Fisher
Reuben Evans
P.A. Thomason
James Beatie
Jonathan Fuson and
William C. Odom
And it is further ordered by the court that the clerk of this court certify
a copy of each allowance to the individual entitle to the same And it is
further ordered by the court that the Trustee of Cannon County pay the same
out of any monies in his hands not otherwise appropriated.

        On motion court then adjorned till tommorrow morning ten oclock.
Samuel Lance
Charman Protem
Reuben Evans
E. Stephens

Tuseday morning December the 5th 1837.
The worshipfull court meet pursuant to Adjornment present the worshipfull
Sam'l Lance
Elijah Stephens
Reuben Evans and
William Bates Esqrs.
Whereupon the following order was made to wit.

James M. Brown Esqr. This presented in open court his resignation as justice
of the peace for Cannon County and the sixth cival district there of which
is received by the court and on motion ordered by the court that the sheriff
of Cannon County proceed proceed to open and hold an election to fill said
vacancy as the law directs.

(p 247) Court then adjorned til court in course.
Samuel Lance
Reuben Evans
Wm. Bates.

January Term 1838

(p 248)
State of Tennessee
        At a county court began and held for the county of Cannon at the House
of John Fisher in the Town of Woodbury On the first Monday (It being the
first day) of January 1838. And of the American Independence the sixty second
year Present The worshipfull
Alexander McKnight
Joseph Simpson
Washington Kenedy
Elijah Stephens
Charles C. Evans
John Melton
William Bates
Thomas Simpson and
Francis Cooper Esqrs.
Whereupon the following the following orders were made, to wit.

        Whereas John C. Martin Chairman of this court being absentm on motion
Elijah Stephens Esqr. wwas called to the chair to preside over the deliberations of the same for the time being.

        William Wright made known to the satisfaction of the court that Phillip
Palmer late of our county is deceased and having no will or Testament, Therefore on motion ordered by the court that the said William Wright be appointed
administrator of the estate of the said deceased who came into court and was
duly qualified as such who together with his securities, Alfred W. Walker and
John Fisher entered into bond in the sum of sixteen hundred dollars conditioned and payable as the Lawdirects.
Whereupon Letters of Administration were Granted &C.

        On motion ordered by the court that
Jonathan C. Doss
William Floyd and
Pleasant A. Thomason
be and they are hereby appointed (p 249) commissioners with full authority
to proceed to and upon the premises of the late Phillip Calmer decd. and then
and there to lay off one years provisions out of the Estate of the said deceased

to the widdow of the said Phillip Palmer deceased. And make report of the same under Oath to the next Term of this court &C.

George Grizzle shiriff of Cannon County by his Deputy Thomas Elkins this day returned into court a certificate of the judges of an election by him held in the sixth district in Cannon County on the 16th day December 1857 to elect a justice of the peace for said district in place of James M. Brown Esq. resigned Also a commission from his Excelency the Governor to Eli A. Fisher who it appeared from said return was duly elected. Whereupon the said Fisher came into court and was duly qualified into office as the law directs.

George Grizzle sheriff of Cannon County by his deputy Thomas Williams this day returned into court a certificate of the judges of an election by him held in the third district in Cannon County on the 30th day of December 1857 to elect a constable in said district to fill the vancancy of Jonathan Bateman removed from which certificate it appeared to the satisfaction of the court, that Wiley Hopkins was duly elected whereupon the said Hopkins came into court and and was duly qualified as such who together with his security, Joseph Simpson entered into bond in the sum of one thousand dollars conditioned and payable as the law directs

(p 250) James O. George and John A. George Executors of the last will and Testament of Robert George decd. this day returned into court an Inventory of the sale of the property belonging to said Estate and were duly qualified to the same, whereupon on motion the same was admitted to reccord.

Lewis Parker administrator of the estate of Ephrian Parker decd. this day returned into court an Inventory of sale of the property belonging to said Estate and was duly qualified to the same whereupon on motion Ordered by the court that the same be admitted to reccord - &C.

William Stone makes known to the satisfaction of the court that her father Usibious Stone late of our county is deceased and having left no will or Testament, On motion Ordered by the court that the said William Stone together with Alexander Higgins be and they are hereby appointed Administrator of said Estate, Whereupon the said Stone and Higgins both came into court and were duly qualified as such who together with their securities Archibald Stone and William West entered into bond in the sum of four thousand dollars conditioned and payable as the law directs.
Whereupon letters of Administration are granted &C.

On motion ordered by the court that Archibald Stone be appointed Guardian of his mother Milly Stone. Whereupon the said Archibald Stone came into court and entered into bond in the sum of two thousand dollars payable to John C. Martin chairman of the county court of Cannon County and his successors in office conditioned as the Law directs. &C

(p 251) Joseph Turney this day produced in open court a commission from his Excelency the Governor, to him the said Turney as a justice of the peace in and for the county of Cannon Whereupon on motion the said Turney came into open court and was duly qualified as such in manner and form as the Law deriots.

On motion and upon application of David Coughanous, George Spears an orphan boy about the age of Ten Years was bond to him to learn the art of Occupation of a farmer. Whereupon the said Coughanous together with his ———— Alexander F. McFerrin came into court and entered into bond and faithfully and truly to perform towards the said George certain stipulations in said bond contained.

On motion and upon the application of Arthur Warren Sr. Thomas Kincaid an orphan boy about the age of twelve years is bound to him the said Warren till he attains the age of twenty one years. Whereupon he the said ――――― together with his security Archibald Stone came into court and entered into bond well and truly to perform to words the said Thoma s certain stipulations in said bond mentioned.

On motion ordered by the court that Joseph Clarke
         William Bates
         John Brown
         John B. Stone and
         Archibald Stone

commissioners appointed by the county court Cannon County at the May Term of said court 1836 to Lay off and sell out the lots in the Town of Woodbury &c and for other purposes be and they are hereby required to make report in writing to the next Term of this court of all their proceedings as commissioners with regard to the duties assigned by law. And that a copy of this order Issue to said commissioners &c.

(p 252)

On motion of Charles C. Evans Esqr. Thomas Elkins Deputy shirriff of Cannon County is released from a fine of five dollars which was Entered against him at the November term of this court 1837, for negligence and absence from the place of Holding Court during the setting of the same.

Milton Sandridge et al)
Power of Attorney   )
William Bates   )   The execution of a power of Attorney from Milton
Sandridge,
Dabney Sandridge
Eliza Sandridge
Huldy Sandridge
Permela Sandridge and
Louisisa Sandridge
to William Bates (the attorney in fact therein names) for certain purposes therein Expressed bearing date the 23rd day of November 1837, was this day duly acknowledged in open court by the said
Milton Sandridge
Dabney Sandridge
Elisa Sandridge
Huldy Sandridge
Permela Sandridge and
Louisa Sandridge
to be their acts and deeds severally for the purposes therein mentioned. Thereupon On motion It is ordered by the court that the same be certified for Registration.
Sam'l J. Garrison clerk of this court for and leave is Granted him to spread upon the minutes of the court his receits for the collection and payment of all the revenue by him collected and payable from the different sources which he is bound by law to collect and account for as also the different statements of the liabilities of other officers concerned in the collection of the State and County Revenue which by law he is bound to report, that is to say from the second day of May 1836 (the time he the said Garrison was qualified (p 253) into office up to the first day of September 1837, to wit

Woodbury Sept. 20th 1836
Received of Sam'l J. Garrison his statement of revenue collected and payable
by him as clerk of Cannon County Court from the 2nd day of May to the 1st of
September 1836.
        (signed) John Stephens Trustee
            by Joseph Clarke his Dpt.

State of Tennessee)
Cannon County   ) Received of Samuel J. Garrison clerk of said county
court the agreeable amount of the Taxes due and payable in said county for
the fiscal year of 1836, this the 1st day of October 1836.
John Stephens Trustee
By Joseph Clarke dept Trustee

           Nashville 30 Sept. 1836
Received of Sam'l J. Garrison his statement of Revenue collected and payable
by him as clerk of Cannon County court from 2nd May to 1st September 1836.
                Dan'l Graham
                Comptoler of the Treasury

(p 254) Nashville 30th September 1836 No. 90
$ 346.91
Received of S. Garrison three hundred forty six dollars and 71 cents audited
to him by No. 90 and due on account of Revenue by him collected as clerk of
county court of Cannon County from 2nd May to 1st September 1836.
                (Signed duplicates)
                Miller Francis
                Treasurer of Tennessee

           Nashville 1 October 1836
Received of Samuel J. Garrison Esqr. clerk of Cannon County court two hundred
and forty three 75/100 dollars monies collected off retailers of spirituous liquors
on licence for the use of common schools for which duplicate recepts are
Given
    R.H. McEwin
    Supt Public Instructions

State of Tennessee)
Cannon County   ) Received of Sam'l J. Garrison clerk of said county court
Ten Dollars our fees for settling with him and Thomas G. Wood clerk of the
Circuit court upon this Revenue accounts for 1836, this 16th Sept. 1836
                Watson Cantrell
                John C. Martin
                Commissioners

Received of Sam'l J. Garrison his statement of the County Revenue for the
year 1837, this 23rd September
              John Stephens
              Trustee for Cannon County

Received of Samuel J. Garrison clerk of Cannon County three hundred and forty
five dollars and forty (p 255) cents in full of the account of Revenue by
him collected from the first day of September 1836 up to the first day of
September 1837 — which appears from the certificate of the commissioners of
the county Revenue this 23rd September 1837
$345.40 ct (signed) John Stephens Trustee for said County

State of Tennessee)
Cannon County   ) Received of Sam'l J. Garrison clerk of said county court
the aggregate amount   of the taxes due and payable in said county for the fiscal year of 1837 - this 23rd September 1837.
                                      John Stephens Trustee
                                      for Cannon County

          Nashville 30th Sept. 1837
Received of Sam'l J. Garrison his statement of Revenue collected as clerk of
Cannon County court 1 Sept. 1836, to 1 September 1837
                                      Daniel Graham
                                      Comptroler &C.

$788.27   Nashville 30 September 1837 No. 397
Received of Sam'l J. Garrison seven hundred and Eighty eight dollars 27 cents
audited to him by No. 397 and due on account of Revenue by him collected as
clerk of the county court of Cannon County, from the 1st of Sept. 1836, 1
Sept. 1837.
        (signed Duplicates)
        Miller Francis Trustee of Tennessee
Received Nashville 30th Sept. 1837, 1837 of Sam'l J. Garrison Esqr. clerk of
the county court for Cannon County, two hundred and ninety two dollars & 50
cents monies collected on lifting licince   from 1 Sept. 1836 to 1 Sept. 1837
in his county appropriated to use common schools for which Duplicate recepts
are Given)
$292.50) R.M. McFwin Supt. &C

(p 256) Thus appearing no further Buisness the worshipfull court adjorned
till tomorrow netning 10 o'clock.
                        E. Stephens
                        John Melton
                        E.A. Fisher
                        Wm. Bates

Tuseday morning January 2nd 1838
The worshipfull court met pursuant to adjornment   present the Worshipfull
Elijah Stephens chrm protem &C
Eli A. Fisher
John Melton and
William Bates Esqrs.

Whereupon the follow Order was made to wit

    On motion Ordered by the court that William Y. Henderson and Joseph
Ramsey be and they are hereby appointed commissioners of the county of Cannon
from the first day of Jany 1838 with full power to settle with the officers
concerned in the collection of the county revenue as the law directs &C.

    There being no further Buisness court adjorned till court in course.
E. Stephens
Wm. Bates
John Melton
E.A. Fisher

(p 257) February Term 1838

State of Tennessee

    At a county court begain and held for the county of Cannon at the
House of John Fishers in the Town of Woodbury (it being a place procured by
said court for the holding of the same until the court househall be finished
for said county) on the first Monday and 5th day of February in the year of
our Lord one thousand Eight Hundred and thirty Eight and of the Independence
of the of the United States the 62nd year. present the worshipful
John C. Martin? chairmn &C

Alexander McKnight

Isaac Finley

Joseph Simpson

Allen Wailey

Washington Kenedy

Elijah Stephens

D.A. Fisher

Charles C. Evans

John Melton

William Bates

Joseph Turney

William Bryson and

Francis Cooper Esqrs.

Whereupon the following orders were made to wit

    On motion and upon the application of John P. Dale he is hereby con-
stituted and appointed Guardain to Charles C. Dale and Thomas H. Dale
(minors) Whereupon the said John P. Dale togeth with his security William
Dale (which being approved by the court) Entered into bond in the sum of five
hundred dollars payable to John C. Martin Chairman of said county court and
his successors in office conditioned for the faithfull performance &C.
Whereas it has this day been made known to the satisfaction of the court that
Thomas Stroud late of our county is deceased and having left no will or
Testament. Therefore on motion (p 258) ordered by the court that Vinsan Gather
be appointed administrator of the state of the said Thomas Stroud decd. who
together with his securities Joseph Simpson and Azariah Gather (who being
approved by the court) entered into bond in the sum of hundred dollars payable
to Newton Cannon Governor and his successors in office conditiond for the
faithful performance of said Administration Whereupon letters of Administration were Granted &C
Wheras It having been made known to the satisfaction of the court that John
Cooper late of our county is deceased and having left no will or Testament
Therefore on motion It is ordered by the court that Silas Cooper be appointed Administrator of the Estate of the said John Cooper deceased who together
with his security James O. George (who being approved of by the court) entered
into bond in the sum of Fourteen Hundred dollars payable to his Excelency
Newton Cannon (Governor) and his successors in office conditioned for the faithful performance of said Administration. Thereupon letters of administration
were Granted &C.
Whereas It having this day been made know to the satisfaction of the court
that Judith Bennett (widdow of the late John M. Bennettdecd.) late of
our county has decd. and having left no will or Testament, Therefore on
motion It is ordered by the court William Patterson be and she is hereby
appointed Administrator of the Estate of the said (p 259) Judith Bennett
deceased who together with his security William Bennett entered into bond in

open court in the sum of three hundred dollars payable to his Excelency Newton
Cannon Governor and his successors in office conditioned for the faithful per-r
formance of said Administration. Thereupon letters of Administration were

ranted &C.

On the petition of Adam Elrod by the Advice of his Counsel he is hereby appointed administrator of the estate of his deceased wife Margaret Elrod who came into court and entered into bond in the sum of three thousand Dollars payable to his Excelency Newton Cannon Governor and his successors in Office conditioned for his faithful performance in said Administration. Thereupon letters of Administration were granted him upon said Estate.

John Tucker)
  Transfer)
John Pendleton)   The execution of a transfered or a assignment upon a plot and certificate of survey of one hundred and fifty acres of land lying in Cannon County, from John Tucker to John Pendleton bearing date the fourth day of Feb. 838, was this day acknowledged in open court by the said John Tucker the assignor to be his act and deed for the purposes therein contained And on motion ordered by the court that the same be certified &C.

John Tucker)
  Transfer)
John Pendleton)   The execution of a transfer or an assignment upon a plat and certificate of survey from John Tucker to John Pendleton for one hundred (p 260) acres of land lying in Cannon County bearing date the 4th day of February 1838, was this day duly acknowledged in open court by the said John Tucker (the assignor) to be his act and deed for the purposes therein contained And on motion Ordered by the court that the same be certified &C.

Arthur Warren)
Henry Warren)
Deed 263)
Thomas Thompson)   The execution of a deed of conveyance from Arthur Warren and Henry Warren to Thomas Thompson for two hundred and sixty Eight acres of land lying in Cannon (originally Warren) County bearing date the 30th day of July 1818 was this day duly acknowledged in open court by the said Arthur Warren and Henry Warren(the bargainor) to be their acts and deeds for the purposes therein contained And on motion ordered by the court that the same be certified for Registration.

William Rea)
Deed 120)
Iverson J. Thomas)   The execution of a deed of conveyance from William Red to Iverson J. Thomas for one hundred and twenty six acres of land lying in Cannon (originally Rutherford county bearing date the 29th day of November 1836 was this day duly proven in open court by the Oaths of Dennison Hagwood and Alexander McKnight subscribing witnesses thereto. And on motion ordered that the same be certified for Registration.

(p 261) Joseph Turney Guardain of Sally S. Campbell, Frances Turney and George Turney, minor heirs of Isaac Turney deceased this day returned in open court an account current showing the situation of the means &C in his hands belong to said heirs, And was duly qualified to the same, And on motion ordered by the court that the same be admitted to reccord.

Susanah Stone)
  Petition)
For Dower)   Susanah Stone, widdow of George Stone decd. this day filed her petition in open court praying the order to be made by the court Ordering the

sheriff of Cannon County to summons a jury of five Good and Lawful men to proceed to and upon the land and premises upon which her husband died seized and possessed of to wit Bounded North by the land of Alexander Higgins west by the land of William James and Thomas Thompson south by the land of James Cantrell and East by the land – Alexander Higgins And it appearing to the satisfaction of the court that the prayer of Petitioner is reasonable and ought to be granted . Therefore on motion Ordered by the court that the shirriff of Cannon County summons a jury of five Good and lawful men free holders and proceed to and upon the primises aforesaid and then and there after being duly sworn to set apart to the said Susanah Stone widdow of the said George Stone deceased as aforesaid the one third part of the land and premises of the said Geo. Stone deed. including the Mansion House out House &C. And make return of the same in writing to the next Term of this court.

(p 262)

William Patterson)
   Petition   )
To Devide Land)   William Patterson
                       Benjamin Bennett
                       William Bennett

for himself and for the minor heirs (children of Joab Patterson And Thomas Bennitt for himself and as Guardain of Rebecca S. Bennitt and Richard S. Bennitt who being severly the Heirs at Law of the Estate of Judith Bennitt deed. This day filed their petition in open court praying that an order be made by the court appointing commissioners to proceed to and upon the Dower lands as laid off and marked out by commissioners appointed for that purpose at a previous Term of this court to the said Judith Bennett Deceased (then the widdow of the late John M. Bennett Decd. And it appearing to the satisfaction of the court that the prayers of the petitioners are reasonable and ought to be granted Therefore on motion ordered by the court that

James Goodner
Jonathan Griffith
Ephriam Garrison
Moses Fite and
Wiley Jones

be and they are hereby appointed commissioners as aforesaid with full power and authority to proceed to proceed on the premises aforesaid and then and there to divide Equally (according to Quality and quanty) among the legal heirs of the said Judith Bennett deed. as aforesaid all the lands and landed premises as heretofore set apart to here as a dower right whereof she the said Judith lately died seized and possessed of And make due return of the same under oath to the next Term of this court.

(p 263) On motion ordered by the court that
James Goodner
Moses Fite
Ephriam Garrison
Moses Allen and
Jonathan Griffith

commissioners appointed at the December ———— of this court 1837, for to devide the lands belonging to the heirs of John M. Bennitt deed. among the said heirs of said Estates respectively and to lay off and set apart the one third part of the lands belonging to the said John M. Bennitt deed. to Judith Bennitt widdow of the said John M. Bennitt deed. as a dower wright be and they are hereby continued as such and that they make report at the present term of this court insted of at the next term after their said appointments for the purposes aforesaid Whereupon Matthias West came into court and presented the reports of the said sad commissioners upon the several appointment s respectively which were In all things confirmed by the court. And admitted to record &C. And the said commissioners Discharged &C.

Whereas It appearing to the satisfaction of the court that in runing the south west boundry line of the county of Dekalb that said line passes through tur to wit the ninth and tenth cival districts in Cannon County and therby very much disranging said districts by Reducing the number of inhabitants and including of one of the justices of the ninth district and both in the tenth district in the county of Dekabb And it appearing also to the satisfaction of the court that a provision was made in the act of Assembly Establishing the county of Dekalb that the county court of said county as also the counties from which the fractions were taken (p 264) to form the county of Dekalb should have the power of regulating the Broken districts through which any of the lines of said County should pass. Therefore On motion It is ordered by the court that in order to amend the two above mentioned Broken districts in Cannon County and for the better convenience of the citizens generally that for the future until altered by a proper authority that the tenth cival district shall commence and be bounded as follows to wit Begining on the line between the counties of Cannon and Dekalb near Henry Powells runing thence West so as to include the said Powells, Archibald McDougle and Miles Spurlock, to a point on the ridge that Devides the waters of Marican Creek from the waters of the sycamore fork Thence with said ridge north so as to include in said tenth district all the Inhabitants residing East of said ridge that were stricken off from the county of Wilson together with the fractional ballance of said tenth District which shall constitute and compose the tenth cival district in Cannon County. And it is further Ordered by the court that the shirriff of Camon County fourthwith proceed to open and hold an Election at the House of Alfred Hancocks Cocks in said district (which shall hereafter be the place of Holding the precent Eliction for said District) to elect two justices of the peace and such other officers whose places places are vacant in said District as are required to be Elected for the people &C.

It is also further ordered by the court that Alfred Hancock be and he is hereby appointed as a Revenue commissioner to take in (p 265) a list of taxable property and poles in said District in such manner as he may think most advisable and to come the nearest to the direction of the law that may be proble from such of the citizens in said district as have not Given alredy to the comissioners appointed in the Original 17th District for the year of 1838, And make return of same at the next term of this court. It is also Ordered by the court that the ballance of the ninth cival District be and remain as the ninth District in Camon County and that the place of Holding the precent elections for said District shall in future be held at the House of John G.G. Poses, And It is also ordered by the court that the Shirff of Cannon proceed fourthwith to open and hold and Election as the law directs at the above place to Elect one justice of the peace for said District to fill the vacancy Occationed by the attachment of John Martin Esqrs. to Dekalb County. It is also further Ordered by the court that Jobe Stephens be and he is hereby appointed as a revenue commissioner to take in a list of the taxable property and poles in said District for the present year of 1838 in the best manner posiable and as near as may be according to the directions of the acts of assembly in such cases made and provided And make return of the same to the next term of this court. It is also further Ordered by the court that the remainder of the seventeenth cival District shall compose one district and be known by the name of District No. Eleven until otherwise altered &C.

(p 266) Pursuant to an order made at the last term of this court Calling upon

William Bates
John Brown
Archabald Stone and
Joseph Clarke
commissioners appointed at the May Term of this court 1836 to lay off and s
sell out the lots in the Town of Woodbury and for other purposes. They have
this day presented in open court said report, which on motion was receved and
ordered on file till the next term of this court for further Examation &C.

Joseph Simpson One of the justices of the peace for the county of
Cannon and third cival district thereof this day tendered in court his resignation as such which was received . And on motion Ordered by the court that the
shirriff of Cannon County proceed forthwith as the Law diriets to open and
hold an Election in said district to fill said vancancy.

There being no further Buisness On motion the worshipfull court then adjorned
till tomorrow morning Eleven O'clock.
E. Stephens
John Melton
E.A. Fisher

(p 267) Tuseday morning February the 6th day 1838.
The Worshipfull Court met pursuant to adjornment present the worshipfull
Elijah Stephens
E.A. Fisher and
John Melton Esqrs.

Whereupon the following order was made to wit.

Whereas from the absence of John C. Martin Chairman of this court-
On motion ordered by the court that Elijah Stephens Esqr. be called to
the chair to preside over the deliberations of the court the ballance of the
term.

There being no further Buisness On motion the worshipfull court adjorned
til court in course.
E. Stephens
E.A. Fisher
John Melton

March Term 1838
(p 268)
State of Tennessee
At a county court begun and held for the County of Cannon at the House
of John Fishers in the Town of Woodbury in the county and state aforesaid on
the first Monday and fifth day of March A.D. 1838, and of the Independence of
the United States the sixty second year present the Worshipfull
John C. Martin Chairm &C
Alexander McKnight
Thomas Hays
Isaac Finley
Blake Sagely
Hugh Reed
Washington Kenedy
Elijah Stephens
Eli A. Fisher

John Melton
Charles C. Evans
Sam'l Lance
William D. Foster
William Bryson and
Francis Cooper Esqrs.
Whereupon the following orders were made to wit.

On motion the court proceeded to the Election of a chairman to preside over there Deliberations until the first Monday in January next, And on counting the votes Given in said Election, It appeared that John C. Martin Esq. had received twelve votes, which being a majority of all of the justices in the county the said John C. Martin was declared to be duly Elected to said office.

James Goodner
Ephriam Garrison
Jonathan Griffith
Wiley Jones and
Moses Fite
commissioners appointed at the last term of this court to lay off and Devide the lands belonging to the Estate of Judith Bennett decd.

(p 260) This day made report of the same in open court of the same in writting and on motion the same is admitted to reccord.

John Melton
George T. Ford
Henry Ford
William D. Evans and
Charles C. Evans
a jury summoned by the sheriff of Cannon County to Lay off and set apart the one third part of the land belonging to the Estate of the late George Stone deceased to the widdow (Susannah Stone) of the said George Stone decd. this day made report of the same in open court in writting And on motion the same is admitted to reccord .

On motion the following justices present to wit
Isaac Finley
John Melton
Charles C. Evans
Alexander McKnight
Thomas Hays
William D. Foster
Eli A. Fisher
Hugh Reed
Washington Kennedy
Elijah Stephens
William and
John C. Martin Esqrs.
twelve in number which being a majority of all the justices in the county voting in the affirmative the following rates were fixed upon for to be paid as a Tax for county purposes indiscriminately for the fiscal year of 1838, to wit.
The one half of the amount of the state Taxes upon all of the priveledges and occupations to authorise which a Licence is required to be collected by the clerk of this court when licencing the ------ And ten cents to the

hundred dollars worth upon all property listed for state Taxation and twenty
five cents (p 270) upon each white listed and subject to Taxation to be
called by the sheriff when collecting the state taxes in the county of Cannon
for the fiscal year of 1838. And on motion It is ordered by the court that
the clerk of this court Calculate and certify the same to the sheriff or
collector of the publick taxes together with the state tax as the laew
directs in such case made and provided.

On motion and upon the application of Thornton Pendergrass he is hereby
constituted and appointed Guardain to Pleasant H. Roberts
                         William Roberts
                         Henry Roberts and
                         John Roberts
Orphan children of ———Roberts deceased , Whereupon the said Thornton Pendergrass together with his security Daniel Duncan (approved by the court) Entered into bond in open court in the sum of one hundred dollars payable to John
C. Martin chairman of the county court of Cannon County for the time being and
his successors in office conditioned as the law dirïcts .

On motion of Joshua Nichols, Robert K. Joy an orphan boy about the age of
nine is Bound by and with the assent of the court to the said Nichols until
he the said Robert K. attains the age of twenty one years. Whereupon the said
Joshua Nichols and John C. Martin Esq. Chrm. of this court entered into Bond
conditi ned as the law directs &C
 (p 271)
Hardy Byford   )
Deed 50   )
Archibald Lewis) The Execution of a deed of conveyance from Hardy Byford
to Archibald Lewis for fifty acres of land lying in Cannon County, bearing date
the 29th day of January 1837, was this day duly proven in open court by the
oaths of William Leigh and William Byford subscribing witnesses thereto . And
on motion ordered by the court that the same be certified for Registration.

Joseph Elledge   )
Deed 101 acres   )
Joseph L. Elledge) The Execution of a deed of conveyance from Joseph Elledge
Sr. to William F. Elledge and Joseph L. Elledge for one hundred and one acres
of land lying in Cannon County bearing date the 9th day of August 1837, was
this day duly proven in open court by the oaths of John Welton and John B.
Parris Jr. subscribing witnesses thereto and on motion ordered by the court
that the same be certified for Registration.

John A. Spurlock)
Deed 300 acres)
Frances Turner) The execution of a deed of conveyance from John A. Spurlock for three hundred acres of land lying in Cannon County bearing date the
3rd day of January 1838 was this day duly proven in open court by the oaths of
Frances Spurlock and Daniel S. Ford subscribing witnesses thereto And on motion
ordered by the court that the same be certified for Registration.

 (p 272)
Frances Turner)
   Deed 40   )
Frances Spurlock) The execution of a deed of conveyance from Frances Turner
to Frances Spurlock for about forty acres of land lying in Cannon County bearing date the 2nd day of January 1838 was this day duly acknowledged in open co
court by the said Frances Turner (the bargainor) to be his act and deed for
the purpose therein contained And on motion ordered by the court that the same

be certified for Registration.

Gabriel Hume)
Power of Atto.)
David Hume   )   The execution of a power of attorney from Gabriel Hume to
David Hume for certain purposes therein stipulated bearing date the — day
of March 1838 was this day duly acknowledged in open court by the said Gabriel
Hume to be his act and deed for the purposes therein Expressed. And upon
motion ordered by the court that the same be certified &c.

William Bryson)
Deed 150 acres)
Stephen Wilson) The execution of a deed of conveyance from William Bryson
to Stephen Wilson for one hundred and fifty acres of land lying in Cannon
County bearing date the 14th day of February 1838 was this day duly proven
in open court by the oaths of R.B. Cooper and Elijah Summar subscribing
witnesses thereto And on motion the same is admitted to be registered.

(p 273) George Grizzle sheriff of Cannon County this day produced in open
court the certificate of an election by him and his deputies held for the
county of Cannon at the several precints in said county on the third day of
March 1838, From which certificate It appeared to the satisfaction of the
court that the following persons had been duly and constitutionally Elected
to the office of constable in their respective districts in said county to
wit

In District No. one ——Charles Porterfield
In District No. two —— James Hollis
In District NO. three ——John Witt
In District NO. four —— Levi Barnett
In District No. five —— James Cherry
In District No. six —— John Brown and William L. Covington
In District No. seven W.D. Allen
In District NO. eight ——James H. Lance
In District No. nine —— Joseph Elledge
In District No. ten —— William A. Hancock
In District No. eleven —— Samuel Corn
And whereas It appearingfurther to the satisfaction of the court upon an
Examination of the constitution of the state, and the acts of assembly in
such case made and provided that the present Term is the proper court for the
above named constables Elect to Enter into bond and security and be qualified
into office as such .
Thereupon the said Charles Porterfield
                Jessie Hollis
                John Witt
                Levi Barnett
                James Cherry
                John Brown
                William L. Covington
                W.D. Allen
                James H. Lance
                Joseph Elledge
                William A. Hancock and
                Sam'l Corn
Constables elect as aforesaid (p 274) came into court together with their
securities severally and entered into bonds severally in the sum of Four
thousand dollars each payable to Newton Cannon Governor in and over the State
of Tennessee for the time being and his successors in office conditioned

severally as the Law directs after which they were severally qualified into office &c.

Higdon R. Jarratt this day came into court and produced in open court a certificate from under the hand of Geroge Grizzle Esq. sheriff of Cannon County. In the following words and Figures, to wit.

I George Grizzle sherriff of Cannon County Do certify that Higdon R. Jarratt was duly and constitutionally Elected sherriff of Cannon County, for the ensuing two years March 5th 1838.——George Grizzle sff. From which certificate It appeared to the satisfaction of the court that the said Higdon R. Jarratt had been duly and constitutionally elected sheriff of Cannon County for the ensuing Term of two years from and after the first Saterday and third day of March 1838. And it appearing also to the further satisfaction of the court from an examination of the constitution of the state, and from the acts of Assembly in such case made and provided that the present term is the property court at which time to take bond and security from the said Jarratt and to qualify him into office. Therefore on motion the Oath of office was administered to him the said Jarratt by the clerk of this court in manner and form as the Lawdirects. After (p 275) which The said Higdon R. Jarratt together with his securities ,
David M. McKnight
Alexander McKnight and
John C?Martin
(who being approved of by the court) Entered into bond in the sum of twelve thousand five hundred dollars - payable to Newton Cannon Governor in and over the state of Tennessee for the Time being and his successors in office which bond is in the following words and Figures to wit -

Know all men by these presents that we,
Higdon R. Jarratt
David McKnight
Alexander McKnight and
John C. Martin
all of the County of Cannon and state of Tennessee are held and firmly bound unto Newton Cannon Governor in and over the state of Tennessee for the time being and his successors in office in the sum of twelve thousand five Hundred ———————— the payment of which well and truly to be made we bind ourselves our heirs Executors Administrators and assigns jointly and severally and firmly by these presents sealed with our seals and dated this 5th day of March 1838.

The condition of the above obligation is such that whereas the above bound Higdon R. Jarratt, has been Elected sheriff of Cannon County, for the term of two years from and after the first Saterday in March 1838. Now if the said Higdon R. Jarrett, shall well and truly Execute, and perform and due returns make upon all process and precepts, to him diricted and shall well and truly collect, and pay over all fees and monies that shallcome into his hands by virtue of his office of sheriff to the office by which the same by the Tenue thereof ought to (p 276) be paid or the person or persons to whom the same shall be due his h r or their agents or attornies And shall well and truly in all other things partaining to his office faithfully Execute the same according to Law, during his continuance therein then this obligation to be void else to be and remain in full force and virture In testimony whereof we have here unto set our hands and seals the day and year first above written.
H.R. Jarratt (seal)
David McKnight (seal)
Alexander McKnight (seal)
J.C. Martin (seal)
          (seal)

Attest. Sam'l J. Garrison, Clerk.

Therebeing no further Buisness the court adjorned til tomorrow morning
12 O'clock.
E. Stephens
Charles C. Evans
John Melton

Tuesday morning March 6th 1838.
The worshipfull Court met pursuant, to adjornment present the Worshipfull
Charles C. Evans
John Melton and
Elijah Stephens Esqqrs.
Whereupon the following order was made to wit.

It is ordered by the court from the absence of John C. Martin chairman of this
court that Elijah Stephens Esq. be called to the chair to preside over the del-
berations of the court for the ballance of the present Term.

(p 277) Isaac W. Elledge this day makes known to the satisfaction of the
court that his father Joseph Elledge late of our county is deceased and
having left no will or Testament. Therefore on the Application of the said
Isaac W. Elledge He is hereby appointed Administrator of the Estate of the
said Joseph Elledge decd. who together with his securities, George Grizzle
and Robert K. Stephens Entered into bond in the sum of four thousand dollars
payable to his Excellency Newton Cannon Governer in and over the state of
Tennessee for the time being and his successors in officeconditioned as the
law deriets . After which the said Isaac W. Elledge was duly qualified as
such. And on motion It is ordered by the court that, letters, of Administration be Granted him upon said Estate.

William Y. Henderson , This day came into open court and produced the certificate of George Grizzle sheriff of Cannon County shewing to the satisfaction
of the court that he the said Henderson had been duly and constitionally
Elected Trustee for the County of Cannon aforesaid for the Term of two years,
next ensuing which certificate is in the following words and figures to wit.

J. George Grizzle sheriff of Cannon County do certify that William Y.
Henderson was duly and constitutionally Elected Trustee for Cannon County
for the ensuing two (p 278) years (dated) March 5th 1838
                              (signed) George Grizzle sff.
Whereupon the said William Y. Henderson together with his securities Entered
into bond in the sum of five thousand dollars payable to John C. Martin chairman of the county court of Cannon County for the time being and his successors
in officeconditioned as the Law dirtcts.

Thomas Elkins This day produced in court a Deputian from H.R. Jarratt sheriff
of Cannon County, shewing to the satisfaction of the court that he was regularly appointed as Deputy sheriff of said county. Thereupon It is ordered by
the court that the clerk of this court qualify the said Elkins as such which
was done accordingly.

Isaac W. Elledge this day produced in Court a deputian from H.R. Jarratt,
sheriff of Cannon County shewing to the satisfaction of the court that he the
said Isaac W. Elledge was regularly appointed as Deputy sheriff of said county
Thereup it was ordered by the court that the clerk of this court qulify the
said Elledge as such whis is accordingly done.

(p 279)
There being no further Buisness the worshipfull --------adjorned til court
in Course.
E. Stephens
Charles C. Evans
John Melton

April Term

State of Tennessee
        At a county court began and held for the County of Cannon at the House
of John Fishers in the Town of Woodbury and County aforesaid on the first
Monday and seconn day of April 1838. And of the Independence of the United
States the sixty second year present The Worshipfull
Thomas Hays
Isaac Finley
Hugh Reed
Moses Shelby
Washington Kenedy
Elijah Stephens
Eli A. Fisher
Charles C. Evans
John Melton
William Bates
William Bryson and
Thomas Cooper Esqre.
Whereupon the following Orders were made towit.

William Wright Administrator of the Estate of Phillip Palmer Deceased this
day returned into court an account current of the sales of the property
belonging to said Estate to which report he was duly qualified in open court.
And on motion the same was admitted to record.

(p 280) Sam'l Derby this day produced in open court a commission from his
Excelency Newton Cannon Esq. Governor of Tennessee Appointing him an acting
justice justice of the peace for the county of Cannon And on motion the oath
of office was duly Administered to him the said Derby after which he took a
seat with the other members of the court and proceeded to the further -----
of the day.

Samuel J. Harrison clerk of this court Give notice to the court that he had
in redinnss a list of the Taxes for the county of Cannon for the year 1838.
And also produced the same in open court. Whereupon Higdon R. Jarratt Sheriff
and collector of the publick Taxes for the County of Cannon came forward in
open court and was duly qualified as such. Who together with his securities
Joseph Ramsey and George Grizzle Entered into two several Bonds to wit. One
payable to Newton Cannon Governor of the state of Tennessee for the time being
and his successors in office in the sum of sixteen hundred and fifty dollars
conditioned for the faithfull collection and payment of the state and school
taxes And one other payable to John C. Martin chairman of the county court of
Cannon County for the time being and his successors in office in the sum of
thirty three hundred dollars conditioned for the faithfull collection and
payment of the County Taxes, Both for the years 1838 & 1839.
Which bonds are in the following words and figours to wit.

(p 281)
State of Tennessee

Cannon County)
         Know all men by these presents that we

Higdon R. Jarratt
Joseph Ramsey and
George Grizzle

All of the state and county aforesaid are held and firmly bound unto Newton
Cannon Governor of the state of Tennessee for the time being and his successors
in office for the use of the said state in the sum of sixteen hundred and
fifty dollars to the payment of which well and truly to be made we bind ourselves our heirs Executors and Administrators jointly and severly firmly by
these presents sealed with our seals and dated the second day of April 1838.

    The condition of the above obligation are these that whereas the above
bound Higdon R. Jarratt has been duly and constitutionally Elected sheriff
and collector of the publick Taxes of said County of Cannon fot two years
from the first Saterday in March 1838. Now if the said Higdon R. Jarratt
shall well and truly Collect all state Taxes and also all Taxes on school
land within said county which by lawhe ought to collect, and well and truly
account for and pay over all Taxes by him collected or which ought to be
collected on the first day of December in the years 1838 and 1839 Respectively then the above obligation to be void otherwise to remain in full force
and virtue.

Attest.   ) H.R. Jarratt (sl)
) Joseph Ramsey (sl)
Sam'l J. Garrison) George Grizzle (sl).
        Clk.)

(p 222)
State of Tennessee)
Cannon County   ) Know all men by the se presents that we
Higdon R. Jarratt
Joseph Ramsey and
George Grizzle

All of the state and county aforesaid are held and firmly bound unto John
C. Martin chairman of the county court of said county for the time being
and his successors in office for the use of said county in the sum of
thirty three hundred dollars to the payment of which well and truly to be
made we bond ourselves our heirs Executors Administrators and assigns jointly and severly firmly by these presents sealed with our seals and dated
this the 2nd day of April 1838.

    The condition of the above obligations are these that whereas the above
bound Higdon R. Jarratt has been duly and constitutionally elected sheriff
and collector of the public Taxes of said county of Cannon for two years from
the first saterday in March 1838. Now if the said Higdon R. Jarratt shall
well and truly collect all County Taxes within said county which by law , he
ought to collect and well and truly account for and pay over all Taxes by
him collected or which ought to be collected, to the county Trustee on the
first day of December in the years of 1838 and 1839 Respectively then the
above obligation to be void otherwise to remain in full force and virtue.
                    Attest.   H.R. Jarratt(seal)
                              Joseph Ramsey (seal)
            Samuel J. Garrison   George Grizzle (seal)

(p 223) William Stone one of the administrators of the estate of Usibous
Stone deceased this day returned into court an account current of the sales
of the property belonging to said Estate and was duly aqualified to the same.
And on motion Ordered by the court that the same be admitted to record.

John Hollinsworth this day makes known to the satisfaction of the court that Sam'l Tittle late of our county is deceased, having left no will or Testament. On motion the said John Hollenswirth is by the request of the widdow of the said deceased and by his own consent appointed Administrator of said Estate Whereupon he came into court and was duly qualified as such who together with his securities Hiram Tittle and Henry Dennis Entered into bond in the sum of two thousand dollars payable to Newton Cannon Governor and his successors in office conditioned for his faithful Administration. Whereupon Letters of Administration were granted. &C.

On motion and upon the application of David T. Warren and by the consent of Charles Beau he the said Charles is by order of the court bond to the said David T. until he attains the age of twenty one years. Whereupon the said David T. Warren together with his securities Henry Warren and John C. Martin Chairman of this court On behalf the court entered into bond as per agreement which is ordered to be filed in the office of the clerk of this court &C.

(p 284) On motion the following justices present to wit.
Charles C. Evans
Sam'l Denby
Hugh Reed
Eli A. Fisher
William Bates
John Melton
Thomas Hays
Isaac Finley
Washington Kenedy
William Bryson
Moses Shelby
Elijah Stephens and
John C. Martin Esqrs.
all voting in the affirmative an allowance is made to Sam'l J. Garrison clerk of this court of the sum of Forty two dollars fifty cents, for Issuing one hundred and fifty two Jury Tickitts to the diferdnt jurors who served at the March July and November Terms of the circuit court 1837 and the March Term of the circuit court 1838 also Recording the revenue commissioners reports of the Taxes for the year 1838. And for furnishing the shiriff and collector of the publick Taxes with a copy of the same And it is further ordered by the court that the county Trustee pay the same out of any monies in his hands not otherwise appropriated.

On Motion the following justices present to wit.
Charles C. Evans
Sam'l Denby
Hugh Reed
E.A. Fisher
William Bakes
John Melton
Thomas Hays
Isaac Stephens and
John C. Martin Esqrs.
All voting in the affirmative an allowance of four dollars is made to Jobe Stephens for the consideration of furnishing his office with Books for the use of the county which the Trustee is ordered to pay out of any monies in his hands not otherwise appropriated &c-

(p 285) On motion the following Justices present to wit.

Eli A. Fisher
Washington Kenedy
Moses Shelby
Thomas Hays
John Melton
Charles C. Evans
Isaac Finley
Sam'l Denby
Hugh Reed
Elijah Stephens
Francis Cooper and
John C. Martin Esqrs.
All voting in the affirmative An allowance of one dollar and fifty cents pr.
day for 1 days services in laying off the county of Cannon into magistrates
districts and in making out a map of the same is allowed Milton Fowler which
the Trustee of Cannon County is ordered to pay out of any monies in his hands
not otherwise Appropriated.

On motion the following Justices present to wit.
Eli A. Fisher
Washington Kenedy
Moses Shelby
Elijah Stephens
Thomas Hays
Sam'l Denby
Charles C. Evans
Isaac Finley
William Bates
John Melton
Francis Cooper
Hugh Reed and
John C. Martin Esqrs.
all voting in the affirmative An allowance of thirty dollars is made to George
Grizale former sheriff of Cannon County for the consideration of his Exoficio
services Ending at the March Term of this court 1838 which the Trustee of
Cannon County is ordered to pay out of any monies in his hands not otherwise
appropriated.

On motion the court proceeded to Elect of their own body three justices
to act as quram judges in holding all the county courts.(p 286) for the county
of Cannon not otherwise provided for until the first Monday in January next
And on counting out the votes poled in said ----
Sam'l Denby
Eli A. Fisher and
Charles C. Evans Esqrs.
were found and declared to be duly Elected.

On motion the court proceeded to appoint the following persons as jurors
to attend and serve at the May Term of the circuit court 1838, to wit
John C. Martin
Alexander McKnight
Thomas H. Windle
George Cannon
James Soap
Silas Cooper
Joseph Simpson
William Ring

Joseph Knox
Hugh Reed
Nicholas Goeding
Baxter D. Pickens
Washington Kenedy
Moses Shelby
Benjamin Pendleton
James Wood
Eli A. Fisher
Joseph Faily
Charles C. Evans
Pleasant Leeary
William Jakes
William Felton
George Grizzle
Peter Daniel
John Hollensworth
Frances Turner
Henry Powell
Joseph Bryson
Warren Davenport and
William Bryson and
James Cherry and
Sam'l Corn Constables to wait upon the court and jury.

On motion it is ordered by the court that John Boyd be released from Double Taxs by the payment of the cost of this Entry.

There being no further buisness the worshipfull court adjorn til tomorrow morning Eleven O'clock.
Samuel Denby
E.A. Fisher
T.L. Turner

(p 287)
Tuesday morning April 3rd 1838.
The Worshipfull court meet pursuant to adjornment present the worshipfull,
Sam'l Denby
Eli A. Fisher and
Thomas L. Turner Esqrs.
Whereupon the following orders were made to wit.

From the absence of John C. Martin chairman of this court, And it appearing to the satisfaction of the court that his seat would be vacant the ballance of the term. On motion Sam'l Denby Esqr. is appointed chairman protem to serve the ballance of the Term.

On motion and upon the application of William Y. Henderson the clerk of this court is permitted to Administer the oath of office to him the said Henderson as Trustee for the county of Cannon the same having been omitted at the last Term of this court at which time he Executed his bond as required by Law.

On motion it is ordered by the court that
Archibald Hicks
Asa Smith and
William Wood

be and they are hereby appointed to Lay off and set apart one years provisions
out of the Estate of Joseph Elledge decd. to the widdow of said deceased,
and make report of the same to the next Term of this court under oath in
writing.
Court then adjorned til court in course.
Samuel Denby
E.A. Fisher
T.L. Turner

May Term 1838
(p 288)
State of Tennessee
        At a county court began and held for the County of Cannon at the House
of John Fishers in the Town of Woodbury, on the first Monday and seventh day
of May 1838 present the Worshipfull
Sam'l Denby
Charles C. Evans and
Eli A. Fisher Esqrs.

Qurum justices
Whereupon the following orders were made to wit.

Vincent Gather Administrator of the Estate of Thomas Stroud decd. this day
returned into ---- an account current of the sales of the perishable property
Belonging to said Estate and was duly qualified to the same And on motion the
same is admitted to reccord.
Lazerous Holeman   )
Deed loo acres   )
Richard L. McKnight)   The execution of a deed of conveyance from Lazerous
Holeman to Richard L. McKnight for one hundred acres of land lying in Cannon
County bearing date the 2nd day of September 1837 was this day duly proven
in open court by the oaths of E.R. Jarratt and Alexander McKnight subscribing
witnesses thereto which is ordered to be certified for Registration.

Henry Sauls)
Deed of Trust)
Jacob Wright)   The execution of a deed of Trust from Henry Sauls to Jacob
Wright upon one grey stud horse , one wagon, two yoke of oxen, one sorrel mare
and yearling (p289) colt, four cows and calves, forty Head of sheep, forty
head of hogs and twenty six bee stands, bearing date the 6th day of April
1838 was this day duly acknowledged in open court by the said Henry Sauls
the (bargainor) which is ordered to be certified for Registration.

John Tucker   )
Deed 30 acres)
John Pendleton)   The Execution of a deed of conveyance from John Tucker to
John Pendleton for thirty acres of land Lying in Cannon County bearing date
the 21st day of June 1836, was this day duly acknowledged in open court by
the said John Tucker (the bargainor) to be his act and deed for the purposes
therein contained which is ordered to be certified for Registration.

        On motion and upon the application of Francis Bryson she is constituted
and appointed as Guardain to her daughter Locky Bryson a minor , Whereupon
the said Francis Bryson together with her securities Francis Cooper and
James Thomas (approved by the court) entered into bond in open court in the
sum of Four Hundred dollars conditioned and payable as the law directs.

A paper writing purporting to be the last will and Testament of John Higgins deod. was this day produced in open court for probate and was proven in part by Nelson Owen one of the suscribing witnesses thereto, And upon the afdavit of John McMin and James Higgins who being also sworn depose and say (p 290) that they were present when said Will was signed by the Testator and that they heard him acknowledge the same to be his last will and Testament and It appearing to the satisfaction of the court that the said paper writing is in fact the last will and Testament of the said John Higginsdeod. It is therefore admitted to record And on motion It is ordered by the court that George Boyle and John McMin be qalified as Executors of said will which being done the said Boyle and McMin Entered into Pond in the sum of Eight thousand dollars together with their securities Joseph H. Boyle and Hiram T. Tittle conditioned and payable as the law directs, Whereupon letters Testamentory were Granted them upon said Estate.

Elijah Higgins)
Deed 50 acres)
John Higgins) The execution of a deed of conveyance from Elijah Higgins to John Higgins for fifty acres of land Lying in Cannon County bearing date the 23rd day of May was this day duly proven in open courts by the oaths of Hiram Tittle and James Milligan subscribing witnesses thereto And on motion It is ordered by the court that the same be certified for Registration.

(p 291)
Elijah Armstrong)
Deed 25 acres)
John Higgins) The execution of a deed of conveyance from Elijah Armstrong to John Higgins for twenty five acres of land lying in Cannon County bearing date the 18th day of October 1830 was this day proven in part by the oath of James Milligan one of the suscribing witnesses thereto the other witness not appearing to qualify.

William Patterson Administrator of the Estate of Judith Bennitt deceased this day returned into court an account current of the sales of the perishable property belonging to said Estate and was duly qualified to the same And on motion the same is admitted to reccord.

On motion It is ordered by the court that
Larkin Keaton
Francis Turner and
Benjamin Hale
be and they are Hereby appointed as commissioners to lay off and set apart one years provisions out of the estate of Sam'l Tittle deod. to Susan Tittle widdow of said deceased And make report to the next Term of this court under oath.

Higdon R. Jarratt sheriff of Cannon County this day produced in open court commissions from his Excelency the Governor to,
David Patton
Danill S. Ford and
Alfred L. Hancock
as justices of the peace for Cannon County who being present came forward and were duly qualified as such.

(p 292) Silas Cooper Administrator of the Estate of John Cooper deceased this day returned into court a report of Blank amount of proceeds arising from said Estate And was duly qualified to the same And on motion the same is admitted to record.

James Taylor and Daniel Tenpenny two of the commissioners appointed at a previous Term of this court to lay off one years provisions out of the Estate of Robert George decd. to the widdow of said decd. this day made report of the same And on motion the same is admitted to reccord.

Benjamin B. Cooper)
Deed 50 acres   )
Cosby Marshall &Co)   The execution for a deed of conveyance from Benjamin B. Cooper to Cosby Marshall &Co for fifty acres of land lying in Cannon County bearing date the 7th day of April 1838, was this day duly acknowledged in open court by the said Benj. B. Cooper (the bargainor) to be his act and deed for the purposes therein contained which is ordered to be certified for Registration.

        Therbeing no further Buisness court adjorned till court in course.
Samuel Denby
Charles C. Evans
E.A. Fisher

(p 293)
State of Tennessee
        At a county court begain And held for the county of Cannon at the House of John Fishers in the Town of Woodbury in the county aforesaid on the first Monday and 4th day of June in the year of our Lord 1838. And of the American Independence the 62nd year, present the worshipful
Sam'l Denby
Charles C. Evans and
Eli A. Fisher Esqrs.   Quoram justices &C.
Whereupon the following orders were made to wit.

Anthony Tittle &)
Nancy Tittle   )
Bill of sale   )
Joseph H. Boyle)   The execution of a Bill of sale from Anthony Tittle & Nancy Tittle to Joseph H. Boyle for a negro girl named Mariah aged about nineteen years, Bearing date the 29th day of May 1838, was this day duly proven in open court as to the said Anthony Tittle by the oaths of George Boyle and Francis Cooper subscribing witnesses thereto And on motion It is ordered by the court that the same be certified for Registration.

George Boyle (may be no Bogle) one of the Executors of the Estate of John Higgins decd. this day made report of the account of sales of the real and personal property belonging to said Estate and was duly qualified to the same in open court And on motion It is ordered by the court that the same be Admitted to record.

(p 294) May term 1838 June Term 1838
Francis Turner
Benjamin Hale and
Larkin Keeton
commissioners appointed at the last Term of this court to Lay off and set apart one years provisions out of the Estate of Sam'l Tittle decd. to the widdow of said decd. this day made report of the Trust reposed in them which having been examined by the court is in all things confirmed therein And on motion the same is admitted to record.

Valentine Simpson)
   Deed 10 acres)
David McGill   )   The execution of a deed of conveyance from Valentine Simpson to David McGill for ten acres of land lying in Cannon County bearing date the 21st day of May 1838, was this day duly acknowledged in open court by the said Valentine Simpson the bargainor, to be his act and deed for the purposes therein contained And on motion the same was admitted to be certified for Registration.

John Wright   )
   Deed 128 acres)
Sam'l C. Bryant)   The execution of a deed of conveyance from John Wright to Sam'l C. Bryant for one hundred and twenty eight acres of land lying in Cannon Caounty bearing date the 8th day of March 1836 was this day proven in part by the oath of J.B. Robinson one of the suscribing witnesses thereto which is ordered to be certified for Registration.

(p 295)
Solomon Brents)
   Deed 37 1/8)
Gabriel Hume   )   The execution of a deed of conveyance from Solomon Brents to Gabriel Hume for thirty seven & 1/8 acres of land lying in Cannon County date the 1st day of June 1838 was this day duly acknowledged in open court by the said Solomon Brents (the bargainor) to be his act and deed for the purposes therein contained And on motion It is ordered by the court that the same be certified for Registration.

Solomon Brents)
Deed 3 acres)
Gabriel Hume)   The execution of a deed of conveyance from Solomon Brents to Gabriel Hume for three acres of land lying in Cannon County bearing date the 1st day of June 1838, was this day duly acknowledged in open court by the said Solomon Brents (the bargainor) to be his act and deed for the purposes therein contained And on motion ordered by the court that the same be certified for Registration &C.

Isaac W. Elledge Administrator of the Estate of Joseph Elledge decd. this day made report of the sales of the personal property belonging to said Estate and was duly qualified to the same and on motion the same is admitted to record

Court adjorned til court in course.
Samuel Denby
E.A. Fisher
Charles C. Evans

(p 296)   July Term 1838

State of Tennessee
     At a county court began and held for the county of Cannon at the House of John Fishers in the Town of Woodbury on the first Monday and Second day of July A.D. 1838. And of the Independance of the United States the Sixty second year present the Worshipful
John C. Martin
Alexander McKnight
Isaac Finley
Thomas Hays
David Patton
Hugh Reed

Washington Keneday
Moses Shelby
Elijah Stephens
Eli A. Fisher
Charles C. Evans
John Melton
William Bates
Samuel Lance
Samuel Denby
Daniel S. Ford
Alfred L. Hancock
William Bryson and
Francis Cooper Esqrs.

Whereupon the following orders were made to wit.

On motion of Archibald Stone leave is granted him and John M. Stone and John Brown (a majority of the commissioners appointed by this court at the May Term thereof 1836 to Lay off and sell the lots in the Town of Woodbury and for other purposes) to make a Report in which they state among other things that they have received the jail and courthouse from the contractors for the building of the same. The terms and condition upon which the same were reced. being stated at full lenght in said Report. And the same being read in open court and by the court fully understood, was in all things confirmed by the court, And ordered to be filed in (p 297) in the office of the clerk of this court the said report bearing date the 2nd day of July 1838. Whereupon the said Archibald Stone on behalf of the commissioners aforesaid came forward in open court and Delivered all the Keys belonging to Both of the said Houses and delivered to the Chairman of this court. Whereupon motion the Court Then adjorned to the court House in the Town of Woodbury in the aforesaid county of Cannon pursuant to the section of an act of the General Assemblyof the state of Tennessee passed at Nashville on the 31st Jany 1836.
Entitled as act to Establish a new county by the name of Cannon &C.

On motion the following justices present to wit
Alexander McKnight
David Patton
Daniel S. Ford
Alfred L. Hancock
John Melton
Washington Kenedy
Samuel Denby
Eli A. Fisher
Thomas Hays
Moses Shelby
Hugh Reed
Charles C. Evans
Francis Cooper and
John C. Martin Esqrs.
being fourteen in number all voting in the affirmative an allowance is made to Samuel J. Garrison, clerk of this court for Exofficia servises for the Term of one year that is to say from the May Term of this court 1837 up to the adjornment of the April Term of this court 1838. And on motion It is ordered by the court that the Trustee of Cannon County pay the same out of any monies in his hands not otherwise appriated.

(p 298) On motion the court prodeeded --- appoint by Ballad a Ranger for the

County of Cannon. Whereupon Elijah Stephens and John Esteswere declared as canidates for the office aforesaid, and on counting the votes taken on the first Balloting JohnnEstus was declared to be duly Elected to said office of Ranger he having Received fifteen votes and the said Elijah Stephens only three votes.

Whereupon the said John Estes came into court and was duly sworn as such together with his securities Francis Cooper and Thomas Elkins (being approved by the court) Entered into Bond in the sum of Five Hundred dollars payable to John C. Martin Chairman of the county clourt of Cannon County and his successors in office conditioned as the law directs. &C.

On motion the court next proceeded to appoint by Ballad a Coroner for the County of Cannon Thereupon Alexander McKnight Declared himselfas a canidate for the office aforesaid. And there being no one else in nomination on counting the votes taken on the Balloting the said McKnight was declared to be duly Elected to said office of Coroner , Whereupon the said McKnight in open court was duly sworn as such who together with his securities William M. Knoxiahd Alexander McKnight Jr. Entered into bons in the sum of twenty five Hundred Dollars pay and conditioned as the Law directs.

(p 299) It is ordered by the court upon the application of Joseph H. Smith that an orphan boy about the age of nine years by the hame of Arthur H. Burket Be bound to him the said Joseph H. Smith as an apprentice til he attains the age of twenty oneyears - to learn the art and mistery of farming, Whereupon the chairman of this court and the said Joseph H. Smith with his securities Joseph Knox Entered into an Indenture containing such stipulations as were agreed upon by the court &C.

It is ordered by the court upon the application of Joseph F. Brown that an orphan Boy by the name of George E. Burket about the age of thirteen years be bound to him the said Joseph F. Brown as an apprentice to Learn the art and mistery of Farming until he attains the age of twenty one years. Whereupon the Chairman by the direction and with the assent of the court together the said Joseph F. Brown and his security David Coughanour Entered into an Indenture containing such stipulations as were agreed upon by the court.

It is ordered by the court that
Sam'l Denby
Eli A. Fisher and
Charles C. Evans
be appointed a committee with full power and authority to meet the commissioners appointed to lay off the Town of Woodbury into lots, sell the same and for other purposes at the court House in said Town of Woodbury at such time as may suit their convenience . And then and there to Examine into and ascertain (p 300) the number of days that each of said commissioners have been necesaryly imployed as such and report the same to any subsequent Term of this court &C.

On motion the following justices present to wit,
Alexander McKnight
Thomas Hays
Isaac Finley
Daniel S. Ford
Sam'l Denby
John C. Martin
Alfred L. Hancock

Moses Shelby
Charles C. Evans
David Patton
John Melton
William Bates and
Washington Kenedy
being thirteen in number all voting in the affirmative an allowance of Ten
Dollars each is made for the Benifit of Catherine Clem and Nancy Clem (paupers)
to be paid by the county Trustee out of any monies in his hands not other-
wise appropriated to such person or persons as may be legally appointed Guard-
ains to the said Nancy and Catherine for the purposes aforesaid.

It is ordered by the court upon the application of David that he is
appointed Guardian to Catherine Clem and Nancy Clem (paupers) Whereupon the
said David Patton together with his security Alexander McKnight Entered
into Bond in the sum of Fifty dollars payble to John C. Martin chairman of
the court of Cannon County and his successors in office conditioned for
the faithful performance of his said Guardainship.

(p 301) On motion the following justices present to wit.
Elijah Stephens
William Bates
Alexander Mcknight
Daniel S. Ford
Washington Kenedy
E.A. Fisher
Thomas Hays
Sam'l Denby
Moses Shelby
William Bryson
Isaac Finley
Hugh Reed and
Charles C. Evans Esqrs.
voting in the affirmative and
Alfred L. Hancock
John Melton
John C. Martin and
David Patton Esqrs.
voting in the negative.
Whereupon It appeared to the satisfaction of the court that twelve justices
had voted in the affirmative therefore an allowance of the sum of thirty six
dollars is made for the Benefit of Thomas Tucker to be paid by the Trustee
for the County of Cannon out of any monies in his hands not otherwise appropri-
ated to such person as may be appointed Guardain for the purposes aforesaid &C

On motion of Green B. Sapp And with the assent of the court he is permitted to enter as Guardain to Thomas Tucker (pauper) who together with his security William Bates entered into bond in open court in the sum of one Hundred
dollars payable to John C. Martin Chairman of the county court and his successors in office conditioned as the law directs. &C.

John Hollensworth Administrator of the Estate of Sam'l Tittle decd. this day
returned into court an account current of the sales of the perishable property
belonging to the Estate of the said decd. together with money and noted on
hand and was duly qualified to the same which is admitted to record.

(p 302) It is ordered by the court that Hereafter the plan of holding the
precinct Elections in the tenth cival district in Cannon County shall be

held at the school House at the forks of the creek near Robert Tittles insted of the House of Alfred L. Hancock as heretofore.

It is ordered by the court,
Joseph Ramsey
Eli A. Fisher and
Thomas C. Ward
be and they are hereby appointed a committeewith full power and authority to Contract upon the faith of the county court on behalf of the county of Cannon with such person or persons as they may think proper upon the best Terms possible to cover the section of the Cupilo of the court House in Woodbury with lead or tin and when the same shall be done present their claims to the county court for allowance.

On motion the following persons are appointed as jurors to serve at the next Term of the circuit 1858 to wit.
Drewry Matthews
John Vance
John Andrews
John Hays
Isaac Finley
John P. Gannon
Thomas Simpson
B.L. McFerrin
Luke Lassetter
William Leigh
William Holt
Zackeriah Push
Jacob Spangler
David D. Hipp
Samuel Vance
Gabriel Williams
Benjamin C. Stephens
James Melton Jr.
Joseph Baily
Joseph Moore
Andrew L. Wood
James W. Burger
Thomas Nookes
Joseph Hale
Francis Spurlock
John W. Summar
L.B. Moore and Armsted Francis

(p 303) On motion the following justices present to wit,
Alford L. Hancock
Daniel S. Ford
Thomas Hayes
Alexander McKnight
Eli A. Fisher
William Bryson
John C. Martin
John Melton
Washington Kenedy
David Patton
Moses Shelby

Moses Shelby
William Pates and
Samuel Lance Esqrs.
being thirteen in number present all voting in the affirmative an allowance
is made to each of the revenue commissioners appointed by the court to take
a list of taxable property and polls for the year 1838 in Cannon County; the
sum of Three dollars each, and is ordered by the court that the county Trustee
pay the same out of any moneys in his hands not otherwise appropriated & it
is further ordered that the clerk of this court certify a copy of this order
to each of said Commissioners respectively &c.

Court Adjorned til tomorrow 12 O'clock.
E.A. Fisher
William Bryson
Isaac Finley
Thomas Hayes

Tuseday July the 3rd 1838
Court met pursuant to adjornment present the worshipfull
Thomas Hays
Isaac Finley
Sam'l Lance
E.A. Fisher and
Williams Bryson Esqrs.
Whereupon on motion E.A. Fisher Esq. was called to the chair to preside over
their deliberations for the time being.

There being no further Buisness   (p304)   the court --------til   court in
course.

E.A. Fisher
Thomas Hays
Isaac Finley
William Bryson

State of Tennessee
        At a county court began and held for the county of Cannon at the Court
House for said County in the Town of Woodbury on the first Monday and fourth
day of August A.D. 1838 And of the Independance of the United State the
Sixty third year present the Worshipfull
Samuel D enby
Charles C. Evans and
Eli A. Fisher Esqrs.
Quoram Justices &C .

When the following orders was made to wit.

Silas Cooper, Administrator of the Estate of John Cooper Deceased this day
Returned into court An account of sales of the personal property belonging
to said Estate and was dulyqualified to the same And on Motion ordered by the
Court that the same be admitted to record.

(p 305) William Williams)
Deed 473 acres   )
        Jacob Spangler)   The execution of a deed of conveyance from William
Williams to Jacob Spangler for four hundred seventy three acres of land lying
in Cannon County bearing date the 7th day of April 1838 was this day duly p
proven in open court by the oaths of James Cherry and George Upley subscribing

witnesses thereto and on motion ordered by the court that the same be certified for Registration.

There being no further Buisness court then adjorned till tomorrow morning 9 O'clock.
Samuel Denby
E.A. Fisher
Charles C. Evans

Tuseday morning August 7th A.D. 1838 present the Worshipful;
Samuel Denby
Charles C. Evans and
Eli A. Fisher Esqrs. Quoram Justices.

And there appearing no further Buisness court then adjorned till court in course.
Samuel Denby
Charles C. Evans
E.A. Fisher

(p 306)
State of Tennessee
At a county court began and held for the county of Cannon in said State at the court House in the Town of Woodbury on the first Monday and third day of September in the year of our Lord one thousand eight hundred and thirty eight and of the Independance of the United States the sixty third year present the worshipful
Charles C. Evans and
Sam'l Denby Esqrs.
Also David Patton Esqrs. who appears in place of Eli A. Fisher Esq. By request of the court, And by the authority of the Acts of Assembly in such case made and provided. Whereupon the following orders were made to wit.

Isaac W. Elledge one of the deputie sheriffs of Cannon County this day returned in open court a certificate of election by him held at the House of John Witks in third cival district in said county on the 1st Inst. to elect a constable in said district from which certificate it appeared to the satisfaction of the court that Joseph F. Brown was duly and constitutionally elected to said office whereupon the said Joseph F. Brown came into court. And together with his securities David McGill and David Coughanour entered into Bond in the sum of four thousand Dollars conditioned and payable as the Law diricts After which ----------- was duly sworn into office as such.

(p 308) (numbered wrong in the original)
David McGill this day makes known to the satisfaction of the court that (his father , James McGill late of our county has deceased, And that having left no will or Testament makes application to the court to be appointed himself jointly with David Patton as Administrators of said Estate which being granted by the court, the said David McGill and David Patton together with their security Joseph C. McGeal entered into bond in the sum of one thousand dollars conditioned and payable as the law dircts after which they were duly qualified as such in open court. And it is further ordered by the court that Letters of Administration be given them upon said said Estate. Which are in the words and Figuers following.
In the name of the state of Tennessee, Cannon County. It being Justices of Cannon County. It being certified to us that James McGill late of said county is deceased and has made no will or Testament, On motion It is order-

ed by the court, David McGill and David Patton have letters of Administration
on the Estate of the said deceased.

These are therefore to authorise and Empower you the said Administrators
to enter into and upon all singular the Goods and chattle rights and credits
of the said deceased, And then into your possession take and an Inventory thereof to render to the court within ninety days from the date hereof and all the
Interest debt of the said decd. to pay so fare as the Estate of the said deceased may extend or amount to and the residue Thereof to deliver (p309)
up to those who have a right to by Law to receive the same . Witness Sam'l J.
Garrison clerk of our said court at office the 1st Monday in September 1838.
Sam'l J. Garrison Clk.

Joseph Ramsey one of the securities of William Moore Guardain of Jacob Moore
This day returned into court a paper writing purporting to be a copy of a
notice to the said William Moore Guardain as aforesaid by him the said Ramsey
Given to him the said Moore to appear at the present Term of this court and Give
other counter security on his said Guardainship And that he the said Ramsey
might be released from further Liability as such, &C. And the said William
Moore being solemly called to come into court and comply with the Requisitions
of said notice came not, But made Default. It is therefore ordered by the court
that a summons Issue to compell the said William Moore to appear at the next
term of this court and Give other Good and sufficient security in place of the
said Joseph Ramsey upon his said Guardainship or otherwise the court will dispose of the said Estate as the Law in such case diricts &C.

Pursuant to the acts of assembly in such case made and provided Sam'l J.
Garrison Clerk of this court presented Before the (p 310) court for confirm-
ation or rejection a settlement by him made with Henry Heart Guardain of
Elizabeth Jane Kelly
William Jasper Kelly and
John R. Kelly
minor heirs of John R. Kelly decd. for the year ending the 2nd Jany. 1838.
Also a settlement made with Harmon James Administrator of the estate of Daniel
James decd. together with the said Administrators of fully (adnterd) Also
a settlement with Joseph Bryson Guardain of John Bryson minor heir of William
Bryson decd. for the year ending the 6th day of March 1838. Also a settlement
with William Moore Guardain of Jacob Moore minor heir of Jessie G. Moore decd
from the 4th day of July 1836 up to the 4th July 1837. Also another settlement
with the same as Guardain of the same from the 4th day of July 1837 up to the
4th day of July 1838. Also a settlement with William Moore Guardain of
Elizabeth Jane Moore decd. and heir at Law of Jessie G. Moore decd. fromthe 4th
day of July 1836 up to the 4th day of July 1837. Also another settlement with
the same as Guardain for the same from the 4th day of July 1837 up to the
4th day July 1838. All of which being red in the presence and fully understood by the court And there appearing no objections to the same from any person interested in the same They were severally in all things confirmed by the
court and ordered to be recorded as the ——dirícts. There being no further
Buisness court adjorned till court in course.
(p 311)
Samuel Denby
Charles C. Evans
David Patton

October Term 1838

State of Tennessee

At a county court began and held for the County of Cannon and state aforesaid
at the court House in the Town of Woodbury on the first Monday and first day
of October in the year of our Lord one thousand Eight Hundred and thirty eight
& od the Independance of the United States the sixty third year present the
Worshipfull
John C. Martin
Sam'l Denby
Elijah Stephens
Eli A. Fisher
Sam'l Lance
David Patton
Francis Cooper
William B. Foster
Daniel S. Ford
John Melton
Isaac Finley
Thomas Hays
William Bryson
Charles C. Evans
William Bates
Washington Kenedy

        Then was the following orders made to wit.

        On motion the following justices present to wit
Francis Cooper
Davied Patton
Daniel S. Ford
William B. Foster
Elijah Stephens
Sam'l Denby
John Melton
Sam'l Lance
William Bryson
Thomas Hays
Isaac Finley
Washington Kenedy and
John C. Martin Esqrs.
Being thirteen in number all voting in the affirmative . An allowance of the
sum of Eighteen dollars and fifty cents (p312) is madeto John Fisher for the
consideration of Furnishing a House for to hold the county court in from Oct-
ober Term thereof in 1837 to the July Term of the said court 1838 inclusive
and also for furnishing a House for the accomodation of the circuit court at
the November Term thereof in 1837 which the Trustee of Cannon County is hereby
ordered to pay out of any monies in his hands not otherwise appropriated.

        On motion the following justices present to wit
Francis Cooper
David Patton
Eli A. Fisher
Daniel S. Ford
William B. Foster
Elijah Stephens
Sam'l Denby
John Melton
Sam'l Lance
William Bryson
Thomas Hays

Charles C. Evans
William Bates
Washington Kenedy
Isaac Finley and
John C. Martin Esqrs.
Sixteen in number all voting in the affirmative. An allowance of the sum of
six Dollars and fifty cents for a book furnished for the use of his office,
which the Trustee of Cannon County is hereby ordered to pay out of any monies
in his hand not otherwise appropriated .

On motion the following justices present to wit.
David Patton
Eli A. Fisher
Daniel S. Ford
William B. Foster
Sam'l Denby
John Melton
Isaac Finley
Thomas Hays
Washington Kenedy
William Bates
Charles C. Evans and
John C. Martin Esqrs.
twelve in number voting in the affirmative and Elijah Stephens and Sam'l Lance
Esq. voting in the negative. An allowance of fifteen dollars is made to
Clement R. Davis for the consideration of Furnishing a House for the accomadation
of the circuit court at the March and July Terms 1837 which the Trustee
of (p 313) cannon County is ordered to pay out of any monies in his hands
not otherwise appropriated.

On motion the following justices present to wit.
Eli A. Fisher
William W. Foster
Elijah Stephens
Sam'l Denby
John Melton
Sam'l Lance
William Bryson
Thomas Hays
Washington Kenedy
Isaac Finley
William Bates and
John C. Martin Esqrs.
twelve in number all voting in the affirmative and
Francis Cooper
David Patton
Daniel S. Ford and
Charles C. Evans
four in number voting in the negative. An allowance of thirty five dollars
is made to Henry Trott for the consideration of Furnishing the clerks of the
different courts and the Register of the county with an office from the first
of June 1836 to sometime in the spring of 1837 which the Trustee of Cannon
County is ordered to pay out of any monies in his hands not otherwise appro-
priated .
Joseph Ramsey
Thomas E. Wood and

Eli A. Fisher
a committee appointed at the July Term of this court 1838 to contract for the
covering with tin the diferent Sixon of the copola of the court House in
the Town of Woodbury made report this day before the court that they had com-
pleted the same And that the same amounted to the sum of sixty four dollars
and twenty cents And ast for an appropriation covering the same. It is there-
fore ordered by the court. The follwoing Justices present to wit.
David Patton
Eli A. Fisher
Daniel S. Ford
W.B. Foster
Elijah Stephens
Sam'l Denby
John Melton
Samuel Lance
Isaac Finley
Thomas Hays
Washington Kenedy
Charles C. Evans
William Bates
Francis Cooper
William Bryson and
John C. Martin Esqrs.
Sixteen in number all voting in the affirmative. An allowance is made to the sa
said Joseph Ramsey, Thomas C. Ward and Eli A. Fisher.
For the consideration aforesaid And it is further ordered by the court that the
County Trustee of Cannon County pay the same out of any monies in his hands
not otherwise appropriated.

Jacob Wright)
  Deed 85   )
Levin Jones)   The execution of a deed of conveyance from Jacob Wright to
Levin Jones for Eighty five acres of Land lying in CannonnCounty bearing date
the 17th day of February 1837 was this day duly acknowledged in open court
by the said Jacob Wright(the bargainor) to be his act and deed for the purposes therein contained And on motion It is ordered by the court that the
same be certified for Registration.

Brinkley Lasseter This day filedoothis petition in open court praying for the
priviledge Granted by an act of Assembly passed at Nashville on the 4th
day of January 1838. Entitled and act to authorize the county courts in
this state to Grant the privilidge of Hawking and pedling without Licence
And the said Brinkley Lasseter having taked the oath In open court as required
by said act And It appearing to the satisfaction of the court that the said
Laseter is unable to make a support by manual Labour and that his means
were otherwise insufficient. It is therefore considered that (p 315) the
said Brinkley Lasseter be permitted to vend Goods , wares merchandize &c
in Cannon County as contemplated by said Act of Assembly.

Higdon R. Jarratt This day made known to the satisfaction of the court that
Drewry Matthews late of our county is deceased and having left no will or Testament . And that said Jarratt also produced in open court a certificate from
the widdow of the said decd. Shewing to the satisfaction of the court that
she had made choice of the said Jarratt to Administer upon the estate of the
said decd. And thereby relinquishing her right to do. It is therefore order-

ed by the court that the said Higdon R. Jarratt be and he is hereby appointed Administrator of the Estate of the said Deceased, who appeared in open court and was duly qualified And entered into bond together with his securities Bennit Rucker and John C. Martin in the sum of Ten thousand ------- conditioned and payable as the law directs. Thereupon Letters of Administration were Granted him upon said estate which are in the following words & Figures to wit In the name of the State of Tennessee Cannon County. By the justices of Cannon County It being certified to us Drewry Matthews late of said county is deceased and has made no will or Testament. On motion it is ordered by the court that Higdon R. Jarratt have letters of Administration on the estate of the said deceased . These are therefore to authorise and empower you the said Administrator to enter into and upon all and singular the goods and chattels rights and credits of the said deceased and then into your possesion take and an Inventory thereof to render to the court within ninty days from the date thereof (p 316) and all the interest debt of the said deceased to pay so far as the estate of the said deceased may amount or extend to And the residue thereof to deliver up to those who have a right to by law to receive the same Witness, Sam'l J. Garrison clerk of our said court at office the 1st Monday in October 1838.

Test. Sam'l J. Garrison clk.

On motion and upon the application of Elizabeth Soape, widdow of the late James Soape deceased she is constituted and appointed Administratrix together with Charles P. Alexander Administrator of the estate of the said James Soape decd. And was duly qualified in open court as such who together with their securities Arther Warren Sr. and Isaac Finley intered into bond in the sum of twenty five hundred dollars conditioned and payable as the Law diricts Thereupon Letters of Administration were granted them upon said estate, in the Following words and Figuers to wit.
In the name of the state of Tennessee, Cannon County

By the justices of Cannon County. It being certified tous that James Soape late of said county is deceased and has left or Testament. On motion It is ordered by the court that Elizabeth Soape and Charles P. Alexandria have letters of Administration on the estate of the said deceased . These are therefore to authorise and empower you the said Administrator to enter into and upon all and singular the Goods and chattles rights and credits of the said deceased to pay so fare as the estate of the said deceased may amount or extend to And the residue thereof to deliver up to those who have a right to by (p 317) Law to receive the same.
Witness Sam'l J. Garrison clerk of our said court at office this first Monday in October 1838

Sam'l J. Garrison

On Motion It is orderd by the court that James Taylor, John Finley and Joseph Warren
be and they are hereby appointed as commissioners to Lay off and set apart one years provisions and of the satete of James Soape decd. to the widdow of the said deceased. And make report to the next Term of this court.

Jesse Hollis one of the constables of Cannon County and 2nd district thereof this day returned into court his resignation as such It ------therefore ordered by the court that the sheriff of Cannon County proceed as the Law directs to open and hold an election to fill said vacancy,-------

William Bryson one of the justices of the peace for Cannon County this day Tendered his resignation as such to the court which was accepted. And ordered by the court that the sheriff of Cannon County proceed to hold an election as the Law directs to fill said vacancy.

Sam'l J. Garrison clerk of this court presented to the court a statement of settlement made by himself with John David Guardain of Elijah Duncan from the 3rd day of October 1836 to the 3rd day of October 1837. Also a statement of settlement with William Bates Guardain of Barkerly Couch (pauper) from the 3rd day of April 1837, to the 3rd day of April 1838. Also a (p 313) settlement with William Bates Guardain of Polly Spicer (pauper) from the 3rd day of April 1837, up to the 3rd day of April 1838. All of which reports being read in the presence of and by the court fully understood and there being no person to object to the same they were in all things severally confirmed and ordered to be spread upon record.

John C. Martin chairman of the court this day by the direction of the court and on their behalf Bond William J. Hall and John W. Hall, orphans to Thomas Young with him to live and work as apprentices to learn the art and mistery of the Taning and Curying Buisness until they attain the age of twenty one years each. Whereupon the said John C. Martin and the said Thomas R. Young entered into an Indenture with sundry conditions therein Expre ssed.

Charles C. Evans
Eli A. Fisher
Sam'l Denby
a committee appointed at the July Term of this court 1838 (to meet the commissioners appointed to Lay off and sell out the lots in the Town of Woodbury & for other purposes) at the court House in the Town of Woodbury at such time at might suit their convenience to ascertain the number of days that each of them were in servis as such this day made report of the result of their investigation in writing which was read in the presence of and by the court fully understood and ordered on file.

(p 319) Joseph Ramsey one of the securitys of William Moore Guardain of Jacob Moore minor heir of Jessie G. Moore decd. This day moved the court to be released from any further-Liability upon said securityship with the said William Moore Guardain as aforesaid And It appearing to the satisfaction of the court that the said Joseph Ramsey had given to the said William Moore a legal notice to appear at the last Term of this court and Give other counter security might be released from any further Liability upon said securityship And the said William failing at the said last Term of this court to appear and comply with the requisitions of said notice, Thereupon the court ordered that a subpeona Issue at the said last Term to compell the said William to appear at this Term of the court and Give other counter security upon said Guardainship in order that the said Ramsey might be released from the same. And It appearing further that a subpeona did Issue from the said last term of this court pursuant to the said order and that the same had been returned Executed by the sheriff of Cannon County. And the said William Moore having as yet holey failed to come forward and comply with the requisitions of said notice or subpeona It is therefore considered by the court that the said Joseph Ramsey be and he is hereby released from all and every future responsibility as security with the said William Moore Guardain as aforesaid, for the said Jacob Moore And that the said William Be allowed the further time of till the second day of the Term to procuré other Good and sufficient counter security upon his said Guardainship or upon failure so to do, His said Guardainship is hereby declared to be forfeited.

(p320) On motion It is ordered by the court, that the sheriff of Cannon County Summons the following persons to serve as jurors to sefve at the January Term of Circuit ——1839 to wit.
Joel Maxey
Levi Parker

Andrew Alexander
Thomas Hays
Henry Dosheur
Henry Hays
Silas A. Robinson, Joseph Hollis. Hugh Robinson
William Haney
John Pendleton
William West
William F. George
John Webb
A. Stone
Thomas Pitman
John Melton
Gabriel Lance
Ezekiel Hammond
William Harcune
Samson Stephens
Sam'l Gunter
Thomas Hale
Archibald McDougle
Joseph Boyle and
Washington Matthews

The Worshipfull court then adjorned til tommorrow morning ten oclock.
J.C. Martin Chairmn.
T.L. Turner
Samuel Lance
E. Stephens

Tuseday morning October the 2nd A.D. 1838.
The worshipfull court meet pursuant to adjornment present the worshipfull
John C. Martin
Sam'l Lance
Elijah Stepehns and
Thomas L. Turner Esqrs.
There was the following order made to wit.

John C. Martin chairman of this court. By the direstion of the court and on
their behalf and by the consent of Onnah Sullivan the mother of Eliza Sullivan
about the nine years of age have this day Bond the said Eliza Sullivanto John
Fisher with him to live and work as an apprentice (p 321) untill she attains
the age of eighteen Whereupon the said John C. Martin chairman as aforesaid and
the said John Fisher signed an Indenture with various conditions and stipulations
therein contained.

Court adjorned till court in course.
J.C. Martin chairn.
Samuel Lance
T.L. Turner
E. Stephens

November Term

State of Tennessee
        At a county court began and held for the County of Cannon in said state
at the court house in the Town of Woodbury on the first Monday and fifth day
of November in the year of our Lord one thousand eight hundred and thirty
eight and of the Independence of the United States the sixty third year.

Present the worshipfull
Samuel Denby
Charles C. Evans and
Eli A. Fisher Esquires.
Quoram Justices &C

Alexander McKnight Coroner of Cannon County returned into open court a report
of a jury of Inquest held under his direction on the 13th day of October 1838
in said county of Cannon over the dead body of a coloured man by the name of
William -- And from the evidence before them they believe he was brought to his
death by a shot from a gun in the hands of Nathaniel Taylor which shot entered
the body of said William aforesaid in the back near the right shoulder on the
10th day of October 1838 as is more fully set forth in said report.

(p 322) And it appearing to the satisfaction of the court that the duties
performed by said Coroner in the above named inquest have been done and performed as the acts of Assembly in such case made and provided. It is therefore
ordered by the court that the clerk of this certify the same to the county
trustee of said county, and that he pay the fees allowed by law for such servise
out of any moneys not otherwise appropriated that may be, or come into his hands.
&C.

Alexander McKnight Coroner of Cannon County returned into open court a report
of a jury of inquest held under his direction on the Twenty 27th day of October
1838 in said county of Cannon over the dead body of Thomas Williams And now
the evidence before them they believe he was brought to his death by William
Holt on the 26th day of October 1838 in the county of Cannon aforesaid then and
 there Feloniously wilfully and in the heat of blood with a stake or Billet
of wood kill and slay the said Thomas Williams against the peace and dynity
of the state --------(blotted out) more fully appears in said report. And it
appearing to the sattisfaction of the court that the duties performed by said
Coroner in the above Inqest have been done and performed as the acts of assembly in such case made and provided.
        It is therefore ordered by the court that the Clerk of this court certify
the same to the County Trustee of said county and that he pay all such as allowed by law for such servise out of any monies not otherwise appropriated that
is or may come into his hands.

(p 323)
Robert J. Summar   )
   Deed 50 acres   ))
Elihue L. Wetherspoon) The execution of a deed of conveyance from Robert J.
Summar to Elihu L. Weatherspoon for fifty acres of land lying in Cannon
County state of Tennessee bearing date the 30th of October 1838 was this day
duly proven in open court by Frances Cooper and Enos Sherel Weatherspoon sub-
scribing witnesses thereto - Ordered by the court that the same be certified
for Registration.

Frances Bryson   )
   Deed of Trust)
James Thomas &   )
Cooper   )   The execution of a deed of Trust from Frances Bryson to
James Thomas and Cooper for her entire interest in all the lands formily
owned by her husband Samuel Bryson at his death, Also her interest in two
negroes one a woman & the other a girl about eleven or twelve years old
named Celie and Tinia which was the property of said Samuel Bryson at his death
all lying and being in Cannon County Tennessee, bearing date the 25th day of

'nw 1338 was this day duly proven in open court by Elihu L. Weatherspoon and Enos G. Weatherspoon subscribing witnesses thereto which is ordered by the court to be certified for registration.

James West   )
Deed 90 acres   )
Adam J. Moore   )   The execution of a deed of conveyance from James West to Adam J. Moore for ninety acres of land lying and being in Warren County, state of Tennessee, bearing date the 16th day of April 1834 was this day duly acknowledged by the said James West (the bargainor) (p 324) in open court to be his act and deed for the purposes therein contained .   Ordered by the court that the same be certified for Registration.

George Bogle   )
Deed 50 acres   )
William Higgins)   The execution of a deed of conveyance form George Bogle to William Higgins for fifty acres of land lying in Cannon County State of Tennessee & district No. 17, bearing date the 13th day of February 1837, was this day duly acknowledged by George Bogle the bargainor to be his act and deed for the purposes therein contained, in open court Ordered by the court that the same be certified for registration.

George Boyle   )
Deed 50 acres   )
William Higgins)   The execution of a deed of conveyance from George Bogle to William Higgins for fifty acres of land lying and being in Cannon County state of Tennessee on Harricane Creek of Sanders fork, bearing date the 13th of February 1837 was this day duly acknowledged in open court by the said George Bogle the bargainor to be his act and deed for the purposes therein contained. Ordered by the court that the same be certified for registration.

William Hollis Jr.)
Deed 50 acres   )
James Taylor   )   The execution of a deed of conveyance from William Hollis Jr. to James Taylor for fifty acres of land lying in Cannon County State of Tennessee, bearing date even herewith was this day duly acknowledged in open court by the said William Hollis Jr. to be his act and deed for the purposes therein contained Ordered by the court that the same be certified for registration.

(p 325) Samuel J.Garrison Clerk of the county court of Cannon County by his deputy Thomas G. Wood presented a statement of settlement with William Patterson administrator of Judith Bennett deceased from the 5th day of February A.D. 1838 up to the 2nd day of November 1838 which report being fully understood by the court And there being no person present to object to the same It is therefore considered by the court that the same be in all things confirmed and ordered to be enrolled on Record .

James P. Todd)
Constable &C)
     Rigdon B. Jarratt sheriff of Cannon County this day returnedin open court the certificate of an election by him held at the election ground of the second district in said County on the 3rd day of November 1838 to elect a constable in said district to fill the vacancy lately occasioned by resignation &C from which certificate it appears to the court that James P. Dodd was duly elected to said office of Constable.

Whereupon the said James P. Todd came into open court and was duly qualified as such who together who together with his securities William S. Porterfield, Elijah Pittard and Jesse Hollis entered into bond in the penal sum of Four thousand dollars payable to his Excellency Newton Cannon Governor of the state of Tennessee and his successors in office conditioned as the law directs &C.

(p 326)   On motion ordered by the court that Alexander McKnight Esquire, Alexander McKnight Sr. and Thomas W. Wendel be and they are hereby appointed commissioners to lay off and set apart one years provisions out of the estate of Drewry Matthews estate to the widow of the said siad Mathis deceased and make report to the next Term of this court.

This day Charles Porterfield returned to the court his resignation as constable in the first civil district of Cannon County - which was accepted by the court.

On motion it is ordered by the court that the sheriff of Cannon County proceed to open and hold an election ground of civil district No. 1 - for the purpose of electing a constable to fill the vacancy occasion by the resignation of Charles Porterfield as the law directs.

Allen Beaty)
Constable)
               Higdon R. Jarratt sheriff of Cannon County by his deputy Isaac W. Elledge this day returned into open court a certificate of an election by him held at the house of Thomas William on the 26th day of October 1838 to elect a constable in civil district number four in Cannonn County to fill the vacancy occasioed by the removal of Levi Barnett from which certificate it appears to the court that Allen Beaty was duly elected as such (p 327) constable- And the said Allen Beaty being called into open court to take the oath of constable and enter into bond as the law directs, moves the court to be discharged- therefore - And it appears to the court that the said Allen Beaty refuses to take the oath and enter into bond as the law directs as constable of Cannon County, Therefore it is considered by the court that he be discharge and that said election be for nothing held.

               On motion ordered by the court that the sheriff of Cannon County open and hold an election to elect one constable in civil district number four as heretofore in Cannon County and make report to the next term of this court.

David Patton &)
David McGill)   Administrators of James McGill decd. This day reported to the court an account of the sales of the perishable proprrtybelonging to said estate together with such other effects that have come into their hands and was duly qualified to the same - And on motion the same is admitted to recoord .

Court then adjourned until nine oclock tomottrow morning.
Charles C. Evans
Samuel Denby
D.A. Fisher
Tuseday   morning November the 6th day 1838
               The worshipfull court met according to adjournment present
Charles C. Evans and
Samuel Denby Esquires.

(p 328)   This day came into court Patsey Stanley and by her request and with the assent of the court and in her behalf the court proceeds to bind to Henry Ford her son and daughter by the names of William Angeline, Whereupon the said Henry

Ford entered into bond in open court for the faithful performances of the covenat mentioned in said Bond which will appear from said Bond filed in the clerks office of this court.

And there being no further buisness before the court court adjourned until court in course.

Samuel Denby

Charles C. Evans

(p 329)   December Term 1838

State of Tennessee

At a county court began and held for the county of Cannon and state aforesaid at the court House in the Town of Woodbury on the first Monday and third day of December in the year of our Lord one thousand Eight Hundred and thirty eight and of the Indipendance of the United States the sixty third year.

Present the worshipfull

Charles C. Evans

Samuel Denby and

Eli A. Fisher Esquires

Then was the following orders made to wit.

It was ordered by the court that the following persons be and and they are hereby appointed as Revenue commissioners to take in a list of the Taxable property and poles in their respective cital districts in Cannon County for the fiscal year of 1839, to wit.

In District No 1 —————John C. Martin Esq.
In District No. 2 ——————— Isaac Finley
In District No. 3 ——————— David Patton Esq.
In District No. 4 ———————Blake Sagely Esq.
In District No 5 ——————— Moses Shelby Esq.
In District No 6 ——————— Eli A. Fisher Esq.
In District No 7 ——————— Charles C. Evans esq.
In District No 8 ——————— William Bates Esq.
In District No 9 ——————— Sam'l Denby Esq.
In District No 10 ——————— Daniel S. Ford Esq.
In District NO 11 ——————— Francis Cooper Esq.

Thomas N. Windle

Alexander McKnight Sr. and

Alexander McKnight Jr.

commissioners appointed at the last Term of this court to lay off one years provisions out of the estate of Drewry Matthews decd. to the widdow of said decd. this day made (p 330) report of the same which is in all things by the court confirmed and ordered to be made of reccord .

Epaproditas Francis)
    Deed 12   )
Arnsted Francis   )   The execution of a deed of conveyance from Epaproditas Frances for twelve acres of land lying in Cannon County state of Tennessee, bearing date the 16th day of June 1838, was this day duly acknowledged in open court by the said Epaproditas Francis (the bargainor) to be his act and deed for the purpose therein contained. And on motion the same is ordered to be certified for Registration.

William Lack & wife)
Deed 37 acres   )
Arnsted Francis   )   The execution of a deed of conveyance from William Lack and his wife Elizabeth Lack to Arnsted Francis for thirty seven acres of land lying in Cannon County state of Tennessee, bearing date the 22nd day of September 1838, was this day duly proven (as to the execution of the said William Lack) in open court by the oaths of Epaproditas Francis and Francis Cooper subscribing witnesses thereto. And it appearing to the satisfaction of the court that the said Elizabeth Lack is unable to appear in open court or before the clerk of this court in order to make her private acknowledgement to said deed, It is therefore ordered by the court that a commission Issue to some justice of the peace for the purposes aforesaid in manner and form as the law directs.

(p 331)
William Lack & wife)
Deed 30 acres   )
Arnsted Francis   )   The execution of a deed of conveyance from William Lack and his wife Elizabeth Lack to Arnsted Francis for thirty acres of land lying in Cannon County State of Tennessee bearing date the 22nd day of September 1838 was this day duly proven (as to the execution of the said William Lack) in open court by the oaths of Epaproditas Francis and Francis Cooper, subscribing wit nesses thereto And It appearing to the satisfaction of the court that the said Elizabeth Lack (the Feme covert) is unable to appear in open court or before the clerk of this court) to make her private acknowledgement to the Execution of the same. It is therefore ordered by the court that a commission Issue to some justice of the peace for the purposes aforesaid in manner and form as by Law direction.

James Higgins)
Bill of sale)
John W. Summar) The Execution of a bill of sale from James Higgins to John W. Summar, for one negro boy by the name of George of yellow complection bearing date the 20th day of November 1838, was this day duly acknowledged in open court by the said James Higgins (the bargainor) to be his act and deed for the purposes therein contained And on motion ordered by the court that the same be certified for Registration.

Higdon R. Jarratt sheriff of Cannon County This day returned into court a certificate of an election by him held in the first cival district (p 332) in Cannon County to Elect a constable in said district to fill the vacancy occasioned by the resignation of Charles Porterfield From which certificate it appeared to the satisfaction of the court that James D. Orr was duly and constitutionally Elected . Whereupon the said James D. Orr came into court and was duly qualified as such together with his securities Alexander Orr.
Alexander McKnight Sr. and
Ephriam Andrews
Entered into Bond in open court in the sum of Four thousand dollars conditioned and payable as the law directs.

Court then adjorned til court in course.
Samuel Denby
E.A. Fisher
Charles C. Evans

January Term 1839
(p333) State of Tennessee
        At a county court began and held for the county of Cannon at the court

House in the Town of Woodbury on the first Monday and seventh day of January
in th year of our Lord one thousand Eight hundred and thirty nine and of the
Indipendance of the United States the sixty third year. Present the Worship-
full.
John C. Martin (Chairman &C)
Isaac Finley
Thomas Hays
David Patton
Hugh Reed
Moses Shelby
Eli A. Fisher
Thomas L. Turner
Elijah Stephens
Charles C. Evans
John Melton
Sam'l Lance
William Bates
Samuel Denby
Daniel S. Ford
Alfred L. Hancock and
Francis Cooper Esqrs.
Whereupon the following orders were made to wit.

On motion the court proceeded to an election to elect achairman to preside
over their deliberations for the next twelve months, And on counting the votes
poled in the first Balloting John C. Martin was found to be duly Elected.

On motion the court proceeded to an election to elect three of their own body
as the statues in such case provides as quoram court, for the Term of twelve
months And on counting the votes poled in the first Balloting.
John C. Martin
John Melton and
Thomas Hays Esqrs.
were found to be duly elected as such.

(p 334) On motion the following justices present to wit.
Sam'l Denby
Hugh Reed
Francis Cooper
David Patton
Elijah Stephens
Daniel S. Ford
Eli A. Fisher
Charles C. Evans
John Melton
Sam'l Lance
Thomas L. Turner
Moses Shelby
Isaac --------
Thomas Hays and
John C. Martin Esqrs.
All voting in the affirmative and appropriation is made to Ramsey & Garrison
for the sum of one hundred and nine dollars & 29 cents for the consideration
of Furnishing and putting up two stoves in the court House for Cannon County
including all appartainances thereunto belonging which the Trustee of Cannon
County is ordered to pay out of any monies that are or may come into his hands
for county purposes --

On motion the following justices present to wit

William Bates
Charles C. Evans
Sam'l Denby
David Patton
Daniel S. Ford
John C. Martin
John Melton
Sam'l Lance
Thomas L. Turner
Moses Shelby
Isaac Finley and
Thomas Hays Esqrs.

all voting in the affirmative and Eli A. Fisher Esq. voting in the negative.
And there being a sufficient number of votes taken in the affirmative to make
an appropriation under fifty dollars. Therefore an allowance of the sum of
one dollar pr. day is made to Sam'l Denby, Charles C. Evans and Eli Fisher
for their servises in Holding the quaram courts for the year of 1838 for so
many days each as the reccord   shew them in actual servis And it is ordered by the court that the clerk Issue separate   certificates to each of them
for the same which the Trustee is ordered to pay out of any money in his hand
not otherwise apporpriated..

(p 335) On motion the court proceeded to Levy a tax for county purposes Indiscriminately in Cannon County for the year 1839, when the following justice
were present to wit.

Charles C. Evans
Hugh Reed
Francis Cooper
Sam'l Denby
David Patton
Daniel S. Ford
Elijah Stephens
Eli A. Fisher
John C. Martin
John Melton
Sam'l Lance
Thomas L. Tur ner
Moses Shelby
Isaac Finley
Thomas Hays and
William Bates Esq.rs

Being sixteen in number and more than two thirds of all the justices in the
county all voting the affirmative the following rates were fixed upon to wit.
Upon all the priviledges and occupation liable to taxation in this state to
Exercise which a licence must Issue, The one half of the amount of the state
Tax upon the same to be paid to the clerk when Licensing the same. Also upon
all theproperty (Both real and personal) subject to taxation in this state,
ten cents upon each hundred dollars the same may be valued at and twenty five
cents upon each white poll Subject to to Taxation in this state to be in-
coparated in the tax Book for the year of 1839, And certified to the Sheriff
and collector of the publick taxes and by him paid to the county Trustee as
the Law directs &C.

On motion It is ordered by the court that James M. Brown and Charles C.
Evans be and they are hereby appointed commissioners of the county Revenue
for the year 1839. And that the clerk of this court Furnish then with a copy

of this order.

(p 336)
Higdon R. Jarratt Administrator of the estate of Drewry Mathews decd. this day returned into court an account current of the sales of the perishable property belonging to said ————— together with such other effects of said Estate as had come into their possession and was duly qualified to the same which on motion was Admitted to record.

George Crockett)
Deed 130 acres)
Joshua Barton)   The execution of a deed of conveyance from George Crockett to Joshua Barton for one hundred and thirty acres of land lying in Cannon County state of Tennessee bearing date the 23rd day of November 1838 was this day duly proven in open court by the oaths of David A. Barton and Azariah Cather subscribing witnesses thereto And on motion the same is ordered to be certified for Registration.

Moses Cummings)
Deed 32½ acres)
William Stone)   The execution of a deed of conveyance from Moses Cummings to William Stone for thirty two and one half acres of land lying in Cannon County State of Tennessee bearing date the 24th day of December 1838 was this day duly acknowledged In open court by the said Moses Cummings (the bargainor) to be his act and deed for the purposes therein contained And on motion the same is ordered to be certified for Registration.

Elijah Stephens one of the acting justices of the peace in and for the County of Cannon and sixth cival District thereof this day returned into court his resignation as such which was accepred by the court. And — motion ordered by the court that the sheriff open and hold an election as the Law directs to fill said vacancy.

(p 337)
Alfred L. Hancock one of the justices of the peace in and for the county of Cannon and tenth cival district thereof this day returned his resignation as such which was accepted by the court. And on motion ordered by the court that the shiriff open and hold an election as the Law directs to fill said vacancy.

William A. Hancock one of the constables of Cannon County and tenth cival district thereof this day returned into court his resignation as such which was accepted by the court. And on motion ordered by the court that the sheriff of Cannon County open and hold an election in said district to fill said vacancy.

Andrew Morrison)
Deed 50)
John L. Chaney)   The execution of a deed of conveyance from Andrew Morrison to John L. Chaney for two tracts of land lying in Cannon County State of Tennessee the first tract containing fifty acres the other not mentioned as to the number of acres, bearing date the 22nd day of December 1837 was this day duly proven in open court by the oaths of Francis Cooper and A.D. Alexander subscribing witnesses thereto to which is ordered by the court to be certified for Registration.

Archibald Stone)
Deed 57 acres)

William Stone) The execution of a deed of conveyance from Archibald Stone to
William Stone for fifty seven acres of land lying in Cannon County State of
Tennessee bearing date the 5th day of July 1828 was this day duly acknowledged in open court by the said Ar. Stone (the bargainor) to be his act and
deed for the purposes therein contained And the same is ordered to be certified
for Registration.

(p 338) Sam'l J. Garrison clerk of this court this day returned into court
a Statement of settlement by him made with John D. McBroom administrator of
the estate of Elizabeth Jane Moore deceased which being red to and by the
court fully understood and there being no person present to object to the same
The said report was therefore in all things by the court confirmed. Also
another Settlement made with Benjamin C. Stephens Admr. of the estate of Joel
Mears deceased with the will annexed which also being red to and by the court
fully understood. And there being no person present to object to the same It
was therefore by the court in all things confirmed. And on motion Both of
said settlements were admitted to record.

On motion And upon the petition of sundry citizens living in the third and
fourth cival districts in Cannon County It is ordered by the court that an
Entire new cival district be made in said County of Cannon to be composed
of parts of the said third and fourth districts and to be Butted and Bounded as follows (that is to say) Beginning at the Holla Spring runing thence
northward with the ridge that divides the waters of Brawleys fork and Carsons
fork til it strikes a low Cap in said Ridge near where Dan'l Pearson lives
Thence with a road that crosses said ridge westwardly to the ford of Brawleys
fork near where William A. Knox now lives Thence the same course to the Rutherford county line, Thence south with said line to where the same strikes the
Coffee County line Thence East with the Coffee County line to a point from
which a line to the Holla spring will include all the inhabitants that use
the waters of Brawleys fork And that the precinct or place of holding the
elections to be held for said District shall shall be held at Bradyville
until otherwise (p 339) provided for. And It is further ordered by the
court that said district shall be known and designated as district No. 12
Number twelve.

On motion it is ordered by the court that Baxter B. Dickins be and he is hereby appointed as a revenue commissioner in the twelvth civil district in Cannon
County for the purposes of taking in a list of the taxableproperty and poles
in said district for the fiscal yearof 1839.. Said district having been layed
off and established at the present term of this court out of parts of the 3rd
and 4th cival districts in Cannon County with the place of voting Established at Bradyville. &C.

On motion and upon the petition of sundry citizens living in the fifth and
Eight districts of Cannon County, It is ordered by the court that Hereafter
the dividing line between said 5th and 8th districts shall be as follows, to
wit.
Begining on the line of the 5th and 6th Districts where the old road from
Woodbury to Jacksborough crosses the same thence with said old road by way of
William Travises to the county line thence with said line &C to the stage road
at John Pendletons, AND that so much of said fifth districts as may lye north
and east of said old road be and the same is hereby attached to the Eight
cival district.

On motion of Edwards J. Rosebury It is ordered by the court that he be released
from all the obligations of a Bond by him Given at a former Term of this ----

upon the binding of Thomas Farles to him as an apprentice.

(p 340)
Alexander McKnight Coroner of Cannon County this day returned into court a report of a jury of Inquest by him laid over the dead body of Nathan Pey on the 11th day of December 1838, who died in the jail House in Cannon County And It appearing to the satisfaction of the court from said report that the said corner had performed all things contemplated by the acts of Assembly in such case made and provided in the holding of said Inquest. It is therefore ordered by the court that the clerk of this court certify the same to the County Trustee for the payment of such fees as he the said Coroner is by law allowed for such services.

Alexander McKnight Coroner of Cannon County this day returned into court a report of a jury of Inquest by him heldover the dead body of John Parkley on the 3rd day of January 1839, whodied ------ his own House And It appearing to the satisfaction of the court that the said Coroner from said reports had well and truly performed all things as contemplated by the acts of Assembly in such case made and provided in the holding of said Inquest. It is therefore ordered by the court that the clerk of this court certify the same to the county Trustee for the payment of such fees as he the said coroner maybe by law allowed for such services ?

This day came William Bryson into court And moved the court to have bound to him as an apprentice Benjamin F. Hoggins an orphan boy about the age of thirteen years and the court agreeing to his several proposuals the same was done until he attains the age of twenty one years. Whereupon the said William Bryson and his security John Bryson entered into an Indenture together with John C? Martin chairm. &C containing sundry conditions therein severally Expressesed.

(p 341) Court then adjorned til tomorrow 10 O'clock.
J.C. Martin Chair.
C.C. Evans
E.A. Fisher
John Melton

Tuseday morning January the 8th 1839
The worshipfull court met pursuant to adjornment Present the worshipfull
John C. Martin Chairman &C.
Charles C. Evans
John Melton and
Eli A. Fisher Esq.
Then was the following orders were made to wit.

Higdon R. Jarratt)
Deed 81 acres   )
Albert McKnight)   The execution of adeed of conveyance from Higdon R. Jarratt sheriff of Cannon County to Albert McKnight for Eighty one acres of land lying in Cannon County state of Tennessee bearing date the 11th day of August 1838. was this day duly acknowledged in open court by the said Higdon R. Jarratt (Sheriff as aforesaid) the bargainor, to be his act and deed for the purposes therein contained And on motion It is ordered by the court that the same be certified for Registration.

This day came Henry Ford Sr. into open court to have bound to him Angaline Standley about the age of eight years til she attains the age of Eighteen

years old And William Thomas Standley about the age of Six years until he
attains the age of twenty one years. And it appearing to the satisfaction of
the court that the mother and step father (p 342) of the said Angaline and
William had give there consent to the same. And the court being also satis-
fied with the proposals   made on the part of the said Ford, the same was
done. Whereupon the said Ford And John C. Martin chairman of the court. This
Entered into Indenture in open court containing sundry stipulations as per
agreement.

Elizabeth Soape Administratrix and Charles P. Alexander Administrator of the
Estate of James Soape deceased, this day appeared in open court and made report
of an account of the sales of the property belonging to said estate with such
other effects as have come into their hands belonging to said estate And were
duly qualified to the same. And on motion the same was admitted to record.

Higdon R. Jarratt sheriff of Cannon County this day produced in open court a
commission from his Excelency   Newton Cannon Governor in and over the state
of Tennessee, to William McFerrin as a justice of the peace in and for the
county of Cannon And the said McFerrin being present was duly qualified as
such.

Court then adjorned til court in course.
J.C. Martin Chairm.
John Melton
E.A. Fisher
C.C. Evans

(p 343)
State of Tennessee
        At a county court began and held for the county of Cannon at the court
House in the Town of Woodbury on the first Monday and fourth day of February
in the year of our Lord one thousand Eight hundred and thirty nine and of the
Independance of the United States the sixty third year. Present The worship-
full
John C. Martin
John Melton and
Thomas Harp Esq. Quoram Justices &C.

Then was the following orders were made to wit.

                              February Term 1839

James Williams)
Deed 80 acres)
John Brewer)   The execution of a deed of conveyance from James Williams to
John Brewer for Eighty acres of land lying in Cannon County state of Tennessee
bearing date the 1st day of April 1837 was this day duly acknowledged in open
court by the said James Williams (the bargainor) to be his act and deed for the
purposes therein contained. And on motion ordered by the court that the same
be certified for Registration.

Robert Marshall)
Deed 100 acres)
Robert W. Landson) The execution of a deed of conveyance from Robert Marshall
to Robert W. Landson for one hundred acres of land (moore or less) lying in
Cannon County state of Tennessee bearing date the 23rd day of January 1839

was this day duly proven by the oaths of John C. Marshall and W.M. Hooper subscribing witnesses thereto And on motion ordered by the court that the same be certified for Registration.

(p 344)

Jonathan Winberly)
Deed 50 acres   )
Henry Trott Jr.   )   The Execution of a deed of conveyance from Jonathan Winberly to Henry Trott Jr. for the one half of a one hundred acres of land lying and being in the 5th District in Cannon County and state of Tennessee bearing date this day 4th of February 1839 was this day duly acknowledged in open court by the said Jonathan Winberly (the bargainor) to be his act and deed for the purposes therein contained And on motion It is ordered that the same be certified for Registration.

Moses Cummings)
Deed 220 acres)
William Cilley)   The execution of a deed of conveyance ---Moses Cunningham to William Cilley for two severall tracts of land lying and being in the county of Cannon state of Tennessee containing two hundred and twenty acres of land bearing date this day the fourth day of February 1839, was duly acknowledged in open court by the said Moses Cummings (the bargainor) to be his act and deed for the purposes therein contained And on motion It is ordered by the court that the same be certified for Registration.

Blake Sagely Esqr. one of the justices of the peace for the county of Cannon this day returned into court his resignation as such which is by the court accepted. And on motion ordered by the court that the sheriff of Cannon County open and hold an Election to fill said vacancy as the Law directs.

John Rigsby   )
Deed 20 acres   )
Charles C. Evans)   The execution of a deed of conveyance from John Rigsby to Charles C. Evans for twenty acres of land lying and being in the county of Cannon and state of Tennessee bearing date the 14th day of September 1838, was this day duly acknowledged in open court by the said John Rigsby (the bargainor) to be his act and deed for the purposes therein contained And on motion It is ordered by the court that the same be certified for Registration.

Charles C. Evans)
Deed 15 acres   )
John Rigsby   )   The execution of a deed of conveyance from Charles C. Evans to John Rigsby for fifteen acres of land lying and being in the county of Cannon and state of Tennessee bearing date this the 4th day of February 1839, was this day duly acknowledged in open court by the said Charles C. Evans (the bargainor) to be his act and deed for the purposes therein contained And on motion it is ordered by the court that the same be certified for Registration.

Hugh Reed   )
Deed 95 acres   )
William Stroud Sr.)   The execution of a deed of conveyance from Hugh Reed to William Stroud Sr. for ninety five acres of land lying and being in the county of Cannon and state of Tennessee bearing date the 1st day of February 1839, was this day duly acknowledged in open court by the said Hugh Reed (the Bargainor) to be his act and deed for the purposes therein contained And on motion It is ordered by the court that the same be certified for Registration.

(p 346)
Jonathan Winberly

Deed of Trust)

James J. Trott) The execution of a deed of trust from Jonathan Wimberly to James J. Trott as Trustee for the benifit of himself and Henry Trott Jr. as merchants trading under the firm and style of H & J.J. Trott nand also for the Benifit of Henry Trott Jr. and Rusel Brower upon the following property real and personal to wit. the one half of a tract of land of one hundred acres (being fifty acres) held in joint Tenency by the said Wimberly and Henry Trott Jr. lying and being in district No. 5 in Cannon County state of Tennessee Also one clay bank about Eigh or nine years old and her colt about ten months old it also being a clay bank and a mare colt , also one sorrel Horse three years old next spring named Farlton, Three cows and two yearlings and fifty head of stock hogs consisting of sows and pigs and year old barrow and speyed sows marked with a swallow fork in each ear and an under bit in the left ear. Also one mans saddle and one womans saddle Also one bed and bedstead bearing date this day the 4th day of February 1839, was this dayduly acknowledged in open court by the said Jonathan Winberly (the baraginor) to be his act and deed for the purposes therein contained . And on motion it is ordered by the court that the same be certified for Registration.

C. Reed Davis)
Deed 129 acres)
Jesse Hollis) The execution of a deed of conveyance from C. Reed Davis (Trustee) to Jesse Hollis for one hundred and twenty nine acres of land (p 347) lying and being in the county of Cannon and state of Tennessee bearing date the 4th day of December 1838 was this day duly acknowledged in open court by the said C. Reed Davis (the bargainor) to be his act and deed for the purposes therein contained And on motion the same is ordered by the court to be certified for Registration.

Isaac W. Elledge one of the deputy sheriffs of CannonnCounty this day returned into court a certificate of an election by him held in the twelvth cival district in said County on the 2nd day of February 1839 to elect a constable in said district from which certificate It appeared to the satisfaction of the court that William Stacey was duly and constitutionally ——— as constable for said district. Whereupon the said William Stacey came forward in open clurt and was duly qualified as such who together with his securities
Silas A. Robinson
Pleasant Cothorn &
Blake Sagely
entered into bond in the sum of four thousand dollars payable to Newton Cannon Governor in and over the state of Tennessee for the time being and his successor in office conditioned for the faithf l performance of his duty as constable.

James M. Brown this day produced in open court a commission from his Excelency Newton Cannon Governor in and over the state of Tennessee to him the said Brown as a justice of the peace in and for the county of Cannon under (p 348) Date of the 25th day of January 1839, And on motion (the said James being in court) The oaths of office were duly administered to him by the clerk of this court and ordered to be made of reccord &C.

Sam'l J. Carridon clerk of this court this day produced in open court a statement of settlement by him made with Alexander Young Administrator of Archibald Edwards decd. which being by the said clerk read to and in the presence of the court . And by the court fully understood and there being no objection raised to the same by any person Interested in said Estate , The said settlement was therefore confirmed by the court And admitted to record,

In which the said Administrator Enters his plea of fully administered &C.

John W. Summar This day produced in open court a commision from his Excelency Newton Cannon Governor in and over the state of Tennessee to him the said John W. Summar as a justice of the peace in and for the county of Cannon, Bearing date the 4th day of January 1839. And on motion (the said John W. Summar being in court) came forward and by the direction of the court the oaths of office were duly administered to him in open court by the clerk of this court. Whereupon It is ordered by the court that the same be made of Reccord &C.

(p 349) It is ordered by the court that the clerk of this court Issue the state writ of venirifacias to the Sheriff of Cannon County commanding him to summons the following persons as jurors for the next term of the circuit court to be holden for the county --- Cannon at the court House in the Town of Woodbury commencing on the second Monday in May next, to wit.
David McKnight
Joseph C. McGee
William Nichols
George W. Thurston
Daniel M. Stewart
William McFerrin
Joseph Simpson
Thomas J. Williams
Hugh Reed
John Craft
Mordica J. Duke
James M. Brown
Edmund Taylor
James Moars
Robert Baily
William Stone
Henry Lance
William Cummings
Job Stephens
William Wood
John Durting
John W. Hailey
Francis Cooper
William C. Odom
Baxter B. Dickens and
Wiley Willis.

On motion it is ordered by the court that Jonathan Hendrickson be and he is hereby constuted and appointed as Guardain for Mary Scribner Whereupon the said Jonathan Hendrickson together with his security John Melton Entered into bond in open court in the sum of three hundred dollars payable to John C. Martin Chairman of this court and his successors in office conditioned for his faithfull performance in his said Guardainship &C.

Court then adjourned til tomorrow morning nine oclock.
J.C. Martin
John Melton
Thomas Hayes

Tuseday morning February the 5th A.D. 1839.
The worshipfull court meet pursuant to adjournment present the worshipfull
John C. Martin
John Melton and

Thomas Hays Esqrs. Quoram justices &C.

March Term

(p 350)

There being no further Buisness before the court , Therefore on motion court adjorned til court in course.

J.C. Martin Chairm.

John Melton

Thomas Hays

State of Tennessee

At a county court began and held for the county of Cannon at the court House in the Town of Woodbury on the first Monday and fourth day of March in the year of our Lord one Thousand Eight hundred and thirty nine and of the Indipendance of the United States the sixty third year, present the worshipfull

John C. Martin

Thomas Hays and

John Melton Esqrs. Quoram justices &C.

When the following orders were made to wit,

On motion It is ordered by the court that Thomas Hale be and is hereby appointed as Administrator of the Estate of John McGee (late of our county deceased Whereupon the said Thomas Hale came into court and was duly qualified as such who together with his securitys John W. Haley and Robert King entered into bond in the sum of six hundred (p 351) dollars payable to Newton Cannon, Governor and his successors in office conditioned as the law directs, Whereupon letters of Administration are Granted &C - which are in the words and Figeurs following to wit.

In the name of the state of Tennessee, Cannon County By the justices of Cannon County. It being certified to us that John McGee late of said county is deceased and has left no will or Testament On motion It is ordered by the court that Thomas Hale have letters of Administration on the Estate ofthe said deceased. These are therefore to authorize and empower you the said Administor to enter into and upon all and singular the Goods and chattles rights and credits of the said deceased and them into your possession take and an Inventory thereof to return to the court within ninty days from the date hereof and all the Interest debt of the said deceased to pay so far as the estate of the said deceased may amount, or extend to - And the residue thereof to deliver up to those who have a right to by law to receive the same. Witness, Sam'l J. Garrison, clerk of our said court at office the first Monday in March 1839.

Sam'l J. Garrison Clk.

On motion It is ordered by the court that,

Benjamin Hale

John Hollensworth and

William Blair

be and they are hereby appointed as commissioners with ful power to proceed to and upon the premises of the late John McGee deceased And then and there out of the estate of said deceased to set apart one years provisions to the widdow of the said Deceased (having due regard to her past manner of living) as also such (p 352) other Articles as are now Exempt from Execution sale in the hands of heads of families If such belong to the estate, which duties they are required to discharge on oath and deliver a memorandom to the Administrator of said deceased which shall not be taken into the account of said Administration.

On motion It is ordered by ———— ———— that Berry Vinson Be and he is hereby appointed Administrator of the Estate of John Darkley late of our county deceased , whereupon the said Berry Vinson came into court and was duly qualified as such, who together with his securities Alexander Vinson and Joseph Warren Entered into bond in the sum of three hund dollars payable to Newton Cannon Governor andhis successors in office conditioned as the Law directs, whereupon Letters of administrations were Granted &C —— which are in the words and figuers following to wit. In the name of the State of Tennessee, Cannon County By the justices of Cannon County, It being certified to us, that John Darkley, late of said county is deceased and has left no will or Testament . On motion It is ordered by the court, that Berry Vinson have letters of Administration on the estate of the said deceased. These are therefore to authorise and em power you the said administrator, to enter into and upon all the singular the goods and chattles rights and credits of the said deceased and them into your possession keep and an Inventory thereof to render to the court within ninty days from the date hereof and all the interest debt of the said deceased to pay so far as the estate of the said deceased may amount or extend to and (p 353) the residue thereof to deliver up to those who have a right by Law to receive the same.Witness, Sam'l J. Garrison clerk of our said court at office the first Monday in March 1839.

Sam'l J. Garrison Clk.

Higdon R. Jarratt, Sheriff of Cannon County by his Deputy Thomas Elkins this day returned into court a certificate of an Election in the tenth cival district in Cannon County on the 15th day of February 1839, to elect one justice of the peace and one constable for said district from which certificate It appeared to the satisfaction of the court that Joseph Hale was duly elected to the office of constable, W hereupon the said Joseph Hale came into court and took an oath to support the constitution of the United States and the constitution of the state of Tennessee and an oath of office, who then together with his securities Thomas Hale and John W.H ailey entered into bond in open court in the sum of four thousand dollars payable to Newton Cannon Governor in and over the state of Tennessee for the time being and his successors in office conditioned for the faithful purformance of his said office.

Higdon R. Jarratt Sheriff of Cannon County by his deputy Thomas Elkins This day returned into court a certificate of an election by him held in the 7th cival district in Cannon County on the 27th day of February 1839, to elect one constable in said ———— from which certificate It appeared to the satisfaction of the court that Thomas D. Pendleton was duly elected to said office Whereupon the said Thomas D. Pendleton came into court & (p 354) took an oath to support the constitution of the United States and the constitution of the state of Tennessee and an oath of office, who together with his securities John Brown and James M. Brown entered into Bond in open court in the sum of four thousand dollars payable to Newton Cannon Governor in and over the state of Tennessee for the time being and his successors in office conditioned for the faithfull performance of his said office.

On motion It is ordered by the court that E.A. Orr, Joshua Nichols and Lewis Jetton be and they are hereby appointed as commissioners with full power and authority to proceed to and upon the primises of the late John Darkely deceased and then and there upon oath set apart, one years provisions out of any of the assetsof the estate of the s id deceased to the widdow of said sadd deceased, as also such other articles as are now exempt from Execution sale in the hands of heads of familys at the same time paying due reguard to her past manner of living. And when the same shall be so set apart deliver a memorandom of the same to the administrator of said Estate, which shall not be taken into the account of said Administration.

John C. Martin chairman of the court by the direction of the court and on their behalf this bound an orphan boy by the name of Richard Holston aged about fifteen years, until he attains the age of twenty one years to Benjamin (p 355) F. Odom with him to live and work as an apprentice to learn the occupation of farming, whereupon the said John C. Martin, Chairman as aforesaid and the said Benjamin F. Odom Entered into an Indenture bearing even date with the reccord contained sundry stipulations as by the court and the said Benjamin F. Odom agreed upon.

It is ordered by the court that William Moore be and he is hereby appointed Guardain of Jacob Moore a minor heir of Jessie G. Moore decd. whereupon the said William Moore came into court who together with his securities,
John R. Sullivan
Sam'l Moore and
Arther Warren
entered into bond in open court in the sum of three thousand dollars payable to John C. Martin chairman of the county court of Cannon County and his successors in office conditioned for the faithfull performance of his said Guardainship.

On motion It is ordered by the court that John C. Martin be and is hereby constituted and appointed as Guardain for
Peggy Bragg
Nancy Bragg
Sally Bragg
Dozier Bragg
Louiza Bragg
Moore Bragg
minor heirs of Thomas Bragg decd. Whereupon the said John C. Martin came into open court and together with his security Higdon R. Jarratt entered into bond in the sum of two thousand dollars payable to John C. Martin chairman of the county court of Cannon County for the time being and his successors in office conditioned for the faithful performance of said Guardainship.

James M. Brown one of the commissionirs of the county Revenue this (p 356) day presented in court a Report of settlement by him and Charles C. Evans (the other commissioner of the county Revenue) made with William Y. Henderson, County Trustee on the 23rd day of February 1839, which was by the court duly Examined and ordered to be recorded in the commissioners Book.

John C. Martin one of the Quoram justices and member of this court is permitted to be absent for the ballance of the presence term. Whereupon James M. Brown Esq. takes his the said Martins place for the ballance of the Term.

Court then adjorned til tomorrow morning nine oclock.
James M. Brown
John Melton
Thomas Hayes

Tuesday morning March 5th A.D. 1839.
Court met pursuant to adjournment present the worshipfull
John Melton
ThomasHays and
James M. Brown Esqrs.

There appearing no further Buisness court adjorned til court in course.
J.M. Brown
John Melton
Thomas Hayes

April Term 1839

(p 357)
State of Tennessee

At a county court began and held for the county of Cannon at the court House in the Town of Woodbury on the first Monday and first day of April in the year of our Lord , one Thousand Eight hundred and thirty nine and of the Indipendance of the United States the sixty third year present the worshipful,

John C. Martin
Alexander McKnight
Thomas Hays
Isaac Finley
William McFerrin
Washington Kenedy
James M. Brown
Charles C. Evans
John Melton
William Bates
Sam'l Lance
Sam'l Denby
William B. Foster
John W. Summar and
Francis Cooper Esqrs.
Whereupon the following orders were made to wit.

Nathan Neely this day produced in open court a commission from his Excelency Newton Cannon Governor in and over the state of Tennessee bearing ———— the 11th day of March 1839, Appointing him the said Neely as a justice of the peace in and ———— the county of Cannon. And on motion It is ordered by the court the clerk of this court administer to him the oaths of office whereupon the said Neely came forward and took an oath to support the constitution of the United States and of the state of Tennessee and the oath of office prescribed by Law.

James Cherry one of the constables of Cannon County this day returned to the court his resignation as such And on motion it is ordered by the court that the sheff of Cannon County open and hold an election to fill said vacancy as the law directs.

(p 358) Sam'l J. Garrison clerk of this day obtained leave of the court to present a Settlement by him made with Thomas S. Bennett Guardain of Rebecca F. Bennett and Richard S. Bennett minor heirs of the estate of John M. Bennett decd. for the Term of one year that is to say from the first Monday of December 1837 and up to the first Monday of December 1838. Also a settlement by him made with William Bennett Guardain of Elizabeth Patterson.

                                        John M. Patterson
                                        William M. Patterson
                                        Judith C. Patterson and
                                        Sophia Bennett

minor heirs of Elizabeth Patterson decd. wife of Joab Patterson also heirs at Law of the estate of John M. Bennett decd. All of which being read to and by the court fully understood were in all things confirmed And admitted to Record

On motion the following justices present to wit.
William B. Foster
Francis Cooper

Alexander McKnight
John Melton
John C. Martin
Thomas Hays
Isaac Finley
John W. Summar
William McFerrin
Sam'l Lance and
Nathan Neely Esqrs.
all voting in the affirmative and being Eleven in number against Charles C.
Evans and Sam'l Denby Esqrs. voting in the negative, An allowance of Forty
dollars is made to Sam'l J. Garrison clerk of this court for his Exofficia
Servises as such for the Term of one year last past and ending with the ad-
jornment of the present Term of this court . It is therefore ordered by the
court that the Trustee of Cannon County pay the same out of any monies in his
hands not toherwise appropriated.

On motion the following Justices present to wit,
James M. Brown
Charles C. Evans
Alexander McKnight
John Melton   (p 359)
John C. Martin
Thomas Hays
Isaac Finley
Sam'l Denby
John W. Summar
William McFerrin and
Washington Kenedy and
Moses Shelby Esqrs.
being twelve in number all voting in the affirmative . Therefore an allowance
is made to Adam Elrod for the sum of three dollars for the consideration of
Furnishing three Loads of wood for the use of the court House during the
January Session of the circuit court 1839 - which the Trustee is ordered to
pay out of any money in his hands not otherwise appropirated.

On motion the following Justices present to wit.
Nathan Neely
Francis Cooper
Alexander McKnight
John Melton
John C. Martin
Thomas Hays
Isaac Finley
Charles C. Evans
John W. Summars
Sam'l Denby
William McFerrin
Sam'l Lance
Washington Kenedy
Moses Shelby and
William Foster Esqrs.
all voting in the affirmative But Charles C. Evans, Sam'l Denby and Washington
Kenedy who voted in the negative.
Therefore an allowance is made to Higdon R. Jarratt Sheriff of Cannon County
of the sum of $60 for the consideration of his Exoficia Servises as such

for the Term of one year last past ending with the adjornment of the February
Term of this court 1839. And on motion It is ordered by the court that the
Trustee of Cannon County pay the same out of any monies in his hands not other-
wise appropriated.

On motion the following justices present to wit,
William B. Foster
Nathan Neely
Francis Cooper
Alexander McKnight
John Melton
John C. Martin
Thomas Hays
Isaac Finley
Charles C. Evans
Sam'l Denby
John W. Summar
William McFerrin
Sam'L Lance   (p 360)
Moses Shelby and
Washington Kenedy Esqrs.
all voting in the affirmative . Therefore an allowance is made to Hixdon R.
Jarratt, sheriff of Cannon County for the consideration of conveying of
Thomas Howerton who was convisted in the circuit court of Cannon County for
the crime of Horse stealing to the jail of Davidson County for the sum of
fifteen dollars and six cents which the Trustee of Cannon County is ordered
to pay out of any money in his hands not otherwise appropriated.

-     On motion the following justices present to wit;
William B. Foster
Alexander McKnight
John Melton
John C. Martin
Thomas Hays
Isaac Finley
Charles C. Evans
Sam'l Denby
John W. Summars
William McFerrin
Sam'l Lance
Washington Kenedy
Moses Shelby and
James M. Brown Esqrs
all voting in the affirmative . Therefore an allowance of the sum of three
dollars & 18¾ cents is made to John Estus jailor of Cannon County for the
consideration of Furnishing a srowd and other Burial clothes for the Inter-
ment of Nathaniel Peay, who died in the said jail House being there confined
under a charge of counterfeiting. It is therefore ordered by the court that
the Trustee of Cannon County pay the same out of any moneys in his hands not
otherwise appropriated.

On motion the following justices present to wit;
James M. Brown
Alexander McKnight
John Melton
John C. Martin
Thomas Hays
Isaac Finley

William McFerrin
Washington Kenedy and
Moses Shelby Esqrs.
being nine in number all voting in the affirmative against ,
Charles C. Evans
Sam'l Denby and
John W. Summars Esqrs.
being only three in number. Therefore an allowance is made   (p 361) to
Gabriel Williams for the sum of four dollars for the consideration of Building
a flat form in order to élivate the Judges seat in the court House in the
County of Cannon , And on motion ordered by the court that the Trustee of
Cannon County pay the same out of any monies in his hands not other wise
appropriated.

On motion the following justices present to wit;
Alexander McKnightA
John Melton
John C. Martin
Thomas Hays
Isaac Finley
Charles C. Evans
Sam'l Denby
John W. Summars
William McFerrin
Sam'l Lance
Washington Kenedy and
Moses Shelby Esqrs.
all voting in the affirmative against James M. Brown voting in the negative
only. Therefore the sum of thirty six dollars is hereby appropriated, that
is to say; three dollars each to the Revenue commissioners appointed by the
court to take in a list of the Taxable property and in their respective cival
districts for the fiscal year of 1859, to wit.
John C. Martin
Isaac Finley
David Patton
Blake Sagely
Moses Shelby
Eli A. Fisher
Charles C. Evans
William Bates
Sam'l Denby
Daniel S. Ford
Francis Cooper and
Baxter D. Dickens.

It is therefore ordered by the court that the clerk of this court issue to
each of the above names commissioners a seperate certificate of the same
which the Trustee of Cannon County is ordered to pay out of any monies in
his hands not otherwise appropriated.

On motion It is ordered by the court that Thomas Cavatt be and he is hereby
Granted the privilidges of building a grist mill on the East fork of stones
river upon his own lands and at his own proper Expence.

(p 362)
Joseph D. Morgan
Title Bond
Thomas R. Young

The execution of a Title bond from Joseph D. Morgan to Thomas R. Young for one hundred acres of land lying in Cannon County state of Tennessee bearing date the 21st day of May 1839 was this day duly acknowledged in open court by the said Joseph D. Morgan (the bargainor to be his act and deed for the purposes therein contained. And on motion It is ordered by the court that the same be certified for Registration.

Albert F. Smithson)
Deed 100 acres   )
Thomas L. Turner   )   The execution of a deed of conveyance from Albert F. Smithson to Thomas L. Turner for one hundred acres of land lying in Cannon Cou County (originall Warren County) bearing date the 13th day of May 1833, was this day duly proven in open court by the oaths of William Cummings and Pleasant D. Cummings subscribing witnesses thereto. And on motion It is ordered by the court that the same be certified for Registration.

Thomas Hale Administrator of the estate of John McGee deceased this day returned to court an Inventory an account of sales of the property belonging to said Estate and was duly qualified to the same in open court therefore the same is admitted to reccord .

Washington Kenedy one of the justices of the peace for the county of Cannon and 5th civl district thereof this day returned his resignation as Auch to the court which was accepted. It is therefore ordered that the shff. hold an election as the Law directs to fill said vacancy.
(numbered wrong in the original)

(p 364)
Silas A. Robinson this day produced in court a commission to himself from his Excelency Newton Cannon in and over the state of Tennessee as a justice of the peace in and for the county of Cannon . And on motion It is ordered by the court that the clerk of this court administer to him the oath of office, Whereupon the said Robinson came forward and took an oath to support to support the constitution of the United States and of the state of Tennessee and a oath of office as required, by Law.

John C. Martin chairman of this court , This day by the direction of the court and on their behalf Bound William C. Hatfield an orphan about the age of fourteen years to Dennison Haywood with him to live and work as an apprentice to Learn the art and mistery of Taning Currying &C until he attains the age of twenty one years. Thereupon the said John C. Martin chairman as aforesaid and the said Denison Haywood entered into an Indenture containing the various stipulations and conditions as agreed to by the court.

John C. Martin chairman of this court by the direction of the court and on their behalf this day bound Thomas Farley an orphan boy about the age of sixteen years to Washington Kenedy with him to live until he attains the age of twenty one years — Work with him the said Kenedy to Learn the art and mistery of Taning Currying &C. Thereupon the said John C. Martin chairman as aforesaid And the said Kenedy entered into an Indenture containing the various stipulations &C as agreed to by the court.

(p 365)
On motion and upon the petition of John Estus jailor of Cannon County It is requested by the court,
Daniel M. Stewart
Gabriel Hune and
James O. George

act as a committee to contract with some person to build Some sort of Fencing Such as they may deem expedient in order better to secure and prevent persons from having or Holding any communication through the windows of the Dungeon room of the jail House in Cannon County and when the same shall be done that they present their account to the court for allowance.

Whereas Thomas G. Wood clerk of the circuit court of Cannon County this day presented to the court 22 different Bills of cost which had accrued in the said circuit court in the different State cases hereinafter mentioned which was adjudged by said court to be paid by the county of Cannon when the county court should allow the same, And whereas It appearing to the satisfaction of the court that the same had been Examined by Thomas C. Whitiside Esq. Attorney General for the 5th Solicitorial district and by him certified to be correct . Therefore on motion the following justices being present to wit.

Alexander McKnight
Charles C. Evans
Nathan Neely
John Melton
John C. Martin
Thomas Hays
John W. Sumner
Sam'l Denby
William McFerrin
Moses Shelby and
James H. Brown Esqrs.

being twelve in number and a majority of all the justices of the county all voting in the affirmative against Silas A. Robinson Esq. voting the negative. An appropriation is made in favour of the said Thomas G. Wood clerk of the circuit court as aforesaid of one hundred and Eighty two dollars &35 cents.

(p 388) Imbracing all the costs liable to be paid by the county of Cannon in the following cases that is to say in the case;

The State of Tennessee vs Willis Almond	$2.00
The State of Tennessee vs James Philips	2.25
The State of Tennessee vs Durham & Potter	5.62½
The State of Tennessee vs John Eddings	3.25
The State of Tennessee vs Eli Preston	2.37½
The State of Tennessee vs David McGill	3.37½
The State of Tennessee vs Henry Lance	4.75
The State of Tennessee vs Michael Free	6.87½
The State of Tennessee vs Ward Barrett	6.00
The State of Tennessee vs Gilbert Williams	13.37½
The State of Tennessee vs John R. Sullivan	15.16
The State of Tennessee vs Bleuford Reynolds	7.62½
The State of Tennessee vs Richard Fouch	7.25
The State of Tennessee vs John Campbell	4.37½
The State of Tennessee vs Augustine Weedon	10.75
The State of Tennessee vs Roswell Soap	8.37½
The State of Tennessee vs Starling Vaughn	8.00
The State of Tennessee-Lewis G. Martin	11.37½
The State of Tennessee vs Andrew McInturf	8.43½
The State of Tennessee vs Henry Bullord	12.47½
The State of Tennessee vs Milton Maxwell	9.02½
The State of Tennessee vs Simon Williams	23.12½
	182.35

which the Trustee of Cannon County is ordered to pay out of any monies in his hands not otherwise appropriated in order that the said Thomas G. Wood may Dispose of the same amongst the witnesses, officers &C who are intitled by

Law to receive the same.
Court then adjorned til tomorrow morning ten oclock.
J.C. Martin Chairn.
Thomas Hays
C.C. Evans
Nathan Neely

(p 367) Tuseday Morning April the Second 1839.
Court met pursuant to adjornment present the worshipfull
John C. Martin
Thomas Hays
Nathan Neely and
Charles C. Evans

And on motion there appearing no further buisness court adjorned   til
court in course.
J.C. Martin Chairn.
Thomas Hayes
C.C. Evans
S. Lance
Nathan Neely

State of Tennessee
       At county court began and held for the county of Cannon at the court
House in the Town of Woodbury on the first Monday It being the Sixth day of
May in the year of our Lord ine thousand Eight hundred and thirty nine,
And of the Independance   of the U ited States the Sixty third year present
the worshipfull;
John C. Martin
ThomasHayes and
John Holton Esqrs.

Then was the following orders made to wit.

Higdon R. Jarratt Sheriff of Cannon County this day produced in open court
Commissions from his Excelency   Newton Cannon Governor to:
Richard U. Lemy
William Bowen and
Robert L. Shaw
being present were severally duly qualified as such.

                       May Term
(P 368)
Thomas Elkins Deputy Sheriff of Cannon County This day produced in open court
a certificate of an election by himself held in the 5th cival district in
Cannon County on the 27th April 1839, to Elect a constable in said district
to fill the vacancy occasioned by the resignation of axes Cherry resign-
ed from which certificate It appears to the satisfaction of the court that
Albert G. Millikin was duly and constitutionally elected to said office
Whereupon the said Albert G. Millikin being present came forward and was duly
qualified as such who together with his securities Joel Cherry and Jessie
Millikin entered into bond in the sum of Four thousand dollars conditioned
and payable as the law directs.

At this Term the court appointed Thomas J. Williams deed who being present
was duly qualified as such who together with his securities John Petty and
John Witt entered into bond in the sum of Three Thousand dollars payable

and conditioned as the Law directs. And on motion ordered by the court that Letters of Administration be Issued to him upon said Estate which are in the words and Figuers following to wit.

In the name of the state of Tennessee Cannon County. It being certified to us that Thomas Williams late of said county is deceased and has made no will or Testament . On motion It is ordered by the court that Thomas J. Williams have letters of Administration on the Estate of (p 369) the said deceased. These are therefore to authorize and empower you the said Administrator to enter into and upon all and singular the Goods and chattles rights and credits of the said deceased and them into your posession take and an Inventory thereof to render to the court within ninety days from the date hereof and all the Interest debt of the said deceased to pay so fare as the Estate of the said deceased may amount or Extend to and the residue thereof to deliver up to those who have a right to by law to receive the same.

Witness Sam'l J. Garrison clerk of our said court at office this 1st Monday in May 1839.

    Sam'l J. Garrison clk.

At this Term of the court Sam'l J. Garrison clerk of this court presented for confirmation a settlement by him made with Moses Shelby Guardain of Elizabeth Spence, from the 6th day of March 1837 up til the time of her death say the 9th day of December 1837, which being by the court Examined and fully understood was in all things confirmed And ordered to be recorded.

    At this Term of the court Isaac W. Elledge deputy shff. of Cannon County produced in open court a certificate of an Election by him held in the 4th civil district in Cannon County on the ——— day of ——— to elect a constable for said district to fill the unexpired time of Levi Parrett Former constable from which certificate It appeared to the satisfaction of the court that John McClain was duly and constitutionally elected to said office whereupon the said John McClain came (p 370) into court and was duly qualified as such who together with his securities Joseph F. Brown and Isaac W. Elledge entered into bond in the sum of four thousand dollars conditioned as the Law directs.

Court then adjorned til court in course.
J.C. Martin chairm.
Thomas Hayes
John Melton

State of Tennessee
    At a county court began and held for the county of Cannon at the court House in the Town of Woodbury on the first Monday and third day of June In the year of Our Lord one thousand Eight hundred and thirty nine and of the Indipendance of the United States the sixty third year present the worshipfull
John C. Martin
John Melton and
Thomas Hays Esqrs.
Then was the following orders made (to wit)
William Patterson Administrator of the estate of Judith Bennett decd. this day produced in court Six refunding Bonds by him taken from the distributors of the said decd. And on motion it is ordered by the court that the same be entered upon the minuits of this court which are in the words and Figuirs to wit.

June Session 1839

(p 371) We acknowledge ourselves indebted to John C. Martin chairman of Cannon County court and his successors in office in the sum of thirty three dollars to be void if Rebeciah F. Bennitt distributee who has this day received from William Patterson Administrator of Judith Bennitt the sum Sixteen dollars & fifty _____ her share of the personal estate of the said Judith Bennett should pay and refund her ratiable part of any debt or debts against said Estate which may be hereafter sued for , recovered or otherwise made to appear, this 7th May 1839 -

No 1 Test) Rebecoah F. Bennett (seal) (her mark)
James Tubb) Thomas S. Bennett (seal)
         Benjamin Bennett (seal)

We acknowledge ourselves Indebted to John C. Martin chairman of Cannon County court and his Successors on office in the Sum of thirty three dollars to be void of Wm. Bennett distributee who has this day received from Wm. Patterson administrator of Judith Bennett the sum of sixteen dollars and fifty cents his share of the personal estate of Judith Bennett should pay and refund his ratiable part of any debt against said estate which maybe hereafter sued for, recovered or otherwise duly made to appear this 7th May 1839.

No.2) Wm. Bennett (seal) (his mark)
Test) Thomas S. Bennett (seal)
James Tubb) Benjamin Bennett (seal)

We acknowledge ourselves Indebted to John C. Martin chairman of Cannon County court and his successors in office in the sum of thirty three dollars to be void if Sopiah Bennett,
     Elizabeth
     John M.
     William M.
(p 372) Judith C. Patterson heirs at Law of Elizabeth Patterson Distributee who has this day received from Wm. Patterson Administrator of Judith Bennett the sum of sixteen dollars and fifty cents their share of the personal estate of the said Judith Bennett should pay and refund their ratiable part of any Debt or debts against said estate which may be hereafter sued for, recovered, or otherwise duly made to appear this 7th day May 1839.
Wm. Bennett Guardain (seal) [Test No. 3)
Thomas/Bennett (seal)   (James Tubb)
Benjamin Bennett (seal)

We acknowledge ourselves Indebted to John C. Martin chairman of Cannon County court and his successors in office in the sum of thirty three dollars to be void if Rich'd S. Bennett distributee who has this day received from Wm. Patterson (p 373) administrator of Judith Bennett the sum of sixteen dollars & fifty cents, his share of the personal property of the said Judith Bennett should pay and refund his ratiable part of any debt or debts against said estate which maybe hereafter sued for, recovered, or otherwise duly made to appear this day May 1839.
Test) Thomas S. Bennett Guardain (seal)
No. 5) Benjamin Bennett (seal)
James Tubb) William Bennett (his mark seal)

We acknowledge ourselves Indebted to John C. Martin chairman of Cannon County court and his successors in office in the sum of thirty three dollars to be viod if Benjamin Bennett distributee who has this day received from Wm. Patterson Administrator of Judith Bennett the sum of sixteen dollars and fifty cents his share of the personal property of the said Judith Bennett, Should pay and refund his ratiable part of any debt or debts against said estate which may be hereafter sued for, recovered or otherwise duly made to appear, this 7th day May 1839.

No. 6 Test (Benjamin Bennett (seal)
James Tubb (Thomas/Bennett (seal)
(Wm. Bennett (his mark) (seal)

Berry Vinson Administrator of John Barkley deceased this day returned into court an account of sale of the personal property belonging to said Estate together with such other assets as have come into his possession and was duly qualified to the same which is admitted to reccord.

(p 374) it is ordered by the court that Leroy Rose be appointed administrator of the estate of John G.W. Rose decd. whereupon the said Leroy Rose being present was duly qualified as such in open court who together with his securities Elisha B. Rose and Joseph Simpson Entered into bond in the sum of five thousand dollarsconditioned and payable as the Law directs Thereupon Letters of Administration were Granted him upon said estate; which are in the words and figuers following to wit.
In the name of the state of Tennessee, Cannon County. By the justices of Cannon County. It being certified to us that John G.W. Rose, late of said county is deceased and has made no will or Testament, On motion it is ordered by the court that Leroy Rose have letters of Administration on the estate of the said deceased.

These are therefore to authorize and empower you the said administrator to enter into and upon all and singular the Goods and chattles , rights and credits of t e said deceased and them into your possession take and an Inventory thereof to render to court within ninety days from the date hereof And all the Interest debt of the said deceased to pay so fare as the estate of the said deceased may amount or extend to and the residue thereof to deliver up to those who have a right to by Law to receive the the same.
Witness Sam'l J. Garrison clerk of our said court at office this 1st Monday in June 1839.
        Sam'l J. Garrison clk.

(p 375) It is ordered by the court that Martin S. Hoover be appointed Administrator of the estate of Daniel Hoover deceased. Whereupon the said Martin S. Hoover being present was duly qualified as such in open court who together with his securities David Patton and William Pace, entered into bond in the sum of six Hundred dollars, conditioned and payable as the Law directs Whereupon letters of administration were Granted him upon said estate which are in these words and Figuers to wit .

    In the name of the State of Tennessee Cannon County by the justices of Cannon County, It being certified to us that Daniel Hoover late of said county is deceased and has made no will or Testament . On motion it is ordered by the court that Martin S. Hoover have letters of Administration on the estate of the said deceased.
    These are therefore to authorize and empower you the said administrator to enter into and upon all and singular the goods and chattle rights and cridits of the said deceased and then into your possession take and an Inventory thereof to render to court within ninty days from the date hereof and all the interest debt of the said deceased to pay so far as the estate of the said deceased may amount or extend to and the residue thereof to deliver up to those who

have a right to by law to receive the same.

Witness Sam'l J. Garriosn clerk of our said court at office this 1st Monday in June 1839.

Sam'l J. Carrison clk.

(p 576) On motion It is ordered by the court that David Patton, William Ring and William Pace

be and they are hereby appointed as commissioners with full power and authority to proceed to and upon the primises of the late Dan'l Hoover deceased and then and there set apart out of any assetts belonging to said estate One years provisions to the widdow of said deceased, paying due reguard to her past manner of living and also to set apart such other articles (if such belong to the estate) as is now exempt from execution sale in the hands of heads of Families.

Thomas D. Pendleton one of the constables in Cannon County and 7th cival district thereof this day returned into court his resignation as such which was accepted by the court. And on motion It is ordered by the court that the shiriff of Cannon County open and hold an election to fill said vacancy as the Law directs.

Sam'l J. Carrison clerk of this court this day produced to the court a statement of settlement by him made with Sam'l Braswell administrator of Nathan Sellers deceased, Which by the court was fully Examined and understood therefore in all things confirmed and admitted to record wherein the said Braswell Administrator as aforesaid enters his Pleas of fully Administered.

(p 377) Whereas at the ------- Term of this court 18--- one Elihu B. Jewell, appeared in court and moved the court to have bond to him one Hugh Thomas an orphan boy to live and work with him as an apprentice to Learn the Blacksmith Buisness And the court agreeing to the several propositions by him made did bind the said Hugh to the said Elihu B. And whereas at the present term of this court, one Sarah Brogan the mother of the said Hugh Thomas appeared in court and charged the said Jewell with having the covanants   by him entered into on the binding of the said Hugh and moved the court to have the said Hugh bond to her. And It appearing to the satisfaction of the court that the said Jewell had mistreated the said Hugh and had in fact Broke the covanants aforesaid. They therefore bind the said Hugh to his mother the said Sarah Brogan. Whereupon John C. Martin chairman of this court on behalf the court and by their direction together with the said Sarah, Thomas Vance and Sam'l Vance entered into Indenture containing sundry stipulations as ther in stipulated.

On motion It is ordered by the court that

Hugh Reed

James Sissom and

Robert Carson

be and they are hereby appointed as commissioners with full power and authority to proceed to and upon the premises of the late Thomas W lliams deceased and then and there to set apart out of any of the assetts   (p 578) Belonging to said estate, to the widdow of the said deceased, one years provisions paying due reguard to her past manner of living. And also such other articles (if such belong to the estate) as is now exempt from Execution sale in the heads of Families,

At this Term of the court, William Y. Henderson Trustee of Cannon County appeared in open court who together with his securities John Henderson and James J. Trott entered into bond in the sum of two thousand four hundred and

forty four dollars payable to R.H. McEwen superintendant of publick Instruction and his successors in office cinditioned for the faithfull receiving and
paying out of all monies that may be or shall come into his hands fot the use
and benifit of common svhools in Cannon County for the year of 1839 —

Court hten adjorned till court in course.
J.C. Martin
John Melton
Thomas Hayes

July Session 1839

(p 379)
State of Tennessee
At a county court began and held for the County of Cannon at the court
House in the Town of Woodbury in the county aforesaid On the first Monday and
first day of July in the year of our Lord one thousand Eight hundred and
thirty nine. And of the Indipendance of the United States the sixty third
year — present the worshipful
John C. Martin
Alexander McKnight
Thomas Hays
Isaac Finley
William McFerrin
William Bowen
David Patton
Charles C. Evans
William Bates
Nathan Neely
John Melton
Robert L. Shaw
Richard U. Lenny
Sam'l Denby
Daniel S. Ford
Sam(l Lance
Hugh Reed and
John W. Summar Esqss.
Thereupon the following orders were made to wit.

On moti n the following justices present (to wit)
Samuel Dehby
Nathan Neely
Richard U. Lenny
Alexander McKnight
David Patton
John C. Martin
Charles C. Evans
Thomas Hays
Isaac Finley
William McFerrin
William Bowen
Robert L. Shaw
John Melton and
John W. Summar Esqrs.
being fourteen in number all voting in the affirmative, Therefore an approria-
tion is made of twenty four dollars to Hannah Henderson wife of Robert Hender-

son Lunatic to be applied to her support for one year from this date. The
Trustee of Cannon County is therefore ordered to pay the same out of any monies
in his hands not otherwise appropriated to such person as maybe appointed
Guardain of the said Hannah Henderson for the purposes aforesaid.

(p 380) Samuel J. Garrison clerk of this court this day prayed and obtained
leave to spread upon record his receits for his statements of settlements by
him made with the proper authorities as also for the publick   Taxes by him
collected and payed out at the close of the fiscal year of 1838, which are in
the words and Figuers following to wit.

Comptrollers office Nashville Tennessee 26th Sept. 1838. Received of Sam'l J.
Garrison his statement of Revenue collected as clerk of Cannon County court
from 1 Sept. 1837 to 1 Sept. 1838.

Amount collected		$546.83
Commissions at 2½	13.66	
paid commissioners		
Denby & Remsey	5.00	18.66
Warrant No 619 this day for		528.17

signed Daniel Graham Comptroller of the Treasury
$528.17 ——— Nashville 26 Sept. 1838. No. 619.
Received of Sam'l J. Garrison five hundred and twenty Eight dollars 17 cents
audited to him by No. 619 and due on account of Revenue b him collected as
clerk of County court of Cannon County from 1st Sept. 1837 to 1st Sept. 1838.
signed duplicates—Miller Francis
Treasurer of Tennessee

Woodbury October 1st 1838
Then received of Sam'l J. Garrison clerk of Cannon County court his statement
of Revenue by him collected as clerk of said county court from the 1st day
of September 1837 up to the 1st day of September 1838. W.Y. Henderson
Cannon County Trustee

(p 381)   Woodbury October 1st 1839.
Then received of Sam'l J. Garrison clerk of the county court of Cannon County
Two hundred and fifty eight dollars and fourteen cents the amount of his li-
ability for Taxes by him collected for the county aforesaid from the 1st day
of September 1837 up to the 1st day of September 1838.
(W. Y. Hnederson
(Cannon County Trustee

 On motion the following justices present to wit
Nathan Neely
Sam'l Denby
Daniel S. Ford
R.U. Lemay
Alexander McKnight
David Patton
John C. Martin
Charles C. Evans
Thomas Hays
Isaac Finley
John Melton
William McFerrin
William Bowen
Robert L. Shaw

John W. Summar and
William Bates Esqr.
fifteen in number all voting in the affirmative therefore an appropriation of
twenty four dollars is made for the benifit of Polly Spicer Daughter of
Hardy Spicer, An Idiot, for the support of the said Polly for the Term of one
year from the date hereof to be paid to such person as may be appointed for
that purpose which the Trustee of Cannon County is ordered to pay out of any
money in his hand not otherwise appropriated.

Sam'l J. Garrison clerk of this court and account of settlement by him made
with Thomas Givens Guardain of William and Henry Braughton minor heirs of Henry
Draughton deed. for two years, the first year from the July Term 1837 and the
2nd year ending with the present Term of this court, which was by the ————
fully examined and understood and was in all things fully confirmed.

(p 382) Sam'l J. Garrison clerk of this court this day produced in open court
a statement of settlements by him made with David Patton Guardain of Nancy
and Catherine Clems for the Term of one year ending with the term of the court
which was by the court duly examined and fully understood which was in all
things confirmed and ordered to be recorded.

On motion thefollowing justices present to wit.
Nathan Neely
Dan'l S. Ford
Richard U. Leray
Alexander McKnight
David Patton
John C. Martin
Charles C. Evans
Thomas Hays
John Melton
Sam'l Lance
William McFerrin
William Bowen
Issac Finley
Robert L. Shaw and
John W. Summar Esqrs.
being fifteen in number all voting in the affirmative therefore an appropriation
is made for the sum of thirty dollars into the hands of David Patton Guardain
of Catherine and Nancy Clem, for their use and benifit for the Term of one year
from this date and in order also to pay back to the said Guardain the sum of
four dollars & 62 cents, an amount by him paid and furnished for his said ward
in the last twelve months over and above the last appropriation by this court
to said ward. And on motion the Trustee of Cannon County is ordered to pay the
same out of any money in his hands not otherwise appropriated.

On motion (the following justices present to wit.
Daniel S. Ford
Richard U. Leray
Alexander McKnight
David Patton
John C. Martin
Charles C. Evans
Sam'l Lance
Thomas Hays
William McFerrin
William Bowen
Robert L. Shaw

John W. Summar and
Isaac Finley Esqrs.
(p 383) being thirteen in number all voting in the affirmative therefore an
appropriation is made to Elijah Stephens of the sum of three dollars for the
consideration of putting two large Iron bars across the jail door of Cannon
County, which the Trustee of said county is ordered to pay out of any money
in his hands not otherwise appropriated.

On motion (the following Justices present to wit
Daniel S. Ford
Richard U. Lemay
Alexander McKnight
David Patton
John C. Martin
Charles C. Evans
Thomas Hays
William McFerrin
William Bowen
Isaac Finley
William Bates
Hugh Reed and
Sam'l Lance Esqrs.
being twelve in number all voting in the afirmative therefore an allowance of
the sum of six dollars is made to Henry D. McBroom for the consideration of
Furnishing an office for the clerk of the circuit court for from four to six
months imediately before the Reception of the court House, which the Trustee
of Cannon County is ordered to pay out of any monies in his hands not other-
wise appropriated.

On motion of Joseph Pinkerton it is ordered by the court that the line between
the third and twelvth cival districts in Cannon County be and the same is so
changed as to includ the said Pinkerton in the third district.

Isaac Finley Esq. one of the justices of the peace for Cannon County and 2nd
cival district therein this day Tendered his resignation as such which was by
the court acceptes and ordered to be made of record.

(p 384) On motion It is ordered by the court that Henry Ford be and he is
hereby appointed as Guardain to Hannah Henderson (lunatic) whereupon the
said Henry Ford came into court and together with his security Thomas Elkins
entered into bond in the sum of forty Eight dollars payable to John C. Martin
chairman of the county court Cannon County for the Time being and his successors
in office conditioned for the faithful performance of his said Guardainship.

On the petition of sundry citizens living in the second and third districts
of Cannon County It is ordered by the court that the line runing through and
dividing the second and third cival districts of Cannon County be and the same
is hereby changed and Established as follows to wit.
Begining at John H. Woods runing thence with the stage road to the river,
Thence up the river to Josephus H. Coms so as to include said Coms own
House Thence on a direct line to the House of George Thurstons, Thence with
the ridge line as to include William Todd and Gideon Duke Thence to the old line
at Jonathan Jones And that the place of Holding the precinct Election shall in
future be established at Joseph F. Browns in place of McFerrins store asform-
ily.

On motion it is ordered by the court that Thomas Elkins Deputy Sheriff be fined the sum of two dollars for absenting himself from the court House during the setting of the court thereby neglecting the buisness of the court contentuously.

(p 385) It is ordered by the court that the following persons be a pointed and summoned by the shuriff of Cannon County as jurors and constables for the september Term of the circuit court 1839, to wit
Jonathan Wherry
John M. McKnight
William Bowen
Joseph Smith
Isaac Finley
John Gannon
John McLain
Allen Beaty
Jonathan Wimberly
Moses Shelby
James O. George
H.M. Taylor
James Wood
Charles C. Evans
Thomas Pitman
Washington Kenedy
Pleasant Essary
Thomas Reaves
Enoch Ferrell
Robert L. Shaw
Hiram Dodd
John W. Summar
Benjamin B. Cooper
Richard Holt and
Jessie B. Robinson and
William L. Covington and
Sam'l Corn
be appointed as constables.

Court then adjorned til tomorrow morning 10 O'clock

Charles C. Evans
Nathan Neely
William Brown

Tuseday morning July 2nd 1839.
Court meet pursuant to adjornment present the worshipfull
Charles C. Evans
Nathan Neely and
William Bowen Esqr s.
Charles C. Evand caled to the chair.
Then was the following orders made to wit.

On motion It is ordered by the court that
George Grizzle
Samson Stephens and
John Stephens
be and they are hereby appointed with full power and authority to proceed to and upon the primises of the late John G.W. Rose deceased and then and there set apart out of the estate of the said deceased one years provisions out of any of

the assets belonging to said Estate to Jane Ross widdow of the said deceased paying due regward to her past manner (p 336) of living. Also to set apart such other articles (if such belong to the estate) as is now exempt from Execution sale in the hands of heads of families And when the same shall be so set apart , deliver a copy of the same to the widdow and another to the Administrator of said Estate.

H.R. Jarratt Sheriff of Cannon County, this day produced in open court a commission from his Excelency Newton Cannon Governor in and over the state of Tennessee to Allen Batey as justice of the peace in and for Cannon County And the said Allen Batey being in court came forward and was duly qualified as such.

On motion of Thomas Elkins by his attorney the fine of two dollars entered against him on the first day of this Term be and the same is hereby relased upon the payment of the cost of this entry and the same and this this entry.

Court then adjourned til court in course.
Charles C. Evans
William Bowen
N. Neely
Allen Beaty.

August Term 1839

(p 337)
At a county court began and held for the county of Cannon at the court House in the Town of Woodbury in the aforesaid County of Cannon on the first Monday and fifth day of August one thousand Eight hundred and thirty nine and of the Indipendance of the United States the sixty fourth year present the worshipful
John C. Martin
Thomas Hays and
John Melton Esqrs.

Then was the following orders made to wit.

On motion It is ordered by the court that Alexander McKnight and David McKnight be and they are hereby appointed administrators of the estate of Charles Porterfield deceased, Thereupon the said Alexander McKnight and David McKnight being present in court entered into bond in the sum of Eight hundred dollars, payable to the Goveror of Tennessee for the time being and his successors in office conditioned for the faithfull performance of their said Administration And on motion It is ordered by the court that Letters of Administration be granted them on said Estate which are in the words and Figuers following to wit.
In the name of the state of Tennessee Cannon County
By the Justices of Cannon County it being certified to us.-
Charles Porterfield late of said county is deceased and has (p 338) left no will or Testament On motion it is ordered by the court that Alexander McKnight and David McKnight have letters of Administration on the estate of the said deceased, There are therefore to authorize and empower you the said Administrators to enter into and upon all and singular the Goods and chattle rights and credits of the said deceased , And them into your possession take and an Inventory thereof to render to the court within ninety days from the date hereof and all the interest debts of the said deceased to pay so far as the estate of the

said deceased may amount or extend to and the residue thereof to deliver up to those who have a right to by law to receive the same.
Witness Sam'l J. Garrison clerk of our said court at office this 1st Monday in Augt. 1839.
(signed) (Sam'l J. Garrison clk.)

On motion It is ordered by the court that Moses McKnight
                                        Robert B. Williams and
                                        Joshua Nichols
be and they are hereby appointed as commissioners with full power and authority to proceed to and upon the primises of the late Charles Porterfield decd. and then and there out of the estate of the said deceased to set apart to the widdow of the said deceased one years provisions paying due reguard to her past manner of living . Also to set apart such other articles (if such belong to the estate) as is now exempt from Execution sale in the hands of heads of Families. &C.

(p 389) Higdon R. Jarratt Sheriff of Cannon County, this day returned into court a certificate of an Election by him held in the Eleventh cival district in Cannon County to elect a constable in said district to fill the vacancy occasioned by the death of Sam'l Corn dec. And from which certificate It appeared to the satisfaction of the court that Benjamin B. Cooper was duly and constitutionally elected as such, whereupon the said Benjamin B. Cooper together with his securities Abraham Cooper and Francis Cooper entered into bond in the sum of four thousand dollars payable to Newton Cannon Governor in and over the state of Tennessee for the time being and his succ essors in office conditioned for the faithfull performance of his duty as an officer when he was duly qualified in open court as such.

On motion It is ordered by the court that William C. Odons
                                        John W. Summar and
                                        L.B. Moore
be and they are hereby appointed Administrators of the estate of Sam'l Corn deceased, Whereupon the said Odom, Summar and Moore came into court and were duly qualified as such who together with their security H.R. Jarratt entered into bond in the sum of fourteen hundred dollars payable to the Governor in and over the State of Tennessee for the Time being and his successors in office conditioned for the faithful performance of their said Administration.

(p 390) Whereupon on motion It was ordered by the court that they have letters of Administration upon said Estate which are in the following words and Figuers to wit.
In the name of the state of Tennessee, Cannon County, It being certified to us that Sam'l Corn late of our said county is deceased and has made no will or Testament On motion It is ordered by the court that
William C. Odom
John W. Summar and
L.B. Moore
have letters of Administration on the state of the said deceased, These are therefore to authorize and empower you the said Administrator to enter into and upon all and singular the goods and chattle rights and credits of the said decd. and then into your possession take and an Inventory thereof to render to the court within ninety days from the date hereof and all the Interest debt of the said deceased to pay so fare as the estate of the said deceased may amount or extend to and the residue thereof to deliver up to them who have a right to by Law to receive the same.
Witness Sam'l J. Garrison clerk of our said court at office this first Monday in Augt. 1839.

(signed) Sam'l J. Garrison. clk.

Henry Trott Jr. Administrator of the estate of John V. Cummings decd, this day returned into court an account currant of the effects belonging to said estate and was duly qualified to the same i open court.

(p 391) On motion It is ordered by the court that Jonathan Jones be and he is hereby constituted and appointed as Guardain to;
Elizabeth Ferrell
Robert I. Ferrell
Jessie Ferrell and
Edmund Ferrell
minor heirs and ophans of James Ferrell deceased Whereupon the said Jonathan Jones together with his securities Henry Trott Jr. and R.R. Jarratt came into open court and entered into bond in the sum of four thousand dollars payable to John C. Martin chairman of the county court of Cannon County and his successors in office conditioned for his faithfull performance as such.

Benjamin Pendleton sr. this day produced in open court a paper writing purporting to be the last will of John Brown deceased , to which It appeared that Thomas G. Wood and James M. Brown were subscribing witnesses who came into open court, andproved the same, And on motion the same is admitted to record. And It appearing to the satisfaction of the court that Benj. Pendleton had been appointed in said will to execute the same the said Benj. Pendleton being in court was duly —————as such who together with his securities ;
Jas. M. Brown
John Melton and
Jobe Stephens
entered into bond in the sum of twenty five hundred dollars, conditiones and payable as the law directs. Whereupon It is ordered by the court that Letters Testamentary be granted him upon said estate which are in the words and Figuers following to wit.

(p 392) In the name of the State of Tennessee.
     At the county court of Cannon County held on the first Monday in August at Woodbury. The last will and Testament of John Brown decd. late of said county deceased was produced and proven in open court in due form of law. Whereupon in thesame manner Benjamin Pendleton has been qualified as Executor. These are therefore to authorize and empower you the said Executor to enter into and upon all and singular the Goods and chattles rights and credits of the said deceased and them into your possession take wheresoever to be found in this state and an Inventory thereof to render to the court according to Law and all the interest debts of the said deceased to pay so fare as the estate of the said deceased may amount or extend to. And the residue the eof to deliver up to those who have a right to by Law to receive the same.

Witness Sam'l J. Garrison clerk of our said court at office this 1st Monday in August 1839 (signed) Sam'l J. Garrison clk.

(p 392) Court then adjorned til tomorrow morning 10 oclock.
John Melton
Thomas Hayes
Nathan Neely

Tuseday Morning August the 6th A.D. 1839.

The worshipfull court met pursuant to adjornment present the worshipfull

John Melton and
Thomas Hayes Esqrs.
(p 393) John C. Martin Esq. the other Quoram justice being absent. Nathan
Neely Esq. appeared and took a set upon the Bench in place of the said Martin
for the remainder of the Term.

There being no further buisness court adjorned til court in course.
John Melton
Thomas Hayes
Nathan Neely

State of Tennessee
At a county court begain and held for the county of Cannon att the court
House in the Town of Woodbury on the first Monday and second day of September
in the year of our Lord one thousand Eight hundred and thirty nine And of the
Indipendance of the United States the sixty fourth year present the worship-
full
John C. Martin
John Melton and
Thomas Hayes Esqrs.
Then was the following order made to wit.

Leroy Rose administrator of the estate of John G.W. Rose deceased this day
appeared in open court and returned an Inventory of the sale and other effects
belonging to the estate of the said decd. And was dully sworn to the same. And
on motion It is ordered by the court that the same be admitted to record.

September Term 1839

(p 394) On motion It is ordered by the court that William Anderson be appointed
Admistrator and that he have letters of Admininstation upon the estate of Patrick
McGenigel decd. And the said William Anderson being present came forward and was
duly qualified as such who together with his securities Robert Anderson and
James Simmons entered into bond in open court in the sum of three hundred dollars payable to Newton Cannon Governor in and over the state of Tennessee for
the time being and his successors in office conditioned for the faithful performance of his said Administration whereupon letters were granted &C . which
are in the words and Figures to wit.
In the name of the state of Tennessee, Cannon County. By the justices of
Cannon County, It being certified to us that Patrick McGenigel late of our
said county is deceased and has made no will or Testament.

On motion It is ordered by the court that William Anderson have letters
of administration on the estate of the said deceased. These are therefore to
authorize and enpower you the said administrator to enter into and upon all en
and singular the Goods and chattle rights and credits of the said deceased
and them into your possession take and an Inventory thereof to render to the
court within ninty days from the date of the said deceased to pay so far as
the estate of the said deceased may amount or (p 395) extend to, and the residue thereof to deliver up to those who have a right by law to receive the same.

Witness Sam'l J. Garrison clerk of our said court at office the first Monday in
September 1839.
(signed) Sam'l J. Garrison, clk. of said county court.

Thomas L. Turner Esq. one of the justices of the peace of the 6th cival district
in Cannon County this day returned to court his resignation as such which was

accepted And on motion It is ordered by the court that the sheriff of Cannon County open and hold an election as the law directs to fill said vacancy.

Higdon R. Jarratt sherriff of Cannon County By his deputy Thomas Elkins this day returned into court a certificate of an election by him held in the sixth cival district in Cannon County on the 24th day of August 1839 to elect one constable for said district to fill the vacancy occationed by the death of John Brwon from which certificate It appeared to the satisfaction of the court that Arthur Youngblood was duly and constitutionally elected to said office Whereupon the said Arthur Youngblood cameinto court and was duly qualified as such, who together with his securities,
James S. James
Melchesedia Williams and
Richard Vensent
entered into bond in the sum of Four thousand dollars payable to Newton Cannon Governor   (p 396) in and over the state of Tennessee for the time being and his successors in office conditioned as the Law directs.

Court then adjorned till court in course.
J.C. Martin chairm.
John Helton
Thomas Hays

State of Tennessee
        At a county court Began and held for the County of Cannon at the court House in the Town of Woodbury in the county aforesaid ON the first Monday and seventh day of October in the year of our Lord one thousand Eight hundred and thirty nine and of the Independance of the United States the sixty fourth year. Present the worshipfull
John C. Martin
Thomas Hays
William Bowen
Allen Beaty
Nathan Neely
James M. Brown
Charles C. Evans
John Helton
William Bates
Richard U. Lemay
Sam'l Lance
William B. Foster &
Moses Shelby Esqrs.

Then was the following orders made to wit.
        On motion of Sam'l J. Garrison clerk of this court leave is Granted him to spread upon record his Egceits for the Revenue by him collected and paid over for the fiscal year ending the first day of September 1839 - which are in the words and -------- &C. (p 397) following to wit.

Woodbury Sept. 30th 1839
        Then received of Sam'l J. Garrison clerk of Cannon County court his statementof settlement by him made with James M. Brown and Charles C. Evans commissioners of the county Revenue) the 19th day of September 1839 - for the revenue by him collected by virtue of his office from the first day of September 1838, to the first day of September 1839. Also Received of said Garrison an aggregate statement of the Taxable property and poles for said County for the fiscal year 1839. (signed) W.Y. Henderson,
                                        Cannon County Trustee.

Woodbury Sept. 30th 1839

Then received of Sam'l J. Garrison clerk of Cannon County court, Eighty three
dollars and 12 cents in full of his Liability for the revenue by him collected for the county afiresaid from the 1st day of September 1838 to the first
day of September 1839 as appears from a statement of Settlement by him made
with the commissioners (no. 2) of the county Revenue on the 19th September
1839.

W.Y. Henderson
Cannon County Trustee.

Comptroller
Nashville Tennessee
30th Sept. 1839 - Receved of Sam J. Garrison his statement of Revenue collected as clerk of Cannon County court from 1st Sep. 1838 to 1st Sep. 1839

Amount collected		$185.13
Commissions	$4.63	
paid Brown & Evans	5.00	9.63
		175.50

October Session 1839

(p 398)

No. 3. Warrant No 905 this day for $175.50
Daniel Graham
Comptroller of the Treasury $175.50.
Nashville 30th Sept. 1839. No. 905.
Received of Sam'l J. Garrison one hundred and twenty five dollars 50 cents.
Audited to him by No. 905 and due on account of Revenues by him collected as
clerk of Cannon County court from 1 Sept. 1838 to 1st Sept. 1839.

No. 4 Signed Duplicate (N. Francis , Treasurer of Tennessee.

James Mears this day came into court and presented a commission from his
exceleney   Newton Cannon Governor to him the said Mears as a justice of the
peace for the county of Cannon And on motion the oaths of office were duly
administered to him as such by the clerk of this court.

On motion the following justices present to wit;
James Mears
David Patton
William Bowen
Allen Beaty
Thomas Hays
John Melton
John C. Martin
Charles C. Evans
Sam'l Lance
Richard U. Leray
William B. Foster
Nathan Neely and
William Bates Esqrs.
all voting in the affirmative and being thirteen in number, therefore an allow-
ance of the sum of one hundred and four dollars and 37 cts. is made to Sam'L
J. Garrison clerk of this court for sundry Items as set Down in his account
and embracing all the charges that he has aganst the county of Cannon either
for Exoficia servises rendered for the county as also for Items of servises
for which (p 399) the Trustee of Cannon County is ordered to pay out of
any monies in his hands not toherwise appropriated.

On motion the following justices present to wit;
Nathan Neely
James Mears
Allen Beaty
David Patton
John Melton
John C. Martin
Charles C. Evans
Moses Shelby
Thomas Hayes
Richard U. Lemay
Sam'l Lance and
William B. Foster Esqrs.
all voting in the affirmative and being twelve in number therefore an allow-
ance is made to Daniel M. Stewart for the sum of Forty nine dollars for the
consideration of Timber by him furnished to pickit in the jail House for
Cannon County, which the Trustee of Cannon County is ordered to pay out of
any monies in his hands not otherwise appropriated.

On motion the following justices present to wit.
Allen Beaty
John Melton
John C. Martin
Moses Shelby
Thomas Hayes
Richard U. Lemay
Sam'l Lance and
William B. Foster Esq.
being Eight in number voting in the affirmative against;
David Patton
Nathan Neely
James Mears and
Charles C. Evans
voting in the negative and it appearing to the satisfaction of the court
that a majority had voted in the affirmative therefore an allowance of the sum
of fifteen dollars is made to Gabriel Hume for the consideration of preparing th
the Timber and selting the same in so as to close in the windows of the jail
House of Cannon County which the Trustee of Cannon County is ordered to pay
out of any monies in his hands not otherwise appropriated.

(p 400) On motion the following justices present to wit.
Nathan Neely
David Patton
James Mears
Allen Beaty
John Melton
John C. Martin
Charles C. Evans
Thomas Hays
Moses Shelby
Richard U. Lemay
Sam'l Lance
William B. Foster and
James M. Brown Esqrs.
all voting in the affirmative and being twelve in number therefore an allow-
ance is made to John A. George of the sum of twelve dollars for the consider-
ation of four days Hauling of the timbers to inclose the windows of the jail
House of Cannon County which the Trustee of Cannon County is ordered to pay out

of any monies in his hands not otherwise appropriated.

On motion the following justices present to wit.
James M. Brown
David Patton
Allen Beaty
James Mears
John Melton
John C. Martin
Charles C. Evans
Moses Shelby
Sam'l Lance
Richard U. Lemay
William Bates and
Thomas Hays
all voting in the affirmative, therefore an allowance is made for the Benifit of Parkley Couch (pauper) which the Trustee is ordered to pay to Moses Shelby Guardain who has this day entered into Bond Before the court as such.

H.R. Jarratt sheriff of Cannon County by his deputy Isaac W. Elledge this day returned into court a certificate of an election by him held in the twelvth civil District to fill the vacancy occasioned by the resignation of William Stacy from which (p 401) certificate It appeared to the satisfaction of the court that William Patton was duly elected to said office of Constable whereupon the said William Patton came into open court and was duly qualified as such who together with his securities David Patton and David McGee entered into bond in the sum of Four thousand dollars conditioned and payable as the Law directs.

John C. Martin chairman of this court this day produced and read in open court the resignation of Sam(1 J. Garrison clerk of this court Bearing this days date and to take effect from and after the meeting of the court tomorrow and after the minuits of the court of this days Buisness is read and signed which was by the court accepted. Whereupon It is ordered by the court that an election be held by the same on Tuesday the second day of this Term as the statues in such case provide to fill said vacancy.

On motion and upon the petition of Joshua Nichols he is released from the obligation a Bond by him entered into before this court on having Robertson Joy bound to him as an apprentice and the said Robertson is hereby Given up to his stepfather John Coop with him to live or dispose of as he may think proper.

Charles P. Alexander this day produced in court a commission (from his Excelency Newton Cannon Governor) as justice of the ------ in and for the county of Cannon (p 402) And on motion the oaths of office were duly administered to him by the clerk of this court.
Court then adjorned til tomorrow morning 12 o'clock.
J.C. Martin Chairm.
John Melton
Samuel Lance

Tuseday morning October 8th 1839.
The court met pursuant to adjournment present the worshipfull
John C. Martin
Thomas Hayes
Charles P. Alexander
William Bowen
William McFerrin

Allen Beaty
David Patton
Silas Robinson
Moses Shelby
Richard U. Lemay
Samuel Lance
William Bates
William B. Foster
Robert L. Shaw
Francis Cooper
Nathan Neely
James Mears
Samuel Denby
Charles C. Evans and
John Melton Esqrs.
this day Sam'l J. Garrison offered to this court his resignation as clerk of
this court and the same being received and excepted and an Election was opened
and held by this court for the purpose of electing a successor to the Said Sam'l
J. Garrison formily clerke of this court whereas upon an the first balloting
James M. Brown received thirteen votes Josiah M. Crane recd. Two votes and
Reason Fowler five votes and it appearing to the court that James M. Brown has
received a majority of the justices of this court and of the county ------ it
is therefore considered by (p 403) this court that the said James M. Brown
has been duly and constitutionally Elected clerk of this court and the said
Election is hereby ratified in all things upon the said James M. Brown entering
into and giving bond and security as the Law directs in such cases made and provided, whereupon came her into court the said James M. Brown and offered the
feloving men as securities to said Bind to wit.
Edmund Pendleton
Benjamin Pendleton
James J. Trott &
Henry Trott Jr.

Know all men by these presence that we;
James M. Brown
Edmund Pendleton
James J. Trott &
Henry Trott Jr.
are held and firmly bound together unto Newton Cannon, Governor in and over the
State of Tennessee and his successors in office in the sum of one thousand
dollars for the true performance and payment of which we bind ourselves our
heirs Administrators or Executors &C the condition of the above obligation
is such that whereas the above bound James M. Brown has this day been appointed Clerke of the county courtof Cannon County, which appointment was made by
the county court of said county for the Term of five months or until the first
Satterday of March of March next or until a successor is choosen and qullified
(p 404) now if the said James M. Brown as clerk of the county court of Cannon
County afforesaid do the well and truly collect all public monies that he is
by Law made to collect as Clerke and well and truly pay over all the public
money by him so collected as clerke afforesaid to those intitled to receive
the same according to Law this this obligation to be void , otherwise to remain
in full force and virtue in law as witness our hands and seals this the 8th day
of October 1839

J.M. Brown (seal)
Edmund Pendleton (seal)
Benj. Pendleton (his mark) (seal)
James M. Trott (seal)
Henry Trott Jr. (seal)

Know all men by these presence that we;
James M. Brown
Benjamin Pendleton
James J. Trott &
Henry Trott Jr.
are held and firmly bound unto Newton Cannon Governor in and over the state
of Tennessee or his successors in office in the sum of five thousand dollars
which payment well and truly to be made we bind ourselves our heirs Administrators &C the condition of the above obligation is such that whereas the above
bound James M. Brown was this day (p 405) appointed clerke of the county
Court of Cannon County which appointment was made by the county court of said
county for the term of five months or until the first Satterday of March next
or until a successor is elected and q alified. Now if the said James M. Brown
as Clerke of the county court of said county of Cannon shall well and truly
discharge the duties as Clerke as afforesaid and do safely keep the public
records of said court as the Law directs, then this obligation to be void otherwise to remain in full force and virtue in Law as witness our hands and seals
this the 8th day of October 1839.
James M. Brown (seal)
Edmund Pendleton (seal)
Benjamin Pendleton (seal) (his mark) x
James Trott (seal)
Henry Trott Jr. (seal)
which bonds was recived by this court and therdupon the said James M. Brown
was duly and constitutionally sworn in as Clerke of the county court of
Cannon County.

On motion it is ordered by the court that Robert K. Stephens be appointed Administrator of the Estate of Archibald McDoogle, he thereupon came into
open court, the said Robert K. Stephens together with (p 406) his securities
David C. Mullins & William Wood who having entered into bond of one thound-
sand dollars payable to Newton ————— Covenor and his sucessors in office
conditioned for the faithfull performance of the said Robert K. Stephens as
administrator afforesaid it is therefore ordered by the court that Letters
of Administration be granted and Issued to the said R. K. Stephens.

On motion bt is ordered by the cout that James Scott be released from
paying the amount of his county and State Tax of this county with the exception of seventy five cents , it appearing to the satisfaction of the court that
there was a mistake in the return of the revenue commision of said Scotts
District.

The Letters of Administration granted to Robt. K. Stephens on the estate of
Archibald McDoogle Deceased are in the words and figurs to wit, in the name
of the state of Tennessee Cannon County it being to certifyed to us that
Archibald McDoogle Late of said county is deseased and has made no will (p
(p 407) or Testament On motion it is nordered by the court that Robert K.
Stephens have Letters of Administration on the estate of the said deseased
these are therefore to authorise and empower you the said Administrator to
enter into and upon all and singular the goods and chattles rights and credits
of the said Deseased and them into your posession take and an Inventory
thereof underto the court within thirty days from the date thereof and all
the interest debt of the said deased to pay so fare as the Estate of the
said deseased may amount or extend to and the residue thereof to deliver up
to those who have a right to receive the same.
Witness James M. Brown Clerk of our said Court at office this/day of October
1839.
        James M. Brown clk.

this day John Finley produced in open court a paper writing porporting to be
the Last will and testament of John Wood deseased to which it appeared that
John Finly
James S. James
Henry Ford
are subscribing witnesses who came into open court and proved the same, and
thereupon came into open court Thomas L. Todd & Jackson Whary heirs at Law
of the said John Wood desead and contested the validity of the said paper
writing purporting the last will and Testament of John Wood deased and says
that the same is not the last will and testament of John Wood Deseased, as the
said John Wood (p 408) Deseased was not of sound mind andmemory, and at the
same time the said Thomas L. Todd & Jackson Whary objected to the said John
Finly , James S. James and
Henry Ford being sworn in open court to prove said paper writing as the Last
will and testament of the said John Wood Deseased and it is therefore considered by the court that the partied contesting the validity of said paper writing
enter into bons and security as the Law directs and thereupon came into open
court Thomas L. Todd & Jackson Whary the contesting parties and took and subscribed on oath required of poore persons to take who are not able to bear the
expens of a law suit, made and provided by an act of the jeneral assembly
pased the in the yeare 1821. And it is further ordered by the court that the
fact of said cintestation togeather with the origicnal will be certified to
the next Circuit court of Cannon County on the second Monday in January 1840.
agreably to an act of the General Assembly in such cases made andprovided pased
the 25th of January 1836, as appears in Nicholson & Caruthers, statue Laws of
Tennessee.

Upon the petition of;
Jackson Whary
Thomas L. Todd
Archibald Stone and
Frederick G. St. John
heirs at Law of John Wood Deseased, it is ordered by the court that Henry Trott
Jr. be appointed Administrator of the Estate of the said John Wood (p 409)
Deseased pendetlite and that the said Henry Trott Jr. enter into bond and
security as the law directs and that Letters of Administration be granted and
Issued.

Thereupon James Wood came into court and prayd an apeal from the order appointing Henry Trott Jr. Administrator pendtelite to the next circuit court to
be holen for the county of Cannon on the second Monday in January next and the
said appeal being granted by said court upon the opelant going security, thereupon came into open court the said James Wood togeather with his security
John H. Wood who was approved of by the court and acknowledged themselves jointly bound unto the said Henry Trott Jr. Adms. pendente lite in the sum of Two
hundred dollars conditioned for the prosecution of said appeal with effect or
to pay all such costs and damages as may be awarded against thereby the circuit
court upon fialing to prosecute said suit with effect.

On motion it is ordered by the court that the folowing named men be
sumoned by the shiriff of Cannon County as jurors for the January Term of the
circuit court next to wit.
Phillip Maxey
Ephriam Andrew
Turner Smith
Ezekiel Hayes
Joseph Knox Esq.
Azariah Gather

John M. Banks
(p 410)
John Petty
Jessee Millikin
William Whitamore
William Preston
James Mears
Benjamin Pendleton
William B. Evans
William Stone
Samuel Lance
William Bates
Enoch Jones
Asa Smith
Hiram U. Dodd
Robert L. Shaw
James Read
James Odom
Jessie Gilley &
William Pace.

Ordered by the court that Henry Trott Jr. be fined two dollars for contempt and Execution Issue for the same the court then adjorned until tomorrow nine oclock.
A. Beaty
John Melton
Charles C. Evans
William Bate
Samuel Lance

Wensday morning October 9th May 1839.
The court met persuant to adjournment present the worshipfull
Charles C Evans
John Melton
Allen Beaty
William Bates
Samuel Lance Esqrs.

On motion it -- ordered by the court that Charles C. Evans in the absence of John C. Martin Chairman be appointed Chairman protemproe, On motion it is ordered by the court that,
Daniel S. Ford
Frances Owen &
Francis Turner
be and they are hereby appointed Commissioners to alot and set (p 411) apart to Martha McDoogle the widow of the Late Archibald McDoogle, Deceased, one years support out of effects belonging to said Estate, and that the said commissioners make report as the Law directs.

At the request of James M. Brown Clerke of the county court of Cannon County on motion it is ordered by the court that Dillard G. Stone be and he is hereby appoint Deputy Clerke of the said county Court Whereupon the said Dillard G. Stone came into open court and took an oath to suport the constitution of the United States and of the state of Tennessee and on oath against dueling, and also on oath -- office which oath was administered by Charles C. Evans Chairman protemproe.

(p 412) On motion it is ordered by the court that the fine of Two dollars

220

inposed on Henry Trott Jr. for contempt on the second day of the present term of the court be and the same is hereby remited.

the court then adjourned untill the next court in course.
C.C. Evans Chr. protem
Charles P. Alexander
William Bates
John Melton
Allen Beaty.

State of Tennessee
    At a court began and held for the county of Cannon at the court House in the Town of Woodbury in the County afforesaidon the first Monday and fourth day of November in the year of our Lord one thousand Eight hundred and thirty nine and of the indapendance of the United States the sixty fourth year . present the worshipful
John C. Martin
John Melton and
Thomas Hayes Esqrs.
Then was thefollowing orders made to wit.
                        November Session 1839.
(p 413) On motion of Henry Trott Jr who was appointed at the October Term of this court Administrator of the estate of John Wood Deseased it is ordered by the court that the said Henry Trott Jr. have Letters of Administration upon said Estate by enter ing into bond and security and qualifying as the law diriota Whareupon the said Henry Trott Jr. togeather with his securities ;
Archibald Stone
David M. Jarratt
Thomas L. Todd and
Jackson Whary
which was approved of by the court entered into bond in the sum of Five thousand dollars payable to James K. Polk Govenor in and over the state of Tennessee for the time being and his successors in office for the faith-full performance of said Administration and thareupon the said Henry Trott Jr. was duly qualified ad Administrator -- ------, in open court, and is fur-ther ordered by the court that the said Henry Trott Jr. have Letters of Admin-istration upon said Estate which are in thefollowing words and (p 414) Figuers to wit.

    In the name of the Stateof Tennessee, Cannon County it appearing to our satidfaction that a proper writing was produced at the October Term of this court 1839 perporting to be the Last will and Testament of John Wood and the same being contested on motion it is ordered by the cout that Henry Trott Jr. have Letters of Administration on the estate of the said Deseased these are therefore to authorise and empower you the said Administrator to enter into and upon all and singular the goods and chattle Rights and credits of the

said deseased and them into your posesion take and on Inventory thareof and all the interest debts of the said deseased to pay so fare as the Estate of the said deseased may amount or extend to and the residue thareof to deliver up to those who have a right to recive the same.
Witness James M. Brown Clerk of our said court this the b fist Monday and 4th day of November A.D. 1839.
            James M. Brown Clk.

(p 415)

Aylett Tunely)
To Deed 158 acres)
Benjamin Sapp) the execution of a deed of conveyance from Aylett Tunely
to Benjamin Sapp for one hundred and fifty Eight acres of Land Lying formerly Warren County nowCannon County Tennessee bearing date 20th March 1830, was
this day duly proven in open cout by the oaths of William Wood and William
Stone subscribing witnesses to the same and ordered to be certified for registration.

On motion and it appearing to the satisfaction of the court that Martin S.
Hoover Administrator of the Estate of Daniel Hoover was not able to attend at
the last Term of this court owing to sickness, to return an inventory of Estate
of the said Daiel Hoover, it is therefore ordered by the court that said Administrator have time to render the same an inventory at the present term of
the court which was returned and sworn this day in open court.

(p 416)
David McKnight)
Alexander McKnight)
Administrators of)
Charles Porterfield) this day returned into open court an Inventory of the Es-
tate of Charles Porterfield Deceased which was sworn to in open court by
said Administrators.

John W. Summars &)
Littlebry Moore) Two of the administrators of the S of Samuel Corn deceased
returned into open cout an Inventory of said Estate which was this day sworn
to in open court.

On motion It is ordered by the court that Thomas Elkins be appointed
Guardan of;
Rebecca Patrick
William Patrick
John Patrick
Jesse Patrick
Lockey Patrick &
Polly Ann Patrick
minor heirs of Levi Patrick Deceased and thereupon the said Thomas Elkins
togeather with his security John Kelton who was approved of — the court
entered into bond in the sum ———— Two hundred and twenty five Dollars payable
to John C. Martin Chaimon &C conditioned as the Law directs. The court then
ajourned until court in course.
                    J.C. Martin Char.
                    Thomas Hays
                    John Kelton

December Term 1839

State of Tennessee)
Cannon County) At a court began and held for the County of Cannon at the
court House in the Town of Woodbury on the first Monday and second day of December in the year of our Lord one thousand Eight hundred and thirty nine and
of the independence of the United States the sixty fourth year.
                    Present the worshipfull
John C. Martin
Thomas Hayes

John Mullins Esqrs.
Then was the Folowing orders made to wit.

On motion it is ordered by the court that Benjamin Pendleton executor of
John Brown Deseased be permitted to return into court an Inventory of the Estate
of John Brown Deseased at the present term of this court in place of the last
time & the said Benjamin Pendleton being present returned into open court an
Inventory of said estate and was swon to the same as the law directs.

Robert K. Stephens
Administrator of
Archibald McDoogle Dsed.) This day returned into open court an Inventory of
the estate of Archibald McDoogle which was duly sworn to by order of the court
Daniel S. Ford
Fountain Owen and
Francis Turner
who was appojnted at the October Term of this court to goe upon the premises
of the late Archibald McDoogle Deseased and alot and set apart to said Mc-
Doogles widow MarthaMcDoogle one years suport returned into open court (p 418)
a report of their proceedings which report showed that they had set apart to
said widow one years suport.

Joseph F. Brown, a constable in the 3rd district of Cannon County this day
offered in open court his resignation as constable afforesaid which are in
the words and figues following to wit.
To the worshipfull the county court of Cannon County now in sesion
would respectfully tender to your worship my resignation as constable of said
county in the 3rd civel district December the 3rd 1839.
                                        Joseph F. Brown
it — therefore ordered by the court that the sheriff of Cannon County open
and hold an Elcotion to fill said vacancy.

(p 419) On motion it is ordered that Lewis Jetton and John C. Martin be and
they are hereby appointed Administrators of Levi Parker Deseased and the
said Lewis Jetton and John C. Martin being present in open court came forward and was duly qualified as such who togeather with their security Doshiro
Pragg. said security being approved of by the court entered into bond payable
to James K. Polk Govenor conditioned as the Law directs.

On motion it is ordered by the court that an order made at the last
Term of this court 1839, appointing Thomas Elkins Guardain of the minor heirs
of Levi Patrick deseased be and the same is hereby resinded it appearing to
the satisfaction of the court that RebeccaPatrick one of the heirs atlaw mentioned in said order was at the time of makeing the same of Lawfull age it
is tharefore ordered by the court that Thomas Elkins be and is hereby appointed Guardain for;
William Patrick
John Patrick
Jesse Patrick
Lockey Patrick and
Polly Ann Patrick
minor heirs of Levi Patrick Deseased the said Thomas Elkins being present
came forward and was duly qualified as such who together with his security John Melton who was approved of by (p 420) the court , entered into
Bond in the sum of Two hundred and Twenty five dollars conditioned as the Law
directs.

On motion it is ordered by the court that,?

John Vance
D.M. Stewart &
Dennis Haywood
be and they are hereby appointed commissioners to goe upon the premises of the
Late Levi Parker deseased, and there alot and set apart to the widow of the said
Levi Parker deseased, one years support out of any of the effects of said Estate
and that they report there proceedings to the next term of this court.

On motion it is ordered by the court that the sherriff of Cannon County
sumon Jas D. Orr and Arthur Youngblood , said Orr to serve upon the grand-
jury and Youngblood upon the court at the January term of the circuit court
for said county.

On motion it is ordered by the court that Letters of Administration
be granted to Lewis Jetton and John C. Martin who was at this term of the
court appointed Administrator of Levi Parker Desoased which are in the words
and figures Following to wit.
(p 421)
State of Tennessee)
Cannon County   )
Whareas it appears to the court here that Levi Parker Late of said county is
dead and having made no will or Testament and aplication being madeby Lewis
Jetton and John C. Martin to have Letters of Administration granted to them
on the Estate of the said Levi Parker deseased they having Given bond and
security as by Law in such cases required the court therefore order that they
have Letters accordingly those are tharefore to authorise and empower you
the said Lewis Jetton and John C. Martin to inter into and uppon all and
singular the goods and chattels, rights and credits of the said Levi Parker
deseased and the same into your posesion take whersoever to be found in
this state and atrue and perfect inventory tharedf make and return into our
ensuing county court on oath and all the just debts of the interstate pay
so far as the said Estate will amount or Extend the residue thareof deliver
to those who have a right thareto by Law.
Witness James M. Brown Clerk of our said court at office the first Monday in
December 1839.
          James M. Brown clk.

(p 422)
The court then adjorned until tomorrow morning Twelve oclock.
J.C. Martin Chm/
John Melton
Thomas Hayes

Tuseday morning December the 3rd the court met pursuant to ajournment present
the worshipfull
John C. Martin
John Melton and
Thomas Hayes Esqrs.
It is ordered by the court that the following persons be and they are hereby
appointed as revenue commisioners to take in a list of Taxable property
and poles in their respective civil districts for the fiscal year 1840.

In District No. 1   Josua Nichols
In District No. 2   Charles P. Alexander
In District No. 3   William Bowen Esq.
In District No. 4   Daniel Finly
In District No. 5   Richard U. Lemay

In District No. 6 James Pears Esq.
In District No. 7 Charles C. Evans
In District No. 8 Josiah M. Crane
In District No.9 William B. Foster
In District No. 10 Robert L. Shaw Esq.
In District No. 11 John W. Summar Esq.
In District No. 12 David Patton Esq.

The court then ajourned until court in course.
J?C? Martin Charm.
Thomas Hayes
John Melton

January Term 1840

(p 423)
State of Tennessee
 At a county court began and held for the county of Cannon at the court House in the Town of Woodbury on the first Monday and sixth day of January in the year of our Lord one thousand eight hundred and forty, And of the independence of the United States the sixty fourth year. Present the worshipful;
J.C. Martin
Richard U. Lenny
A. McKnight
S. Lance
J. Melton
J.W. Summar
D. Patton
A. Beaty
C.C. Evans
Wm. B. Foster
N. Neely
D.S. Ford
WM. Bates
J. Pears
J.M. Brown
S. Denby
Wm. McFerrin &
T. Hays Esqrs.

On motion the court proceeded to elect a chairman to preside over their deliberations for the next twelve months and on counting the votes polled in the first ballotting David Patton was found to be duly elected.

On motion the court then proceeded to elect three of their own body as a quorum court for the term of twelve months and on counting the votes in the first balloting David Patton & Charles C. Alexander McKnight was elected as one of the quorum.

(p 424) On motion the court proceeded to levy a tax for county purposes in the county of Cannon for the year 1840, when (the following justices being present (to wit)
Wm. Bates
Richard U. Lenny
J.W. Summar
S. Lance
J. Melton

D. Patton
C.C. Evans
S. Denby
D.S. Ford
T. Hays
A. McKnight
J.C. Martin
Wm. McFerrin
Wm. B. Foster &
J.M. Brown Esqrs.

it was moved that the county and poor tax be assessed at ten cents upon each hundred dollars worth of Taxable property and Twenty five cents on Each white poll upon which motion the following justices voted in the affirmative viz;

R.U. Lemay
J.W. Sumner
S. Lance
D. Patton
C.C. Evans
S. Denby
D.S. Ford
T. Hays
A? McKnight
J.C. Martin
Wm. McFerrin
Wm. B. Foster &
J.M. Brown Esqrs. 13

Wm. Bates & John Melton voting in the negative 2. And by the same vote (i.e.) in the affirmative

R.U. Lemay
J.W. Sumner
S. Lance
D. Patton
C.C. Evans
S. Denby
D.S. Ford
T. Hays
A? McKnight
J.C. Martin
Wm. McFerrin
W.B. Foster &
J.M. Brown

and in the negative Wm. Bates & John Melton Esqrs.) the poll tax was assessed at 37½ cents pr. head

On motion it is ordered by the court that Daniel Tenpenny be and he is hereby appointed Administrator of the estate of David Tenpenny Deceased, ---- Whereupon the said;
Daniel Tenpenny
Samuel Burke &
Arthur Warren

being present in court entered (p 425) into bond in the sum of six hundred dollars payable to the governor of Tennessee for the time being and his successors in office conditioned for the faithful performance of said Administration And on motion it is ordered by the court that letters of Administration be granted him upon said estate, which are in the words and and figures following to wit.

State of Tennessee

Cannon County) At January 1840
Whereas it appears to the court that David Tenpenny is dead and having made
no will or testament and application being made by Daniel Tenpenny to have
Letters of Administration granted to him on the estate of the said David Tenpenny deceased, he having given bond and security as by Law in such is required.
The court therefore order that he have letters accordingly. These are therefore
to authorise and empower you the said Daniel Tenpenny to enter into and upon
all and singular the goodsand chattels, Rights and credits of the said David
Tenpenny deceased and the same into your possession take whatsoever to be found
in this state, and a true and perfect inventory thereof make and return into
our next county court on oath, and a l the just debts of the intestate pay so
far as the said estate will amount or extend, the residue thereof deliver to
those who have a right thereto by law, herein fail not.
Witness James M. Brown clerk of our said court at office the first Monday
in January 1840.
                James M. Brown clk.

        On motion it is ordered by the court that Matthew Whitfield & Temperance
Willis be and are hereby appointed administrator & administratrix of the Estate
of Wiley Willis deceased, whereupon the said Matthew Whitfield
                                        Temperance Willis
                                        Thomas Y. Whitfield &
                                        Armstrong Carter
being present in court entered into bond in the sum of six hundred dollars
payable to the governor of Tennessee for the time being and his successors
in office conditioned for the faithful performance of said Administration And
on motion it is ordered by the court that letters of administration be granted
them upon said estate which are in the words and figures following, to wit.

State of Tennessee)
Cannon County   }   January Session 1840.
Whereas it appears to the court that Wiley Willis is dead, and having made no
will or testament and application being made by Matthew Whitfield ,
                                        Temperance Willis
to have letters of administration granted to them on the estate of the said
Wiley Willis, they having given bond and security as by law in such case is
required, The court therefore order that they have letters accordingly.

        These are therefore to Authorise and empower you the said Matthew
Whitfield and Temperance Willis to enter into and upon all and singular the
goods and Chattels, rights and credits of the said Wiley Willis deceased and
the same into your possession take, whatsoever to be found in this state And
a true (p 427) and perfect inventory thereof make and return into our ensuing county court on oath and all the just debts of the intestate pay so far
as the said Estate will amount or extend to The residue thereof deliver to
those who have a right thereto by law - herein fail not. Witness James M.
Brown Clerk of our said court at office the first Monday in January 1840
                                        James M. Brown Clk.

Higdon R. Jarratt by his deputy Isaac W. Elledge This day returned into court
a certificate of an election by him held in the third civil district of the
County of Cannon on the 4th day of January 1840 to elect one constable for
said District to fill the vacancy occasioned by the resignation of J.F. Brown
from which certificate it appeared to the satisfaction of the court that Hampton Sullivan was duly elected to said office.
Whereupon the said Hampton Sullivan came into court and was duly qualified as
such who together with his securities;

J.F. Brown
J.W. Roberts &
Isaac W. Elledge
entered into bond in the sum of four thousand dollars payable to Jas. L. Polk
t e Governor of the State of Tennessee for the time being and his successors in
office conditioned as the law directs.

J.M. Brown Clerk

(p 428) J.C. Martin Chairman of the county court for the year 1839 (the coroner
being absent) returned into court a report of a jury of inquest by him held
over the dead body of Abraham Sands on the 4th day of December 1839, who died
in the county of Cannon, And it appearing to the satisfaction of the court
from said report that the said chairman had performed all things contemplated
by the acts of Assembly in such case made and provided in the holding of said
inquest. It is therefore ordered by the court that the clerk of this court
certify the same to the county trustee for the patment of such fees as he the
said chairman is by law allowed for such services.

On motion the following justices being present and all voting in the
affirmative (to wit)
Wm. Bates
R.H. Lemay
J.W. Sumner
S. Lance
J. Melton
D. Patton
C.C. Evans
S. Denby
D.S. Ford
T. Hays
A. McKnight
Wm. McFerrin
(being twelve in number) an allowance of one dollar per day each was voted to
the quoram of 1839 composed of;
J.C. Martin
J. Melton &
T. Hays
for their services in said capacity And that the clerk of this court certify
the same to the county trustee for the payment of the said allowance.

(p 429) On petition of sundry citizens of the 6th 7th & 8th civil districts
of Cannon County. It is ordered by the court that a part of the 6th & 8th
districts be attached to the 7th. The line changed to run as follows, Commencing at the corner of the 7th & 8th districts where Thomas Cabotts formerly
lived, from thence to Thomas Rigsby a d Henry Lances from thence to the house
of Wm. Stones where R. Sullivan lived last year above Wm. Cummings thence to
the House where ThomasL. Turner formerly lived so as to include James Miles
thence with the meander of the top of the ridge between Thomas Elkins and Solomon Travenses to the mouth of the rock house fork including all the points
named in the 7th district.

This day H.B. Jarratt produced in open court a paper writing purporting to be
the last will and testament of Abraham Souls deceased to which it appeared
that H.B. Jarratt and Moses McKnight one subscribing witness who came into
open court and proved the same And on motion the same is ordered to be recorded and it appearing to the satisfaction of the court that Michael West had
been appointed in said will to execute the same, the said Michael West being
in court failed to come forward and enter into security as is in such case re-

quired by law.

(p 450) Henry Trott Jr. came into court and tendered his resignation as Administrator pendente lite, of the estate of John Wood deceased which resignation was accepted by the court.

At the October term 1839 of this court a paper writing purporting to be the last will and Testament of John Wood Deceased was duly proven in open court Thereupon Thomas L. Todd & Jackson Wherry contested the same. And it was then ordered by the court that the contestation be certifyed by the clerk of this court and together with the will be sent up to the circuit court to be proceeded with as the law in such cases directs. And it now appearing to the satisfaction of the court that the said T.L. Todd and Jackson Wherry no longer contest the same (and that a compromise has been effected between the heirs at law) and no objection being made by any one else, It is ordered by the court that the said paper writing purporting to be the last will and testament of said John Wood deceased be recorded in the proper book And thereupon James Wood the executor appointed in said will to execute the same together with his securities;
Archibald Stone
Thomas G. Wood and
John H. Wood
entered into bond in the sum of fifteen thousand dollars conditioned to carry out the will according to in agreement entered into by the heirs at law of said John Wood deceased.

(p 451) On motion it was ordered by the court that;
J.C. Martin
Daniel S. Ford and
Joseph Ramsey be appointed a committee to settle with the commissioners that were appointed to superintend the publick building in Woodbury and make report to the next term of this court & Also that the clerk shall issue an order of the same.

Thomas R. Young, came into open court this day and surrendered to the court William J. Hall and John W. Hall minor heirs of John Hall deceased who was at a previous term of this court bound to the said Thomas R. Young as apprentices to Lean the trade of Taning which surrender was accepted by the court The court then ajourned until tomorrow morning Ten oclock.
David Patton Chairman
Charles G. Evans
Richard U. Leray

Thomas Hays an acting justice of the peace for Cannon County this day came into court and offered his resignation which was received by the court in the words following (to wit) To the worshipful the county court of Cannon County now in session.

The petition of Thomas Hayes an acting justice of the peace for said County would respectfully Repre sent to your worship (p 432) his intentions to resign and Tender this his Resignation as such respectfuly submitted January 6th 1840.
Thos Hayes
The court then ajorned until tomorrow morning ten oclock.
David Patton Chairman
Richard U. Leray
James Mears.

(p 433) Tuesday morning January 7th 1840
The court met pursuant to ajournment present the worshipfull
David Patton Chairman
John Melton
Charles C. Evans
Samuel Lance
William Bates
William B. Foster
Daniel S. Ford
Nathan Keely
James Mears
Allen Beaty
Richard U. Lemay

On motion ordered by the court that
William F. George
John Finly and
Isaac Finly
be and they are hereby appointed commisioners to goe upon the premises of
the Late David Tempenny Deseased, and alot to the widow and family of said
Deseased one years provisions out of eny of the effects of said Dseased
Estate and make report of the same.

       On motion ordered by the court that
David Patton
William King and
Armstrong Carter
be and they are hereby appointed commissioner to goe upon the premises of
Wiley Willis Deseased and alot and set apart one years provisions to Tem-
perance Willis widow of said Dec. & her family out of said estate said Wily
Willis Decd. sized or posesed of and report their proceedings to the next
term of this court.

It appearing to the satisfaction of the court that Michael West had been appointed executor of a paper writing which was produced and proven on the
first day of the present (p 434) Term of this court said paper writeing
parporting to be the Last will and Testament of Abraham Sauls and the said
West being in court was duly qalified as executor who togeather with his securities David M. Jarratt and Jacob Wright entered into bond in the sum of Two
Thousand Dollars payable and conditioned as the Law directs ordered that Letters
Testamentary be granted said West on said Estate which are in the words and
figurs following to wit.

In the name of the State of Tennessee at a county court of Cannon County held
on the first Monday in January 1840 at Woodbury the Last Will and Testament
of Abraham Sauls late of said County, Deseased was produced and proven in open
court in due form of Law whareupon in the same Michael West has been duly
qualified as executor. These are therefore to authorise and empower you
the said executor to enter into and upon all and singular the goods and chattels Rights and credits of the said deseasedand them into your posesion take
wharesoever to be found in this state and on Inventory thareof to the court
(p 435) acording to law and all the interest debts of the said desedaed
to pay so fare as the Estate of the said Deseased may amount or extend to and
the residue thareof to deliver up to those who have a right to by law to
recive the same.
Witness James M. Brown Clerk of our said Court at office this 7th day of January 1840.
         James M. Brown clk.

On motion James Wood came into court and qualified as executor of the last will and Testament of John Wood deceased. Whereupon it was ordered that he have letters testamentary which are in the words and figures following .

In the name of the State of Tennessee At the County court of Cannon County held on the first Monday in January 1840 at Woodbury the last will and testament of John Wood late of sd county decd. was produced at a former session of this court in due form of Law. Whereupon in the same manner James Wood has been qualified as executor. These are therefore to authorise and empower you the said executor to enter into & upon all and singular the goods and chattels Rights and credits of the said Deceased and them into your possession take wheresoever to be found in your state.

(p 436) And a true and perfect Inventory thereof to render to the court according to the law and all the interest debts of the said deceased may amount or extend to and the residue thereof to deliver to those who have a right by law to receive the same.

Witness James M. Brown Clerk of our court at office this the 7th day of January 1840.

James M. Brown Clk.

The court then ajourned until tomorrow morning at 9 oclock.
David Patton Chairman
Charles C. Evans
James Pearse.

(p 437) Wendsday morning January 8th A.D. 1840
The court met pursuant to ajournment present the worshipfull
David Patton chairman &C
Charles C. Evans and
James Pearse Esqrs.

James M. Brown Clerk of this court this day produced in open court a settlement by him made with William Wright Administrator of the Estate of Philip, Palmer deseased which was read to the court and in all things confirmed.

On motion it was ordered that Letters of administration granted to John D. McBreon upon the estate of Elizabeth J. Moore Dec. 1836, be and the same are hereby revoked. And it is further ordered by the court that Isaac W. Elledge Esq. be and is hereby appointed administrator de bonis now of the estate of Elizabeth J. Moore deceased, whereupon the said Isaac W. Elledge together with his securities Benjamin Pendleton and David Patton being present in court entered into bond in the sum of three thousand dollars payable to the Governor of Tennessee for the time being and his successors in office conditioned for the faithfull performance of said administration, and it is (438) further ordered by the court that letters of Administration be granted him upon sd estate which are in the words and figures (to wit)

In the name of the State of Tennessee Cannon County - By the justices of Cannon County, it being certified to us that Elizabeth Jane Moore late of said county is dead, and has made no will or testament on motion it is ordered by the court that Isaac W. Elledge have letters of administration on the estate of the said deneased, These are therefore to authorise and impower you the said administrator to enter into and upon all and singular the goods and chattels Rights and credits of said deceased and them into your possession take and an Inventory thereof and all the interest debt of said deceased to pay so fare as the Estate of said deceased may amount or extend and the residue thereof deliver up to those who have a right to by law to recive the same.

Witness James M. Brown clk.

of our said court at office the 8th day of January 1840.

James M. Brown.

(p 439) On motion and petition of He ry Trott Jr. the foregoing order is made
appointing Isaac W. Elledge administrator of Estate of Elizabeth Jane Moore
for said Trotts relief as security of John D. McBroom former Administrator
of the Estate of the said Elizabeth Jane Moore deceased as it appeared in
said petition to the satisfaction of the co rt that he is in great danger of
being damaged by being any longer bound as security afforesaid and it also
appearing to the satisfaction of the court that said McBroom had abused his
Trust as Administrator afforesaid.

The court then ajourned until court in course.

David Patton Chairman
James Mears
Charles C. Evans

(p 440)

State of Tennessee)
Cannon County   )   At a county court began and held for the county of Cannon
at the court house in the Town of Woodbury on the first Monday and third day
of February in the year of our Lord one thousand Eight hundred and Forty and
of the American Indipendance the sixty fourth year.

Then was the following justices present to wit.

David Patton Chairman
Charles C. Evans
Alexander McKnight Esqrs.

On motion ordered by the court that the shirriff of Cannon sumon the following named men as jurrors for the May Term of the circuit court Cannon County
1840 to wit.

John C. Martin
Moses McKnight
Charles P. Alexander
Jesse Hollis
Absolem Bowen
James R. Taylor
John A. Brown
David McGill
Hugh Craft
Mordicah J. Duke
Josiah Neely
James K. Edson
William Young
William Raylson
J. Boyd
Josiah M. Crane
William West
Samuel Denby
Elijah Scott
Daniel S. Ford
Richard Hancook
Robert Marshall
Thomas D. Sumar
Blake Sagely &
Silas L. Roberts

(p 441)   On motion ordered by the Court that Samuel Denby and Joseph Ramsey
be and they are hereby appointed commissioners of the Revenue for the year 1840

to settle with the county Trustee County Court and Circuit Court clerks of
Cannon County.

Ordered by the court that Francis Cooper Esq. be and he is hereby appointed
Revenue commissioner in the place of John W. Summar to take in a list of Taxable property and poles in district Number Eleven for the year 1840.

It appearing to the satisfaction of the court from the certificate of Thomas
Elkins deputy shirriff of Cannon County that an election had by him been
held in District Number 7 to assertain by a vote of the qualified voters
of said District a place for the holding of elections in said district which
certificate it is ordered by the court be spread upon the journal of the
county. Which certificate is in the words and figures following to wit, I
certify that I opened and held an election an election at the House of John
Meltons in the 7th district of Cannon County to vote and say when the place
of voting should be held in said district, It appears often comparing the votes
it appears that Robert Bailey was the wish of the people Jan. 5th 1840.

Thomas Elkins D. Shff.

(p 442) Upon the petition of Henry Trott Jr. one of the securities of J.D.
McBroom administrator of Elizabeth J. Moore, it is ordered by the county
court that a summons be issued against said John D. McBroom for whom the petitioner stands bound returnable to the next term of this court, to compel said
J.D. McBroom to give other sufficient or county security to be approved by
said court or to deliver up said estate to the said petitioners or to such
other person as the court shall direct.

It appearing to the court upon the statement of the clerk of this court, that
D.G. Stone his deputy intended leaving the county, and that said clerk wished
to appoint another it is ordered by the court that he is permitted to make
said appointment , Whereupon R.M. White was duly appointed said deputy, and
being in court on oath was administered to him by the chairman of this court
to support the constitution of the united States — the constitution of the
State of Tennessee together with the oath of office.

David Patton chairman of this court by direction of this court and on their
behalf this day bound an orphan boy by the name of Barnett G. Smith aged about
13 years, untill he attains the age of twenty one years, to Daniel B. Nichols
with him to live and work as an apprentice whereupon the said David Patton
chairman as aforesaid and the said Daniel B. Nichols together with his security
(p 443) Wm. Nichols entered into an indenture bearing even date with this record
containing the stipulations as by the court. And the said Daniel B. Nichols
agreed upon.
The court then ajourned until tomorrow morning 10 oclook.
David Patton
Charles C. Evans
Alexander McKnight

Tueseday morning February 4th 1840
The court met pursuant to ajournment present the worshipfull
David Patton chairman
Charles C. Evans &
Alexander McK ight Esqrs.
James M. Brown clerk of this court produced in open court a settlement by
him made with Vinson Gather Administrator of Thomas Stroud desseased which was
in all things confirmed by the court there being no objection to the same.
The court then ajourned untill court in course.

David Patton
Charles C. Evans
Alexander McKnight

March Term 1840

(p 444)   State of Tennessee)
          Cannon County   )   At a county court began and held for the county of
Cannon at the court house in the Town of Woodbury on the first Monday and second
day of March in the year of our Lord one thousand Eight hundred and forty and
of the American Indipendence the 64th year.

Then was the following orders made to wit.
David Patton Chairman
Charles C. Evans
Alexander McKnight Esqrs.

Ordered by the court that Eli Nicholl be and he is hereby appointed revenue
commissioner in place of Joshua Nichols Deseased, to take in a list of Taxable property and poles in District No. 1 and make Report to the next term of
this court

Alexander McKnight Coronor of Cannon County this day returned into open court
an Inquest by —— held on the 19th day of February 1840 over the dead body of
James McAdoo which are in the words and figurs to wit.

State of Tennessee)
Cannon County   )   We being duly elected empowered sworn and charged by the
coroner (p 445) of Cannon County as a jury of Inquest to inquire how when
and in what manner James McAdoo came to his death on our oaths do say that the
said James McAdoo on the 19th day of February 1840 in the County of Cannon came
to his death by being dashed from his horse against a tree on his own plantation
And not otherwise. Given and rendered by us this the 19th day of February 1840.

John W. Summar (seal) foreman of jury of inquest.
B.W. Hail (seal)
James Odom (seal)
Moses Standy (seal)
John Willard (seal)
William Wharton (seal)
Wily Davenport (seal)
Armsred Francis (seal)
Alexander A. Smith (seal)
R.L. Molem (seal)
Benjamin Sapp (seal)
Nelson Owen (seal)
Alexander McKnight (seal)
Coronor of Cannon County

(p 446) Michael West Executor of Abraham Sauls deced. this day Returned into
open court an Inventory of said Estate and was duly sworn to the same. The
same was ordered to —— Recorded in the proper book.

Matthew Whitfield Administrator of Wily Willis Deseased, this day Returned into
open court an Inventory of the Estate of Wily Willis Deseased. and was duly
sworn to the same. It is ordered that the same be Recorded in the proper book.

John C? Martin one of the administrators of the Estate of Levi Parker Deceased this day returned into open court an Inventory of said Estate and was duly sworn to the same ordered by the court that the same be record in the proper book.

Charles P. Alexander this day produced in open court this day a paper writing purporting to be the Last will and Testament of Moses Shelby Deceased to which it appeared that James Cherry and ———————— were subscribing witnesses and it also appearing that said witnesses were not at this time Redidents of the State of Tennessee and thereupon by and with the assent of the court David D. Hipp and Richard C. Price come forward into open (p 447) court and proved said paper writeing to be the last will and Testament of said Moses Shelby (Deceased) by Testifying that they believe the signature purporting to be Moses Shelby they belived to —— genuine. On motion the same is admited to Record and it appearing to the satisfaction of the court that William Bates and Charles P. Alexander had been appointed in said will to Execute the same the said William Bates and Charles P. Alexander being in court came forward and was duly qualified as such who togeather with their securities Richard C. Price & Woodson Northcutt entered into bond in the Sum of Two thousand dollars conditioned and payable as the law directs whareupon It is ordered by the court that Letters Testamentary be granted them upon said Estate which are in the words and figures following to wit.

In the name of the State of Tennessee at the county court of Cannon held on the first Monday in March at Woodbury the last will and testamnt of Moses Shelby Late of said County Deceased was produced And and aproven in open court in due form of Law whareupon in the same manner William Bates & Charles P. Alexander (p 448) has been qualified as Executor these are tharefore to Autherise and empower you the said Executors to enter into and upon all and singular the goods and chattels Rites and credits of the said Deceased and them into your posesion take wharesoever to be found in this State and an Inventory thareof to render to the court according to Law and all the interest debt of said deseased to pay so fare as the said Estate of the said Desceased may amount or extend to and the residue thareof to deliver up to those who have a wright by Law to Receive the same.
Witness James M. Brown Clerk of our said court at office this Monday in March 1840.
   (signed) James M. Brown clk.

On motion it is ordered by the court that Richard C. Price be and he is hereby appointed Administrator of the Estate of Elizabeth Couch desceased whereupon the said Richard C. Price and William Bates being present in court enter into Bond in the sum of three hundred dollars payable to the govenor of the state for the time being and his successors in office conditioned for the faithful performance of his said Administration and on ——— it is ordered by the court that Letters of Administration be granted him upon said Estate, which are in the figures and words following to wit.

State of Tennessee)
Cannon County   )   March Sesion 1840
Whareas it appears to the court that Elizabeth Couch is dead and having made no will or testament and application being made by Richard C. Price to have Letters of Administration granted him on said Estate of the said Elizabeth Couch he having given bond and security as by Law in such cases is Required the court tharefore order that he have Letters accordingly. These are tharefore to Autherize and empower you the said Richard C. Price to enter into and upon all and singular the goods and chattels Rights and credits of the said Elizabeth Couch Deceased and the same into your posesion take wharesoever to be found in this state and a true and perfect Inventory thareof make and

return into our insuing county court on oath and all the just debts of the intestate pay so fare as the said Estate will amount or extend the residue thereof deliver to those who have a right thereto by law Herein fail not Witness J
James M. Brown clerk of our said court at office the first Monday in March 1840

J.H. Brown clk.

(p 450) Hugh Robinson this day produced in open court a paper writing perporting to be the last will and Testament of Thomas Thrower (Deseased) and it appearing to the court that Hugh Robinson and James Williams was subscribing witnesses to the same who came into court and proved the same it is therefore ordered by the court and proved the same he admited to Record.

It appearing to the satisfaction of the court that a summons had been Issued by the clerk of this court upon order made at the last term of this court requiring John D. McBroom to come in at the present term of this court to give other or better security for his administration on th e Estate of Elizabeth Jane Moore Deseased or deliver up said estate to Henry Trott one of said McBrooms securities , And it also appearing to the satisfaction of the court that said summons had been served on said McBroom by a Lawfull officer of this county and the said McBroom having failed to appear agreable to said summons to the present term of this court and Give other or counter security or deliver up said Estate. It is therefore ordered by the court that letters of Administration granted (p 451) said McBroom on the Estate of the said Elizabeth Jane Moore be revoked the court then ajourned until tomorrow morning Ten oclock,
David Patton
Charles C. Evans
Alexander McKnight

Tuseday morning March 3rd 1840
The court met pursuant to ajournment present
David Patton Chairman
Charles C. Evans
Alexander McKnight Esqrs.

     Ordered by the court that Gabriel Williams be and he is hereby appointed a juror in the plan of James K. Eason to serve at the May term of the circuit court next.
The court then adjourned until court in course.
David Patton
Charles C. Evans
Alexander McKnight

Aprile Session 1840

(p 452)
State of Tennessee
     At a county court Began and held for the County of Cannon at the court House in the Town of Woodbury on the first Monday and sixth day of April in the year of our Lord one thousand Eight hundred and forty and of the Indipendance of the United States the sixty fourth year present the worshipfull
David Patton chairman
John C. Martin
Alexander McKnight
Charles P. Alexander

William McFerrin
William Bowen
Allen Beaty

Richard U. Leray
James Mears
James M. Brown
Nathan Neely
Charles C. Evans
John Melton
Sam'l Lance
William Bates
Sam'l Denby &
Daniel S. Ford Esqrs.

Whereupon the following orders were made to wit.

Rezin Fowler this day produced in open court a certificate from Alexander Mc-
Knight Esq. Coroner of Cannon County from which it appeared to the satisfaction
of the court that he the said Fowler (upon the first Saterday in March 1840)
had been duly and constitutionally Elected clerk of Cannon County court for
the term of four years from that time Whereupon the said Fowler Being pre sent
On motion It was ordered by the court that he be qualified as such which being
performed by David Patton Esqrs Chairman of the court He the said Fowler together with his securities;
Joseph Knox
Isaac Finley
(p 453)
William Preston and
Nathan Finley
(who being approved by the court) Entered into Bond in the sum of seven thousand dollars payable to James K. Polk Governor in and over the state of Tennessee
for the time being and his successors in office for the faithfull performance of his said office which bond is in the words and figuers following to
wit.
        Know all men by the presents that we;
Regin Fowler
Isaac Finley
William Preston
Nathan Finley and
Joseph Knox.
all of the county of Cannon and state of Tennessee are held and firmly bound
unto James K. Polk Governor in and over the State of Tennessee for the time
being and his successors in office in the sum of seven thousand dollars ——
to which payment well and truly to be made we bind ourselves our heirs Executors Administrators and assigns jointly and firmly severally by these presents sealed with our seals and dated this day 6th of April 1840. The conditions of the aboveobligation is such that whareas the above bound Regin Fowler has been duly and constitutionally elected clerk of the county court of
Cannon County for the term of four years from the first Saterday in March 1840.
        Now therefore If the said Regin Fowler shall well and truly keep all the
reccords of said court properly belonging to his office according to Law
during his continuance therein And shall well and truly collect and pay over to
the State Treasur and county Trustee all monies that shall come into his hands
(p 454) By virtue of his office afforesaid then the above obligation to be
void otherwise to remain in ful force and virtue.
(signed)
David Patton) Rezin Fowler (seal)
Cannon County) Joseph Knox (seal
Court   ) Isaac Finley (seal
                Nathan Finley (seal)
                William Preston (seal)

James O. Georgethis day produced in open court the certificate of Alexander
McKnight Esq. Coroner of Cannon County from which it appeared to the satisfaction of the court that the said George had been (upon the first saterday
in March 1840) duly and constitutionally elected sheriff of Cannon County for
the term of two years from that time. Whereupon the said James O. George being
present was duly qualified as such who together with his securities;
John A. George
Benjamin Hayes
Ezekiel Hays
James J. Trott and
Thomas Vance
who being approved by the court, Entered into Bond in the sum of twenty five
thousand dollars payable to James K. Polk Governor in and over the state of
Tennessee for the time being and his successors in office for the faithfull
purformance of his said office which bond is in the words and Figures follow-
ing to wit.

Know all men by these presents that we;
James O. George
John A. George
Benjamin Hays
Ezekiel Hays and
Thomas Vance
all of the county of Cannon and state of Tennessee are held and (p 455) and
firmly bound unto James K. Polk Governor in and over the state of Tennessee
for the time being and his successors in office in the penal sum of twenty five
thousand dollars to which payment well and truly to be made we bind ourselves
our heirs, Executors, Administrators jointly and severally, firmly by these presents sealed with our seals and dated the 6th day of April 1840.
The conditions of the above obligation is such that whereas the above
bound James O. George has been duly and constitutionally elected sheriff of
Cannon County for the term of two years from the first saterday in March 1840.
Now therefore If the said James O. George shall well and truly Execute
and due returns make of all process and precepts to him directed and pay and
satisfy all and sums of money by him received or levied by virtue of any process in the proper office by which the same by the tenor thereof ought to be
paid or to the person or persons to whom the same shall be due his, her or
their Executors Administrators or attornis or agents and in all things well
and truly and faithfully Execute the said office of sheriff during his continuance therein then the above obligation to be void otherwise to remain in
full force and effects.

James O. George (seal)
John A. George (seal)
Benjamin Hays (seal)   Attest. Rezin Fowler Clk.
Ezekiel Hays (seal)
James J. Trott (seal)
Thomas Vance (seal)

(p 456)
Isaac Finley this day produced in open court the certificate of Alexander Mc-
Knight Esq. Coroner of Cannon County from which it appeared to the satisfaction
of the court that the said Isaac Finley had been duly and constitutionally
elected upon the first saterday in March 1840, as Register of Cannon County
for the term of four years from that time, Whereupon the said Isaac Finley
being present was duly qualified as such in open court who together with his
securities;
William Cummins

Thomas G. Wood
Dabrey Ewell
Nathan Finley and
Ezekiel Hays
who being approved of by the court entered into bond in the sum of twelve thousand five hundred dollars, payable to James K. Polk of the state of Tennessee and his successors in office conditioned for the faithful performance of his said office of Register which Bond is in thewords and figures following to wit.

Know all men by these presents that we
Isaac Finley
William Cummins
Thomas G. Wood
Ezekiel Hays
Nathan Finley &
Dabrey Ewell
all of the county of Cannon and State of Tennessee are held and firmly bound unto James K. Polk Governor of the State of Tennessee and his successors in office in the sum of twelve thousand five hundred dollars, for which payment well and truly to be made, we bind ourselves, our heirs, executors and administrators jointly severally firmly by these presents sealed with our seals and dated the 6th day of April 1840.
The condition of the above obligation is such that whereas (p 457) the said Isaac Finley has been duly and constitutionally elected Register for Cannon County for the four ensuing years, from the first saterday in March 1840, Now if the said Isaac Finley shall and well and truly and faithfully execute all the duties of his office as also to keep safe the records all thatt belong to his office during his continuance therein Then this obligation to be void otherwise to remain in full force and virtue.

Isaac Finley (seal)
William Cummins (seal
Thomas G. Wood (seal)   Attest. Rezin Fowler Clk.
Dabrey Ewell (seal)
Nathan Finley (seal)
Ezekiel ^his^ X ^mark^ Hays (seal)

Job Stephens this day produced in open court the certificate of Alexander McKnight Esq. Coroner of Cannon County from which it appeared to the satisfaction of the court that the said Job Stephens, had been duly and constitutionally elected Trustee for said county for the term of Two years from the first Saterday in March 1840. Whereupon the said Job Stephens being present was duly qualified as such in open court who together with his securities;
Joseph Ramsey
Archibald Stone and
Robert Daily
(p 457) who being approved of by the court entered into bond in the sum of five thousand dollars payable to David Patton chairman of Cannon County court and his successors in office conditioned for the faithful performance of said office of Trustee which bond is in the words and figures following to wit.

(p 458)
Know all men by these presents that we;
Joseph Ramsey
Job Stephens
Archibald Stone and

Robert Baily
all of the county of County of Cannon and state of Tennessee are held and firmly bound unto David Patton Chariman of Cannon County Court and his successors
in office in the sum of five thousand dollars for which payment well and truly
to be made we bind ourselves our heirs, executors and administrators jointly
and severally firmly by these presents, sealed with our seals and dated the 6th
day of April 1840. The condition of the above obligation is such that whereas
Job Stephens has been duly and constitutionally elected Trustee for Cannon
County for the term of two years from the first Saturday in March 1840. Now
if the said Job Stephens shall well and truly and faithfully account for and
disburse all county monies that shall come into his hands by virtue of his
office of county Trustee during his cintinuance therein and shall in all
things appertaining to his office discharge the duties of his said office of
county Trustee according to law, Then this ovligation to be void, otherwise to
remain in full force and virtue.

Job Stephens	(seal)
Joseph Ramsey	(seal)
Archibald Stone	(scal)
Robert Baily	(seal)

Attest. Rezin Fowler Clk.

(p 459)
Alexander McKnight Esq. Coroner of Cannon County this day returned into court
a certificate of an Election by him and his deputies held on the first Saturday and seventh day of March 1840 in the different cival districts in Cannon
County from which the certificate It appeared to the satisfaction of the court
that the following persons wereduly and constitutionally elected ac constable
in their respective districts to wit

In District No. one   James D. Orr
In District No two   James P. Todd
In District No third   Thomas E. Jones
In District No fourth   John McLain
In District five   Isham Pelham
In district No. Sixth   William L. Covington and Arthur Youngblood
In District No seven   William Elkins
In District No. Eighth   James H. Lance
In District No. nine   Jas, L. Elledge
In District No. ten   Joseph Hale
In District No. Eleven   Benjamin B. Cooper
In District No.twelvth   Aaron Byford

Whereupon the said constables (Except James P. Todd and Isham Pelham) being
present in court were severally duly qualified as such who severally, together
with their respective securities (being approved of By the court, Entered into
bond severally in the sum of Five thousand dollars conditioned and payable
as the Law directs.

James Wood Executor of John Wood deceased this day reported to court an
account current of the estate of the said decd. and qualified to the same
which is admitted to record.

(p 460)
Dabrey Ewell)
Bill of sale)
Zacheriah Bush) The execution of a quit claim Bill of sale from Dabrey Ewell
to Zachriah Bush fot two negro slaves One a girl about fifteen years old
named Winney, the other a boy about six or seven years old and named Washington —Bearing date the 3rd day of February 1840 was this day duly acknowledged in open court by the said Dabrey Ewell (the bargainor) to be his act and

deed for the purposes therein contained And on motion the same is ordered to
be certified for Registration.

On motion the following justices present to wit.
Alexander McKnight
John Melton
Willaim Bates
David Patton
Charles P. Alexander
Sam'l Denby
William Bowen
Richard U. Lemay
Nathan Neely
James Mears and
Allen Patey Esqrs.
all voting in the affirmative against Charles C. Evans Esq. voting in the
negative. And there being a sufficient number of the justices voting in the
affirmative , Therefore an appropriation of the sum of fifty dollars is made
for the support and maintainance of Parkley Couch pauper which theTrustee of
Cannon County is ordered — pay to such person as may hereafter be appointed
Guardain to the said Parkley out of any monies in his hands not otherwise
appropriated.

On motion the following justices present to wit.
Alexander McKnight
Charles C. Evans
James Mears
William Bates
David Patton
John Melton
Sam'l Denby
Nathan Neely
Wm. Bowen
(p 461)
Allen Patoy
Charles P. Alexander and
John C. Martin Esqrs.
all voting in the affirmative therefore an allowance of the sum of Sevebty one
dollars and thirty seven and a half (cents &C that is to say - is made to James
M. Brown clk. for Issuing twenty Eight jury tickets making one dollar and seven-
ty five cents for copying one pauper allowance fifty cents for entering two jury
list of Reccord seventeen road orders and Issuing copys of same two dollars
and twelve and a half cents for making two copys of Taxes thirty six dollars—
For half years servises Exoficio twenty dollars - for recording constables certificates of Elections of school commissioners ten dollars which the Trustee of
Cannon County is ordered to pay out of any monies in his hands not otherwise
appropriated.

On motion the following justices present to wit.
James M. Brown
Alexander McKnight
Daniel S. Ford
James Mears
William Bates
David Patton
Charles P. Alexander
John Melton

William Bowen
Sam'l Denby
John C. Martin &
Allen Batey Esqrs.
all voting in the affirmative against Charles C. Evans Esq. voting in the negative therefore an allowance of the sum of Forty dollars is made to H.R. Jarratt
for the consideration of his Exoficio servises for the year of 1839. Which the
Trustee of Cannon County is ordered to pay out of any monies in his hands not
otherwise appropriated.

(p 462)
On motion the following justices present to wit
James M. Brown
Alexander McKnight
Daniel S. Ford
James Mears
William Bates
David Patton
Charles P. Alexander
John Melton
Willaim Bowen
Sam'l Denby
John C. Martin and
Alleh Batey Esqrs.
all voting in the affirmative against Charles C. Evans Esq. voting in the
negative t erefore an allowance is made to Higdon R. Jarratt late sheriff
and collector Cannon County of the sum of twenty dollars & ninty   four cents
It being the two thirds and the amount of the county Taxes included in a list
of insolvents that he the said Jarratt this day returned into court which stand
upon the Tax list for the year 1839 And unpaid And that he has paid and account-
ed for the County Trustee for the same which allowance the Trustee of Cannon
County is ordered to pay to the said Jarratt out of any monies in his hands
not otherwise appropriated in the way of reimbursing him of the same.

Whereas having been this day made known to the satisfaction of the court that
Joshua Nichols of our county is deceased and whereas Mary A. Nichols the widow
of the said deceased by her order having notified the court thatshe had waved
all right that she by law has to administer on said estate. Therefore on
motion it is ordered by the court that Ephriam Andrews and Thomas H. Youree
be and they are hereby appointed administrators of the estate of the said deceased who being present were duly gallified (p 463) as such and together
with their securities H.R. Jarratt and Alexander McKnight being approved of
by the court entered into bond in the sum of one thousand dollars conditioned
and payable as the law directs. And thereupon letters of administration were
granted them upon said estate which are in words and figures following to wit.

        In the name of the state of Tennessee Cannon County by the justices of
Cannon County it being certified to us that Joshua Nichols late of said county
is deceased and has made no will or testament, On motion it is ordered by
the court that Ephria- Andrews and Thomas H. Youree have letters of Administration on the estate of the said deceased these are therefore to authorize
and empower you the said administrator to enter into and upon all and singular
the goods and chattels, rights and credits of the said deceased and then into
your possession take and an Inventory thereof to render to the courts within
ninety days from the date hereof and all the interest debt of the said decd.
to pay so far as the estate of the said deceased may extend or amount to and
the residue thereof to deliver up to these who have a right to by law receive
the same. Witness James M. Brown clk. of our said court at office this first

Monday in A^Pril 1840.
                    James M. Brown clk.

(p 464)
On motion of John C. Ransom Esq. the court appoint;
James M. Brown
James J. Trott
Joseph Ramsey &
Archibald Stone
(p 464) Trustees of Laurens Academy at Woodbury and that the clerk of this
court issue a copy of this order and deliver it to the said Trustees.

Wheras at the January term of this court 1840 the time prescribed by Law for the
Leving of Taxes for county purposes the court omitted the leving a Tax upon
privileges and occupations for county purposes. And whereas it is also provid-
edby Law that if the court should fail or omit to lay a Tax at the Term of the
court above mentioned they may do so at April Term following. It is therefore
ordered by the court the following justices present to wit,
Allen Batey
James M. Brown
Charles C. Evans
Alexander Mc Knight
Daniel S. Ford
James Mears
William Bates
David Patton
Charles/Alexander
John Melton
William Brown
Sam'l Denby
John C. Martin and
Richard U. Lemay Esqrs.
all voting in the affirmative And being a majority of all the justices in the
county that a Tax of the amount of the state tax fixed by Law be laid on all
the privileges and occupations liable to Taxation in the state for county pur-
poses And the clerk of this court collect the same, when Issuing license for
the same and collecting the state Taxes.

(p 465) Edmund Barton this day produced in court a certificate from James O.
George Esq. sheriff of Cannon County from which it appeared to the satisfaction
of the court that he the said Barton had been duly appointed as deputy sheriff
of Cannon County, Therefore on motion he was by the clerk of this court duly
qualified a such according to Law.

Court then adjourned till tomorrow ten oclock.
                              David Patton
                              James Mears
                              Samuel Denby

Court met on Tuesday morning April the 7, 1840 pursuant to adjournment present
the worshipful
David Patton Chairman
John C. Martin
Alexander McKnight
Charles C. Evans
Samuel Denby

James Mears
James M. Brown and
Nathan Neely Esqrs.

On motion of Isaac Finley Esqr. Register of Cannon County Thomas G. Wood was permitted to be qualified as deputy Register And ordered that the same be made of Record.

James P. Todd who was reported on the first day of the present Term of this court by Alexander McKnight Esqr. Coroner of Cannon County to have been duly and constitutionally Elected Constable in the second cival dostriot, in Cannon (p 466) County for the Term of two years from the first Saturday in March 1840 And who failed to appear in court on the said first day of this Term to qualify &c.

This day came into court and on motion the oaths of office were duly administered to him by the clerk of this court, After which he, together with his securities who being approved by the court, Entered into Bond in the sum of five thousand dollars conditioned and payable as the law dirlots.

James M. Brown Esq. former clerk of this court this day reported to court the following settlements by him made with the following persons to wit. with David Patton and David McGill administrators of James McGill deceased; with John Hollensworth admr. of Samuel Tittle deceased; with Henry D. McBroom and Benjamin Sapp executors of the estate of James Barkley deceased; with William Stone and Alexander Higgins administrators (p 467) of Usibious Stone deceased with William Bennett Guardain of Sophia Bennett; with William Moore Guardain of Elizabeth Jane Moore minor heir of Roben Moore deceased; with William Moore Guard. of Jacob Moore minor heir of Jessie G. Moore deceased, with Thomas S. Bennitt Guardain of Richard S. Bennitt heir at Law of John M. Bennett and Judith Bennitt decd. all of which being Emanied and by the court fully understood are in all things confirmed.

Whereas John D. McBroom administrator of Elizabeth Jane Moore having at the last term of this court Been removed from his said administrationship upon the petitionnof one of his securities to wit, Henry Trott Jr. Now therefore It is ordered by the court that John C. Martin and Isaac W. Elledge be and they are hereby appointed Administrators deboures non of the estate of the said Elizabeth Jane Moore deceased who being present were duly qualified as such; And together with his securities Henry D. McBroom and Isaac Finley being approved of by the court Entered into bond in the sum of thirty five hundred dollars payable to James K. Polk Governor in and over the state of Tennessee for the time being and his successors in office conditioned for the faithful purformance as such whereupon It is ordered by the court that they have letters of administration upon said estate which are in the words and Figures following to wit- (p 468) State of Tennessee, Cannon County Whereas It appearing to the satisfaction of the court that Elizabeth Jane Moore is dead and that wheras one John D. McBroom having been appointed administrators of the Estate of the said deceased, And having been at the last Term of this court removed And application by John C. Martin and Isaac W. Elledge being made to the court, They are hereby appointed Administrators deboures non of the estate of the said deceased, These are therefore to authorise you the said Administrator to enter into and upon all and singular the Goods and Chattels rights and credits of the said deceased, And them into your possession take and an Inventory render to the court within ninety days from the date hereof and all the debts of the Intestate, pay so far as the estate may amount or extend and the rest and residue thereof pay over to such person or persons as have a right by Law to receive the same.

Witness Rezin Fowler clerk of our said court at office the 1st Monday in April 1840.
Rezin Fowler clerk.

Court then adjourned till tomorrow morning ten oclock.
David Patton
James M. Brown
James Mears

(p 459) Court met on Wednesday morning April 8th 1840 pursuant to adjournment
The worshipful
David Patton chairman
James M. Brown
James Mears Esqrs.

Then was the following orders made to wit.

Elijah Nealy)
vs)
Henry D. McBroom)   Executor James Barkley Dec.
&)
Benjamin Sapp
This day came the parties with their Attorney and on motion of Elizabeth Nealy for a reconsideration it was refused, and prayed as <u>appeal</u> to the circuit court of Cannon County to be held at Woodbury in the county aforesaid on the 2nd Monday in May 1840 which was granted.

Court then adjourned till court in course.
David Patton
James M. Brown
James Mears.

Hay Term 1840

(p 470)
State of Tennessee
     At a county court began and held for Cannon County at the court House in the Town of Woodbury on the first Monday and fourth day of May in the year of our Lord one thousand eight hundred and forty and of the <u>Independance</u> of the United States the sixty fourth year. Present the worshipfull
David Patton chairman
Alexander McKnight
Charles C. Evans
quoram justices.

Then was the following orders made(to wit.)

William Moore this day produced in open court a commission from his Excellency Governor in and over the state of Tennessee to him the said William Moore as justice of the peace for Cannon County. And on motion the said William Moore came forward and the oath of office was duly administered to him by the clerk of this court whereupon it was ordered by the court that the same be made of Record.

     On motion it is ordered by the court the worshipful,
David Patton

Alexander McKnight and
Charles C. Evans
being present all voting in the affirmative. The thanks of the court were
voted to James Taylor, (sen) Esqr. for his public spirit in placing at his
individual expense, a stone step at the front door of the court house of said
county and that the order be made of Record.

(p 471)
George Boyle, one of the executors of John Higgins (deceased) this day reported to court a Supplemental account of the effects of the said (deceased) and
being quallified to the same which was admitted to record.

Bezin Fowler Clerk of this court this day presented to the court a settlement
by him made with James Malone administrator of Winney Scrivener (deceased)
which being examined by the court in all things confirmed.

Richard C. Price administrator of Elizabeth Couch (deceased) this day reported
to court an account current of the sales and other effects of the said (deceased)
and being qualified to the same which was admitted to record.

William Bates Esq. one of the executors of the estate of MOses Shelby (deceased)
this day reported to court an account of the sale and other effects of the estate – said deceased and being duly quallified to the same- which was admitted
to record.

On motion of John C. Ransom Esq. the court appoint
James H. Brown
James Wood
Joseph Ramsey
Archibald Stone and
James J. Trott
be and they are hereby appointed Trustees of Lawrens Academy for the term of
two years, and that the clerk of this court Issue a copy of this order and de-
liver it to the said Trustees.

(p 472) Ordered by the court that the report of Alexander McKnight Coroner at
March Term of this court 1840 is conclusive that he has performed all the duties contemplated by the Act of the Assembly in holding an Inquest over the
dead body of James McAdoo and that the clerk of the court certify the same to
the county Trustee.

David McGill this day produced in open court a paper writing purporting to be
the last will and Testament of Nancy McGill decd. from which it appeared to the
satisfaction of the court that the said David McGill and John McCrary were
appointed to Execute the same who being present were duly qualified as such
And together with their securities entered into bond in the sum of Four thousand
dollars payable to the Governor for the time being and his successors in office
conditioned as the law directs, Whereupon letters Testamentary were Granted
them upon said estate which are in the words and Figures to wit.

In the name of the State of Tennessee at the county court of Cannon County
held on the first Monday in May at Woodbury the last will and Testament of Nancy
McGill late of said county (deceased) Whereupon in the same manner David Mc-
Gill and John McCrary has been quallified as executors. These are therefore
to authorize and empower you the said executors to enter into and upon all and
singular the goods and chattels, rights and credits (p 473) of the said deceased and them into your possession take wheresoever to be found in this
state and an Inventory thereof to render to the court according to law and all

the interest debts of the said (deceased) to pay so far as the estate of the s
said (deceased) may amount or extend to and the residue thereof to deliver up
to those who have a right to by law receive the same. Witness Rezin Fowler Clerk
of our said court at office this first Monday in May 1840.

R. Fowler Clk.

On motion It is ordered by the court that Richard Tenpenny be and he is
hereby appointed administrator of the estate of John Vance (deceased) whereupon the said Richard Tenpenny came into court together with his securities J.C.
Martin and Joseph Ramsey who entered into bond in the sum of five hundred dollars payable to James K. Polk governor in and over the state of Tennessee and
his successors in office conditioned for the faithful performance of his said
administration and it is ordered by the court that letters of administration
granted him on the said estate which in the words and figures following (to wit)

State of Tennessee)
Cannon County)
By the justices of Cannon County it being certified to us that John Vance
late of said county (is deceased) and has left no will or Testament On motion
it is ordered by the court that Richard Tenpenny have letters (p 474) of administration on the estate of the said (deceased) These are therefore to authorise and empower you the the said administrator to enter into and upon all
and singular the goods and chattels, rights and credits of the said deceased
and them into your possession take and an Inventory thereof to render to the
court within ninety days from the date hereof, and all the interest debt of
the said deceased, to pay so far as the estate of the said (deceased) may
a,ount or extend to, and the residue thereof to deliver up to those who have
a right to by law to recive the same.-
Witness Rezin Fowler Clerk of our said court at office this the first Monday
in May 1840.
R. Fowler. Clk.

On motion It is ordered by the court that John M. Alexander be and is hereby
appointed administrator of the estate of James McAdoo, deceased, whereupon the
said John M. Alexander came into court together with his securities J.W. Marshall and J.W. McAdoo who being approved of by the court entered into bond in
the sum of two hundred dollars payable to James K. Polk governor in and over
the state of Tennessee for the time being and his successors in office conditioned for the faithful performance of his said administration granted him on
the said Estate which are in the words and figures following (to wit)

(p 475)
State of Tennessee)
Cannon County)
By the justices of Cannon County It being certified to us that James
McAdoo late of said county is deceased, and has left no will or tesyament
On motion it is ordered by the court that John M. Alexander have letters of
administration on the estate of the said deceased. These are therefore to
authorise and empower you the said administrator to enter into and upon all
and singular the goods and chattel rights and credits of the said deceased
and them into your possession take and an Inventory thereof render to the
court within ninety days from the date hereof and all the interest debt of the
said deceased to pay so far as the estate of the said deceased may amount or
extend and the residue thereof to deliver up to those who have a right to by
Law to receive the same.
Witness Rezin Fowler Clk. of our said court at office the first Monday of May
1840.
R. Fowler.

On motion It is ordered by the court that Richard B. Price be and he is hereby appointed as Guardain of Barkely Couch (a pauper) who together with his security William Bates came into court and Entered into bond in the sum of one hundred dollars conditioned and payable as the law diriots.

(p 476)
Court then adjourned till Court in course.
David Patton
Charles C. Evans
Alexander McKnight.

June Term 1840

State of Tennessee

At a county court began and held for the county of Cannon at the court house in the Town of Woodbury on the first Monday and first day in June in the year of our Lord one thousand eight hundred and forty And of the Independence of the United States the sixty fourth year, present the worshipfull
David Patton Chairman
Charles C. Evans
Alexander McKnight Esqrs. Quorum Justices.

Then was the following orders made (to wit)

Samuel Greear this day came into court and produced a commission from his Excellency the governor in and over the state of Tennessee To him the said Samuel Greear as justice of the peace for Cannon County And on motion the said Samuel Greear came forward and was duly quallified as such by the Clerk of this court Whereupon it was ordered by the court that the same be made of Record.

Richard Tenpenny Administrator of the estate of John Vance deceased) this day reported an account current of the sale and other effets of the said deceased. And on motion was duly quallified (p 477) to the same, and that the same be Recorded in the proper Book.

Charles P. Alexander an acting justice of the peace for Cannon County this day tendered his resignation as such to the worshipful court, which are in the words and figures following (to wit)

June Term of the county court 1840,
To the chairman of Cannon County Court I now tender to you my resignation as a justice of the peace for the second district of said county given under my hand on June 1st 1840.
C.P. Alexander

Rezin Fowler Clerk of this court this day presented to the worshipful court for their confirmation or Rejection The following Settlements by him made (to wit) one with John McMinn and George Doyle the executors of the Estate of John Higgins (deceased) and one with Thomas Givens guardain of William and Henry Bratton minor heirs of Henry Bratton (deceased) which being examined and understood by the court was in all things confirmed.

Henry D. McBroom &)
Benjamin Sapp Executors)
of James Barkley decd.)
    vs)
Elijah Neely) Settlement of Executor ———
                 Clerk of the county court &C
On motion of the Defendant by his attorney it is ordered by the court that the clerk of this court proceed forthwith without regard to a former settlement made

by the executors aforesaid with James M. Brown former clerk of this court and settle with said executor according to Law.

(p 478) On motion it is ordered by the court that the sheriff of Cannon County summon the following named persons as jurors for the September Term of the circuit court of said county 1840.

District No 1 Rigdon Jarratt and Lewis Jetton

District No. 2 — Dennis Haywood and John Hollis

District No. 3 — William Bowen and A.F. McFerrin

District NO. 4 — Thomas J. Williams and John H. Banks

District No. 5 — E.A. Orr and Jonathan Marchbanks

District No. 6 — Isaac Mc Breen, Benjamin Sapp and John L. Taylor.

District No. 7 — C.C. Evans and Thomas Elkins

District No. 8 — John Parles and John Tucker

District No. 9 — Wm. B. Jones and Luke Shirley.

District No. 10 — Lewis Hancock and Robert King

District No. 11 — John W. Summars and James Reed

District No. 12 — Isaac W. Elledge and William Ring

Constables--------- William Elkins and Aaron Byford

On motion of James O. George Sheriff of Cannon County, Franklin Coleman came forward and was duly qualified as collector of the public taxes for said county by the clerk of this court whereupon It is ordered by the court that and the same be made of record.

James O. George Sheriff and collector in and for Cannon County This day came forward together with his securities and entered into the following Bonds, for the faithful collection and paying over the State and County Taxes of said County for the year 1840. Which Bonds are in the words and figures following (to wit)

Know all men by these present that we (p 479)
James O. George
E. Berton
Isaac Finley and
William L. Covington
All of the county of Cannon and State of Tennessee are held and firmly bound unto James K. Polk governor in and over the State of Tennessee for the time being and his successors in office for the use of the state in the sum of eight hundred and twenty five dollars to the payment of which well and truly to be made, we bind ourselves, our heirs Executors and Administrators jointly and severally firmly by these presents sealed with our seals and dated the 4th day of June A.D. 1840.

The condition of the above obligation is such that whereas the above bound James O. George has been duly and constitutionally elected sheriff and collector of the public Taxes of said County of Cannon for the Term of two years from the first Saturday in March 1840 - Now if the said James O. George shall well and truly collect all State Tax, And also all Taxes on school lands within said County

which by law he ought to collect and well and truly account for and pay over all
Taxes by him collected or which ought to be collected. On the first day of January 1840.

Then the above obligation to be void. Otherwise to remain in full force
and virtue.

Signed
J.O. George (seal)
E. Barton (seal)
Isaac Finley (seal)
Wm. L. Covington (seal)
Attest. Rezin Fowler Clk.

(p 480)
Know all men by these presents that we;
James O. George
James Mearn
Isaac Finley and
William L. Covington
all of the county of Cannon and State of Tennessee are held and firmly bound
unto David Patton Chairman of said county and his successors in office for the
use of said county in the sum of sixteen hundred and fifty dollars, to the payment of which well and truly to be made we bind ourselves our executors and adm
ministrators jointly and severally firmly by these presents sealed with our seals
and dated the 1st day of June A.D. 1840.

The condition of the above obligation is such that whereas the above
bound James O. George has been duly and constitutionally Elected Sheriff and
collector of Cannon County for the Term of two years from the first Saturday in
March 1840. Now if the said James O. George shall truly collect all county Taxes within said county which by law he ought to collect and well and truly
Collect and account for and pay over all Taxes by him collected to the County
Trustee of said county on the first day of December in the year 1840. Then the
above obligation to be void, otherwise to remain in full force and virtue.

Signed
J.O. George (seal)
James Mearn (seal)
Isaac Finley (seal)
Wm. L. Covington (seal)

(p 481)
Court then adjourned till tomorrow morning nine oclock
David Patton
Charles C. Evans
Alexander McKnight

Tuseday morning June the 2nd 1840
The worshipful Court met persuant to adjournment present the worshipful
David Patton Chairman
Charles C. Evans
Alexander McKnight
Quoram Justices.

Then was the following orders made (to wit)
James O. George this day presented to this court. The Tax Book – which was
received by the court and on motion it is ordered by the court that the matter
be made of Record.

There appearing no further buisness to be done the court then adjourned
till Court in Course.

David Patton
Charles C. Evans
Alexander McKnight

State of Tennessee
    At a county court begun and held for the County of Cannon at the court
House in the Town of Woodbury on the first Monday and sixth day of July in the
year of our Lord one thousand eight hundred and forty and the Independance of
the United States the sixty fifth year – present The worshipful
David Patton Chm.
Samuel Denby
William Moore
John D. McBroom
Richard U. Leway
James M. Brown   (p 482)
James Moore
Nathan Neely
E.A. Orr
William Bowen
Alexander McKnight
John C. Martin
Charles C. Evans
John Melton
Daniel C. Ford
John W. Sumner and
Silas A. Robinson Esqrs.

Then was the following orders made (to wit)

James C. George Sheriff of Cannon County this day produced in open court the
following Commissions from his Excellency the governor in and over the State
of Tennessee to the following persons (to wit) John D. McBroom and Eleazer
A. Orr as justices of the peace in and for said County of Cannon whereupon the
said McBroom and E.A. Orr came forward into court and the oath of office was
duly administered to them by the clerk of this court – And on motion it was
ordered by the court that the same be made of record.

David McGill and John McCrary Executors of the last will and Testament of Nancy
McGill Deceased This day Reported to court — an account Current of the sales
and other effects of the said (deceased) and was duly qualified to the same
by the clerk of this court And on motion it is ordered by the court that the
same be Recorded in the proper book.

(p 483)
On motion the following present (to wit)
Alexander McKnight
John C. Martin
William Bowen
Richard U. Leway
Eleazer A. Orr
Nathan Neely
James M. Brown
James Moore
John Melton
Charles C. Evans
Sam'l Denby
John W. Sumner
David Patton

William Moore and
John D. McBroom Hears.

all voting in the affirmative . Therefore the sum of thirty six dollars is
hereby appropriated that is to say three dollars each to the Revenue Commiss-
ioners appointed by the court to yake in a list of Taxable property in and for
their respective civil districts for the fiscal year 1840- (to wit)
Charles P. Alexander
William Bowen
Daniel Finley
Richard U. Lenay
James Hears
Charles C. Evans
Josiah M. Crane
William B. Foster
Robert L. Shaw
Francis Cook
David Patton and
Eli Nichols

It is therefore ordered by the court that the Clerk of this court Issue seperate
orders to each of the above named commissioners for the same - and that the
Trustee of Cannon County is ordered to pay the same out of any money in his
hands not otherwise appropriated.

John M. Alexander Administrator of the estate of James Mc Adoo Deceased, This
day reported to court an account Current of the Sales and other effects of
the said deceased and was duly quallified to the same.- And on motion it
was ordered by the court that the same be recorded in the proper Book --

(p 424)
On motion the court proceeded to elect a County Surveyor for Cannon County And
on counting the votes polled at the first Pallading John Andrews was found
to be duly and constitutionally Elected to the said office of County Survey-
or of Cannon County.

On motion the court proceeded to elect a Coroner in and for the Cannon County
and on Counting the votes polled - at the first Pallading John Fisher was
found to be duly and constitutionally elected to the said office of Coroner for
Cannon County.

On motion the court proceeded to the Election of a Ranger in and for Cannon
County and on counting the votes polled at the first Pallading John Estus
was found to be duly and constitutionally Elected to the said office of Ranger
in and for Cannon County.

Herod Holt   )
    To   )
Aaron Byford   )
Deed 200 acres.) The execution of a deed of conveyance from Herod Holt to
Aaron Byford for two Hundred acres of land lying in Cannon County and State of
Tennessee bearing date the 19th of October 1838 - was this day duly acknow-
ledged by the said Holt the Bargainor And on motion it is ordered by the court
that the same be certified for Registration.
William Whitamore
    To
William Howard
Deed 70 acres

The execution of a deed of conveyance from Herod Holt to Aaron Pyford for two hundred acres of land lying in Cannon County, and State of Tennessee bearing date the 12th of October 1838 - was this day duly acknowledged by the said Holt the Bargainor - And on motion it is ordered by the court that the same be certified be certified for Registration.

William Whitamore)
    To)
William Howard)
  Deed 70 acres) The execution of a deed of conveyance from William Whitamore to William Howard for seventy acres of land (p 485) lying in Cannon County and State of Tennessee Bearing date the 1st day of December 1838 was this day duly proven by the oath of James D. Holt and Hugh Robinson Esqr. two of the subscribing witnesses to the same - And on motion it is ordered by the court that the same be certified for Registration.

William and Franky Howard)
    To)
Aaron Pyford)
Deed 70 acres) The execution of a deed of conveyance from William and Franky Howard to Aaron Pyford for seventy acres of land lying in Cannon County and State of Tennessee Bearing date the 29th day of June 1840 - was this day duly proven by the oath of Baxter B. Dickeys and Joseph Nivens - two of the subscribing witnesses to the same - And on motion It is ordered by the court that the same be certified for Registration.

The State of Tennessee)
    vs)
Frederick Hoover) Recognizance for Bastardy, This day came the defendant by J.C. Ransom Esquire his attorney, and moved the court to quash the proceedings in this cause on the ground of irregularity, which motion was overruled by the court, and thereupon the court ordered the defendant to inter into bond with good and sufficient security to support the bastard child of Mary Ann Joy ans indemnify the County of Cannon against all expenses that have or may accrue in supporting said child, And the defendant by his attorney from all of which prayed an (p 486) appeal to the next circuit court to be holden for said County of Cannon on the third Monday in September next which is granted by the court upon the defendant entering into bond with security according to law for the prosecution of the same to effect.

    Court then adjourned till tomorrow morning nine o'clock.
David Patton
Richard U. Lemay
Charles C. Evans
Ja C. Martin

Tuesday morning July the 7th 1840
    The worshipfull court met pursuant to adjournment present the Worshipfull
David Patton Chairman
John D. McBroom
Richard U. Lemay
Charles C. Evans
Joh C. Martin and
Nathan Neely Esqrs.

Then was the following orders made (to wit)

Pursuant to the Acts of the Ceheral Assembly in such cases made and provided

Benjamin Fowler Clerk of this court this day presented to the court for their confirmation or rejection, the following Settlements by him made with the following named persons (to wit) With Joseph Bryson guardan of John Bryson, minor heir of William Bryson, deceased, with Robert K. Stephens Executor of the last will and Testament of Robert Stephens deceased and with David Patton guardian of Katherine and Nancy Glen All of which being examined and by the court fully understood are in all things confirmed.

(p 437)
John Estus who was duly Elected on the first day of the rpesent Term of this court as Ranger in and for Cannon County for the Term of two years from this date this day came into court – And on motion the oath of office was duly administered to him by the Clerk of this court after which he together with his securities Jessee Trower and Franklin Coleman who being approved of by the court – Entered into bond in the sum of five hundred dollars conditioned and payable as the law directs – Also John Fisher who was duly and constitutionally elected Coroner in and for Cannon County for the Term of two years from this date – In like manner came into court and the oath of office was duly administered to him as such – who together with his securities Isaac Finley and John Estus being approved of by the court Entered into Bond in the sum of twenty five hundred dollars conditioned and payable as the law directs.

On motion the court proceeded to Elect one Entry taker in and for Cannon County And on counting the votes polled on the first Ballading John C. Ranson Esq. was found to be duly and constitutionally elected to said office of Entry Taker for Cannon County Whereupon the said John C. Ranson came into court together with his securities James O. George and Henry Trott being approved of by the court and entered into bond in the sum of two thousand dollars conditioned and payable as the as the law directs. And Whereupon was duly quallified as such.

Majot John Andrews who was duly Elected Surveyor in and for Cannon County, on the first day of the present Term of this court this day came into (p 488) court together with his securities Joseph Ramsey and John C. Martin who being approved of by the court Entered into Bond in the sum of ten thousand dollars conditioned and payable as the law directs – And on motion was duly quallified as such.

H.C. Helroani &
Benj. Camp Exec. of)
James Barkley dcod.) This day the clerk of this court produced to the court the settlement with the plaintiff as executor aforesaid which was axcepted of by the court and ordered to be affirmed and the defendant by his attorney excepted to the opinion of the court in confirming the settlement and filed his bill of exceptions which was signed by the chairman of the court and ordered to be made a part of the record in this cause And prayed an appeal to the next circuit court of the county of Cannon to be held at the court house in the Town of Woodbury on the third Monday in September next which to him is granted he having entered into Bond to prosecute said appeal to effect according to law.

John C. Martin and Isaac B. Elledge Adm. Debonusnon of the Estate of Elizabeth Jane Moore decased this day Reported to court an Inventory of said estate and was duly quallified to the same and on motion it is ordered by the court that the same be recorded in the proper Book.

(p 489)
Court then adjourned till court in course.
David Patten
Charles C. Evans

J.C. Martin

August Term 1840

State of Tennessee

At a county court began and held for the County of Cannon At the court
House in the Town of Woodbury On the first Monday and third day of August
in the year of our Lord One thousand Eight hundred and forty and of the Indep-
endance of the United States the Sixty fifth year — present the worshipful
David Patton Chairman and
Charles C. Evans Quorum Justices.

Then was the following orderes made(to wit.)

Alexander McKnight, one of the quoran justices of this court being absent, the
court called John D. McBroom Esq. to the Bench to sit for the present Term of
this court in room of said McKnight afforesaid.

On motion of John C. Ranson Esq. be it remembered that this day August
Weisert presented a petition to the worshipfull court of Cannon County praying to be admitted as a citizen of t e United States for a longer period of
time than five years — And the said Weisert swearing that he will forever renounce all alleginace and fidelity to his majesty the King of (p 490) Germany and all other foreign Princes Potentates States and soverign ties — and
support the Constitution of the United States It is thereofre ordered by the
court that August Weisert be admited to all to all the rights and priviloges
of a citizen of the United States.

State of Tennessee)
Cannon County   )   Then personally appeared in court August Weisert and makes
oath that he will renounce forever all allegiance and fidelity to his Majesty
the King of Germany and all other foreign Princes potentates, States and Sover-
igns whatsoever and that he will support the constitution of the United States
— this the third of August 1840.
August Weisert
Sworn to and suscribed in open court — August Term of the county court 1840.
                                        Rezin Fowler Clerk.

Thomas Elkins guardian of the minor heirs of Levi Patrick deceased — this day
reported to the court an account current of the effects which had come into
his hands as guardian afforesaid   and was duly quallified to the same. And
on motion it is ordered by the court that the same be recorded in the proper
Book.

On motion it is ordered by the court that Elihu L. Wetherspoon be and
is hereby appointed administrator of the estate of Ebenezer A. Wetherspoon
(deceased) Whereupon the said Elihu L. Wetherspoon came forward into open
court — together with his securities John Andrews and Milas F. Travis who being
(p 491) approved of by the court entered into Bond in the sum of one thousand
dollars conditioned and payable as the Law directs for the faithful performance of his said administration and on motion it is ordered by the court that
the said Elihu L. Wetherspoon have letters of Administration granted him upon
the estate of the said (deceased) which are in the words and figures following
(to wit)

State of Tennessee)
Cannon County   )

By the Justices of Cannon County it being certified to us that Ebenezer A. Wetherspoon late of said county is (deceased) and has made no will or Testament — On motion it is ordered by the court that Elihu L. Wetherspoon have letters of Administration on the State of the said deceased — These are therefore to authorize and empower you the said Administrator to enter into and upon all and singular the goods and chattels rights and credits of the said (deceased) And them into your possession take and an Inventory thereof render to the court within ninety days from the date hereof and all the interest of the said deceased, to pay so far as the estate of the said deceased may amount or extend to and the residue thereof to deliver up to those who have a right ti by law to recive the same.

Witness Rezn Fowler, Clerk of our said court at office this first Monday and 3rd day of August — 1840.

Rezin Fowler Clk.

(p 492)

John Melton one of the acting justies of the peace in and for said County of Cannon this day Tendered to the court his resignation as such which was accepted by the court And on motion it is ordered by the court that the Sheriff of Cannon County open and hold an election to fill said vacancy, persuant to the acts of the general Assembly in such cases made and provided, Rezin Fowler Clerk of this court this day produced to the worshipful Court for their confirmation or Rejection the following Settlements by him made with the following persons (to wit) With Allen Whirfield Administrator of Willia Whitfield deceased one with Henry Hart administrator of Michael Etherage the will annexed and one with Silas Cooper Administrator of the estate of John Cooper, deceased which being examined and fully understood by the court was in all things confirmed.

Job Stephens this day came into court together with his securities (to wit) Robert Baily and David Patton who being approved of by the court entered into Bond in the sum of Twenty four hundred and thirty six dollars payable to R.R. Currin superintendant of public instruction conditioned for the faithful Receiving and paying out all school monies that shall (p 493) come into his hands for that purpose for the scholastic year 1840.

Court then adjourned till court in course.

David Patton, Char.
Charles C. Evans
John D. McBroom

September Term

State of Tennessee

At a county court Began and held for the county of Cannon at the court house in the Town of Woodbury on the first Monday and sevebth day in September, in the year of our Lord One thousand eight hundred and forty, And of —— Independance of the United States the sixty fifth year, present the worshipful David Patton Chm.
Charles C. Evans and
Alexander McKnight Esqrs.
Quoram Justices

Then was the following orders made to ade to wit.

Alexander McKnight one of the quoram justies of this court beged leaved of the court to Absent himself for the present Term of this court, which was granted. Whereupon John C. Martin Esq. was called to the Bench to sit for the present Term of this court.

Thomas Elkins this day produced in open court a Commission from his Excellency

James K. Polk governor in and over the State of Tennessee To him the said Elkins
as justice of the peace for Cannon County Whereupon the said Thomas Elkins came
forward and the oath of office was duly administered to him by the clerk of
this court. Whereupon it is ordered by the court that the same be made of Record.

(p 494) On motion of James O. George Sheriff of Cannon County Eli Baily came
forward into open court & was duly quallified as Deputy Sheriff of said County
Whereupon it was ordered by the court that the same be made of Record.

Pursuant to the Acts of Assembly in such cases made and provided Rezin Fowler
Clerk of this court presented to the worshipful court for their confirmation
or rejection or Settlement by him made with John C. Martin guardian of the minor
heirs of ThomasBragg deceased which being examined and fully understood by the
court was in all things confirmed.

Whereas Robert J. Summars who had an orphan boy by the name of Tetitha Summars
bound unto him at the May Term of this court 1837, This day sent to the court
by the hand of James Duggan a line praying to -------released from said indenture and that said Tetitha requested to live with the said Duggan. On motion
it is ordered by the court that James Duggan enter into Bond as the law directs
and that the clerk of this court deliver up the original Bond given by the said
Summar to the said Duggan Whereupon the said James Duggan came forward into
court together with his security Approved of by the court, to wit Benjamin B.
Cooper And entered into Bond payable to David Patton chairman faithfully perform the conditions therein mentioned.

Gabriel Hume this day makes known to the satisfaction of the court that an orphan
girl by the name of Polly Anne Patrick needed their protection And proposed to
have the said Polly Anne (p 495) Bound unto him till she attains to the age
eighteen years. Whereupon the said Gabriel Hume came forward together with
his security, John Harris who being approved of by the court And entered into
Bond payable to David Patton Chn. and his successors in office faithfully to
perform the conditions specified in said Bond.

On motion and on application of John Harris the court appoint Sarah Harris
administratrix and John Harris Administrator of Nicholas Harris Deceased
whereupon the said Sarah and John Harris came forward into open court together
with their securities, Adam Elrod and Gabriell Hume who being approved of by
the court entered into Bond in the sum of four Hundred dollars conditioned and
payable as the law directs for the faithful performane of their administration
on the estate of the said deceased, And on motion it was ordered by the court
that the said John and Sarah Harris have letters of administration granted
them on the estate of the said deceased, which was in the words and figures
to wit.

State of Tennessee)
Cannon County   ) By the justice of Cannon County It being certified to us
that Nicholas Harris late of our said county is deceased and has left no will
ot Testament On motion it is ordered by the court that Sarah and John Harris
have letters of Administration granted them on the estate of the said deceased.
These are Therefore to authorize and empower you the said Administrators to
enter into and upon all and singular the goods and chattels rights and credits
of the said deceased, And them into your possession take (p 496) And an Inventory there thereof render to the court within ninety days from the date hereof, And all the interest debt of the said deceased may amount or extend to,
and the residue thereof deliver up to those who have a right by law to receve
the same.
Witness Rezin Fowler Clk. of our said court at office this first Monday and

seventh day of September 1840.
   Rezin Fowler Clk.

On motion it is ordered by the court that Joseph Ramsey and Wm. West be and they
are hereby appointed Administrators of the estate of Wm. James deceased whereupon the said Ramsey and West came forward into open court, together with their
securities to wit.
Thomas Elkins and Job Stephens, who being approved of by the court, entered into
Bond in the sum of four hundred dollars, conditioned and payable as the law
directs, for the faithful performane of their said Administration on the estate
of the said deceased and on motion it is ordered by the court that the said
Joseph Ramsey and Wm. West, have letters of Administration granted them on the
estate of the said deceased - which are in the words and figures following to
wit.

State of Tennessee)
Cannon County) By the justices of Cannon County It being certified to us
that William James late of our said county is deceased, and has left no will
or Testament On motion it is ordered by the court that Joseph Ramsey & Wm.
West have letters of administration ------- them on the estate of the said deceased These are therefore to authorize and empower you the (p 497) said Administrators, to enter into and upon all and singular the goods and chattels
rights and credits of the said deceased, and then into your possession take,
and an Inventory thereof render to the court within ninety days from the date
hereof, And all the interest debts of the said dec. to pay so far as the estate
of the said deceased may amount or extend to And the residue thereof deliver
up to those who have a right by law to receive the same. Witnes Rezin Fowler
Clerk of our said court at office the first Monday and seventh day of September 1840.
   Rezin Fowler Clk.

On motion it is ordered by the court that
Thomas Elkins
Solomon Travis and
Archibald Stone
be and they are hereby appointed commissioners with full power to go upon the
premises of the late Wm. James decd. And then and there lay off on set apart
oneyears provisions; from the death of the said deceased, for his said widow
paying due regard to her former manner of living. And make due return thereof to the next Term of this court.

It is ordered by the court that
Wm. Kirk
Alexander McBroom and
Wm. Young be and they are hereby appointed commissioners, with full power and
authority to go upon the premises of Nicholas Harris decd. and then and there
allot and set apart to the widow of the said deceased one years provisions
paying due regard to her former manner of living together with the articles
that is exempt from from (p 498) from Execution agreeable to the statutes
in such cases made and provided.
   Court then adjourned till court in course.
David Patton Chairman
Charles C. Evans
J.C. Martin

State of Tennessee
   At a county court began and held for the county of Cannon at the court

House in the Twon of Woodbury on the first Monday and fifth day of October in the year of our Lord One thousand eight Hundred and forty And of the Independance of the United States the sixty fifth year, present the worshipful

David Patton
Alexander McKnight
John C. Martin
Samuel Grecar
Wm. Bowen
Charles G. Evans
R.U. Leray
Sam'l Denby
Samuel Lance
Thomas Elkins
Wm. Moore
John W. Summar
Nathan Neely and
James Mears E'qrs.

Then was the following orders made to wit.

On motion Sam'l J. Garrisons receits are permitted to record.

Woodbury Sept. 12th 1840.

Then received of Sam'l J. Garrison clerk of Cannon County nineteen dollars & fifty ———— in ful of his Liability for Revenue by him collected from the first day of September 1839 - up to the 9th October 1839 as appears from the commissioners report of settlement with him on the 3rd Sept. 1840 -$19.50

Job Stephens Trustee of Cannon
County.

Comptrollers office Nashville
Sept. 28th 1840

Received from Sam J. Garrison former clerk of Cannon County court his statement of Revenue collected as clerk aforesaid from 1st Sep. to 7th October 1840.

(p 499)	Amount collected	$42.01
	Commissions	1.05
		40.96

Warrant No. 1161 - this day for Daniel Graham, Comptroller.

$40.96 - Nashville 28th Sept. 1840 No. 1161 -
Received of Sa Garrison Forty dollars - 96 cents audited to him by No. 1161 and due on account of Revenue by him collected as clerk of Cannon County from 1st September to the 7th October 1839. Signed

M. Francis Treasurer of Tennessee.

On motion of Rezin Fowler he was permitted to spread upon the minutes of the court his receipts for the Revenue by him collected as clerk from the 6th day of April up to the 1st day of September 1840. which are in the words and figures following to wit.

Woodbury, June the 13th 1840.

Then received of Rezin Fowler an aggregate Statement of property polls and State and county Tax of said county for the fiscal year 1840 -

Job Stephens Trustee of Cannon
County.

Woodbury September the 12th 1840

Then Received of Rezin Fowler Clerk of Cannon County court Forty two dollars & 41½ cents, in full of his liabilities for Revenue by him collected from the 6th day of April 1840 upto 1st day of Sept. 1840 as appears from the commissioners Report of Settlement with him on the 3rd September 1840. $42.41½

                                  Job Stephens Trustee of
                                  Cannon County.

(p 500)   Comptrollers office
                          Nashville Tennessee 28th Sept.1840

Received from Rezin Fowler his statement of Revenues collected as clerk of Cannon County court from the 6th April to 1st September 1840.

Amount collected $92..04
Commission $2.30
Paid Denby and Ramsey $5.00   7.30
Warrant No. 1162 this day for 84.74 cents
                          Daniel Graham, Comptroller.

$84.74 Nashville 28th September 1840 No. 1162.
Received of Rezin Fowler Eighty four dollars & 74 cents auditted to him by No. 1162, and due on account of Revenue collected as clerk of Cannon County Court from the 6th day of April to the 1st September 1840.
                          Signed duplicates
                          M. Francis Treasurer of Tennessee.

On motion it is ordered by the court that Judith Cox be and she is hereby appointed Administratrix on the estate of James Cox deceased, whereupon the said Judith Cox came into court and was duly quallified as, who together with her securities Erasmus Jones and Joseph Ramsey came into court and entered into Bond in the sum of Two hundred dollars conditioned and payable as the Law directs, for the faithful performance of her said Administration granted her on the estate of the said deceased, Thereupon it was ordered by the court that the said Judith Cox have letters of Administration on the estate of the said deceased, which are in the words and figures following to wit.

State of Tennessee)
Cannon County   ) By the Justices of Cannon County it being certified to us that James Cox late of said county is deceased and has (p 501) made no will or Testament On motion it is ordered by the court that Judith Cox have letters of Administration on the estate of the said deceased. These are therefore to authorize you the said Administratrix to enter into and upon all and singular the goods and chattels rights and credits of the said deceased, and them into your possession take, and an inventory thereof render to the court within ninety days from the date hereof and all the interest debts of the said deceased to pay so far as the estate of the said deceased may amount or extend, and the residue thereof to deliver up to those who have a right to by law to recive the same.
Witness Rezin Fowler Clerk of our said Court at office this first Monday and 5th day of October A.D. 1840.
              Rezin Fowler Clerk.

Elihu L. Wetherspoon administrator of the estate of Ebenezer A. Wetherspoon deceased this day reported to court an account current of the sales and other effects of the said deceased, and was duly quallified -- the same. Whereupon it was ordered by the court that the same be recorded in the proper Book.

On motion and application of Joshua Barton the court appoint him administrator on the estate of Edmund Barton Deceased, Whereupon the said Joshua Barton came into court together with his securities Wm. Barton and John C. Martin being approved of by the court and entered into bond in the sum of Three thousand dollars conditioned and payable as the law directs for the faithful perform- ance of his said administration granted him on the estate of the said deceased Whereupon it was ordered by the court that the said Joshua Barton have letters of administration grantedhim on the estate of the (p 502) said deceased, which are in the words and figures following to witt.

State of Tennessee)
Cannon County   )   It being certified to us that Edmund Barton late of our sa said county is deceased, and has made no will or Testament On motion it is ordered by the court that Joshua Barton, have letters of Administration, on the estate of the said deceased.
These are therefore to authorize and empower you the said administrator to en- ter into and upon all and singular the goods and chattels rights and credits of the said deceased, and them into your possession take and an Inventory thereof to render to the court within ninety days from the date hereof, and all the interest debt of the said deceased, to pay so far as the estate of the said deceased may amount or extend to, and the residue thereof deliver up to those who have a right by law to receive the same.
Witness Rezin Fowler lerk of our said court at office the first Monday and 5th day of October A.D. 1840.
        Rezin Fowler Clk.

On motion the follwoing justices present to wit;
Samuel Greear
Alexander McKnight
Charles C. Evans
Richard U. Lepay
David Patton
Wm. Bowen
Allen Beaty
Samuel Lance
John W. Summar
John C. Martin
Thomas Elkins
Wm. Moore and
Nathan Neely Esqrs.
all voting in the affirmative Thereofre an appropriation of fifty dollars is made to Nancy Patrick a pauper, which the county Trustee of Cannon County is ordered to pay to the person who may be appointed guardian for the said Nancy out of any monies in his hands not otherwise appropriated.

(p 503) On motion the following justices present to wit -
Alexander McKnight
Samuel Greear
Richard U. Lepay
James Mears
David Patton
Wm. Bowen
Allen Beaty
John W. Summar
Wm. Moore
Nathan Neely
Samuel Lance
John C. Martin and
Thomas Elkins Esqrs.

all voting in the affirmative against Charles C. Evans in the negative, Therefore the sum of thirty one dollars is appropriated for the benefit of Barkely Couch pauper, untill the next January Term of this court which the Trustee of Cannon County is ordered to pay unto the guardian of the said Barkely out of any monies in his hands not otherwise appropriated.

On motion of Robert Baily and it appearing to the court, that he is bound and liable as security of Job Stephens, Trustee of Cannon County, as appears of Record and moves the court to be released from all liability as his said security from henceforth, And thereupon motion Joseph Ramsey and Sampson Stephens came into court and entered into bond conditioned and payable as the law directs in the room and stead of the said Robert Baileys.

On motion the following justices present to wit
Wm. Moore
Alexander McKnight
Samuel Cuear
Charles C. Evans
David Patton
John W. Surrar
R.U. Loney
Wm. Bowen
Thomas Elkins
John C. Martin
Allen Beaty
Samuel Lance &
Nathan Neely Esqrs.
all voting in the affirmative against James Tears and Samuel Denby voting in the Negative, therefore the following order was made to wit.

(p 504) Ordered by the court that Thomas G. Wood Clerk of the Circuit Court be allowed for himself and others entitled to the same the following sums of money and Bills of costs to wit -- In the case the State vs Elizabeth Spence on a bill of indictment for keeping a Bandy House $16.12½
The State vs Nathan Jarrell on a Bill of indictment for assault and Tresspass $23. 56¼

The State vs. Adam Elrod Indictment for neglect of duty as overseer of a public road $8.25

The State vs. Alfred Tenpenny and others Indictment for an assault $19.00

The State vs. Wm. King on a Bill of Indictment for an affray $14.87½

The State vs. John Brown $18.37½ cents

The State vs William James Indictment for an assault and battery $15.45 cents

The State against Allen Beaty Indictment for assault and battery $12.31 cents

The State vs James Williams and others Indictment for an assault battery $17.93 cts

The State vs. Henry Persey Indictment for an affray $8.62½ cents.

The State vs. Wm. Weedon Indictment for an affray $16.31

The State vs. Samuel Adams Indictment for an affray $14.50 cents

The State vs. George Reaves for Tresspas & c $9.41 cents

The State vs. Gideon Anderson for assault and Battery $19.12½

The State vs. Wm. H. Robinson presentment for gaining $18.00

The State vs. John Craft Indictment for assailt and battery $16.75

The State vs. Elizabeth Hass presentment for Lendress $24.00

The State vs. Selina Reaves Indictment for Tresspass & C $12.12½ cents

The State vs Mark A. Pope for Indictment for Drunkeness $12.00

The State vs. A.F. Tood & Hugh P. Neely $8.00

The State vs. John Adams presentment for drunkeness $12.12½ cents
which was all certified by the Attorney General to be correct. And that the
Trustee of Cannon County is ordered to pay the same out of any monies that is
or may come into his hands not otherwise appropriated.

(p 505) On motion the following justices present to wit.
Alexander McKnight
Samuel Greear
Nathan Neely
Charles C. Evans
David Patton
John C. Martin
Richard U. Lemay
John W. Sumrar
Samuel Lance, Samuel Denby
Thomas Elkins
Wm. Bowen
Wm. Moore and
James Mears Esqrs.
all voting in the affirmative Therefore the sum of eleven dollars is appropri-
ated to Thomas G. Wood. Clerk of the circuit court for the consideration of a
Record Book procured by him for the use of his office, which the Trustee of
Cannon County is ordered to ——— out of any monies in his ——— not otherwise
appropriated.

On motion and petition of the minor heirs of Henry Wiley deceased viz. Frances
Anne and Henry Wiley By their next friend James J. Trott and upon notice given
and it appearing to the satisfaction of the court, that James H. Brown, who
was appointed guardian of said minor heirs by the county court of Warren county
before the new county of Cannon was made, and he had wasted the estate of the
said heirs and had privately arseonded from the county. It is therefore considered and ordered by the court that the said James H. Brown be removed as
guardian of said minor Heir and that James J. Trott be appointed guardian of
said Frances Ann and Henry Wiley deceased, Whereupon the saind James J. Trott
came forward together with his securities to wit.
Henry Trott Jr.
C.R. Davis
Benjamin Sapp and
Wm. Barton
who being approved of by the court entered into bond in the sum of one thousand
dollars conditioned and payable as the law directs, for the faithful perform-

ance of the same.

On motion it is ordered by the court that James J. Trott Te and he is hereby
constituted and appointed guardian to (p 506) minor heirs of John Brown deceased to wit.
James Brown
Ann Brown and
May Brown
whereupon the said James J. Trott came into court together with his securities
to wit.
Henry Trott Jr.
C.R. Davis
Benjamin Sapp and
Wm. Barton
who being approved by the court entered into bond in the sum of one thousand
dollars conditioned and payable as the law directs for the faithful performance of the same.

On motion it is ordered by the court that
John W. Summar
Medford Caffey and
Joseph Ramsey
be and they are hereby appointed commissioners with full power and authority
to go upon the premises of the late James Cox deceased, and then and the allot
and set apart to the widow of the said deceased, One years provision paying
due regard to her past manner of living and also such articles as are exempt
from execution sale in the Heads of Families and make due returns thereof to
the next Term of this court.

On motion and on petition of sundry citizens of the Sixth civil district of
Cannon County It is ordered by the court, that the district lines be so
changed that a certain portion of the said District No. Six be attached to
District No 8th, to wit, Beginning on the line between James H. Lances and
James Mileses on the line the 8th District, and Running to William Whitlocks
leaving Joel and Gabriel Mears in the 8th District also leaving Whitlock in
the 8th and attacting Thomas L. Turner to the 7th, Thence to Isaac Browns
leaving him In the 8th thence to the old coal ground near Andrew McAdoos.

It is ordered by the court that the clerk of this court Issue the State writ
of venire facies to the Sheriff of Cannon County commanding him to Summon the
following named persons as jurors for the Term of the circuit court to be Hold-
en for the county of (p 507) Cannon at the Court House in the Town of Woodbury on the third Monday in January next, to wit.

District No. 1 Alexander McKnight and Edward Bragg

No. 2   Wm. Hollis and David Warren

No. 3   Miles Saffle and Abner Adams

No. 4th   John Petty and Wm. Lee

No. 5th   Woodson Northcutt & David D. Hipp

No. 6th   Daniel Tenpenny and James Vinson and Alexander McBroom

No. 7th   John N. Baily & James H. Stone

No. 8th   Washington Kennedy & Wm. Cummings

No. 9th   Milton Ward and James H. Carl

No. 10th   John Hollensworth and Robert L. Shaw

No. 11th   B.F. Odom and Erasmus Jones

No. 12th   B.B. Dickens and John Williams sen.

Constables, James N. Lance & A. Youngblood
Court then adjourned till tomorrow morning Ten o'clock.
David Patton
Richard U. Lemay
James Mears
William Moore

Tuesday morning October the 6th 1840.
Court met pursuant to adjournment present the worshipfull
David Patton
James Mears
Richard U. Lemay and
Wm. Moore Esqrs.
    Then was the following orders made to wit.
There appearing no further Buisness before the court – Court then adjourned till
court in course.
David Patton
James Mears
Richard U. Lemay

(p 508)   November Term 1840
State of Tennessee
    At a county court began and held for the County of Cannon at the Court House in the Town of Woodbury On the first Monday and second day of November in the year of our Lord one thousand eight hundred and forty. And of Independance of the United States the sixty fifth year present the worshipful
David Patton
Alex. McKnight and
Charles C. Evans
quoram justices. Then was the following orders made to wit.

James O. George Sheriff of Cannon County this day produced in open court a Commission from his excellency James K. Polk Governor in and over the state of Tennessee To Wm. R. James as justice of the peace in and for said County. Whereupon the said Wm. R. James came into court and was duly quallified as such by the clerk of this court. Thereupon it was ordered by the court that the same be made of Record.

On motion it is ordered by the court that Mariah Johnson be appointed Administratrix of the estate ------John Johnson deceased, whereupon the said Mariah Johnson came into court and was duly quallified as such, who together with her securities Benjamin Early and Blake Sagely who being approved of by the court entered into Bond in the sum of three Hundred dollars conditioned and payable as the law directs for the faithful performance of her said administration, granted on the estate of the said deceased, which are in the words and figures following to wit.

(p 509)
State of Tennessee)
Cannon County   )   By the justices of said County.
It being certified to us that John Johnson late of our said county is deceased and has left no will or Testament On motion it is ordered by the court that Mariah Johnson have letters of Administration on the estate of the said deceased. These are therefore to authorize and empower you the said Administratrix to enter into and upon all and singular the goods and chattels rights and credits of the said deceased and them into your possession take. And an Inventory thereof render to the court within ninety days from the date hereof. And all the interest debt of the said decd. to pay so far as the estate of the said decd. may amount or extend to and the residue thereof deliver up to those who have a right by law to receive the same.
Witness Rezin Fowler Clerk of our said cour at office this first Monday and 2nd day of November A.D. 1840.
                    Rezin Fowler Clk.

On motion it is ordered by the court that;
David Patton
Hugh Robinson and
Blake Sagely
be and they are hereby appointed commissioners with full power and authority to go upon the premises of the late John Johnson deceased, and then and there allot and set apart to the widow of the said deceased, One years provisions paying due regard to her former manner of living together with the articles which are now exempt from execution sale in the Heads of Families if such there be and make due return thereof to the next Term of this court.

(p 510) On motion of James O. George Sheriff of Cannon County Samuel Vance was permitted to be quallified as deputy Sheriff of said County. Whereupon it is ordered by the court that the same be made of record.

Pursuant to the Acts of the General Assembly in such cases made and provided Rezin Fowler Clerk of this court this day presented to the worshipful court for the confirmation or Rejection, the following settlements by him made with the following names persons to wit.
With Francis Bryson guardian of Locky Bryson minor Heir of Samuel Bryson deceased, and with Thomas Elkins Esq. guardian of the minor heirs of Levi Patrick deceased, which being examined and fully understood by the court was in all things confirmed.

On motion it is ordered by the court that Thomas Barrett be appointed guardian of Nancy Patrick, pauper whereupon the said Thomas Barrett came into court together with his securities entered into Bond in the sum of one hundred dollars conditioned and payable as the law directs, for the faithful performance of the same.

On motion and upon application of John R. Sullivan the court appoint him Administrator of the estate of Alexander Sullivan deceased, Whereupon the said John R. Sullivan came into court and was duly quallified as such who together with his securities John Fisher and Alexander Tassey being approved of by the court entered into Bond in the sum of one Hundred dollars conditioned and payable as the law (p 511) directs for the faithful performance of the same Whereupon letters of Administration were granted him on the estate of the said deceased which are in the words and figures following to wit.

State of Tennessee)
Cannon County   ) By the justices of said county It being certified to us that Alexander Sullivan late of our said county is deceased and has left no will or Testament, On motion it is ordered by the court that John R. Sullivan have letters of Administration on the estate of the said deceased. These are therefore to authorize and empower you the said Administrator to enter into and upon all and singular the goods and chattels rights and credits of the said deceased and them into your possession take and an Inventory thereof render to the court within ninety days from the date hereof. And all the interest debt of the said deceased to pay so far as the estate of the said deceased may amount or extend to. And the residue thereof deliver up to those who have a right to by law to receive the same. Witness, Rezin Fowler, Clerk of said court at office this first Monday and 2nd day of November A.D. 1840.
                                Rezin Fowler Clk.

It is ordered by the court that;
Dozier Bragg
Milas F. Travis and
John Bragg
be and they are hereby appointed commissioners with full power and authority to go upon the premises of the late Alexander Sullivan deceased and then and there allot & set apart to the widow of the said deceased, one years provisions paying due regard to her former manner of living , together with the articles (p (p 512) which are now exempt by lae from execution sale in the Heads of families And make due return thereof to the next Term of this court.

John Harris and Sarah Harris Administrators of the estate of the estate of Nicholas Harris decd. this day reported an account current of the sale and other effects of the said deceased, And was duly quallified to the same by the clerk of this court Whereupon it is ordered by the court that the same be recorded in the proper Book.

Court then adjourned till court in course.
David Patton
Charles C. Evans
Alexander McKnight
                        December Term 1840
State of Tennessee)
Cannon County   )
        At a county court began and held for the County of Cannon at the court House in the Town of Woodbury on the first Monday and seventh day of December in the year of our Lord one thousand eight hundred and forty. And of the Independance of the United States Sixty fifth year Present the worshipful.
David Patton
Alexander McKnight and
Charles C. Evans Esqrs.
        Then was the following orders made to wit.

Judith Cox Administratrix of the estate of the late James Cox deceased, this day reported to the court an account current of the sales and other effects of the said deceased and was quallified to the same. Whereupon it was ordered by the court that the same be recorded in the proper Book.

(p 513) On motion it is ordered by the court that Higdon R. Jarratt be appointed guardian to Johnanna Elizabeth and Mary Eliza Mathews, minor heirs of Drewry Mathews Deceased, whereupon the said H.R. Jarratt came into court together with his securities Alexander McKnight and Ephriam Andrews who being approved of by the court entered into Bond in the sum of Ten Thousand dollars payable to David Patton Esq. chairman of said court, and his successors in office conditioned as the law directs for the faithful performance of the same.

David McGill, one of the administrators of James McGill deceased this day presented to the court a Note given by the said James McGill deceased, and payable to Joseph Thompson & Jonathan Hall, Administrators of James Thompson Deceased for $81.50 cents, And due the 11th day of August 1814 which appeared to the satisfaction of the court that the same had been paid by the said David McGill from the oath of Joshua Barton Esq. who made an affidavit to that effect who was an acting justice of the peace At the time said note was paid and And whereas there Had been a that a judgement was rendered before him the said Barton on said final Settlement made with the said David McGill and David Patton Esqrs. Administrators of the said James McGill deceased, with the former clerk of this court , and the same above mentioned note had been omitted in the former Settlement to be allowed as a credit in favor of said Administrators, And it appearing to the satisfaction of the court that the said note ought to have been admitted as a credit in said Settlement, whereupon it is ordered by the court that the said note and affidavit be recorded at full length in the Invoice Book in the clerks office of said county and that same be allowed the said Amt. as a credit in the above named settlement together with (p 514) All lawful interest from the day that the afforesaid note fell due.

Pursuant — the acts of the general Assembly of the State of Tennessee, Rezin Fowler clerk of this court this day presented to the worshipfull court for their confirmation or Rejection the following settlements by him made with the following named persons to wit.

With Isaac W. Elledge Adm. of Joseph Elledge deceased

With Higdon/Jarratt Administrator of Drewry Mathews deceased and

With James O and John A. George Executors of the last will and Testament of Robert George decd. all of which being examined severally by the court was in all things confirmed.

Dozier Bragg and Milas F.Travis of the commissioners appointed by the court to Lay off , one years suport to the widow of the late Alexander Sullivan deceased this day made report the court of the same pursuant to said order which was by the court in all things confirmed and ordered by the court to be made of recorded.

Aaron Byford one of the constables of Cannon County in district no. 12th this day tendered his resignation as such, which was accepted by the court, And on motion it was ordered by the court that the Sheriff of Cannon County open and Hold an Election to fill said vacancy according to Law and make due return thereof to the next Term of this court.

(p 515)
David McKnight)
    To   )
John M. McKnight)
Deed 20 acres of)   The execution of a deed of conveyance from David McKnight

to John M. McKnight for twenty acres of land lying in Cannon County and State
of Tennessee has this day duly proven in open court by the oath of Alexander
McKnight Esq. and Andrew M. McKnight subscribing witnesses to the same, the
said deed bearing date the twenty fifth day of September 1840.

And on motion it was ordered by the court that the same be certified for Registration.

On motion it is ordered by the court that the following named persons be and
they are hereby appointed Revenue commissioners for the purpose of taking in
a List of taxable property and polls in their respective civil districts in
Cannon County in the fiscal year of 1841 to wit

In District No. 1st   Alexander McKnight Esq.

In District No. 2d   William Moore Esq.

In District No. 3d   William Bowen Esq.

In District No 4th   Samuel Greear Esq.

In District No 5th   Richard U. Lemay

In District No. 6th   Wm. R. James

In District No. 7th   Charles G. Evans Esq.

In District No. 8th   Samuel Lance Esq.

In District No. 9th   Wm. B. Foster Esq.

In District No 10th   Daniel S. Ford Esq.

In District No. 11th   John W. Gunner Esq.

In District No. 12th   Silas A. Robinson Esq.

Pursuant to the first section of an act of the Generall Assembly of the
State of Tennessee passed the 22nd of January 1836. Intitled an act to authorize the clerks of the county courts to make settlements with Executors, Administrators and guardians and (P 516) for other purposes the court appoint,
James Feers
Wm. R. James and
Nathan Neely Esq.
commissioners to call on Elizabeth Soape Administratrix and Charles P. Alexander Administrator of James Soape deceased. And cause them to come before
them at the court House in the Town of Woodbury on same day to be set by said
commissioners for the purpose of closing their account as Adm. of the said
deceased, And that the said Commissioner s are hereby authorized to make the
settlement with the said Administrators under the same rules as the clerks are
authorized to make in said act, It appearing to the court that the clerk of
this court is wholly incompetent to make said settlement on account of the
relationship existing between him and one of said Adm.s
And the said settlement, when made, Report to the next Term of this court as
contemplated in said act, for their confirmation or relection. And that the
clerk of this court Issue a copy of said order to one of the said commissioners
Isued.

On motion and on application of Ephriam Andrew the court appoint him and Thomas
H. Youree, Administrators of the Estate of Mary A. Nichols deceased, Whereupon
the said Andrew and Youree came into court and was duly quallified   as such
together with their securities, Rigdon R. Jarratt and B.A. Orr who being approved of by the court entered into Bond in the sum of three hundred dollars conditioned and payable as the law directs for the faithful performance of their
said Administration on the estate of the said deceased, which are in the words
and figures following to wit.

(p 517)
State of Tennessee)
Cannon County   ) By the Justices of said county It being certified to us
that Mary A. Nichols late of our said county is deceased and has left no will
or Testament. On motion it is ordered by the court that Ephriam Andrew and
Thomas H. Youree have letters of Administration on the estate of the said deceased. These are therefore to authorize and empower you the said Administrators to enter into and upon all and singular the goods and chattels rights
and credits of the said deceased and them into your possession take, and an
Inventory thereof to render to the court within ninety days from the date hereof and all the interest debt of the said deceased, may amount or extend, and
the residue thereof deliver up to those who have a right by law to receive the
same.
Witness, Rezin Fowler Clerk of our said court at office this first Monday and
7th day of December A.D. 1840.
                    Rezin Fowler Clk.

Wm. Pace   )
   To   )
John Haney   )
Deed 72 acres)   The execution of a deed of conveyance from Wm. Pace to John Haney
for seventy two Acres of land lying in Cannon County and State of Tennessee,
bearing date November the 30th 1840, was this day duly acknowledged in open
court by the said William Pace the bargainor Whereupon it was ordered by the
court that the same be certified for Registration.

(p 518)
Job Stephens one of the securities of Benjamin Pendleton as Executor of the last
will and Testament of John Brown deceased, This day appeared in open court
and filed his petition together with his affidavit that he conceved himself
in danger of becoming liable on the condition of said bond given by said Pendleton as Exo. as afforesaid And moved the court to be released from all liability as such Security, Whereupon it is ordered by the court that a summons
Issue against the said Benjamin Pendleton, for whom the said petitioner Stands
bound — Signed by the clerk of said court, returnable at the next Term of
this court to compel the said Benjamin Pendleton to give other sufficient
or counter securities to be approved of by said court, or to surrender up said
estate to the said petitioner, or to such other person as the court shall direct.
——————Issued. ——

Court then adjourned till tomorrow morning ten oclock.
David Patton
Charles C. Evans
Alexander McKnight

Tuesday morning December the 8th A.D. 1840.
The worshipful court met pursuant to adjournment, present the worshipful
David Patton

Charles C. Evans and
Alexander McKnight Esqrs.
Then was the follwoing orders made to wit.

Joseph Ramsey one of the Administrators of the estate of William James, deceased, this day reported to the worshipfull court, an account current current of the sales of the personal property of said deceased and was duly qualified to the same which was admitted to record.

(p 519)
Court then adjourned till court in course.
David Patton
Charles C. Evans
Alexander McKnight

State of Tennessee)
Cannon County   ) Be it remembered that at acounty court began and held for the county of Cannon, at the court House, in the Town of Woodbury on the first Monday and fourth day of January in the year of our Lord one thousand Eight hundred and forty one; And of the Independance of the United States the Sixty fifth year – present the worshipful.
David Patton (chairman)
Alexander McKnight
John C. Martin
Wm. Moore
John D. McBroom
Wm. Bowen
Wm. McFerrin
Samuel Greear
Richard U. Lemay
Wm. R. James
James Mears
 athan Neely
Charles C. Evans
Thos. Elkins
Samuel Lence
Wm. Bates
Samuel Denby
Wm. R. Foster
Robert L. Shaw
Daniel S. Ford and
Silas A. Robinson Esqrs.

Then was the following orders made to wit.

On motion the court proceded to an election to elect a chairman to preside over their deliberation for the ————twelve months, And on counting the votes polled at the fifteenth Balloting David Pattons Esq. was found to be duly elected.

On motion the court then proceded to an election to elect three of their own body as the Statutes in such cases provides as a quoram for the term of twelve months, And on counting the votes polled at the first Balloting David Patton Esq. was found to be duly elected. And the second (p 520) Balloting, John C. Martin and Jams Mears Esqr. was found to be duly elected.
Pursuant to an act of the General Assembly of the State of Tennessee passed

January the 29th 1840 Entitled an act to provide for the taking the enumeration of the free white male inhabitants of the State of Tennessee, the court proceded to an Election to elect a commissioner to take the enumeration of the free white male inhabitants of Cannon County who are twenty one years and upwards - And on counting the votes polled on the ninth Palloting, John Betus was found to be duly elected.

Woodson Northcutt)
   To Power of Atto.)
Jessee Q. Seawell) The execution of a power of Attorney from Woodson Northcutt to Jessee Q. Seawell to receive and and receipt for all monies due the said Northcutt for distributing the Acts and Journals of the Legislature of the State of Tennessee for the Eastern Division of said State Pearing date December the 28th 1840, was this day duly acknowledged in open court By the said Northcutt the ----------Thereupon it is ordered by the court that the same be certified.

On motion of Charles P. Alexander the court appoint Richard U. Leway guardian for Diadema and Selina C. Shelby minors and Heirs at law of Moses Shelby deceased, Whereupon the said Richard U. Leway came into court together with his security James Mears Esq. who being approved of by the court. Entered into Bond in the sum of one hundred and fifty dollars conditioned and payable as the law directs for the faithful performance of the same.

On motion the following justices present to wit.
John C. Martin
Alex McKnight
Richard U. Leway
David Patton
Wm. Bates
Sam'l Lance
Wm. Bowen
Wm. M. McFerrin
Wm. R. James
Silas A. Robinson
Wm. B. Foster
Charles C. Evans
Sam'l Grecar and
Wm. Moore Esqrs.
All voting in the affirmative, Therefore the sum of forty five dollars is appropriated for the Penefit of Parkely Couch a pauper (p 521) for the term of six months from the date which the Trustee of Cannon County is ordered to pay to the person who may be appointed His guardian - out of any money in his Hands not otherwise appropriated.

James O. George Shff. of Cannon County By his deputy Eli Bailey this day reported to the court a certificate of an Election by Him Held in the 12th cival District of Cannon County on the 19th of December 1840, for the purpose of electing a Constable in said district to fill out the unexpired time of Aaron Dyford, resigned from which certificate it appeared to the satisfaction of the court that Mathew B. Ford was duly and constitutionally elected as such. And thereupon the said Mathew B. Ford came into court, And was duly qualified as such by the clerk of this court, who together with his securities;
Ira L. Blair
Wm. Ring and
David Patton
who being approved approved of by the court entered into Bond in the sum of

five thousand dollars conditioned and payable as the law directs for the faithful performance of the duties of his said Office.

On motion the following justices present to wit.
Charles C. Evans
Wm. B. Foster
John C. Martin
John D. McBroom
Robert L. Shaw
Alex McKnight
Richard U. Leray
David Patton
Samuel Lance
Wm. Bowen
Wm. R. James
Wm. McFerrin
Samuel Greear
Silas Robinson
Wm. Bates
Thomas Elkins Esqrs.
All voting in the affirmative against Daniel S. Ford in the negative therefore the sum of two Hundred and seventy three dollars and thirty three and one third cents. - is appropriated to Henry Trott for the consideration of his services in surveying and laying off the county of Cannon, And for the consideration of his employing chain carriers C.C. to Help do the same - And for his expense money paid out of His own pocket Horse Hire which the Trustee of Cannon County is ordered to pay out of any money in His Hands not otherwise appropriated.

(p 522) Joshua Barton Administrator of the Estate - Edmond Barton decd. this day reported to the court an account current of the sales and other effects belonging to the estate of the said deceased, And was duly quallified to the same whereupon it is ordered by the court that the same be recorded in the proper Book.

On motion the court proceeded to Levy a Tax for county purposes indiscriminately in Cannon County - for the fiscal year 1841, when the following justices beng present to wit.
Charles C. Evans
Daniel S. Ford
Wm. B. Foster
John C. Martin
John D. McBroom
Robert L. Shaw
Alex McKnight
Richard U. Leray
David Patton
Sam'l Lance
Wm. Bowen
Wm. R. James
Wm. McFerrin
Samuel Greear
Silas A. Robinson and
Wm. Bates Esqrs.
Being Sixteen in number. All voting in the affirmative - therefore the following rates are fixed upon to wit.
    On all the priveleges and occupations liable to taxation To exercise which a License must Issue ---- One half of the amount of the State Tax on the same. Also on all the property (Both real and personal) Subject to taxation in said county - Ten cents on each hundred dollars the same may be valued at.

And twenty five cents upon each white poll, Subject to taxation in said county To be incorporated in the Tax Book for the year of 1841, And certified to the Sheriff and collector of the public Taxes, And by him paid to the county Trustees the lawdireots. Court then adjourned till tomorrow morning nine O'clock.
David Patton
Wm. B. Foster
James Mears
Jno. D. McBroom
Richard U. Lemay
Samuel Lance
Silas A. Robinson

(p 523)   Tuseday Morning January the 5th 1841.
        The worshipfull court met pursuant Adjournment present the worshipful.
David Patton Chrm.
James Mears
Charles C. Evans
Silas A. Robinson
John D. McBroom
Richard U. Lemy
Samuel Denby
Wm. R. Jones
Wm. B. Foster
Samuel Lance
Nathan Neely
Wm. Bates and
Sam'l Greear Esqrs.
Whereupon the following orders were made to wit.

It is ordered by the court that Samuel Denby Esq. and Franklin Coleman, be and they are hereby appointed commissioners of the Revenue to settle with the Trustee of Cannon County and with clerk of the county and circuit court of said county for the year April 1941.

On motion it is ordered by the court that Willie F. Couch, be and He is Constituted and apointed guardian to His brother Darkely Couch, a pauper, Thereupon the said Willie F. Couch came into court together with his securities John C. Smith, who being approved of by the court entered into bond in the Sum of ninety dollars, conditioned and payable as the law directs.
        Thomas N. Jones constable in the 3rd civil District of Cannon County this day tendered to the court His resignation as such which was accepted by the court , Whereupon it is ordered by the court that the Sheriff od said county open and hold an Election to fill said vacancy, And make due return thereof to the next Term of this court.

(p 524)   On motion it is ordered by the court that;
James Mears
Charles C. Evans and
Nathan Neely Esqrs.
Be and they are hereby appointed commissioners, to purchase a suitable tract of land in Cannon County at the expense of Cannon County for the purpose of having a poore house and have the same built as soon as the nature of the case will admit, And that the clerk of this court furnish the said commissioner with a copy of said order copied Jan. 7th 1841

On motion the following justices present to wit.

Samuel Greer
David Patton
Wm. R. James
S las Robinson
Wm. Bates
Charles C. Evans
Richard U. Lemay
James Mears and
Samuel Denby Esqrs.
all voting in the affirmative and there being a sufficient to make an appropri-
ation under fifty dollars Therefore the sum of one dollar per day is appropri-
ted to;
David Patton
Alexander McK ight and
Charles C. Evans Esq.
for the consideration of their services as the quoram court for the year 1840,
which the Trustee of Cannon County is ordered to pay out of any monies in his
Hands not otherwise appropriated. And the clerk of the court Issue seperate
orders to Each of the afforesaid justices And certify the same to the county
Trustee.

John Fisher Esq. Coroner of Cannon County this day returned into court a report
of a Jury of Inquest by Him held over the dead body of an infant coloured child
from which report it apeared that the same was murderedBy a certain coloured
woman by the name of Ruth - then in the possession of Enoch Jones which appeared to the satisfaction of the court that the said Coroner Had performed all
the duties as contemplated by the Acts of Assembly in such cases made and provided in Holding of said Inquest, It is therefore ordered by the court that the
clerk of this court certify the same to the county Trustee for the payment
of such fees as he the said Coroner is allowed by law for such services.

(p 525) On motion it is ordered by the court that Joseph Ramsey C. Reed Davis
and Silas A. Robinson,
be and they are hereby commissioners of the Town And make settlement with
them according to law, And make return thereof to the next April Term of this
court? And that the clerk of this court furnish one of the said commissioners
with a copy of said order.

It is ordered by the court that Wm. Bates be and He is Hereby appointed guardian to Polly Spicer a pauper - whereupon the said Wm. Bates came into court
together with his securities James J. Trott who being approved of by the court
entered into Bond in the sum of fifty dollars conditioned and payable as the
law directs for the faithful performane of his said guardianship.

On motion the following justices present to wit.
Wm. B. Foster
Wm. Bates
Silas A. Robinson
Charles C. Evans
John D. McBroom
James Mears
Richard U. Lemay
David Patton
Samuel Denby
Wm. R. James
Samuel Greear and
Nathan Neely Esqrs.

all voting in the affirmative Therefore the sum of $28 and twenty five cents
is appropriated to Reuin Fowler clk. for the consideration of his services as
such - that is to say to appointing 10 jurys of view 25cents each. $2.50 To-
Recording the settlement with commissioners of the revenue and the county Trustee $1.00 for entering of record 3 paupers allowances and copy thereof 50 cents
each $1.50 cents To Issuing 41 road orders 12½ c. each, $5.12½ .
To recording Settlement with the commissioners of the Revenue and himself $1.00.
To recording settlement with commissioner T.G. Wood circuit clk. $1.00

To recording in the Revenue docket the Settlements with commissioner of the Revenue and James H. Brown and Samuel J. Garrison former clerks $1.00 each $2.00
(p 526)
To entering of record 2 venira facias for the circuit court & copy thereof 50
cents. Each $1.00

To issuing 50 jury tickets at 6¼ cts. each $3.12½.

To recording certificates of elections of common school commissioners, And Trans-
mitting a certified copy of all the common school commissioners reports made to
him;

To the Superintendant of public Instruction for the year 1840 $10.00
which the Trustee of Cannon County is ordered to pay out of any monies in his
Hands not otherwise appropriated.

On motion the following justices present to wit.
Nathan Neely
Charles C. Evans
Richard U. Lemmy
James Mears
Wm. Bates
David Patton
Samuel Denby
Samuel Greear
Wm. R. James and
Wm. B. Foster Esqrs.
all voting in the affirmative.
Therefore the sum of fifteen dollars is appropriated for the Benefit of Polly
Spicer a pauper for the next six months, which the Trustee of Cannon County
is ordered to pay out of any monies in his hands not otherwise appropriated.

Nathan Neely and James Mears Esqrs. two of the commissioners, appointed at the
December Term of this court to make settlement with Elizabeth Soape and Charles
P. Alexander, Administrators of the estate of James Soape decd. this day pre-
sented to the court a settlement by them made with the said Admrs. for their
confirmation or rejection And the following justies being present to wit.
Wm. Bates
Samuel Lance
James Mears
Nathan Neely
Silas A. Robinson
Richard C. Lemmy
David Patton
Saml Greear
Saml Denby
Wm. R. James
Charles C. Evans and

John D. McBroom Esqrs.

all voting in the affirmative , therefore the following additional credits were admitted into the afforesaid settlements to wit.

To the amount to wit $50.00 which the widow of the said deceased paid for a mare at the sale of the said decd. which the court consider that should Have been alloted (p 527) to her when her years suport was laid off And that the sa said fifty dollars together with interest from the day that the sale money fell due be allow'd as a credit amounting principal and interest together to $56.00 Also one other claim which the said Administrators was chargeable within said settlement It being an account against Isaac Scape for $5.00 And it appearing to the court that from every circumstance that the same had been paid to the said deceased in His life time, And that he ought to be allowed also as a credit in said settlement together with all lawful Interest from the date that the sale notes of said Estate fell due.

Pursuant to an order made at the December Term of this court command a summons to Issue to Benjamin Pendleton Ex. of the last will and Testament of (blotted out) to appear at the present Term of this court, And give other sufficient or county security in room of Job Stephens or surrender up the Estate of the said deceased to such other person as the court might order, This day the clerk of this court presented to the court the afforesaid Summons, And it appeared to the Satisfaction of the court that the same had been duly Executed by the sheriff of Cannon County on the said Benjamin Pendleton Exr. as afforesaid on the 11th day of December 1840. And Also the said Benjamin Pendleton, appeared in open court, And surrendered His said executorship to the court to make any disposition of the matter they might think best; And Thereupon the court proceeded to appoint James J. Trott, Administrator with the will annexed in room and stead of the said Benjamin Pendleton Ex. as afforesaid whereupon the said James J. Trott being in court, together with His securities Wm. Bates and Wm. L. Covington entered into bond in the sum of Three thousand dollars conditioned and payable as the law directs for the faithful performance of the same.

(p 528) Whereupon letters of Administration are granted Him on the estate of the said deceased, which are in the words and Figures following to wit.

In the name of the State of Tennessee, Cannon County.
Whereas it appears to the satisfaction of the court that John Brown is deceased, And that whereas one Benjamin Pendleton was appointed in the will of the said deceased, to execute the same, and having been at the present Term of this court removed; And James J. Trott, having been appointed Administrator with the will annexed, to cary out His said Administration. These are therefore to authorize and empower you the said Administrator to enter into and upon all and singular the effects of the said decd. and then into your possession take and make all suplemental report not Heretofore by the said Execution been made. And all the Interest debt of the said deceased to pay so far as the estate of the said decd. may amount or extend and the residue thereof deliver up to those who have a right by law to receve the same.
Witness, Rezin Fowler clerk of our said court at office this first Monday and 4th day of January A.D. 1841. And of the Independance of the United States the 65th year, R. Fowler Clk.

It is ordered by the court that,
James K. Mason
Jessee L. Scawell and
Ivie J.C. Haynes
be and they are hereby appointed commissioners to settle with Benjamin Pendleton

Exr. of the last will and Testament of John Brown deceased, And to ———— as near as possible the condition of said Estate and make due return thereof to the clerk of this court on or before the fifteenth of this instant (p 529)

And the settlement when made it shall be the duty of the clerk to deliver a copy of the same to the Administrator of said estate. And fill the original in his office And also furnish the said commissioners with a copy of this order forthwith (copied Jan 7th 1841)

Archibald Stone
Wm. Bates and
Joseph Clark
this day filed their petition in open court praying that the court would make some disposition of two several lots in the Town of Woodbury Known on the plan of said Town as lots No. 26 and lot No. 18 — whereupon It is ordered by the court that
Joseph Ramsey
James K. Eason and
C. Reed Davis
be and they are hereby appointed commissioners with full power and authority to Advertise and sell said lots No. 26 and No. 18 to the Highest bidder on a credit of twelve months, And Have discretionary power to Divide lot No. 26 into four parts, or any number less so as to make it the most saleable. And that the said commissioners Have three months to advertise and endispose of the afforesaid lots and that the clerk of this court furnish the said commissioners with a copy of this order.
Court then adjourned till tomorrow morning 10 O'clock.
James Mears
N. Neely
Wm. R. James

Wednesday morning January the 6th 1841
the worshipful ———— met pursuant to adjournment present the worshipful
Nathan Neely
James Mears
Wm. R. James Esq.

Thereupon the following orders were made to wit.

James J. Trott, who was appointed Administrator (p 530) with the will annexed in room of Benj. Pendleton Ex. of the last will and Testament of John Brown deceased, on the 2nd day of this Term, this day appeared, i open court And the Administrators oath was duly Administered to Him by the clerk of this court it appearing that same had been had been imitted on the 2nd day of the January present Term of this court.

The clerk of this court this day presented to the court, for their confirmation or rejection, the following Settlements by Him made with the following named persons — to wit.
With Henry R. Perry Administrator of Jessee L. Perry deceased and with Joseph Simpson guardian of the minor heirs of David Faulkenberry deceased,

With James Odom guardian of Sarah Odom formerly Sarah Owens and

With Wm. Moore guardian of Elizabeth Jane Moore minor and Heir at law of Jessie G. Moore decd.

With Jonathan Hendrickson guard. of May Scribner, now deceased,

With Charles F. Alexander guard. of Heirs at law of Wm. Sullivan ded. And
with Joseph Bryson guardian of John Bryson minor and Heir at law of Wm. Bryson deceased, which being examined by the court was in all things confirmed,
court then adjourned till court in course.

James Mears
Wm. R. James
W. Neely

February Term 1841.

State of Tennessee)
Cannon County   )

    Be ot remembered that at a county court began and held for the county of
Cannon at the court house in the Town of Woodbury on the forst Monday of February in the year of our Lord one thousand Eight Hundred and forty one, And
of the Independance of the United States the sixty fifth year present the
Worshipful,

Richard U. Lemay
James Mears and
John D. McBroom Esq.
Then was the following orders made to wit.

On motion and it appearing to the satisfaction of the court, that David Petton
Esq. Chariman of this court, was absent. Whereupon it is ordered by the court
that Richard U. Lemay Esq. Be called to the chair, to preside over the deliberations of the court for the rpesent Term.

On motion it is ordered by the court, that the clerk of this court Issue the
State writ of Venires facies to the sheriff of Cannon County commanding Him
to summon the following named persons to serve as jurors, for the next Term
of the circuit court, to be Holden for the county of Cannon at the court
House in the town of Woodbury on the third Monday in May next to wit.

In Dist. No. 1st   John H. Andrews and John C. Martin

In Dist. No. 2d   Samuel Burke and George Walker

Dist. No 3rd   Wm. McFerrin and James R. Tayler

Dis. No 4th   Thomas J. Williams and John A. Brown

Dist. No 5th   Isaac Young and Wm. Whitamore

Dist No. 6th Wm. R. James, Jesse Q? Seawell and Wm. Kirk

Dist No. 7th   John Melton and Alexander Higgins

Dist No. 8th   Wm. West and Samuel Edmondson

Dist No. 9th   Archibald Hicks and Sampson Stephens

Dist No. 10th   John W. Haley and Francis Turner

Dist No. 11th   Wm. C. Odom and Joseph Bryson sen.

Dist No. 12th   Richard Holt and Benjamin Welber

(p 532) And James P. Todd Constable to wait on said jury and Wm. L. Covington to wait upon the court.

Pursuant to the acts of the General Assembly in such casses made and provided the clerk of this court this day presented to the Worshipful court for their confirmation or rejection, the following settlements by Him, made with the following named persons to wit.

With Hugh Robinson Esq. Exr of the last will and Testament of John Pullard decd.

With Woodson Northcutt Adm. of Francis Northcutt decd. and with Jonathan Jones guardian of the minor heirs and Heirs at law — James Terrell deceased, which being examined and fully understood, was by the court in all things confirmed.

Leroy Rose Administrator of the estate of John G.W. Rose deceased, this day reported to the court a supplemental Inventory of the effects of the said deceased and was duly quallified to the same. Whereupon it is ordered by the court that the same be recorded in the proper Book.

On motion it is ordered by the court that Elizabeth Soape be and she is Hereby constituted and appointed guardian Bond to her sons and daughters being severally named in the —— the Heirs at law of James Soape decd. who together with Her security James C. George being approved of by the court entered into bond in the sum of eight hundred dollars conditioned and payable as the law directs.

(p 533)
Court then adjourned till court in course.
Richd. U. Lemay
John D. McBroom
James Mears

March Term 1841

State of Tennessee)
Cannon County) Be it remembered that at a county court began and held for the county of Cannon at the court House in the Town of Woodbury — On the first Monday and first day of March, in the year of our lord one thousand Eight hundred and forty one, And of the Independance of the United States the Sixty fifth year present the Worshipful,
David Patton Chrm.
John C. Martin ord
Samuel Mears Esqrs.
Then was the following orders made to wit.

Pursuant to the acts of Assembly in such cases made and provided the clerk of this court this day presented to the worshipful court for their confirmation or rejection A Statement of settlement by him made with Thomas Hale Administrationof of John McGee Decd. which being examined and fully understood by the court was in all things confirmed.

David McGill and John McCrary Executors of the last will and Testament of Nancy McGill decd. this day reported to the court a Suptental Inventory of the effects of said decd. and was duly quallified to the same Whereupon it is ordered by the court that the same be admitted to Record.

Michael West Exr. of the last will and Testament of Abraham Sauls decd. this day reported to the court A suplemental report of the effects of the said estate and was duly quallified to the same which was admitted to record.

(p 554) On motion it is ordered that Daniel S. Ford Esqr. be and He is Hereby constituted appointed guardian to Nancy McGhe deceased, Thereupon the said Daniel S. Ford came into court together with His Security Francis Spurlock who being approved of by the court entered into Bond in the sum of Eighty dollars conditioned and payable as the law directs for the faithful performance of the same.

Mariah Johnson Administratrix of the estate of John Johnson deceased, this day reported to the cout an account current of the sales and other effects Belonging to the Estates of the said John Johnson decd. And was duly quallified to the same by the clerk of this court.
Thereupon it is ordered by the court that the same be recorded in the proper Book.
Court then adjourned till tomorrow morning ten o'clock.
David Patton
James Mears
Nathan Neely

Tuesday morning March the 2d 1841.
        The worshipful court met pursuant to adjournment present the worshipful
David Patton Chm.
James Mears and
Nathan Neely Esqrs.

Then was the following orders made to wit.

James O. George Shff. of Cannon County this day produced in open court a commission from his Excellency James K. Polk Governor in and over the state of Tennessee to Martin Frater, as justice of the peace in and (p 535) for the county of Cannon, And the said Martin Frater being in court, the oath of office was duly administered to Him by the clerk of this court And thereupon it was ordered by the court that the same be made of record.

On motion of James O. George Sheriff of Cannon County The following order was produced by Him to wit. with a request that it be spread upon the minutes of this court to wit.

Be it known to all whom it may concern, that I have revoked and do Hereby revoke the authority given by me to Eli Bailey, to perform the duties of the Office of Deputy Shff. of Cannon County and that the said Eli Bailey is no longer to perform any of the duties belonging to said office. Given under my hand this the 2d day of March 1841.
                    (signed) James O. George.

Thereupon it was ordered by the court that the clerk of this court issue a copy of said record and deliver the same to the said Eli Baily Dep. Shff.

James O. George Shff of Cannon County by his Deputy Eli Baily this day produced in open court a certificate of an Election by him held in the 3d Civil District in Cannon County from which certificate it appeared to the satisfaction of the court that Thomas Hodge Had been on the 13th of February 1841, duly elected to serve as constable to fill out the unexpired time of Thomas E. Jones resigned. And it appearing to the satisfaction of the court that the said Thomas Hodge Had failed to attend and enter into Bond and quallify as the law directs.

Whereupon it is ordered by the court that the sheriff (p 536) of Cannon County open and hold an Election in the said 3d civil District, to Elect another constable in the room and stead and to fill out the unexpired time of the said Thomas E. Jones, resigned And make due return thereof to the next Term of this court.

Court then adjourned till court in course.

David Patton
James Mears
Nathan Neely

April Term 1841

State of Tennessee)
Cannon County   )   Be it remembered that a county court began and held for the county of Cannon at the court House in the Town of Woodbury on the first Monday and fifth day of April in in the year of our Lord one thousand Eight Hundred and forty one, And of the Independance of the United States the sixty fifth year present the Worshipful

David Patton Chairman &C.
Danill S. Ford
Samuel Lance
Samuel Denby
Charles C. Evans
Nathan Neely
Wm. R. James
Wm. McPerrin
Martin L. Frater
John C. Martin
James Mears
John D. McBroom and
Samuel Creear Esqrs.

Then was the following orders made to wit.

James O. George Sheriff of Cannon County this day produced in open court a commission from his Excellency James K. Polk governor of the state of Tennessee to David D. Hipp as justice of the peace, in and for the county of Cannon, And the said David Hipp being present in court, the oath of office was duly Administered to Him by the clerk of this court, Whereupon it was ordered by the court that (p 537) the same be made of record, And that the said David D. Hipp take His seat upon the Bench.

Samuel Denby Esq. and Franklin Coleman commissioners of the Revenue this day reported to the court a statement of settlement by them made with Job Stephens Trustee of Cannon County from the 6th day of April 1840 up to the 6th day of March 1841 which being examined and understood by the court was in all things confirmed, And And ordered to be recorded in the commission book.

Sussannah Adams   )
     To   )
Benjamin Webber   )
Deed 60 Acres Land)   The execution of a deed of conveyance from Sussannah Adams, to Benjamin Webber for Sixty acres of land lying in Cannon County and State of Tennessee Bearing date March the 30th 1841 was this day duly proven in open court by the oath of John Hollis and Young G. Smith, Suscribing witnesses thereto,

Whereupon it was ordered by the court that the same be certified for registration.

On motion the following justices present to wit.
John C. Martin
Martin L. Prater
Daniel S. Ford
David Patton
James Mears
Wm. R. James
Sam'l Denby
David Hipp
Wm. McFerrin
Samuel Greear
John D. McBroom and
Nathan Neely Esq.
all voting in the affirmative, Therefore, the sum of thirty six dollars is appropriated, that is to say three dollars each to the Revenue commissioners for the fiscal year 1841 to wit.
Alex. McKnight
William Moore
Wm. Bown
Samuel Greear
Richard U. Lemay
Wm. R. James
Charles C. Evans
Samuel Lance
Wm. B. Foster
Daniel S. Ford
John W. Summar and
Silas A. Robinson Esqrs.
which the Trustee of Cannon County is ordered to pay out of any monies in His Hands not otherwise appropriated. Adn that the clerk of this court issue seperate orders to each of them and certify the same to the County Trustee.

(p 538)
Joseph Knox   )
    To   )
Edmond Lamberth)
Deed 69 acres)   The execution of a deed of conveyance from Joseph Knox to Edmond Lamberth for Sixty nine Acres of Land lying in Cannon County and state of Tennessee, bearing date March the 11th 1841 was this day duly acknowledged in open court By the said Knox the Bargainor which on ——— it was ordered by the court that the same be certified for registration.

On motion the following justices present to wit.
John C. Martin
John D. McBroom
Martin L. Prater
Daniel S. Ford
David Patton
James Mears
Wm. R. James
Samuel Denby
David D. Hipp
Wm. McFerrin

Samuel Creear
Nathan Neely &
Charles C. Evans Esqrs.
all voting in the affirmative, Therefore the following Appropriation is made
to Rezin Fowler clerk &c. That is to say for the consideration of His exoficio Services for the term of one year ending with the present term of this
court Forty dollars for making a record of the Revenue commissioners reports for
the year 1841 and calculating Each persons Taxes $18.00 making out a true tran-
script of the same and certifying the same to the sheriff of Cannon County for
collection $18.00 For furnishing a Tax record Book for the use of His office
$1.00 To making of record two pauper allowances and copies thereof .50 cents
each $1.00.
To Issuing 52 jury tickets $3.25.
To Issuing 5 road orders 12½ cents each, 62½ for making record the veniras
facias, for the circuit court for it May Term 1841 and copy thereof 50 — which
the Trustee of Cannon County is ordered to pay out of any monies in His Hands
not otherwise appropriated (copied)

On motion the following justices present to wit.
John D. McBroom
Nathan Neely
John C. Martin
Daniel S. Ford
Martin L. Prater
David Patton
James Mears
(p 539)
Wm. R. Jones
Samuel Denby
Wm. McFerrin and
Samuel Creear Esqrs.
all voting in the affirmative therefore the sum of $3.00 is appropriated to
Thos. G. Wood clk. of the circuit court for the consideration of his furnish-
ing 2 Blank Books for the use of his office which the Trustee of Cannon County
is ordered to pay out of any monies in His Hands not otherwise appropriated.

On motion the following justies being present and all voting in the affirm-
ative to wit.
David D. Hipp
John D. McBroom
Nathan Neely
John C. Martin
Daniel S. Ford
Martin L. Prater
David Patton
James Mears
Wm. R. Jones
Charles C. Evans
Samuel Denby
Wm. McFerrin and
Samuel Creear Esqrs.
Therefore the sum of sixteen dollars and sixty two and a Half cents is appropri-
ated to James O. George shff &C for the consideration of His repairing the court
House $16.00 .
6 panes of glass 12½ cents each, 75 cents.
Fixing the jail room —$3.00

Furnishing 3 cork Inkstands 62½ . To six quares of paper for the circuit court
82.25 cts and 4 loads of wood $14.00
which the Trustee of Cannon County is ordered to pay out of any monies in
Hands not otherwise appropriated.

On motion the following Justies present to wit.
John D. McBroom
David D. Hipp
Nathan Neely
John C. Martin
Daniel S. Ford
Martin L. Prater
David Patton
James Mears
Wm. R. James
Charles C. Evans
Samuel Denby
Wm McFerrin and
Samuel Greear Esqrs.
all voting in the affirmative therefore, the sum of forty dollars is appropri-
ated to James O. George shff &c for the consideration of His Exofficio services
for the term of one year ending with the present term of this court - which the
Trustee of Cannon County is ordered to pay out of any monies in His Hands not
otherwise appropriated.

(p 541)
John Estus)
    To   )
Allowance)
$5.37½   )   On motion the following justices present to wit.
Nathan Neely
James Mears
Martin L. Prater
David Patton
David D. Hipp
Samuel Lance
Charles C. Evans and
Samuel Greear Esqrs.
All voting in the affirmative , Therefore the sum of five dollars and 37½ cents
is appropriated to John Estus jailor of Cannon County. That is to say for the
consideration of Bonding Dawson McGlocklin a prisoner in the jail of said county
nine days $4.37½ and two Turnkeys 50 cents each, —$1.00 which the Trustee of
Cannon County is ordered to pay out of any monies in His Hands not otherwise
appropriated.

Citizens of Woodbury)
Exempt from working)
on County Roads   )   On motion and petition of John C. Ranson Esq. It is
ordered by the court that the citizens of the Town of Woodbury be and they
are Hereby Exempted from working on any of the public roads of Cannon County
Except in the Streets of said Town of Woodbury.

William Elkins)
    To   )
Allowance)   Thomas Elkins Esqr.
              Moses Cummings

William Elkins Esqr.

Thomas Pitman

WM. Foster

John D. Elkins and

James H. Stone

This day reported to court an Inquest Held by them over the dead body of an Infant child at the House of Patton Farles on the 6th day of March 1841--report upon their oath that the said Infant came to its death by the visitation of God and not otherwise - And whereupon the following justies being present to wit.

David Patton

Sam'l Lance

Sam'l Greear

Martin L. Prater

David D. Hipp

Nathan Heely

John D. McBroom and

(p 541)

James Mears Esqrs.

all voting in the affirmative therefore the sum of one dollar and sevebty cents is appropriated to William Elkins constable for the consideration of His services in summoning said jury which the Trustee of Cannon County is ordered to pay out of any monies not otherwise appropriated.

It is ordered by the court that

Joseph Ramsey

Silas A. Robinson and

Clement R. Davis

the commissioners Be and they are Hereby authorized and required to receve and appropriate the amount of money that is due to John Brown decd. for services rendered to the county, as county commissioners to the payment of the money that the said John Brown decd. now owes the county of Cannon at the time they settle with the said county commissioners And that the clerk of this court deliver a copy of this order to said commissioners Instanter.

Pursuant to the second section of an act of the General Assembly of the state of Tennessee passed January the 28th 1840 making it the duty of the clerks of the several county courts to call on the Shff. of their respective counties to Renew their Revenue Bonds. Rezin Fowler clerk of this court this day called on James O? George Sheriff of Cannon County to renew His revenue Bond for the faithful collection and paying over the state and county Taxes for said county for the fiscal year 1841 - Thereupon the said James O. George shff. &C came into court and was duly qualified as collector of the public Revenue for the afforesaid year, who together with his securities (p 542) Being approved of by the court Entered into two several Bonds, which are in the words and figures following to wit.

Know all men by these present that we;

James O. George

John Andrews

Wm. F. George

Adam Elrod

Wm. L. Covington and

James K. Eason

all of the county of Cannon and State of Tennessee are Held and firmly bound unto James K. Polk, governor in and over the state of Tennessee, for the time being and His successors in office for the use of the state in the sum of Eight Hundred and twenty five dollars to the payment of which we bind ourselves, our heirs, Executors and Administrators jointly and severally firmly by these pre-

nents sealed with our seals and dated the 5th day of April 1841 – The condition
of the above obligation is Such that whereas the above bound James O. George
Has been duly and constitutionally Elected sheriff and collector of the public
Taxes – Cannon County for the Term of Two years from the first saturday in
March 1840. Now if the said James O. George shall well and truly collect all
state Taxes within said county which by law He ought to collect for the year 1841
And well and truly account for and pay over all state Taxes by Him collected on
which ought to be collected on the first day of January 1842. Then the above
obligation to be void, otherwise to be and remain in full force and virtue.
Signd

John Andrews (seal)
Adam his mark Elrod(seal)   Attest, Rezin Fowler clk.
Wm. L. Covington (seal)
James K. Mason (seal)

(p 543)
Know all men by these presents that we;
James O. George
Samuel Vance
John Andrews
Wm. F. George
Adam Elrod
Wm. L. Covington and
James K. Mason
all of the county of Cannon County and state of Tennessee are Held and firmly
bound unto David Patton Esq. chairman of Cannon County court and His successors
in office for the use of said county in the sum of sixteen Hundred and fifty
dollars to the payment of which well and truly to be made, we bind ourselves,
our Heirs, Executors, and Administrators, jointly and severally, firmly by
these presents, sealed with our seals and dated the 5th day of April 1841.

The condition of the above obligation is such that whereas the above
bound James O. George Has been duly and constitutionally Elected sheriff &
collecotr of the public Taxes of Cannon County for the Term of two years from
the first Saturday in March 1840. Now if the said James O. George well and
truly collect all county Taxes for the county which by law he ought to collect
and account for and pay over all Taxes by Him collected for the use of said
county to the Trustee thereof, On the first day of January 1842, Then this
obligation to be void, otherwise to be and remain in full force and ————
                                 (signed)
                                 James O. George (seal)
                                 Samuel Vance (seal)
                                 John Andrews (seal)
                                 Wm. F. George (seal)
                                 Adam Elrod (seal)(A— his mark)
                                 Wm. L. Covington (seal)
                                 James K. Mason (seal)

(p 544)
Court then adjourned till court tomorrow morning April the 6th 1841.
The Worshipful court met pursuant to adjournment present the worshipful,
David Patton chairman &C
James Mears and
John D. McBroom Esqrs.
Then was the following orders made to wit.

This day the clerk of this court presented to the worshipful court for their

confirmation or rejections the following settlements by him made with the follow-
ing named persons to wit.
With Berry Vinson, Administrator of John Parkely deceased and
With Joseph Bryson guardian of John Bryson, minor heir at law of Wm. Bryson decd.
which being severally examined and fully understood by the court, was in all
things confirmed.
Court then adjourned till tomorrow morning twelve O'clock.
David Patton
N. Neely
James Mears
Wednesday morning April the 7th 1841.
The worshipful court met pursuant to Adjournment present the worshipful
David Patton chrm &C.
James Mears
Nathan Neely
Wm. R. James
Samuel Gresar
Allen Beaty and
Silas A. Robinson Esqrs.
Then was the following orders made to wit.

(p 545)
Pursuant to an order made at the January Term of this court;
Joseph Ramsey
C.R. Davis and
Silas Robinson Esq.
this day presented to the court a statement of settlement by them made with
Archibald Stone et al commissioner of the Town of Woodbury, which being read
and fully understood by the court was in all things confirmed, And ordered to
be spread upon the minutes of this court which settlement are in the words and
figures following to wit.
          We the undersigned being appointed at the January Term 1841 - of the
county court of Cannon County as commissioners on the part of the county to
make settlement with;
Archibald Stone
John B. Stone
Joseph Clark
Wm. Bates and
James J. Trott
Adm. of John Brown decd. commissioners of the Town of Woodbury Report that at
examination we find them chargable with the sales of fifty six Lots In the town
of Woodbury June the 13th 1836 and notes Taken in the same due June 13th 1837th
--- -Liabil. which amounted to the sum of $12,304.81½
Credits -- Intrest on the same-------------- 2,809.59
                                             ─────────
                                             15,114.40½   Credits
1st By voucher for money paid W.D. McBroom & I. Taylor and Martha Gannon
for Land bought   . . $946.20
Interest on the same   216.04   216.04
Do..By Parker F. Stone for his own note   530.00
Interest on the same   121.01½
Do.. By P.F. Stones receipt for cash   270.00
Interest on the same   61.65
Do.. By P.F. Stones receipt dated Oct. 28th 1837,   1677.33
Interest on the same   345.26
Do.. By Woodenpyle & Bates receipt dated November the 9th 1837,
paid at due time   2502.46½
Interest o n the same   537.27

(p 54)	Credits	Liabilities
Do. By Hoodenpyle & Bates receipt dated Janr. the 21th 1838	$511.10	
Interest on the same	98.88	
Do. By Hoodenpyle & Bates receipt dated January the 2d 1838	1700.00	
Interest on the same	349.05	
Do. By Hoodenpyle & Bates receipt dated May the 14th 1839, paid at different times	1444.01	
Interest on the same	243.80	
Total	11,643.62½ –	$15,114.40½
Do. By tot Bid off by John H. Wood and fell back on the county	$955.00	
Interest on the same	218.06	
Do. By Cooks Bill for printing stationary	7.97	
Interest on the same	1.80	
Do. By J.W. Words receipt for printing	20.00	
Interest on the same	4.56	
Do. By the receipt of S. Nye & Co. dated July the 9th 1837	4.00	
Interest on the same	1.01	
Do. By receipt for recording and Registering January the 21st 1837	9.28	
Interest on the same	2.11	
Do By Charles Readys receipt dated January the 14th 1839, for Atto. fees	63.50	
Interest on the same	12.52	
Do. By Covington & Youngbloods for services in going to see Rusworm and Webster to procure deeds, January the 28th 1837	17.76	
Interest on the same	3.55	
Do By Hill's Burton Receipt for Atto. fees dated September the 24th 1840	100.00	
Interest on the same	3.00	
Do. By Hugh Robinsons receipt for surveyor fees (p 547) dated July the 18th 1837	30.00	
Interest on the same	6.75	

	Credits	Liabilities
Do. By Woodson Northcutts receipt for auctioneering, August the 16th 1839	$12.50	
Interest on the same	2.43	
Do. By error in calculating interest on a note, Received By Bates	3.76	
	115,145.18½	
Balance due		1971.22

And find the following debts outstanding, which the commissioners Report they have heretofore been unable to collect (viz) on debt on Abiathir Capps and others amounting to $140.00

Interest on the same 51.97

171.97

The return of the sheriff on the debt is Illegal

Amt. Brt. up of balance due $1971.22

Amount of credits in an unsettled state 171.97

Do. By claim against John Dunn & others due January 15th 1837 360.00

Interest up to Sept. 13th 1838 (at which time $101.00 was received 100.00

Do. To amount of Interest calculated on $260 for 31 months 40.30

Do. By one claim against Henry Trott Junr and others 405.06

Interest on the same to April 3d 1841 92.74

Total amount of uncollected claims 1098.14¾

Dr. to one claim against J.M. Brown and H. Trott 100.00

Also a claim against John D. McBroom and Nathan Neely 50.00

which said last two mentioned in dotutful and not included in this settlement

(p 548) Amount Brt. forward $1098.14¾

Deduct the unsettled claims 2072.22

which leaves a balance of------ 974.08

Upon careful examination we believe the above calculations to be correct, subjected, However to the correction of errors if any there be All of which is respectfully submitted

C.R. Davis

Joseph Ramsey

Silas A. Robinson

Court then adjourned till court in course.

David Patton

Nathan Neely

James Mears

May Term 1841

State of Tennessee)
Cannon County   ) Be it remembered that at a county court began and held for
the county of Cannon at the court House in the Town of Woodbury on the first
Monday and third day of May, in the year of our Lord one thousand, Eight hun-
dred and Forty one, And of the Independance of the United States the Sixty
fifth year Present the worshipful,
David Patton chrm
John C. Martin and
James Mears Esqrs.

Then was the following orders made to wit.

The clerk of this court, this day presented to the court the following Settlements by him made with the the following named persons (to wit) one with
(p 549) William Bennett, guardian of Sophia Bennett, minor heir of Elizabeth
Patterson decd. and Heir at law of John M. Bennett, Decd. and the other with
Thomas S. Bennett, guardian of Rebecca F. Bennett, and Richard S. Bennett minor
Heirs and heirs at law of John M. Bennett, Deceased, Both for the Term of one
year from the 1st day of December 1859, which being examined and understood
by the court was in all things confirmed.

On motion and on application of Amual Rains the court appoint him guardian to
Daniel and Amos Travis, minor Heirs and heirs at law of Amos F. Travis decd.
Whereupon the said Rains together with his securities, John Patty and Woodson
Northcutt who being approved of by the court entered into Bond in the sum of
five hundred dollars conditioned and payable as the law directs for the faith-
ful performance of his said guardianship/

Martin S. Hoover)
Adm. of   )
Daniel Hoover decd.) Supplemental Inventory
            Martin S. Hoover Adm. of Daniel Hoover decd. this day re-
turned a Supplemental Inventory of the effects of the said deceased, And was
duly quallified to the same, Whereupon it is ordered by the court that the
same be recorded in the proper Book.

On motion of James O. George Esq. Sheriff of Cannon County col, Woodson Northcutt was permitted to be quallified as Deputy Shff. of Cannon County And thereupon it is ordered by the court that the same be made of record.

(p 550) On motion of James Desary Esq. David Patton chairman of Cannon County
court, by the direction of the court and on their behalf, bind an orphan girl
by the name of Sarah Jane Couch, unto Willis F. Couch with him to live and work
untill she attains the age of Eighteen years, And at the expiration of the time
the said Willis F. is to give her a good feather bed and good wheel and cards,
during the the time the said Sarah Jane lives with the said Willis, he is to
learn her to read an write &C And the said Willis F. Couch entered into bond together with his security James Desary Aproved by the court faithfully to perform said agreement.

On motion it is ordered by the court that Richard C. Price be and he is hereby

constituted and appointed guardian to Willis F. Couch, Wm. H. Couch, Darkely Couch, Thoms D. Couch and Sarah Jane Couch, And thereupon the said rice entered into Bond together with his securities, James Bosary. Being aproved by the court in the sum of $300.00 for the faithful performance of his said guardianship.
Court then adjourned till court in course.
David Patton
James Mears
J.C. Martin

June Term 1841

(p 551)
State of Tennessee)
Cannon County   )   Be it remembered that at a county court Began and held for the county of Cannon at the court House in the Town of Woodbury on the first Monday and seventh day of June, one thousand Eight hundred and forty one, And of the Independance of the United States the Sixty fifth year, present the Worshipful
David Patton Esq. Chrm.
James Mears and
John C. Martin Esqrs.

Then was the following orders made(to wit.)

Thos. J. Williams   )
Adm. of   )   Supplemental Inventory
Thomas Williams decd.)   Thomas J. Williams, Administrator of Thomas Williams deceased, This day reported to the court an account current of the proceeds of sales of land and Negroes &C Belonging to said Estate and was duly quallified to the same; which was admitted to record.

Martin S. Hoover   )
    To   )
Guardian Appointment)   On motion it is ordered by the court that Martin S. Hoover He and he is hereby constituted and appointed guardian to Thos. Hoover, Sally Hoover
Mary Anne Hoover and
William Hoover
minor Heirs, and Heirs at law of Daniel Hoover, Deceased, thereupon the said Martin S. Hoover, came into court together with his security David Patton who being approved of by the court entered into Bond in the sum of Two hundred and fifty dollars conditioned and payable as the law directs for the faithful performance of his said guardianship.

(p 552)
On motion it is ordered by the court that the sheriff of Cannon County, Summon the following named persons to serve as jurors at the next September Term of the circuit court for said county to be Holden at the court House in the Town of Woodbury on the third Monday in said month 1841 - to wit.

In Dist. No. 1st   John F. Hare and William C. McLinn

Dist No 2nd   Akelus Alexander and William Moore

No. 3rd   William Bowen and William McFerrin

No. 4th   John Petty and James Sisson

No. 5   David D. Kipp and John Craft

No. 6th   James Mears, Gabriel Hume and John Webb

No. 7th   Charles C. Evans and Thomas Elkins

No. 8th   Washington Kennedy and John Pendleton

No. 9th   George Grizzle and Samuel C. Burger

No. 10   Thomas Nokes and Larkin Keaton

No. 11th   Francis Cooper and James Odom senr.

No. 12th David Patton and Hugh Robinson and Constables Wm. L. Covington to
wait upon the court & James Odom to wait upon the jury.

Pursuant ——— the Acts of the general Assembly in such cases made and provided the clerk of this court this day presented to the worshipful court for
for their confirmation or rejection the following Statements of settlements
by him made with the following named persons to wit.
With Martin S. Hoover, Administrator of Daniel Hoover deceased, and
With Thomas Givens, guardian of William and Henry Bratton minor Heirs and
Heirs at law of Henry Bratton decd. which being read and understood by the
court, was in all things confirmed.

(p 553)
Hugh Thompson   )
    To   )
Apprentice Indenture) Whereas at the April Term of this court 1839 – There
was an apprentice By the name of William C. Hatfield, Bound unto Dennison
Haywood with Him to live and work as an apprentice to learn the art and
mistery of the Tanning Buisness &C, And the said Dennison Haywood this day
appeared in open court and prayed to be released from any further Liability
on said Indenture, and also stated that the said William C. Hatfield was
willing to live and enter into an Indenture with one Hugh Thompson And David
Patton chairman of Cannon County Court– Entered into Indenture containing the
various stipulations and conditions as agreed to by the court, And thereupon
It is ordered by the court that the said Dennison Haywood be and He is Hereby
released from any further Liability on said Indenture.

John Fisher Esq. Coroner of Cannon County this day reported to the court aReport
of ajury of Inquest By Him Held over the dead body of one Parson McGlocklin,
who died in the Cannon jail of Cannon County. And it appearing to the satisfaction of the court, That the said Coroner, Hand performed all the duties as
contemplated By the Acts of Assembly in such cases made and provided. Thereupon it is ordered by the court that the clerk of this court certify the same.
to the Trustee of Cannon County for the payment of such fees as are allowed by
law for similar services.

John Fisher Esq.   )
    To   )
Report of Inquisition) John Fisher Esq. Coroner of Cannon County this day
Reported to Court a jury of Inquest by Him Held over the dead body of one
Lydia Sullivan who died at her own House on the 29th day of May (p 554)

And it appearing to the satisfaction of the court that the said Coroner Had performed all the duties as contemplated by the Acts of Assembly in such cases made, -- provided, in Holding said Inquisition, Thereupon it is ordered by the court, that the clerk of this court certify the same to the Trustee of said County for the payment of such fees as are allowed by Law for such services.

Thomas G. Wood)
)
Apprentice Indenture) Whereas, at former Term of this court There was Two orphans Bound unto one Henry Ford, By the name of Angeline Stanley and Thomas Stanly with Him the said Ford to live and work untill the attain at Lawful age -- And the said Henry Ford, apeared this day in open court, and moved the court to be released from any further Liability on said Indenture, And makes known to the satisfaction of the court that the said orphan is willing to live and work with Thomas G. Wood and thereupon the said Thomas G. Wood and David Patton Esq. Chairman of Cannon County court Entered into Indenture containing various stipulations and conditions as agreed to by the court, And thereupon it is ordered By the court that the said Henry Ford Be released from any further Liability on said Indenture.

David McGill)
        To   )
Guardian Appointment) On motion of David McGill the court Apoint Him guardian to John Pogue minor orphan Whereupon the said David McGill together with His security David Patton, Being approved of by the court entered into Bond in the sum of five Hundred dollars conditioned and payable as the (p 555) Law directs for the faithful performance of His said guardianship.

Henin Fowler clerk of the county court of Cannon County this day appointed Thomas G. Wood Deputy clerk of this court, who came into court and took the oath of office and the oath against dueling.
David Patton
J.M. Martin
James Moore

www.ingramcontent.com/pod-product-compliance
Lightning Source LLC
Chambersburg PA
CBHW081429270326
41932CB00019B/3134